ENGLAND AND ITS RULERS
1066–1307

BLACKWELL CLASSIC HISTORIES OF ENGLAND

This series comprises new editions of seminal histories of England. Written by the leading scholars of their generation, the books represent both major works of historical analysis and interpretation and clear, authoritative overviews of the major periods of English history. All the volumes have been revised for inclusion with the series and many include updated material to aid further study. *Blackwell Classic Histories of England* provides a forum in which these key works can continue to be enjoyed by scholars, students and general readers alike.

Published

Roman Britain
Third Edition
Malcolm Todd

England and Its Rulers: 1066–1307
Third Edition
M. T. Clanchy

Crown and Nobility: England 1272–1485
Second Edition
Anthony Tuck

Church and People: England 1450–1660
Second Edition
Claire Cross

Politics and Nation: England 1450–1660
Fifth Edition
David Loades

Politics without Democracy: 1815–1914
Second Edition
Michael Bentley

ENGLAND AND ITS RULERS
1066–1307

M. T. CLANCHY

THIRD EDITION

Blackwell
Publishing

BLACKWELL PUBLISHING
350 Main Street, Malden, MA 02148-5020, USA
9600 Garsington Road, Oxford OX4 2DQ, UK
550 Swanston Street, Carlton, Victoria 3053, Australia

First edition published 1983 by Fontana Paperbacks
Second edition published by 1998 by Blackwell Publishing Ltd
Third edition published 2006 by Blackwell Publishing Ltd

3 2010

Library of Congress Cataloging-in-Publication Data
Clanchy, M. T.
  England and its rulers, 1066–1307 / M. T. Clanchy.—3rd ed.
     p. cm.—(Blackwell classic histories of England)
  Includes bibliographical references (p.   ) and index.
  ISBN 978-1-4051-0649-8 (alk. paper)
  ISBN 978-1-4051-0650-4 (pbk. : alk. paper)
  1. Great Britain—History—Medieval period, 1066–1485. 2. Great
Britain—History—Norman period, 1066–1154. 3. Great Britain—
History—Angevin period, 1154–1216. 4. Great Britain—History—
Henry III, 1216–1272. 5. Great Britain—Kings and
rulers. I. Title. II. Series.
  DA175.C57 2006
  942.02—dc22
                                        2005036416

A catalogue record for this title is available from the British Library.

Set in 11 on 13.5 pt Bembo
by SNP Best-set Typesetter Ltd, Hong Kong
Printed and bound in Singapore
by Markono Print Media Pte Ltd

For further information on
Blackwell Publishing, visit our website:
www.blackwellpublishing.com

Contents

Preface to the Third Edition

In this edition I have added three new chapters: 'The Creation of Wealth', 'The Matter of Britain' and 'Lordship and the Structure of Society'. I have also updated the Suggestions for Further Reading and made other minor corrections.

This edition is dedicated to the memory of Patrick Wormald (1947–2004), my colleague in the University of Glasgow, who read the first draft of this book and improved it considerably.

M. T. Clanchy
Institute of Historical Research
University of London

Preface to the Second Edition

This book was commissioned by Sir Geoffrey Elton in 1977 for his 'Fontana History of England' as part of a larger whole. It accompanied H.E. Hallam's *Rural England 1066–1348* and A. Tuck's *Crown and Nobility 1272–1461*. My remit was to write a political narrative up to the death of Henry III, as the accompanying volumes addressed the economy and social structure and events after 1272. Now, as a Blackwell book, *England and its Rulers* accompanies M. Chibnall's *Anglo-Norman England 1066–1166* and R. Mortimer's *Angevin England 1154–1258*. It is not a comprehensive history of Anglo-Norman England, still less of Britain, as that was not what Elton required. To link it with current textbooks on the later Middle Ages, I have added an epilogue on Edward I and in the 'Suggestions for Further Reading' I have listed recent work on all aspects of the period 1066–1307.

Preface to the First Edition

This book is intended both as an outline narrative of political history for students and as a new interpretation of the period. Within a necessarily limited format I have been able to give references for all quotations but not for every statement made. I have aimed throughout to keep the reader in contact with the sources (particularly the monastic chroniclers) and to provide a commentary on the views of historians since the time of William Stubbs a century ago. His *Constitutional History* remains the best single work on this period despite its faults.

I wish to thank Mrs M. Sword for her expert typing, my colleague Mr C.P. Wormald for commenting on the book in draft, and Professor G.R. Elton for his encouragement throughout.

The picture on the cover comes from the Bible given to Durham cathedral by Bishop Hugh du Puiset (1153–95) and is reproduced by permission of the Dean and Chapter (Durham Cathedral Library MS A.II.i). It illustrates the campaigns of Alexander the Great, as recounted in the Book of Maccabees, and shows for the purposes of this book the terror that knights inspired.

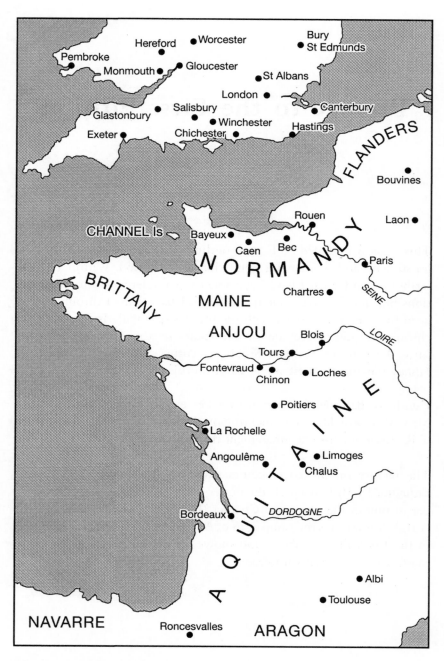

Map 1   *England and France*

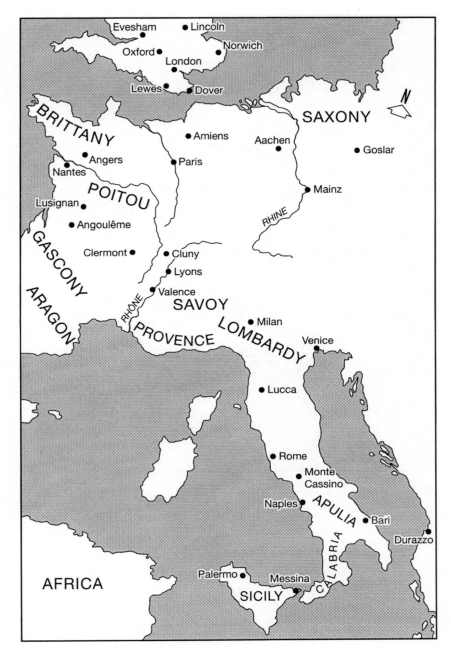

Map 2 England and the Mediterranean

Map 3   Edward I's kingdom in Britain

I

England's Place in Medieval Europe

This book concerns the rulers of England and their aspirations in the period between the Norman Conquest of 1066 and the death of Edward I in 1307. During these two and a half centuries England was dominated by men from overseas. This trend had begun before 1066 with the rule of the Danish king Cnut (1016–35) and of the half-Norman Edward the Confessor (1042–66), and it lingered on after 1272 in the French-speaking court of Edward I (1272–1307) and his successors. Nevertheless the most significant period of overseas domination of political and cultural life in the English kingdom followed the Norman Conquest and continued into the twelfth century and beyond. When the Norman dynasty failed in the male line with the death of Henry I in 1135, England became the battleground between two of William the Conqueror's grandchildren, Stephen and the Empress Matilda. On Stephen's death the kingdom was inherited by Henry II (1154–89), who was count of Anjou in his own right and duke of Aquitaine by marriage. The area of the king of England's political concern had therefore widened beyond William the Conqueror's Normandy to include Anjou and the huge lands of Aquitaine and Poitou south of the Loire. This extension of power is described by historians – though never by contemporaries – as the 'Angevin Empire', implying an overlordship by the dynasty of Anjou over England and half of modern France. According to Gerald of Wales, Henry hoped to extend his rule beyond France to Rome and the empire of Frederick Barbarossa.

In leading Christendom in the crusade against Saladin, Richard I (1189–99) was following in the footsteps of the Angevin kings of

Jerusalem as well as fulfilling promises made by Henry II. His death in the struggle with Philip Augustus of France and King John's subsequent loss of Normandy to Philip did not bring an end either to overseas influence in England or to the ambitions of its kings, as John hoped to regain Normandy from his base in Poitou and Aquitaine. He established the strategy, which was vigorously pursued by his successor Henry III (1216–72), of using Poitevins as administrators and war captains in England. Through them and the support of the papacy Henry hoped to construct a system of alliances which would win his family the huge inheritance in Italy and Germany of the greatest of the medieval emperors, Frederick II, and thus surpass the achievements of Henry II and Richard I. 'We wish', wrote Pope Alexander IV in 1255, 'to exalt the royal family of England, which we view with special affection, above the other kings and princes of the world.'[1]

The rebellion of 1258 against Henry's Poitevins and papal ambitions compelled both king and barons to recognize the separateness of England: the king by conceding the Norman and Angevin lands to Louis IX of France in 1259, and the barons by forming their revolutionary commune of England. As if to emphasize the persistence of overseas influence, that commune was led by a Frenchman, Simon de Montfort. This period of rebellion and civil war marked a turning point in the definition of English identity. Its rulers thereafter continued to pursue overseas ambitions, first in France in the Hundred Years War and then as a worldwide maritime power, but they did so now as heads of an English nation and not as alien warlords like William the Conqueror and Henry II. In order to emphasize the influence of outsiders and at the same time to provide a chronological framework, this book is divided into parts comprising three periods each of about seventy years' duration: the Normans (comprising the reigns of William the Conqueror, William Rufus and Henry I); the Angevins (the reigns of Stephen, Henry II and Richard I); the Poitevins (the reigns of John and Henry III). The titles 'Normans', 'Angevins' and 'Poitevins' are not intended to suggest that the rulers came exclusively from these regions, but that the king of England's predominant overseas connections shifted from Normandy in the eleventh century through Anjou in the twelfth to Poitou in the thirteenth. Edward I gave as high a priority as his predecessors to his possessions in France, while at the same time conducting large-scale wars in Wales and Scotland.

England and its conquerors

The English had developed a settled identity precociously early among the European powers. The Anglo-Saxon kings of the tenth century, building on the achievements of Offa in Mercia and Alfred in Wessex, had created a single kingdom. At its best, a sacrosanct king headed a well-defined structure of authority (consisting of shires, hundreds and boroughs), which used a uniform system of taxation and coinage and a common written language in the Anglo-Saxon of writs and charters. Even the fragility of these achievements, in the face of the Danish and Norman invasions of the eleventh century, encouraged a sense of common identity in adversity, as the kingdom's misfortunes were attributed in such works as Wulfstan's *Sermon of the Wolf to the English* to the sinfulness of the people rather than to the shortcomings of the political system. Monastic writers were therefore able to transmit to their successors the hope that the English kingdom would emerge intact from foreign domination. Thus Orderic Vitalis, who was sent to Normandy when still a child to become a monk, nevertheless identified fiercely with England's woes. Describing Norman atrocities after the rebellion of Edwin and Morcar, he upbraids the Normans who 'did not ponder contritely in their hearts that they had conquered not by their own strength but by the will of almighty God, and had subdued a people that was greater, richer and older than they were'.[2] This sense of Englishness, transmitted like the English language as a mother tongue despite its disappearance in official circles, persisted as a powerful undercurrent throughout the twelfth century to emerge as a political force in the thirteenth. The isolated monks who continued with the Anglo-Saxon Chronicle after the Norman Conquest, noting for example that the year 1107 was the 'forty-first of French rule in this country', and the gregarious mothers and wet nurses who naturally spoke to their infants in English had together saved the nation's identity.

The unity of the English kingdom at the time of the Conquest was a sign not of its modernity by eleventh-century standards but of its antiquity. Its centralized government was based on the models of imperial Rome and the Carolingian empire, whereas the tendency of the tenth and eleventh centuries had been away from royal centralization and towards aristocratic feudalism. Power had shifted from kings and their hierarchies of officials towards self-sufficient knights in their castles. Similarly the clergy were beginning to question the value of sanctified kings as their protectors and were demanding instead to be free from lay domination. 'Who does not know', asked Pope Gregory VII in 1081, 'that kings and dukes originated from those who, being ignorant of God, strove with blind greed and insufferable presumption to dominate their equals, that is their fellow men, by pride, violence, treachery and murder? And when they try to force the priests of the Lord to follow them, can kings not best be compared to him who is the head over all the children of pride? The devil.'[3] With the Norman Conquest and the civil wars of Stephen's and Henry II's reigns, England was therefore brought into the mainstream of European politics, where knights waged war from stone fortresses and clergy, educated at reformed monasteries and the new universities, claimed to be above royal power. The values and style of life of the two most admired Englishmen of the twelfth century, William the Marshal, the model of the new knighthood, and Thomas Becket, the martyr of the reformed clergy, would scarcely have been comprehensible to an Anglo-Saxon thane or bishop of a century earlier.

Such was the power of the new knights and clergy that they reshaped the traditional order of Europe in the eleventh and twelfth centuries. England was not unique in experiencing foreign conquest. At the same time as William the Conqueror was establishing Norman rule in England, other Normans led by Robert Guiscard were forming a new lordship in southern Italy and Sicily by overawing the pope and the abbot of Monte Cassino and defeating the Byzantines and the Moslems. Similarly in 1085 Alfonso VI of Castile and Leon entered Toledo as conqueror of the Moslems and in 1099 the army of the First Crusade triumphantly entered Jerusalem. Although these conquests were not directly related to each other, they were due – whether in England, Italy, Spain or Palestine – to the superiority of mounted knights when inspired by a militant clergy.

In the opinion of the conquered people such invaders were no better than a rabble of robbers. This is how at first the English saw their Norman conquerors, how the Byzantines and the popes saw Robert Guiscard, and how the Moslems saw the Cid in Spain and the crusaders in the east. But in each case the invaders demonstrated that they were more than raiders and looters, as they established strong and resilient forms of government which, while depending on the use of force, tempered and directed it through the disciplines of feudalism and the idealism of the reformed clergy. Feudal values, as enunciated in the *Song of Roland* (which is contemporary with the Norman Conquest and may have been sung at the battle of Hastings), gave knights a sense of hierarchy and of loyalty to their lords as well as an irrepressible pride and delight in their warhorses, armour and other instruments of bloodshed. Clerical idealism, as enunciated by Pope Urban II in his sermons launching the First Crusade (and before him by Gregory VII), acknowledged the savagery of knights but aimed to point them in a similar direction to the *Song of Roland*: they would be a *militia* fighting for Christ instead of a *malitia*, the servants of the devil and the embodiment of malice. Although the knights' new sense of righteousness brought only misfortune to those whom they killed, maimed and ransomed, it did make them a sufficiently disciplined and motivated force to build on the ruins of war. Often, too, their sense of realism as fighting men encouraged them to learn from those they conquered. The Normans in England took over and strengthened the Anglo-Saxon taxation and writ system, just as their counterparts in the Moslem lands of Sicily, Palestine and Spain benefited from the superior civilizations over which they ruled.

This book concentrates on the rulers of England and not on the peasants, or 'natives' as the lords called them. The peasants were 'natives' in the sense both of belonging to a subjugated nation, the English, and of being tied by their inferior birth to the land on which they lived and worked. This social and economic structure is described in Marjorie Chibnall's *Anglo-Norman England* and Richard Mortimer's *Angevin England* in the Blackwell 'History of Medieval Britain' series. Unlike the great majority of the population who were rooted to the soil, the lords exhibited their superior status by moving freely on horseback from place to place, as their life was spent in hunting and collecting levies of money and produce from their tenants. They exercised their power not only through physical force as knights but through intellectual superiority as clergy. The ideology and resources of the church were as essential to lordship as the skills and equipment of knighthood. The local bishop or abbot was often the brother or kinsman of the lord of the land. King Stephen, for example, depended frequently on his brother, Henry of Blois, who was bishop of Winchester for more than forty years (1129–71). This book therefore includes the higher clergy within its purview because they were worldly lords and rulers despite the insistence of ecclesiastical reformers on being a caste apart.

The power and aspirations of lordship, both clerical and lay, were manifested in buildings and works of art as well as through the personal presence of the knight on horseback and the cleric with his sacred scripture. Much of what most impressed people at the time has disappeared: the burnished war helmets and jewel-encrusted reliquaries, the robes and hangings of silk and ermine, the iron strong-boxes filled with gold. Nevertheless enough remains, particularly in the outer forms of castles and churches, to recall this lost way of life. Above all, illuminated manuscripts, many of which are almost perfectly preserved, radiate from their pages not only the colour and brilliance of Romanesque and Gothic art but the thought-worlds of their medieval creators. These works were the supreme products of lordship, the legacy which was deliberately left to posterity as a tribute to divine power from men who recognized their own skills. 'I am the prince of writers,' the inscription in the frame around Eadwine of Canterbury's portrait declares in c.1150, 'neither my praise nor my fame will die hereafter . . . The beauty of this book displays my genius; God accept it as a gift pleasing to him.'[4] The book which this portrait accompanies is a text of the psalms with three variant Latin texts (Gallican, Roman and Hebrew) and English and French translations. It illustrates very well the mastery of the rulers and the way they were part of the civilization of western Christendom as well as building on English traditions.

Europe and the world

Knowledge of England's place in space and time was the speciality of monks and other clerical writers who inspired the men of action to their pilgrimages and crusades and recorded their deeds in chronicles and histories. Although much of this knowledge was inaccurate and some of it was fictitious, like Geoffrey of Monmouth's popular *History of the Kings of Britain*, which elaborated the story of King Arthur, it nevertheless gave the rulers a yardstick by which to measure their endeavours and achievements. Varying Voltaire's epigram, if Arthur did not exist it would be necessary to invent him. The monks of Glastonbury recognized this in 1191 when they discovered and exhumed the alleged bodies of Arthur and Guinevere. Arthur or no Arthur, it is a mistake to underestimate the range of knowledge which medieval writers claimed to have or to dismiss altogether the existence of now lost books such as the one which Geoffrey of Monmouth said he had used. His contemporary, the historian William of Malmesbury, assumed a wide knowledge in his reading public. Defending in 1125 his decision to produce a history of the English bishops, he wrote: 'It was certainly slothful and degrading not to know the names of the principal men of our province when our knowledge otherwise extends as far as the tracts of India and whatever lies beyond, open to the boundless ocean.'[5]

In William's time the world was pictured schematically in *mappae mundi* as a circle with Jerusalem at the centre and the three continents of Asia, Africa and Europe placed around it. Asia occupies the top half of the circle while Africa and Europe are placed in the bottom right- and left-hand quarters respectively. (Neither medieval Europeans, nor the Romans and Greeks who preceded them, had any certain knowledge of Africa south of the equator or of America and Australasia.) The whole circular landmass is surrounded by the 'boundless ocean' to which William of Malmesbury refers. What he meant by saying that our knowledge extends to India is that the conventional representation of three continents had been handed down from ancient geographers via the encyclopedist Isidore of Seville. William and his fellow western Christians had no knowledge from experience of either Asia or Africa, although that was beginning to change now that crusaders and Italian merchants were establishing themselves all around the Mediterranean. Representations of the earth in the form of Jerusalem-centred world maps were a step back rather than forwards from the point of view of geographical science. Thus the large circular wall-map at Hereford cathedral, attributed to Richard of Haldingham and drawn in the late thirteenth century, is less accurate in its representation of Britain, though it is more detailed, than the square map in the British Museum (MS Tiberius B.v) which dates from about AD 1000.

Jerusalem-centred maps showed the world as planned by God rather than according to what was known about it by physical scientists. Sometimes God, as the creator of heaven and earth, is depicted hovering protectively above the map with his angels in the star-filled universe. Such maps represent with accuracy not the relationships of places as measured by fallible men but the words of scripture: 'Thus saith the

Lord God: this is Jerusalem; I have set it in the midst of the nations and countries that are round about her.' St Jerome comments on this passage from Ezekiel (5:5) that Jerusalem is sited in the centre of the world because it is the umbilical cord which connects divine life with earthly life. Jerusalem-centred maps, which become the standard form in the twelfth century, also represent contemporary aspirations. In William of Malmesbury's account of Urban II's speech at Clermont launching the First Crusade the pope uses the image of the *mappa mundi* of three continents, with Asia occupying half the circle and Europe only a quarter. He describes how the Moslems are threatening to take over the whole world, as they already have Asia, which was the cradle of Christianity, and Africa, which produced so many of the fathers of the church. 'The learned will know what I am talking about,' the pope assures his audience: 'thirdly there is the remaining region of the world, Europe, of which we Christians inhabit only a small part.'[6] The pope's comment is strange at first sight, as the Moslems in 1095 possessed only the southern half of Spain together with the Balearic islands and Sicily. But it becomes explicable in the light of his next statement: 'For who will say that all those barbarians who live in the remote islands of the glacial ocean are Christians, as they lead a monstrous life?' Northern Europeans, some of whom in Norway and Sweden had indeed not been converted to Christianity at the time of Urban's speech, are therefore equated by the Mediterranean pope with the sea monsters who live at the world's end.

According to the Jerusalem-centred world view, England bordered the remote islands in the glacial ocean such as Iceland and the Orkneys. England was on the perimeter of the circle, 'the outer edge of the earth's extent' as the Anglo-Saxon Aelfric had described it.[7] Wales and Ireland were consequently on the furthest borders of the world (according to Gerald of Wales), and beyond Scotland there was no habitation (in the words of the Declaration of Arbroath). In the thirteenth century the schoolman Robert the Englishman was obliged to acknowledge in his lectures on cosmology that England was too far north to be included in the recognized climes or regions of geographers. 'But the reason for this', Robert explains, 'is not because it is unfit to live in, as some will have it, but because it was not inhabited at the time of the division into climes.'[8] This slur on England's good name leads Robert, like other medieval writers, to launch into a paean praising the country's fertility and climate.

The elements of such patriotic descriptions had remained much the same since Bede (himself drawing on the works of Nennius and Gildas) set the pattern for them in the opening chapter of his *Ecclesiastical History of the English People* in the early eighth century. Indeed just as Jerusalem-centred maps of the twelfth and thirteenth centuries were less accurate than those of the earlier Middle Ages, so descriptions of England's geographical characteristics show a decline in precision. This is because even those learned in astronomy and the physical science of the time, like Robert the Englishman, preferred Geoffrey of Monmouth's exaggerations to the circumstantial work of Bede. Geoffrey, describing Britain rather than England as such, calls it 'the best of islands'.[9] It provides in unfailing plenty everything that is needed: all sorts of minerals, all kinds of crops from the rich soil, every variety of game in its forests; there are fat cattle on its pastures and green meadows, bees gathering honey from its beautiful flowers, plentiful fish in its rivers and lakes, and people lulled happily to sleep on the banks of its babbling brooks. (Geoffrey borrowed this last image from Gildas, who had written in the sixth century.) Britain also – and this is Geoffrey's main subject – has an extraordinarily distinguished history, beginning with its formation by the Trojan Brutus and progressing through Lear and Cymbeline to Arthur who had dominated Europe.

All this is of course exaggerated and some of it is absurd. Nevertheless such optimism was echoed by other writers. For example Richard of Devizes in the 1190s describes a French Jew persuading a fellow Frenchman to go to England, that land flowing with milk and honey where no one who strives to make an honest living dies poor. Although by modern European and American standards life in the Middle Ages was poor, nasty, brutish and short, that was not the universal opinion of those who experienced it. They veered between extremes of delight in the bountifulness of the earth and its seasons, like William the Conqueror's fellow ruler the troubadour William IX of Aquitaine, and by contrast deep awareness, among reforming monks like St Bernard in particular, of the transitoriness of life and the immediacy of divine retribution. Over the centuries patriotic historians and writers developed Geoffrey of Monmouth's ideal of the best of islands into the famous description in Shakespeare's *Richard II* of:

This blessed plot, this earth, this realm, this England,
This nurse, this teeming womb of royal kings ...

In one way at least England actually was pleasanter in the twelfth century than now, and that was in its climate. In his description of the Vale of Gloucester, William of Malmesbury comments that 'the frequency of vines there is more concentrated, their produce more fruitful, and their taste sweeter than in any other area of England.'[10] This implies, and there is other evidence to support it, that viticulture was quite common in twelfth-century England. Even the Anglo-Saxon Chronicle's pessimistic account of how things went from bad to worse during the nineteen years of Stephen's reign concludes with a description of the Norman abbot of Peterborough, Martin of Bec, planting a vineyard as part of his improvements to the abbey. William of Malmesbury adds that the wines from the Gloucester area could bear comparison with French ones, whereas by implication those from less favoured areas could not. He wrote this in the 1120s when northern Europe was still enjoying a relatively warm period before cold and rain began to predominate in the latter half of the thirteenth century. At the time therefore when England was ruled by incomers from France, its climate (in the south at least) would not have made such a strong contrast with their own. Nevertheless England never was a large wine-producing country. Medieval Englishmen characteristically drank beer and they were notorious abroad for consuming too much (see pages 233–4 below).

England's destiny

England's place in the medieval world could be viewed in different lights. Certainly England was physically remote from the centre and seemed to those who had only theoretical knowledge of it to be on the outer periphery of civilization. On the other hand it was reputed to be rich, in both minerals and agricultural produce, and its climate was benign. Although the wealth of England was probably exaggerated both at home and abroad, it served as a strong inducement to conquerors and adventurers. Eadmer of Canterbury tells a story of how in the reign of Cnut the bishop of Benevento in central Italy went on a fund-raising tour on behalf of his church, which claimed to possess the body of the apostle St Bartholomew: the bishop was offering for sale an arm from this precious relic. Passing through Italy and France he decided to proceed to England when he heard talk of its wealth and of how he was likely to get a better price there than anywhere else. In this the bishop succeeded, selling the arm to Queen Emma for several pounds of silver. Eadmer uses this story to illustrate how in those days, before the coming of Lanfranc and the Norman reformers, the English valued relics above everything. For us the story illustrates England's reputation for wealth, which Eadmer thought a commonplace as he was writing in the reigns of William Rufus and Henry I when the treasures of England and the loot amassed by its Norman conquerors were the talk of Europe.

Throughout the twelfth century the kings of England were reputed to be wealthier than the Capetian kings of France. William Rufus, writes Abbot Suger of St Denis, was 'opulent, a spender of the treasures of the English and a marvellous dealer in and payer of knights', whereas his own king, Louis VI, was short of money.[11] To display their wealth and power the Norman kings built on an unprecedented scale. The Tower of London, completed by Rufus in 1097, was the greatest stone keep yet built in western Europe. Similarly Westminster Hall, which was also the achievement of Rufus, was the largest roofed space (238 feet × 68 feet), being more than twice the size of the emperor's hall at Goslar. Yet Rufus is reported to have commented that it was only 'half as big as it should have been'.[12] The new cathedral at Winchester (533 feet long), where Rufus was brought for burial after being killed in the New Forest, was surpassed in length only by the third abbey church of Cluny, which was nearing completion at the same time.

Such displays of power gave a sense of reality to beliefs that the kings of England were destined to play a dominant role in European politics. William of Malmesbury states that, if belief in the transmigration of souls were permitted, the soul of Julius Caesar had entered Rufus. 'He had huge ambitions,' writes William, 'and he would have achieved them if he could have spun out the tissue of the Fates, or broken through and escaped from the violence of fortune. Such was his force of mind that he was audacious enough to promise himself any kingdom whatsoever.'[13] The best monastic historians like William enjoyed composing obituaries of this sort which evoked the antique world of pagan heroes striving against the gods. Such writing in a classical idiom was as Romanesque as the sculpture and painting of the time; it used classical motifs but the essentials were medieval. The image of Rufus as a conquering Caesar, cut off in his prime, was taken further by Gaimar in his romantic history of the English, which was written in c.1140 in French rhyming couplets and is here translated into prose: 'On account of his great nobleness all his neighbours were subject to him, and if he could have reigned longer he would have gone to Rome to claim the ancient right to that country which Brennius and Belinus had.'[14] Gaimar here associates the career of Rufus with Geoffrey of Monmouth's *History of the Kings of Britain*, which had just been published. Brennius and Belinus, the sackers of Rome in 390 BC, were (in Geoffrey's version) British kings who had first conquered the Gauls and the Germans before uniting against Rome. The fantastic achievements of this pair, like those of Arthur himself, fulfilled (in Geoffrey's story) the prophecy of the goddess Diana, who had told the Trojan Brutus to seek an island in the ocean beyond the setting of the sun and the realms of Gaul; there he would found a second Troy and from him would descend a line of kings who would make subject the 'circle of the whole earth'.[15]

Geoffrey's prophecy of Diana is a myth which explains the ambivalent position of Britain. It is an island which lies on the periphery of the earth, beyond the setting of the sun as seen from the centre, but its rulers originate from the centre and are destined to return there to rule. It is impossible to know how much of this myth Geoffrey made up and how much of it derived from oral traditions or writings in books now lost. What is not in doubt, however, is the popularity of Geoffrey's work: it is extant in over two hundred medieval manuscripts (more than Bede's *History*), fifty of which date from the twelfth century. It was translated from Geoffrey's Latin into French, English and Welsh and one-third of the total number of manuscripts are in continental Europe. These facts make Geoffrey's history the most popular work emanating from medieval Britain and perhaps the most popular of all medieval histories.

As significant as Geoffrey's popularity is the credence he was given by reputable and scholarly writers. Thus Robert the Englishman includes Geoffrey's prophecy of Diana in his lectures as an explanation of why England is prosperous despite its lying beyond the climes. By his time Geoffrey's history had been incorporated into numerous English chronicles, along with the Old Testament and miscellaneous late Roman sources, in narratives of the seven ages of the world from its creation up to the Christian era. This illustrates the medieval scribal tendency to add new information to old rather than to evaluate it critically. The acceptance of Geoffrey is the more remarkable considering that William of Newburgh in the latter half of the twelfth century had put forward the objections which modern critics repeat. William compares Geoffrey's narratives with Bede's and concludes that Geoffrey 'has dressed up in colourful Latin style under the honest name of history tales of Arthur taken from old British legends and augmented by his own inventions'.[16] Geoffrey's history triumphantly survived such criticism because William's comments had a very limited circulation (a problem for any critic of a popular work before the invention of printing) and also perhaps because Geoffrey told people what they wanted to hear. He put the history of Britain into a grand and dynamic context which fed the ambitions of the Anglo-Norman conquerors. Although Geoffrey's book concerned Britain rather than England and might have been interpreted as Celtic propaganda against the Normans, it was dedicated to Robert earl of Gloucester, Henry I's distinguished bastard son. Indeed Geoffrey went further and wished to attribute the work not to his humble self but to Earl Robert, so that it too would be the offspring of the illustrious king.

The best illustration of how Geoffrey's history inflated Englishmen's sense of their own importance is William Fitz Stephen's description of London in the time of Becket. It is the most famous city in the world according to William. To it merchants bring gold from Arabia, oil from Babylon, gems from the Nile, silk from China, wines from France, and furs from the Baltic lands and Russia. The references to gold from Arabia and gems from the Nile were certainly clichés of the time rather than a factual description of trade goods. On the other hand French wines and a variety of northern furs were imported. As in Geoffrey's work fact, fiction and classical allusions are inextricably mixed together in William's account. He reveals his debt to Geoffrey by stating, 'on the good faith of chroniclers', that London is far older than Rome because it was founded by the Trojan Brutus.[17] William likewise cites the prophecy of Diana concerning Brutus, though he ascribes it to the oracle of Apollo. In this version the second Troy of the prophecy is London, and the ruler from Britain in particular who subjected the world is Constantine, the greatest of the emperors from a Christian point of view.

A modern scientist rightly dismisses as nonsense medieval *mappae mundi* which make Jerusalem the centre of the world and histories which claim that London was founded by the Trojans. Nevertheless appreciation of such ideas is essential to a historian because they gave twelfth-century people, however erroneously, a concept of their place in space and time. England's rulers believed that they lived on the edge of the world and increasingly in the twelfth century they aspired to reach the centre, that Jerusalem which was both a real place and a symbol of contact with the divine, the umbilical cord of the earth. Viewed in this way, the aims of Richard I in particular can be seen in their medieval perspective. His ten-year reign (1189–99), of which only six months were spent in England, was not an aberration from the practice of his predecessors but a progression from it. The Norman kings (William the Conqueror, William Rufus and Henry I) had spent less than half their time in England and Richard's father, Henry II, did likewise. Richard was not much criticized by chroniclers for going on crusade and taxing England so heavily. On the contrary, his exactions were blamed on his counsellors and he himself was written about as a hero who had raised England's name by fighting for Jerusalem. His successors, King John and Henry III, spent much more of their time in England but that was not from choice. Rather it was because they were being driven out of their continental lands and out of Mediterranean politics by their rivals, the great French kings, Philip Augustus and St Louis.

The ambitions of England's rulers were fed by a variety of historical myths and chance circumstances. Paradoxically they were given literary shape during Stephen's reign (1135–54) when the kingdom was torn by civil war. This is the time of Geoffrey of Monmouth's *History of the Kings of Britain*, of Gaimar's *Estoire des Engleis*, and of the speech made at the battle of the Standard in 1138 which celebrated the defeat of the Scots. In the earliest report of this speech, which is attributed to the bishop of the Orkneys, the 'great men of England and the distinguished men of Normandy' are reminded of their pre-eminence: 'No one resists you with impunity; brave France has tried and taken shelter; fierce England lay captive; rich Apulia flourished anew under your rule; renowned Jerusalem and noble Antioch both submitted themselves to you.'[18] This is one of the few sources which explicitly links the Normans who conquered England with the achievements of Robert Guiscard in Italy and of his son, Bohemond, who became prince of Antioch during the First Crusade. If this speech were made by the bishop of the Orkneys (in another version it is attributed to the Yorkshire baron Walter Espec), it would have served also to link these islands on the edge of the world with the centre in Jerusalem, as the Normans had reached both. In the versions in which it has come down to us this speech, like Urban II's at Clermont before the First Crusade, is too literary and learned to have directly inspired knights on the battlefield. What it does indicate, however, is the way the Norman victories of the eleventh century had developed into a mythology of conquest in the twelfth which united English and Norman ambitions. All the people of England, according to the chronicler Henry of Huntingdon, replied 'Amen! Amen!' to this speech.

Interpretations of English history

Historians of the nineteenth and twentieth centuries, like their medieval counterparts, have reacted ambivalently to the fact that England was placed on the edge of the medieval world. Some Victorians proudly emphasized England's splendid isolation, while others welcomed the Norman Conquest. Thomas Carlyle's approach was as extravagant as anything in Geoffrey of Monmouth. Without the Normans and Plantagenets, he asked, what would England have been? He trenchantly replied: 'A gluttonous race of Jutes and Angles, capable of no great combinations; lumbering about in potbellied equanimity; not dreaming of heroic toil and silence and endurance, such as leads to the high places of the Universe and the golden mountain-tops where dwell the Spirits of the Dawn.'[19] Edward Freeman, on the other hand, with prejudices almost as explicit, saw the strength of England coming not from the forceful drilling of the Normans but from its endurance of this fiery trial. For Freeman England belonged to the Teutonic north; indeed it is a more purely Teutonic country than Germany itself. 'We Englishmen', he wrote, 'live in an island and have always moved in a sort of world of our own.'[20] This gave the natives the strength to resist and absorb the incomers: first the Normans, then the accession of the Angevins 'which was almost equivalent to a second conquest', and finally the 'fresh swarms of foreigners under Henry III'. Where Carlyle and Freeman agree is in crediting the conquerors with encouraging English unity.

Popular Victorian historians like Carlyle and Freeman could not avoid a polemical style when discussing England's medieval identity because they wrote for an audience imbued with national feeling.

Historians of all the European powers in the nineteenth century laboured to produce scholarly editions of the records of their peoples and to explain their national significance to the public. The problem was that the facts of medieval history were often at variance with the pattern of nineteenth-century national states. Who did Charlemagne belong to, for example, France or Germany? And how did the most powerful government of the twelfth and thirteenth centuries, the papacy, fit into this nationalist scheme? French and German scholars coped with the overlap in their record sources sometimes by agreement but more often by printing the same documents in the *Recueil des Historiens des Gaules et de la France* and in the *Monumenta Germaniae Historica*. English historians faced a more manageable task, as the Anglo-Saxon kingdom had developed a distinct identity precociously early and some medieval writers had believed (with Freeman) that Englishmen moved in a sort of world of their own. The special problem for English national history came with the Norman Conquest, as it appeared at a stroke to destroy the distinctiveness of England and subject it to continental domination in military, ecclesiastical and cultural terms. Furthermore, as Freeman points out, this domination persisted beyond the Normans through the Angevins and into the reign of Henry III.

The most influential Victorian historian to tackle the problem of England's medieval identity was William Stubbs in his authoritative *Select Charters*, first published in 1870, and in the three-volume *Constitutional History*, which followed between 1873 and 1878. These works were overtly nationalist, as their purpose was to make English students understand their own institutions as well as those of ancient Greece and Rome on which they had been reared. These institutions, Stubbs argued, 'possess a living interest for every nation that realizes its identity, and [they] have exercised on the wellbeing of the civilized world an influence not inferior certainly to that of the classical nations'.[21] In other words, English national consciousness was to be identified and nurtured by studying the origins of its monarchy, law courts and parliament. At his most ambitious Stubbs was proposing an alternative curriculum for higher education in which the future rulers of England at Oxford and Cambridge would read their Latin in Magna Carta and Matthew Paris instead of Cicero and Livy. This would serve to make history respectable as a subject for academic study and it would also be a better preparation for governing because (in Stubbs's opinion at least) English history was more relevant than that of Greece and Rome.

Stubbs was too knowledgeable and intelligent a scholar not to know that the flaw in his approach was that in the period on which he concentrated, between the Norman Conquest and the reign of Edward I (the same period as this book concerns), many English institutions were similar to continental ones in their outward forms and nomenclature. Royal courts of justice, fiefs, ecclesiastical councils, parliaments, communes and liberties were not unique to England. Although Stubbs admitted the deep and wide basis which medieval England shared with the continent, he argued that it was a mistake to think that customs 'are borrowed or derived in their matured form by one national system from another'.[22] Taking his metaphor from the railways, which were such a prominent feature of Victorian England, he argued instead that 'the history of institutions, as of nations, runs through occasional tunnels'.[23] These hide the continuous line by which for example medieval boroughs grew out of Anglo-Saxon burghs, or parliament out of the witan. Twelfth- and thirteenth-century institutions were of course connected with their Anglo-Saxon predecessors. Stubbs was mistaken not in this assertion but in his insistence that institutional practice could not be derived by one system from another. Boroughs and parliament in his view had to progress in a single line from their Anglo-Saxon beginnings, even if parts of the line were concealed from view. They could not be significantly influenced by Flemish towns or the French *parlement*, however close the similarities and nomenclature might appear to be, because it was an axiom that each national system created its own institutions and gave to its people a unique and inimitable character. This axiom derived from the fashionable Hegelian philosophy of the time and it also justified Stubbs's hope that English students would realize their identity by studying their history. If that identity were confused with that of France, Germany or Spain, the wrong conclusions might be drawn.

To ensure that only the right message reached his readers Stubbs avoided expressions which belonged in his opinion 'more properly to French and German history'.[24] He disliked the word 'commune', for example, as a description of an association because it was French. Consequently when the rebel barons of 1258 formed 'le commun de Engleterre' Stubbs translated this as 'the commonalty of England'. Whereas 'commune' had associations with revolution and France, both in the thirteenth century and in the nineteenth, 'commonalty' was an archaic English term for a corporation (the mayor and 'commonalty' of a borough) and also for the common people (the commons as distinct from the lords). These usages suited Stubbs's purpose, as 'commonalty' sounded distinctively English and its archaism suggested something conservative rather than revolutionary. Nevertheless this translation was misleading, as the 'commune' of 1258 was in origin a conspiratorial association of barons associated in particular with the Frenchman Simon de Montfort (as explained in chapter 13 below). Its antecedents were in revolutions in continental towns in the twelfth century rather than in the common folk of England.

Although the materials for medieval English history have not substantially changed since the Victorian period, attitudes to it have. The medieval past no longer has to bear the burden which Stubbs imposed on it of justifying England's imperial mission and demonstrating the unique value of its constitutional arrangements. Instead of insisting on a linear growth of institutions from Anglo-Saxon roots, this book emphasizes how England's rulers were influenced by movements of power and ideas from overseas. These influences would have been felt even without the Norman Conquest and the Angevin kings, as they were transmitted by clergy and scholars as much as by knights. Nevertheless the fact that England, like southern Italy and the kingdom of Jerusalem, was conquered by aliens helped to accelerate and reinforce change. Highlighting foreign rule in this way does not obscure England's identity. On the contrary, it clarifies and accentuates it by viewing it as far as possible through medieval eyes. In that Jerusalem-centred world England stood on the outer rim of Europe and its rulers were drawn towards the centre. They knew the world was round, but they viewed it not as a mere fact of modern cartography but as an image of faith and hope. Like the rose windows and circular mazes found in the great Gothic cathedrals, or the round table of King Arthur, the Jerusalem-centred world radiated supernatural power and mystery.

England and Britain

What exactly was meant by England? Where were its frontiers? How did it fit into Britain? These were contentious questions which went far beyond geography. Britain could be readily represented on a medieval map as the island on the edge of the world which the Romans had called *Britannia*. England's boundaries were not so easily defined. The word *Englalond* is not recorded in Old English until the eleventh century, when it describes the territory of 'the kingdom of the English' (*regnum Anglorum* in Latin). The ideal of a united English people (the *Angelcynn* in Old English) had brought together the different Anglo-Saxon kingdoms into a single unit which by 1050 formed a country called 'England'. The territory of this English kingdom was clearly defined to the south and the east by the sea, though it was also true that the greatest threats of invasion came from these directions: from Normandy, Flanders, Denmark and Norway.

Within Britain there were no firm land frontiers to the west and north designating the limits of England, though there were old boundary lines in the form of Offa's Dyke and Hadrian's Wall. The English described their opponents to the west as the Welsh, which originally simply meant 'foreigners'. They were perceived as different especially because they spoke their own language, which fed a whole literature and rich culture with its roots in the Romano-British past. Welsh intellectuals described themselves as Britons. In the north was the kingdom of the Scots, which was growing in power by 1050 as it incorporated part of English Northumbria as well as the old Pictish–Scottish kingdom. Whereas the Welsh were relatively homogenous in their Celtic culture, the Scots were extraordinarily diverse as they incorporated Anglo-Saxon, Celtic, Pictish and Norse elements. The Norwegian kings were as great a threat to the Scots as the English, as their sea power extended all round the Scottish coasts and islands. In 1098 King Edgar conceded to Magnus Barelegs king of Norway all the islands to the west of Scotland, including the holy island of Iona which was the burial place of the early Scottish kings.

The characteristics which made the English a distinct people or nation had been articulated in Bede's *Ecclesiastical History of the English People* in the eighth century and constantly repeated by historians since. The message of Bede's history, which was all the more effective because of his careful chronology and use of documents, was that the English people were deservedly superior to the Britons and Celts, who had betrayed the incoming English by neglecting to convert them to Christianity. By the just judgement of God, the argument ran, the Britons had been driven westwards to the peripheries of the island (to the shores of Cornwall and the Atlantic Ocean and to the inhospitable mountains of Wales and Scotland), where they eked out a wretched existence as herdsmen and shepherds. This made sense of the political and economic geography of Britain where the English had by far the most arable land.

The English sense of their predominant power within Britain had led Anglo-Saxon kings to lay claim to the whole island, even though they could not enforce such a claim on the ground. The significance of the Norman conquerors was that they might succeed where their predecessors had failed. By establishing himself as the lawful successor of Edward the Confessor (1042–66), William the Conqueror took on his purported role as king of the whole of Britain. Most remarkably, in a document from Winchester Edward the Confessor had been entitled 'the industrious king of the English and of all the islands and all the peoples existing roundabout'.[25] If the English king were to make good this claim he would have to defeat the Norwegians' sea power as well as a variety of kings in Wales, Scotland and Ireland. Nevertheless the Normans were quick to take up the English claim to jurisdiction over the whole of Britain, even in its extended sense of the British Isles. At the council of Winchester in 1072 Lanfranc, the lawyer from Italy and Norman abbot who was William the Conqueror's archbishop of Canterbury, had passages from Bede's *Ecclesiastical History of the English People* read out loud in order to demonstrate that Canterbury had jurisdiction 'over the whole island which they call Britain and over Ireland as well'.[26]

In response, Pope Gregory VII authorized Lanfranc in 1073 to extirpate vice among the Irish in particular, 'but also in the island of the English'.[27] The papal injunction to extirpate alleged Celtic sexual vices was significant, as this was the justification in the twelfth century for Henry II's invasion of Ireland. In calling Britain 'the island of the English' the drafters in Rome of Gregory VII's letter were probably not making a careless geographical error. Rather, prompted by Lanfranc's envoys who had learned their Anglo-Saxon history, the pope was making a political claim. The Latin translation of the Anglo-Saxon Chronicle done in the 980s by Ealdorman Aethelweard declared that 'Britain is now called England, thereby assuming the name of the victors'.[28] By describing Britain as English and giving the see of Canterbury moral authority over the Irish, Gregory VII gave the Norman conquerors authority to extend their power throughout the British

Isles. Paradoxically the Normans attempted to conquer Britain in the name of the English whom they themselves had conquered.

This was the complex ideological basis for the remarkable expansion of 'England' within the 'British Isles', which Sir Rees Davies has called *The First English Empire*. He dated the beginning of this empire from 1093, when Normans were involved in the killing of Máel Coluim Cenmór (Malcolm III 'Canmore'), king of Scots, and Rhys ap Tewdwr, king of Deheubarth or South Wales. In the long term the struggles of the twelfth and thirteenth centuries were to show that Britain could not be reduced to an 'island of the English'. War and colonization clarified and emphasized the cultural differences between England and its neighbours. In place of an undifferentiated island of Britain, the maps made by Matthew Paris in the thirteenth century (see p. 236 below) show England (*Anglia*), Wales (*Wallia*) and Scotland (*Scotia*) as distinct territories. This was to be the enduring reality of English history and identity.

PART I

The Normans (1066–1135)

The Normans took their name from the 'Northmen', the Viking pirates who had attacked both England and France in the ninth century. In the same way as King Alfred acknowledged Viking settlement in the northern part of England, the Frankish king, Charles the Simple, ceded his northern territory at the mouth of the Seine in 911 to Rollo, whom the Normans recognized as their first duke. Norman history in the next century is very obscure. By the time William the Conqueror was born, however (in 1027 or 1028), the Normans had created a distinct identity for themselves. Their earliest historian Dudo of St Quentin recorded a story about the homage done by Rollo to Charles the Simple. The Frankish bishops insisted that Rollo should kneel down and kiss the king's foot. Rollo refused, although he permitted one of his warriors to approach the king. This man indeed kissed the royal foot, but he did so without kneeling down by tipping the king backwards off his throne amidst the laughter of the Normans.

This story reveals more about the Normans of William the Conqueror's time than about the events of 911. They were proud and ferocious warriors without respect for rank or tradition other than their own. It was as a typical Norman that Robert Guiscard took the pope prisoner at Civitate in 1053 and went on to become duke of Apulia and Calabria ostensibly by the grace of God and St Peter. His son Bohemond impressed himself similarly on the memory of Anna Comnena, the daughter of the Byzantine emperor Alexius, when he towered above both crusaders and Greeks in the imperial tent inspiring admiration and terror: 'A certain charm hung about the man but it was marred by a general sense of the horrible. For in the whole of his body he showed himself implacable and savage both in his size and glance. He was no man's slave, subject to none of all the world; for such are great natures, people say, even if they are of humble origin.'[1] These Mediterranean Normans, descendants or followers of Tancred of Hauteville, were only remotely connected with the conquerors of England. Nevertheless there were contacts between them. When William the Conqueror's half-brother, Odo of Bayeux earl of Kent, was arrested in 1082, he was believed to have been planning an expedition to Italy to make himself pope, which would have linked up the Normans in England with those in Italy. The similarities between the two groups moreover were noticed by medieval writers, even if only as wishful thinking. William of Poitiers in his account of the conquest of England (written within a decade of the battle of Hastings) mentions Norman triumphs in Italy and Byzantium, and the author of *The Song of the Battle of Hastings* (which may not be strictly contemporary) has William the Conqueror exhort his men before the battle as: 'Apulian and Calabrian, Sicilian, whose darts fly in swarms; Normans, ripe for incomparable achievements!'[2]

The Normans had a mixture of contradictory qualities which chroniclers delighted to describe. In Italy Geoffrey Malaterra (who may have been of Norman origin himself) commented on their passion for wealth and power, though they despised what they had and were always looking for more. Another contradiction was their love of flamboyant dress and their impulsiveness; and yet, when necessity demanded, they could endure all the rigours of a disciplined military life. In England William of Malmesbury, independently of Geoffrey, described similar contradictions: 'The Normans were – and still are [William was writing in about 1125] – proudly apparelled and delicate about their food, though not excessively. They are a race inured to war and scarcely know how to live without it ... They live in huge houses with moderation. They envy their equals and wish to excel their superiors. They plunder their subjects, though they defend them from others. They are faithful to their lords, though a slight offence makes them perfidious. They measure treachery by its chance of success.'[3] Such contradictions were resolved by the logic of war. The Normans were so formidable because they were warlords operating in a Europe that was beginning to be more settled and prosperous. As descendants of the Vikings they were the last barbarian invaders. But they had learned a great deal since the time of Rollo's legendary act of insubordination to the Frankish king. The art of war, like the art of building in stone or the 'liberal arts' of the schoolmen, had become more sophisticated in the eleventh century, and Norman knights were its chief exponents.

The best monument to Norman military methods is the Bayeux Tapestry, though it was probably made by English artists. Its most striking and recurrent features are the groups of knights in chainmail, equipped with long shields and lances, charging on their warhorses. They give the same impression of vigour and ferocity which Anna Comnena observed in Bohemond. The 'general sense of the horrible' is conveyed too in the Tapestry in its lower border where the dead are depicted in terrible postures lying amid a litter of abandoned shields, broken swords and wounded horses. The importance of eating well, which William of Malmesbury had commented on, is also graphically illustrated in the Tapestry. The first action the Normans take on landing on English soil is to seize livestock, slaughter it with their battle axes, roast it on spits and serve it up at a banquet presided over by the warrior bishop, Odo of Bayeux. From there the Normans move on to building a castle at Hastings and burning villages. The Tapestry's emphasis on the practicalities and daily routines of war indicates the Normans' professionalism. Duke William, like the duke of Wellington, knew that battles are won by attention to details of supply. A large section of the Tapestry shows the Normans' thorough preparation for the invasion: trees being cut down and made into planks; ships being specially built and launched; the loading of supplies (coats of mail, swords, lances, helmets); and finally the putting into the ships of the Norman knights' most precious possession, their highly trained warhorses. Almost as many horses as men are shown in the ships crossing the Channel and Duke William's own charger is individually depicted at the start of the battle.

In the Bayeux Tapestry the invaders are not described as 'Normans' but as 'Franci', that is 'Franks' or 'Frenchmen'. Similarly the Anglo-Saxon Chronicle describes them as 'Frencyscan'. In its account of the events of 1066 King Harold defeated the Normans (the 'Normen', that is, the Norwegians) at Stamford Bridge, before himself being killed by the French at Hastings. Similarly the Norman kings of England invariably addressed their people in charters as 'French and English' and not as 'Normans and English'. These usages raise doubts about the cohesion of Norman identity, despite Norman and other chroniclers' descriptions of themselves. The solution lies in the relative position of the observer. The Normans were generally described as Frenchmen in England to distinguish them from the Northmen and because they came from France (Francia). Furthermore a fair number of the 'French' who fought at Hastings were not Normans anyway, but men from Brittany, Maine, Picardy and Flanders. In France itself, on the other hand, they were described as Normans to distinguish them from Angevins, Poitevins, Gascons and so on. Although the Normans are called a 'race' (*gens*) by some contemporaries (Orderic Vitalis, for example), their cohesion lay essentially in their beliefs about themselves rather than in genealogy or blood relationships. Scarcely any Norman family could reliably trace its descent back before the year AD 1000, and their greatest duke was generally known in the Middle Ages not as the Conqueror but as William the Bastard.

Their lack of distinguished ancestry made the Normans' ideology of war and power all the more important to them. They had to fight all the harder to dominate the oldest institutions in Europe (the papacy, the Byzantine Empire and the Anglo-Saxon kingdom) and they were ready to absorb men and ideas from any quarter which would help them. In military terms they embodied the greatness of the barbarian Franks who had conquered Roman Gaul and created the Carolingian empire. But they reflected too the new French knighthood whose prowess was enshrined in the *Song of Roland*. By the twelfth century, as a consequence rather than a cause of their success, the victors of Hastings were: 'You whom France famed for nobility has bred, chivalrous warriors, renowned young men whom God chooses and favours!'[4]

Although the Normans were essentially warlords, they were a force much more complex than mere barbarians or brigands. A contradiction at first sight is the way they succeeded in attracting the two greatest churchmen and intellectuals of their time, Lanfranc and Anselm from south of the Alps, to their cause. These two men built up the new monastery at Bec in William the Conqueror's time into one of the most famous and enterprising schools in Europe, and they became in succession archbishops of Canterbury. This paradox between the Normans' love of war and their advancement of religion did not escape the notice of William of Malmesbury. He says, exaggerating the contrast between the old and the new, that 'by their arrival in England they revived the observance of religion which had grown lifeless.

Everywhere you see churches in villages, and monasteries in towns and cities, erected in a new style of architecture.'[5]

The great Norman churches, epitomized by Durham cathedral above all, are now the best memorial to the aspirations of the Normans. Their ambition and love of display are seen in the massive proportions of the nave; their blend of the traditional and the new in its Romanesque arches and cylindrical pillars on which is imposed the first rib-vault to roof a European cathedral; the demands of war dictate the choice of site on a precipitous peninsula, which is further defended by the bishop's huge castle alongside the cathedral. The Normans built their churches and castles beside each other on fortified hills, as if the surrounding population were pagan hordes instead of native Christians of long standing. Building stone had never before been massed on such a scale to symbolize both man's mastery of his environment and the individual's puniness in the face of power. In a brilliant and ultimately inexplicable interlude the Normans commanded the forces of their time and identified divine authority with themselves.

2

The Norman Conquest
(1066–87)

In the centuries before 1066 England had experienced numerous over-seas invasions and it was ruled by the Danish dynasty of Cnut between 1016 and 1042. William the Conqueror's invasion was the second of the year. A few days before William crossed the Channel in September 1066, Harold of England had defeated at Stamford Bridge in Yorkshire as formidable an invasion force led by the Norwegian king Harold Hardrada and Earl Tostig, who was Harold of England's brother. Duke William moreover came ostensibly not as a foreign conqueror but as the recognized heir of Edward the Confessor. Nor as a Norman was he entirely a stranger. Edward the Confessor, whose mother was a Norman, had introduced Normans into high places, most notably by making Robert of Jumièges bishop of London and archbishop of Canterbury. According to Edward's biography men from France became his most secret counsellors and the controllers of business in the royal palace. Seen from this viewpoint, Harold's death at the battle of Hastings was simply the elimination of a usurper and Duke William was crowned king of the English in Westminster abbey on Christmas Day 1066 as the lawful successor of Edward the Confessor. William described Edward as his kinsman and he claimed to rule over the 'country [*patria*] of the English by hereditary right'.[1]

Immediately after the Conquest

If these were the circumstances, it is surprising that the battle of Hast-ings became so memorable and that William of Malmesbury and other

English writers of the twelfth century looked back on it as 'that fatal day for England, the sad destruction of our dear country [*dulcis patria*]'.[2] The change of attitude is best accounted for by the events of the decade following William's coronation. In the Normans' opinion the English were disloyal to their lawful king and betrayed him by rebelling. The Anglo-Saxon Chronicle on the other hand maintains that William did not behave like an English king, as he let his foreigners oppress the people. The coronation itself had not gone smoothly and it was a presage of what was to come. The Normans had introduced a new element into the ceremony whereby the congregation were asked, as in France, whether it was their wish that William should be crowned as their lord. But this acclamation of the new king only emphasized the division between the English and the Normans, as the question had to be put twice: first by the archbishop of York in English and then by the bishop of Coutances in French. Furthermore the shouting within the church sounded so sinister that the Norman guards outside took fright and started setting fire to London.

Much of the Normans' oppressive conduct in the next decade can be explained by nervousness of this sort. They found they were unwelcome and so they took steps to defend themselves. This 'primitive state of the kingdom after the conquest' is graphically recalled by Richard Fitz Nigel in the twelfth century: 'What were left of the conquered English lay in ambush for the suspected and hated race of Normans and murdered them secretly in woods and unfrequented places as opportunity offered.'[3] Such killers subsequently became the heroes of folk legend, like Hereward the Wake, and then merged into the Robin Hood tradition of free Englishmen lying in wait under the greenwood tree for cruel Norman sheriffs and fat prelates. The Normans themselves reacted by punishing whole districts with murder fines when one of their men was killed. The crime of murder now meant killing Normans. In these early years the Normans were obliged to behave as an army of occupation, fortified in their new castles and sallying out in groups to interrogate people and cow them into submission. The Anglo-Saxon Chronicle concludes its annal for 1066 with the comment that the Norman regents, Odo of Bayeux and William Fitz Osbern, 'built castles far and wide throughout the land, oppressing the wretched people, and things went continually from bad to worse'.[4]

Immediately after the Conquest things went from bad to worse for the Normans as much as for the English. William was in a most hazardous position. His rule in England was threatened not only by sporadic native rebellions but by the Scots and the Welsh and much more seriously by the Danes. Furthermore in the long term he was far from secure in Normandy where his own family, the outlying areas of Norman rule and the French monarchy were all potential threats. After 1073 William spent most of his time in Normandy, not peacefully at home enjoying his triumphs but in wars with the men of Maine (1073), the Bretons (1076), the Angevins (1077–8 and 1081) and the French (1087). In the years 1067–72 he had spent more time in England but this too was primarily in order to suppress rebellions. The earliest of these occurred in 1067–8 and were directed against Odo of Bayeux in Kent and William Fitz Osbern, and then in 1068 Exeter rebelled. In 1069–70 there were larger risings which looked in retrospect like a national rebellion. The Northumbrians joined forces with a Danish fleet and with the English claimant to the throne, the Atheling ('prince') Edgar, and captured York where they killed 'many hundreds of Frenchmen' (according to the Anglo-Saxon Chronicle).

This led to the notorious 'Harrying of the North', when King William in the winter of 1069–70 systematically burned the countryside and destroyed villages so that Danish or Norwegian fleets in future would find nothing to live off. How permanent such damage was and whether the numerous deaths of men and livestock from disease were directly caused by William's policy are matters for debate. Certainly wastelands were prominent in the north in Domesday Book fifteen years later. Although William showed himself ruthless towards the peasants of the north, he was lenient towards the English earls, Gospatric and Waltheof, who had taken part in the revolt. This proved a mistake, as they both subsequently betrayed William and in 1069 two other English earls, Edwin and Morcar, also rose in rebellion. From 1070, the year in which William suppressed these rebellions and appointed Lanfranc (a Lombard by origin and a Norman monk by adoption) as archbishop of Canterbury, government in England became more ruthless and more closely identified with Norman rather than native interests. This is the time too when English was superseded by Latin as the written language of government, presumably because Lanfranc and other foreign clerics found it uncouth and could not understand it anyway. William's most impressive achievement was to march up into Scotland as far as the Tay in 1072 and compel King Malcolm to submit to him. This action was essential for controlling

Northumbria and it also helped Lanfranc's claim to be primate of all Britain.

In retrospect in the twelfth century these rebellions against William and his suppression of them were seen in nationalistic terms. For example, Orderic Vitalis described the beheading of Earl Waltheof for treason in 1076 as if he were a martyr. The execution was held at dawn to prevent the English rescuing 'so noble a compatriot' and Waltheof was venerated as a saint at Crowland abbey where he was buried.[5] His head was miraculously restored to his body and in a vision this man who had been an earl on earth appeared as a king in heaven. Orderic himself composed an epitaph stating that Waltheof had been done to death by Norman judges. Despite Orderic's enthusiasm Waltheof was not a simple English patriot. His father was a Dane, he himself had supported the Danish invasion of 1069, and he was suspected of doing the same in 1075. He had twice been pardoned and reinstated by William, once after the battle of Hastings and again after the rising of 1069–70. The opposition William faced from earls like Waltheof was directed against him not necessarily as a Norman oppressor but as an English king. Edward the Confessor had experienced similar rebellions. The difference was that William suppressed them with such vigour and ruthlessness that his methods were felt in retrospect to be un-English.

Debates about the Conquest

No event in English history has been more continually or fiercely debated than the Norman Conquest. Disagreement started at the time of the Conquest itself in the contrast between the eulogy of William the Conqueror by William of Poitiers and the harsh verse obituary given him in the Anglo-Saxon Chronicle. Many of the essential facts, let alone interpretations, are in dispute and the truth is now impossible to establish. Did William have a legitimate claim to the throne, for example? William of Poitiers, the Bayeux Tapestry and other Norman sources imply that William had been promised the kingdom by Edward the Confessor, whereas the Anglo-Saxon Chronicle and Florence of Worcester make no mention of this. Did the English chroniclers suppress this information, or not know about it, or did they fail to mention it simply because Edward never made such a promise? The right answer is anybody's guess and any answer implies that someone was a liar. The Normans themselves overcame this problem in the end by arguing that they ruled by right of conquest anyway. They were accustomed to testing disputed evidence by appealing to the supernatural through an ordeal. God would allow the just man to be unharmed by hot iron or water or to triumph in trial by combat. The ordeal of the battle of Hastings was the supreme trial and the result proved who had the better right.

In the twelfth century, however, such appeals to the supernatural began to be distrusted and schoolmen argued that it was better to inquire into things by human reason. Thenceforward debating about the Norman Conquest became a matter for academics and there it has remained. Commentators in the twentieth century have been less concerned with the rightness or wrongness of William's claim than with the effects of the Conquest. This discussion gives scope to the most diverse points of view. As with the succession question, it is more useful to state the problems than to attempt to resolve them. The following contradictory statements by professional historians illustrate how opinions can differ. 'At the level of literate and aristocratic society,' Sir Richard Southern says in a presidential address to the Royal Historical Society, 'no country in Europe, between the rise of the barbarian kingdoms and the twentieth century, has undergone so radical a change in so short a time as England experienced after 1066.'[6] On the other hand H.G. Richardson and G.O. Sayles in *The Governance of Medieval England* state that 'if the Conqueror's will had prevailed and the dukedom of Normandy had gone to his eldest son (Robert) and his line and the kingdom of England to his second son (William Rufus) and his line, the Norman Conquest would have been a transitory episode and the foreign element it had introduced would, we make bold to say, have been absorbed into English society almost without trace'.[7]

Such diversity is possible because opinions differ about what made society distinctively English or Norman. If castles, feudalism, bureaucratic government, foreigners in high places, monastic reform and an active urban life were all characteristics of Anglo-Saxon England (as is argued by some), then the Normans cannot have been responsible for cataclysmic change because these were already features of their own society and indeed of all advanced European states of their time. The significant time of change, it can be argued, was not 1066 but the rule earlier in the century of Cnut and his Danes, or the period earlier still when Alfred and his successors organized a unified kingdom in reaction to the first Danish invasions. Just as plausibly on the other hand it can be argued that the significant period of change reflecting overseas movements came in the twelfth century with the government of Henry I, the civil wars of Stephen's reign and the reorganization of the kingdom by the Angevin Henry II. The first Norman conquerors could be absorbed (Richardson and Sayles argue) 'almost without trace', just as the Danes had been absorbed before them, whereas the cross-Channel monarchy of the twelfth century made greater demands and transformed English society.

Southern and others who argue the case for radical change as an immediate consequence of 1066 marshal equally attractive arguments. The Old English aristocracy was eliminated by William the Conqueror. Although this was not an immediate consequence of the battle of Hastings, by the time of the Domesday survey in 1086 only two Englishmen, Thurkill of Arden and Colswein of Lincoln, held tenancies of the first order under the king himself. Some aristocrats had been killed, many dispossessed, and others were exiles: in Scotland and Denmark, and even in Russia and in the imperial guard in Byzantium. In 1081 English exiles defended the Byzantine territory of Durazzo against Robert Guiscard and his Normans. Similarly nearly all bishops and abbots were foreigners by 1086 and as a consequence the English language ceased to be used as the written language of government and of the religious life. The few who persisted with English, like the writers of the Anglo-Saxon Chronicle, were therefore making a deliberate effort to preserve their culture in the face of foreign hostility. Such a cataclysmic and pessimistic view of the consequences of the Conquest also reflects medieval opinion. For William of Malmesbury the day of Hastings was that *dies fatalis* for England.

But even William of Malmesbury's words can be interpreted in another way. The day was fatal, he says, because of the changeover to new lords. Historians have argued that the new Norman lords had neither the wish nor the ability to change everything. On the contrary, they readily stepped into the places of their predecessors and they did their best to maintain and strengthen Anglo-Saxon institutions because they had no governmental ideology of their own. The fact, for example, that the royal Chancery used Latin instead of English for its writs from the 1070s onwards was simply a change in the medium of communication. The form and meaning of the writs, with their stark instructions, continued to reflect the authoritarianism of Anglo-Saxon royal government. Similarly the basic institutions of counties and hundreds, with their officers and courts, remained essentially unchanged. The Norman rulers simply called earls 'counts' and sheriffs 'viscounts'; such well-established royal offices were too useful to abolish. Above all, William the Conqueror continued with the English taxation and coinage systems because from a king's point of view these were the best in Europe. They gave England its reputation for huge wealth and allowed the Norman kings to pay their armies.

If this line of thought is pursued very far, however, it raises the question of how the Normans overcame a kingdom that was so well organized. The answer often given is to argue that, once William had become king, he could use the strength of the royal administration to advance the Conquest. At the regular meetings of county and hundred courts, for example, he and his men could discover who the property-owners were and who opposed the Normans. Domesday Book on this line of argument is the greatest monument to the efficiency of Anglo-Saxon government and it underlined continuity by asking how things stood on the day that Edward the Confessor had died. It may even have been based on Anglo-Saxon documents which were simply translated into Latin by the Normans. William's success therefore arose from his initial victory at Hastings and not from superior Norman administrative talents. It is not even necessary to argue that the Normans were superior warriors, as their success at Hastings can be attributed to luck. Harold and his men were exhausted and unprepared because they had just rushed down from the battle against the Norwegians at Stamford Bridge.

The argument that William was lucky comes back to the medieval notion that his victory was a divine judgement, either to punish the Anglo-Saxons for their sinfulness or to demonstrate William's righteousness, or both. The concept of the Anglo-Saxons' sinfulness which was expounded by William of Malmesbury (for example, he says that the nobility had been drunken and lustful, while the clergy enjoyed food and fancy vestments), has been developed by some historians into the larger idea that the Anglo-Saxons were politically decadent. Thus D.C. Douglas, a leading authority on the Norman Conquest, put forward as an agreed proposition that 'there can be little doubt that

England was politically decadent in 1066' and that this explained why it was unable to defend its civilization.[8] As Douglas knew, this notion went back to Carlyle's 'gluttonous race of Jutes and Angles' (see page 15 above) and this in its turn (via Milton and others) back to William of Malmesbury. As a foil to the decadent Anglo-Saxons, the Normans have sometimes been seen as supermen (either admirable or vicious according to taste) and this view too can be found in medieval sources in the Normans' opinion of themselves: Orderic Vitalis describes them as a warlike race, who continually struggle for mastery, and in the battle speeches recorded by their chroniclers Norman leaders insist on their superiority.

The Norman Conquest supplies a point of interest and identification for almost any point of view and this explains the variety of the problems and the difficulty of resolving them. Those who believe that battles can decisively alter history point to Hastings, while those who think change comes slowly and imperceptibly can argue that the battle by itself had little effect. Similarly those who favour authority and military discipline can recognize these traits in the Normans, while liberals and democrats (particularly in the nineteenth century and earlier) feel some kinship for the Anglo-Saxons. (In fact both Normandy and Anglo-Saxon England were warrior societies and all medieval groups had consultative assemblies.) Nationalist sentiments can likewise be used in a variety of guises. The Normans are either the oppressors of the English nation and language or its revivifiers. Although the Normans might not have recognized themselves in some of these guises, they would no doubt have been pleased that an interest was still being taken in them a thousand years later, as they liked to be noticed and intended to be remembered.

English feelings about the Normans

Judging from the evidence of the Anglo-Saxon Chronicle and of twelfth-century monastic writers, the Norman Conquest caused bitter resentment. The difficulty is to gauge how long this continued and to evaluate the testimony of monks who themselves lived under Norman rule. Orderic Vitalis, for example, describes England as being 'subjected' to William as a conqueror and to the foreign 'robbers' who were his supporters. Orderic's most recent editor, Dr Chibnall, finds this too inflammatory a statement and translates the Latin *praedonibus* not as 'robbers' but as 'invaders'.[9] Nevertheless it was probably robbery that Orderic meant, as later on in his book he reports that the Norman monk Guitmund refused preferment in England and told William the Conqueror to his face that 'the whole of England was like the hugest robbery [*praedam*]'.[10] According to Orderic, the words of this monk who had called the Norman acquisition of England 'robbery' were repeated all over the country. The distinction between plunder and legitimate spoils of war was a fine one. The Normans made no secret of the spoils they took. William of Poitiers says that English treasures were distributed to churches up and down France as well as in Normandy itself. King Harold's banner, which was woven of the purest gold, was sent as a thank-offering to Rome. The penances which were imposed by the Norman bishops on the invaders – for war of any sort was recognized to be a lapse from Christian perfection – are realistic about the conditions which prevailed at the time of the invasion. Not only are those who killed or wounded men in the battle itself to do penance but also those who killed resisters when foraging through the countryside or plundering.

Like the distinction between plunder and legitimate spoils, the difference between lawful taxation and theft depended on one's point of view. In its verse obituary of William the Conqueror the Anglo-Saxon Chronicle makes avarice his besetting sin and accuses him of piling up gold and silver taken from his subjects without justice or need. The arbitrariness of taxation is one of the Chronicle's continual themes, as is injustice. But the writer's tone is rhetorical rather than specific and inconsistencies are self-evident. Under the year 1086, for example, the collapse of law and order is castigated (the more just laws were talked about, the more unlawful things were done), whereas the entry for the next year admires the harshness of William's rule, which instilled such fear that an honest man could travel throughout the country with his pockets full of gold. Considering how much the king and his Normans coveted gold and silver in the Chronicle's opinion, it is surprising that there was anything left for honest travellers. The voice of the Anglo-Saxon Chronicle, which had always been pessimistic because it had started at the time of the Danish invasions in Alfred's reign and was composed by monks who looked forward to a better life in heaven, reached new depths of depression after 1066. The writer frequently concludes his record of the misfortunes of the year (storms, famine, disease, oppression) with an invocation to God to relieve the wretched people.

Such misfortunes were not necessarily new and neither were they all caused by the Normans, though William the Conqueror did use destruction of the countryside as a defensive tactic, not only in his Harrying of the North in 1070 but also in reaction to the threatened Danish invasion of 1085. The peculiar circumstances of the Norman Conquest, which made the lords of the land into an alien people as well as a ruling class, give this part of the Anglo-Saxon Chronicle its distinctive tone. Although it was written by monks who normally identified with the rulers, alienation after 1066 caused them to enunciate something which came close to a peasant or popular voice. The writer describes the sufferings of the people in the countryside and castigates the robber barons, most notably in the description of the troubles of Stephen's reign. This unusual tone disappears from English writing later in the twelfth century, once Norman and English ecclesiastics had begun to cooperate, and it does not reappear until the fourteenth century with the Peasants' Revolt and *Piers Plowman*. The Anglo-Saxon Chronicle therefore articulates a feeling which may have been deeper and more widespread than national sentiment. It voices the bitter helplessness of the labourers in the fields, who contended with the arbitrariness of nature exacerbated by the demands of lords.

A particular point of resentment against William the Conqueror was his introduction of the forest laws. The Chronicle's verse obituary devoted its principal attention to this. William protected deer and wild boar and let the hares run free by contrast with his meanness to people. In fact both Cnut and Edward the Confessor had maintained royal forests. Nevertheless the strict regulation of areas like the New Forest was undoubtedly Norman. The purpose may have been governmental as much as protective of royal prerogatives and pleasures. William was certainly not a modern conservationist, as his ravaging of the countryside makes clear; but the forests were the refuge of the patriots and outlaws, in both legend and fact, who carried on a guerrilla war against Norman rule and lordship. By the end of the twelfth century the royal forests covered about a quarter of England and they can therefore be seen as the most important Norman innovation. They gave the king revenue and recreation as well as jurisdiction over dangerous terrain. Furthermore, as head of a hunting band, the Anglo-Norman king represented the most ancient form of authority known to man.

Given the significance of the forest, it was appropriate that the destiny of England in 1066 should have been symbolized by a green tree. The earliest biographer of Edward the Confessor, who wrote at the time of the Norman Conquest, described how when the king lay dying he had a vision in which God cursed the English kingdom for its sinfulness. Edward asked when there would be a remission of God's anger and received the reply that the troubles would continue until a green tree, which has been cut down, is restored to its trunk and begins once more to bear fruit. The green tree was understood to symbolize the English nation, which had been cut down by the battle of Hastings. The interest of the dream lay in the conditions it required for a restoration between the ancient trunk and the severed top. William of Malmesbury interpreted the dream to mean that the tree would never be restored: 'We now experience', he wrote in 1125, 'the truth of this prophecy, as England today is made the home of foreigners and the domain of aliens.'[11]

Nevertheless when Ailred of Rievaulx came to consider the same dream in his new life of Edward the Confessor (written in the 1160s), he found in it the symbolism of reconciliation and pride in being English: 'The tree signifies the kingdom of the English, adorned in glory, fertile in riches and delights, excelling in the sublimity of royal dignity.'[12] The green top had been restored to its trunk by the marriage of Henry I to Matilda, who was descended from the English royal family, and it had borne fruit in Henry II. 'He, rising as the light of morning,' wrote Ailred, 'is like a cornerstone joining the two peoples. Now certainly England has a king of the English race.' This was special pleading, as few of Henry's roots were in England. But Ailred's interpretation fits other comments of the latter half of the twelfth century which suggest that the distinction between Normans and English no longer mattered. Thus Richard Fitz Nigel explained that 'nowadays, when English and Normans live together and intermarry, the nations are so mixed that it can scarcely be decided who is English by birth and who is Norman'.[13] Fitz Nigel made the significant proviso, however, that he was speaking of freemen only. Serfs, *Anglicani* (English) or *nativi* (natives) as they were called, were still a living reminder of how lords were essentially Norman and peasants were English.

Names and languages

One reason why it was difficult to decide who was Norman and who was English by Fitz Nigel's time was that most freemen by then used non-English personal names like 'Richard' and 'Robert'. Striking evidence of this comes from Winchester, where information is available from the years 1066, 1110, 1148 and 1207. At the time of the Norman Conquest 29 per cent of property-owners in Winchester had foreign names. This proportion increased to 62 per cent by 1110, 66 per cent by 1148 and 82 per cent by 1207. Comparable rates of increase occur at Canterbury, where about 75 per cent of the names listed in the rent surveys of the 1160s are non-English and this increases to about 90 per cent by 1206. Greater foreign influence would of course be felt in Winchester and Canterbury than elsewhere, as these two cities were respectively the governmental and ecclesiastical centres of the Anglo-Norman lordship. What is most significant in these figures is the increase in the twelfth century. Evidently each new generation gave a larger proportion of its children foreign names, as Norman rule and French fashions became more normal, until by 1200 the great majority of freemen in southern England at least had ceased to bear English names. This information, because it is derived from a large number of individuals, is a better indicator of attitudes to foreign rule than are isolated statements in chronicles. A fact of comparable signifi-cance is that 'William' became and remained the single most common recorded name in the twelfth century, which suggests that William the Conqueror and William Rufus were not as unpopular as the Anglo-Saxon Chronicle made out. Peasant families in the countryside (most of whose names are unrecorded), as distinct from householders in cities like Winchester and Canterbury, were presumably much slower to adopt foreign names although they can be found doing so by the thirteenth century.

The increasing use of foreign names by the upper classes has a paral-lel in the way the English language lost status in the century after 1066. As with other changes in the wake of the Conquest, there is consider-able room for debate as to how quickly and how profoundly the lan-guage was affected. Because William the Conqueror claimed to be the legitimate heir of Edward the Confessor, he at first issued his written instructions in English just like his Anglo-Saxon predecessors. But in the 1070s, after the numerous rebellions had caused William to rely more on foreigners (as already discussed on page 30 above), English ceased to be the written language of government, although a few royal charters for Canterbury continue to be recorded bilingually (in Latin and English) until Henry II's reign in 1155. Simultaneously the use of English sharply declined for literary purposes. Some Old English works continued to be copied (indeed some texts only survive in twelfth-century copies) in monastic houses and there was a little new composition, of which the most striking example is the Anglo-Saxon Chronicle, which continued to be compiled at Peterborough until 1154. Nevertheless the text of the Chronicle proves the rule that the status of English was changing. Up to the year 1121 it is written in standard Old English, but thereafter it displays local east midlands variants whose spelling and script depart further from standard forms as the years advance. The problem for the Chronicle's later writers, isolated in the fens of Peterborough, was that they no longer had a consistent standard on which to model their prose. Before 1066 Old English in its principal written form had been a uniform language whose quality was maintained by the royal government and the church. The effect of the changes of the 1070s was to remove – for better or worse – these constraints on written English. As it was no longer an official centralizing language, its forms proliferated into a wealth of local variations. Latin (which had already been very influential before 1066) replaced English as the standard language of government records and literature and remained dominant for two centuries.

In the long term it can be argued that the Norman Conquest, so far from damaging the English language, gave it new life: first by releasing it from official constraints and then by enriching its vocabulary with numerous words derived from French and Latin. The latter phenomenon is brilliantly illustrated by F.W. Maitland in his history of English law, where he shows how modern legal vocabulary is primarily of French origin (*agreement*, *burglary*, *court*, *debt*, *evidence* and so on): 'In the province of *justice* and *police* with its *fines*, its *gaols* and its *prisons*, its *constables*, its *arrests*, we must – now that *outlawry* is a thing of the past – go as far as the *gallows* if we would find an English institution.'[14] In the short term, in the century after 1066, the English language suffered a setback, measured by its written extant output. But such a measure takes no account of literary works which have been lost, and furthermore the written use of a language is an inadequate indicator of total use. The amount and variety of English being spoken (as distinct from written) probably increased in the twelfth century, because the population was larger and the incomers intermarried and learned some English.

It is a mistake to assume that French replaced English as the common language of people in England. It cannot even be proved that the Norman conquerors in the second and subsequent generations spoke French as their mother tongue, although there is no doubt that French had great status as a social and literary language in England in the thirteenth century (see chapter 12, page 239 below). The chronicler Orderic Vitalis, who was born near Shrewsbury in 1075 and was the son of a priest from Orléans and an English mother, never learned French in England. He remarks that when he was sent to Normandy to become a monk at the age of ten he felt an exile, like Joseph in Egypt, because he heard a language which he could not understand. Orderic's ignorance of French before he went to Normandy is the more remarkable considering that his father was a counsellor of Roger Montgomery and special pains had been taken with his basic education. He had been put in the charge of an English priest at the age of five who taught him Latin. The neglect of French in Orderic's early education suggests that instruction in it was not thought a matter of importance by his father, as French (unlike Latin and English) had not yet developed as a literary language. Furthermore, as Orderic remarks, the Normans until the time of William the Conqueror had devoted themselves to war and not to reading and writing. By 1200 every educated man needed to know French, but that was not so in 1066. The literary language to which the Norman Conquest gave new life and discipline was not French but Latin, primarily through the influence of the archbishops of Canterbury, Lanfranc and Anselm, who were northern Italians in origin.

The effects of the Norman Conquest on language in England are therefore rich in paradoxes. English declined in the short term as a literary language and yet it gained new life as the spoken language of the people and re-emerged, enormously enriched, two centuries later. French, from being a despised vernacular in 1066, became in the twelfth century a literary language of high status. Its use by both the Norman and Angevin rulers of England may have contributed to this. For example, the earliest and best text of the *Song of Roland* is English (Bodley MS Digby 23), although its language is French, and other early French texts emerge first in English contexts. As for Latin, the consequence of its revival was that authors of English origin were again appreciated abroad, which they had not been since the days of Bede or Alcuin. Such Latinists as John of Salisbury and the rhetorician Geoffrey de Vinsauf (an Englishman despite his name) sought an international and predominantly clerical audience and therefore had no wish to restrict themselves to an English or French vernacular. To what extent these changes were caused by Norman actions, or were a reaction to them, remains a matter primarily for speculation, as language is shaped by many diverse influences.

Domesday Book

The greatest single achievement of William the Conqueror was his undertaking the Domesday survey in 1086, a year before he died. This description of the land, county by county, was done with such thoroughness that the Anglo-Saxon Chronicle commented with pardonable exaggeration that there was not one ox nor one cow nor one pig which was left off the record. Such detailed and consistent information was achieved by requiring jurors representing each hundred to answer a battery of questions such as: what is this manor called, how many villeins are there, how many freemen, how much woodland is there, how much meadow, how many mills, what is the estate worth, how much does each freeman have? These and many other details were to be answered for at three different dates: when Edward the Confessor was alive (1065), when William the Conqueror granted the estate (depending on when that was), and at present (1086).

Such an unprecedented and searching inquisition gave the book its name Domesday because it reminded the natives (according to Richard Fitz Nigel) of 'Doomsday', that Last Judgement when Christ in majesty would judge the living and the dead. This was an appropriate comparison, as the Domesday survey sought information about the dead (the Anglo-Saxon landowners who had been killed or died between 1065 and 1085), as well as the living, and its text was meant to serve as a final judgement about every disputed property. Fitz Nigel in the twelfth century recorded a tradition emanating from Winchester, where Domesday Book had been compiled, that it was intended as the finishing touch to William the Conqueror's plan 'to bring the subjected people under the rule of written law', so that each person in future would be content with his own rights and not encroach unpunished on those of others.[15]

Whether the Domesday survey had any more immediate purpose than a general though extraordinarily detailed survey of the land has been much debated. In 1085 William the Conqueror's rule was threatened by a joint invasion from Denmark and Flanders, and he brought over from Normandy the largest army which had ever been seen in England. It has therefore been argued that the purpose of the Domesday survey was to reassess the Anglo-Saxon tax of Danegeld to pay for defence. But this hypothesis does not have clear contemporary support and furthermore much of the information in Domesday Book is irrelevant to such a purpose. Although the Anglo-Saxon Chronicle reports the billeting of William's army and the planning of the Domesday survey as successive events, it does not explicitly link the two and neither does it mention Danegeld in this context. Such an elaborate survey was certainly intended to raise money but not necessarily from traditional Anglo-Saxon sources. A current hypothesis (by Sally Harvey) questions the originality of the survey. So far from being unique, Domesday Book was the last in a series of Anglo-Saxon royal land surveys, representing a practice which may have extended back to the time of King Alfred. These earlier surveys have been lost because they were in Old English and became obsolete once Domesday Book was made. The problem with this hypothesis is that it is difficult to distinguish between records which are an ancillary product of the Domesday survey (those describing the state of particular properties in 1065, for example) and those which were actually made in the Anglo-Saxon period.

To acknowledge that the making of the Domesday survey was the special achievement of William the Conqueror is not to assume that the Normans were efficient and energetic administrators, whereas Anglo-Saxon government had been decadent and illiterate. Domesday Book could not have been made without the Anglo-Saxon organization of shires and hundreds and the habit of settling property disputes at meetings of the county court in the presence of royal officers. The most interesting fact about Domesday Book is that William the Conqueror delayed twenty years before having it made. Why was it necessary in 1086? The best explanation, though this again is a modern hypothesis (by R.H.C. Davis), is that William needed the Domesday survey because the process of the conquest and redistribution of lands had been chaotic. The impression is often given in school textbooks that after the battle of Hastings William distributed the conquered land among his followers in an orderly and peaceful manner, giving so much to each and requiring specific services from them. But he cannot have done this in 1066 or 1067 because his hold on the country was still insecure and he and his men would have had only the haziest notion of how big England was or of who owned what. Orderic Vitalis (who wrote in the twelfth century) attributes the systematic redistribution of the land not to the years 1066–7 but to 1071–2 after the defeat of Edwin and Morcar.

Orderic's statement suggests that it was as a consequence of the rebellions of 1067–71, and not of the battle of Hastings, that William decided that he was entitled to dispossess English landholders on a massive scale. Even then the dispossession cannot have been an orderly process. Scarcely any charters or writs are known in which William grants English lands to laymen. The redistribution depended on verbal instructions. Typically the property of a dispossessed Anglo-Saxon magnate would be granted as a whole to one of William's magnates, such as Roger Montgomery or Hugh of Avranches. Such a man would often have already been in possession of some of the property, and it was now up to him and his knights to identify and occupy the rest of it. This would be done by going in force to the county court and then to specific villages extorting information. In the words of R.H.C. Davis, 'a Norman could not very well ride round an English shire "alone and palely loitering" asking in every village if Ulf or Tovi had held any land there'[16] because he would have been cheated or murdered. This primitive state of the kingdom, when the 'English lay in ambush for the suspected and hated race of Normans', is vouched for by Fitz Nigel (see page 29 above).

The purpose and achievement of the Domesday survey was to bring order out of the inevitable chaos caused by the Norman Conquest. The survey was a model of efficiency, but of efficiency imposed after the event and necessitated by the unprecedented disorganization caused by the Conquest. The purpose of asking for precise details of each estate and at three different times (before, during, and since the Conquest) was to find out who now possessed what, and what title they claimed other than force. Domesday Book declared the results of the Conquest like the results of a cricket match. It showed that the royal family possessed about one-fifth of the land, the church about a quarter, and ten or eleven lay magnates another quarter. Altogether it is estimated that by 1086 there were about 2000 foreign knights (or 10,000 new settlers in total) in a population of about one and a half million (some estimates make the population as high as two million or more). The obvious points here are how small a proportion the incomers were, when compared with the total population, and how wealth was concentrated in very few hands: the king's family, a handful of lay magnates (men such as Roger Montgomery, Hugh of Avranches, William de Warenne and Geoffrey de Mandeville), less than 50 prelates, and another 170 persons with estates worth more than £100 per year. In other words the land was controlled by about 250 individuals. This concentration of power did not differ much from the situation in Edward the Confessor's reign. The difference was that nearly every one of these 250 by 1086 was an incomer. Controversy about the effects of the Norman Conquest turns ultimately upon how much, or how little, can be achieved by such a tiny ruling elite.

The Conquest, in all its savagery at Hastings and in the Harrying of the North, proved the Normans' power. Domesday Book entitled them to rule, literally in the sense that it recorded the titles to their lands and symbolically in the sense that it demonstrated their capacity to organize. Legally, if not in reality, the Conquest marked a new start; for no one except the king now possessed a title to property from earlier than 1066 and everyone's rights stemmed from the Conquest. In the twelfth century, when a dispute arose about the charters of Battle abbey (which had been built as a war memorial on the field of Hastings), the chief justiciar told Henry II that even if all documents perished, 'we should all ourselves be its charters, for we are the feoffees from that conquest made at Battle'.[17] The Norman Conquest left a memory which has never been erased.

3

Norman Government
(1087–1135)

By the time he died in 1087 William the Conqueror had firmly established his rule in England, as Domesday Book clearly demonstrated.
Nevertheless the continuance of strong government was far from
certain. William left three surviving sons: Robert, William Rufus and
Henry. Robert, the eldest, claimed Normandy as his paternal inheritance and he had also perhaps been designated duke of Normandy by
his father. William Rufus was left the symbols of English royalty
by William the Conqueror on his deathbed and he legally acquired
Normandy when Robert pawned it to him in 1096 on his departure
for the First Crusade. Henry succeeded Rufus as king in 1100 when
Rufus was killed. But Robert was still alive and returned from the
Mediterranean to defend his inheritance. He was captured by Henry I
in 1106 and imprisoned until his death in 1134. These events suggest
that the union of England and Normandy was preserved largely by
accident and that from the first it had to be defended by almost
continual warfare. Both William Rufus and Henry I, once they had
acquired Normandy (in 1096 and 1106 respectively), spent much more
of their time there than in England, and this fact suggests an order of
priority or necessity.

Each of the three sons aspired to follow his father in being both
king and duke, because neither the practice of primogeniture (which
would have given everything to Robert) nor that of division of the
property between the children was firmly established. In this confusion
the royal family was no different from any other aristocratic family of
the time. The feeling was that all a man's children, but particularly
boys of legitimate birth, shared the inheritance of their father. After

his death they came to what arrangements they could by compromise or war. According to Norman sources, William the Conqueror left England only to God, because he had acquired it through God's help at Hastings, but he hoped God would give it to Rufus. The future Henry I was also intended to get something, and William of Malmesbury (who was writing with the advantage of hindsight) reports that William the Conqueror said to the boy when he was being bullied by one of his elder brothers: 'Don't cry, you too will be a king!'[1] William of Malmesbury also comments that the kingdom seemed particularly to pertain to Henry because he was the only son of William the Conqueror to have been born after 1066. He had therefore inherited royal blood, sanctified by the ceremony of coronation and anointing, whereas his brothers had not. These differing opinions show how far contemporaries were from the concept of automatic inheritance by the eldest son.

Rivalry between the three sons of William the Conqueror might easily have led to chaos in England and incessant civil war. That this did not occur was partly a matter of chance (Robert had gone off to the crusade), but also a consequence of the exceptional ability of the younger sons, William Rufus and Henry I. They as much as their father were responsible for establishing strong government in England. This was a matter of necessity for them, for in order to survive in Normandy they had to exploit English sources of wealth and power to their uttermost. Each depended on a Norman chief minister: Rufus on Ranulf Flambard, and Henry on Roger bishop of Salisbury. As a consequence, in the half-century between 1087 and 1135 the financial system centred on the Exchequer was created, and the legal system was strengthened through the Chancery. These institutions combined Anglo-Saxon governmental traditions with the most modern administrative expertise from the French schools. William the Conqueror had won a kingdom for his sons. They consolidated the Norman hold on England and developed institutions which have survived in name until the present day.

William Rufus and Henry I

These two kings have conventionally been presented as opposites. In the opinion of the Anglo-Saxon Chronicle Rufus was wicked and came to a fitting end by being killed without time to repent, as he was an oppressor of the church and of the poor. Henry on the other hand was a good man, who made peace for man and beast, and no one dared injure another in his time. Other contemporary sources similarly contrast the two rulers, but they draw a more subtle picture. What the clergy saw as vices in Rufus were the virtues of knighthood: he was generous to his men and let them make war. Henry by contrast was the clergy's idea of a king. Although the name *Beauclerk* was not given him until later, he had been educated in Latin and (unlike Rufus) did not relish fighting in person, defending himself with the Latin tag that 'My mother bore me to be a commander not a soldier.'[2] Rufus is described by William of Malmesbury as a model knight, whose promise was spoiled by the impetuousness of youth and the corruption of power. His early death meant that he had no time to live down his mistakes. He was of outstanding physical strength and had been trained in the knightly skills of riding with a lance. He always wanted to be the foremost in any fight and the first to challenge an adversary. Archbishop Lanfranc had made him a knight and to Lanfranc too he owed his throne. At the siege of Rochester in 1088 (when Odo of Bayeux rebelled), he taunted the English that they would be judged as *nithing*, 'worthless', if they did not aid their king. Similarly at the siege of Mont St Michel, Rufus (fighting the future Henry I) rewarded the man who unhorsed him saying: 'By the Holy Face of Lucca, henceforth you shall be mine and, included in my roll of honour, you shall receive the rewards of knighthood!'[3] William of Malmesbury compares Rufus on this occasion to Alexander the Great, and on another occasion, when he released a prisoner so that he could fight another day, Rufus is compared to Julius Caesar.

All this would have reminded twelfth-century readers of the heroes of chivalrous epic as in the *Song of Roland*. Such knights were loyal to their lords (as Rufus was consistently loyal to his father, according to William of Malmesbury), they were of superhuman strength and endurance (Rufus was dragged by a horse which died under him but leapt onto another one without assistance), and they were motivated in battle by honour rather than caution (Rufus returned to the siege of Le Mans without assembling all his troops, knowing that his young men would follow him). Above all, Rufus was famed for his generosity to his men, so that his reputation extended throughout the west and knights came to join him from many provinces. He was, as the chronicler of Battle abbey (which was necessarily committed to the Norman cause) called him, that *vir praeclarus militiaque strenuus*, 'that celebrated man, vigorous in knighthood'.[4]

This early generation of knights to which Rufus belonged was only on the threshold of being converted, in the opinion of church propagandists, from *malitia* (wickedness) into a Christian *militia*. Rufus did not respond to the pope's appeal for the crusade in 1095; instead he took advantage of it to acquire Normandy from Robert. Because knighthood had not yet been sanctified, clerical writers of the time could acknowledge that Rufus was a great knight by secular standards while condemning his conduct. Thus Orderic Vitalis joined William of Malmesbury in disapproving of the extravagant fashions of Rufus's courtiers (particularly their long hair and pointed shoes with curled-up ends), but he also recorded that Rufus was a masterful and brave man who delighted in the honours of knighthood. Rufus's generosity to his knights is likewise consistent with the Anglo-Saxon Chronicle's image of him as an oppressor of the church and the poor, as chivalrous standards were applied by knights to their own class only and not to peasants.

The ruler with whom Rufus is most comparable is his contemporary William IX count of Poitou and duke of Aquitaine. Indeed, according to William of Malmesbury, Rufus said the day before he was killed that he intended to spend Christmas in Poitou, which William IX was going to pledge to him before going on crusade. Like Rufus, William IX had a reputation as a freethinker, maintaining that events were governed by chance and not by divine providence, and he too was an anti-clerical. He was the first of the troubadours, the knightly poets who voiced an alternative ethic to the church's teaching. He sang of his delight in worldly things: in physical love, horses, furs and the changing seasons. There could be no greater contrast between the joyous yet fragile aristocratic spirit of William IX's songs and the lugubrious moralizing tone of the Anglo-Saxon Chronicle. With his exotic oath ('by the Holy Face of Lucca') and large ambitions, Rufus looked out into a wider world than either England or Normandy. Like William IX, he loved *cavalaria et orgueill* ('chivalry and pride'), and he too could say:

De proeza et de joi fui
Mais ara partem ambedui.
[I have lived in prowess and joy
but now we both part company.][5]

Rufus was brought down at the height of his power in 1100 when he was killed while hunting in the New Forest. Whether his death was an accident, and who was really responsible for it, cannot now be established. What is certain is that the future Henry I, who was also hunting in the forest, moved fast and that the death came at an opportune moment for him, as his elder brother Robert was on the way back from the crusade. Henry took control of the treasury at Winchester within hours of Rufus's death and he was crowned king at Westminster three days later.

From a legal point of view Henry was in a weaker position than Rufus had been on his accession, as he could not claim that his predecessor had designated him king, and furthermore he had been crowned neither by the archbishop of Canterbury (as Rufus had been) nor by York (as William the Conqueror had been) but by the bishop of London. Anselm of Canterbury had been exiled by Rufus, and Henry was obliged to send him a submissive letter claiming that he had been chosen (*electus*) king by the clergy and people of England. At the same time Henry sent a circular letter around the counties stating similarly that he had been crowned king by the common counsel of the barons of the whole kingdom. This document, which subsequently became known as Henry's 'coronation charter', made a series of promises in its bid to win support. It therefore indicates the sort of complaints which property-owners had against the government of Rufus. The principal points were that Henry undertook not to tax vacant churches, whereas Rufus had derived up to one-fifth of his revenues from this source, and not to make arbitrary charges on the inheritances and marriages of his barons. This was a move towards acknowledging that inheritance was a right and not a privilege. To the lesser royal tenants, the knights, Henry made the large concession that they should be exempt from taxation (the geld) and other non-military burdens. As a pledge of good traditional government Henry granted the so-called *Laws of Edward the Confessor*, subject to the emendations made by William the Conqueror. To give substance to these promises Henry dismissed Rufus's minister Ranulf Flambard and imprisoned him in the recently completed Tower of London. Only on one point did Henry explicitly make no concessions: the royal forests were to be retained as in the time of William the Conqueror. To the New Forest Henry owed his kingdom.

These concessions, taken together with the cost of winning the compliance of Robert duke of Normandy and of the count of Flanders, probably lost Henry one-third of Rufus's annual revenue. He could not afford to act with the cheerful abandon of Rufus and he had learned caution in his brother's reign, when he had stood awkwardly between the rivalry of Robert and Rufus. Although the capture of Robert at Tinchebrai in 1106 won Henry Normandy, it soon led to further strife with Robert's son and heir William Clito, with Fulk count of Anjou who claimed Maine, with Flanders and with Louis VI of France. In many years (notably in 1112, 1117–19, 1124 and 1128) the Anglo-Saxon Chronicle recorded that Henry remained the whole year in Normandy. A characteristic annal is that for 1118:

> All this year King Henry stayed in Normandy because of the war with the king of France and the count of Anjou and the count of Flanders. Because of these hostilities the king was very much distressed and lost a great deal both in money and also in land. But those who troubled him most were his own men, who frequently deserted and betrayed him and went over to his enemies and surrendered their castles to them to injure and betray the king. England paid dear for all this because of the various taxes, which never ceased in the course of all this year.[6]

The annal illustrates three constant themes of Henry's reign. First, he was never strong enough to defeat decisively his rivals in France despite successes like his victory over Louis VI at Brémule in 1119. Secondly, rebellions in both Normandy and England were common among the barons, as they manoeuvred for new positions in case Henry's power collapsed. This problem was made more acute after 1120 by the drowning of Henry's only legitimate son in the White Ship disaster off the coast of Normandy. Thirdly, the alienness of Norman rule in England was reinforced in Henry's reign by the feeling that the heavy taxes were being used to fight foreign wars. William of Malmesbury was unique in viewing the battle of Tinchebrai as an English victory and a tit-for-tat for the battle of Hastings forty years before. Henry's new men raised 'from the dust' were not native English but Normans (from the Cotentin and the west in particular), like Roger bishop of

Salisbury, Geoffrey of Clinton, and Ralph and Richard Basset. Richard Basset is described returning to his native village in Normandy 'bursting with the wealth of England'.[7]

Although in retrospect the Anglo-Saxon Chronicle and other clerical sources (notably Henry of Huntingdon) saw Henry's reign as a time of peace and order compared with the civil wars which followed, Henry seemed to many of his contemporaries to be avaricious and cruel. Most chroniclers comment on the gruesome penalties which he used to instil fear. Thus he blinded the count of Mortain, who had fought against him at Tinchebrai, and thieves were likewise blinded and castrated. In 1124 all the moneyers (minters of coin) in England were sentenced to have their right hands cut off and be castrated. Although such penalties were characteristic of the Middle Ages, Henry's application of them must have been unusually severe to have merited comment. He was believed to live in fear. Abbot Suger of St Denis reports that Henry was so frightened of plots that he frequently changed the position of his bed and had his sword and shield hung near to hand. In this he was like his contemporary and kinsman Vladimir prince of Kiev, who advised his sons never to lie down to sleep without first looking behind them. Henry's fears are strikingly depicted in drawings in John of Worcester's chronicle, where his nightmare of a rebellion by all three orders of society (peasants, knights and clergy) is described. Each order complains of oppressive taxation and towers above the bedside of the sleeping king wielding instruments appropriate to their class. The peasants carry a scythe, a two-pronged fork and a spade, the knights their arms and armour, and the bishops and abbots their croziers.

The positive side of Henry's fearful severity was the reputation he acquired as a maintainer of law and order, despite the concessions he made at the beginning of his reign and the rebellions which continued until the end. He was the 'Lion of Justice', as John of Salisbury and others called him. Nevertheless even this epithet is double-edged, as it derives from the prophecies of Merlin in Geoffrey of Monmouth's Arthurian history. The characteristics of this lion, according to the prophecy, do not refer to law and order but to its shaking of the towers of Gaul and the squeezing of gold from the lily and silver from cattle. In other words Henry was identified as the 'Lion of Justice' because he fought the French and extracted money from his subjects. The image was the more appropriate because after the Lion would follow a time of bloodshed, which could be identified with Stephen's reign. Rather better evidence of Henry's authority is the attribution to him, in the legal text called the *Laws of Henry I*, of *tremendum regie majestatis imperium*, 'the tremendous power of the royal majesty'.[8] To compensate for his insecurity Henry developed from the traditions of William the Conqueror and the Anglo-Saxon past a commanding tone in his letters which became the characteristic tone of the English Chancery henceforward. This is best heard in an often quoted instruction which Henry addressed to the authorities in Worcestershire in *c.*1110. Even when it is weakened by translation from Latin, the emphasis on personal authority remains: 'I order my county and hundred courts to sit where and when they sat in King Edward's time. I forbid my sheriff to make them sit anywhere else to suit some need of his. But I myself, whenever I wish, may have these courts summoned for my lordly needs at my will.'[9] Henry needed to insist that the courts and their officers were his, and that his prerogative was superior to their customs, in order to counteract the strong pulls of localism and seignorial power.

The development of institutions

Although contemporaries tended to contrast Rufus and Henry I, the long-term consequences of their combined reigns were much the same. Both kings were plagued by rebellions and had to spend huge sums on holding Normandy. They succeeded by giving away crown lands in exchange for support. Thus Rufus created the earldom of Surrey for William de Warenne during Odo of Bayeux's rebellion in 1088, and among the new men rewarded by Henry was Richard de Redvers who was given lands which became the earldom of Devon. To compensate for loss of revenue from land, which had been such a prominent part of royal wealth in Domesday Book, Rufus and Henry had to exploit the crown's rights from such sources as the county farms, feudal dues, profits of justice, and incomes from vacant churches. To do this required detailed and continuous records of who had paid how much for what and when. Domesday Book was insufficient for this purpose, as it went out of date almost before it was made. Instead, lists needed to be compiled and kept from year to year.

In addition to better record-keeping the governments of Rufus and Henry had also to ensure that sheriffs really acted as royal officers in each county and not as local barons. Hence the tone of Henry's letter to Worcestershire insisting on *my* courts and *my* sheriff. That letter was witnessed by 'Roger the bishop'. The man who was well known enough to be described in this way, without specifying where he was bishop of, was Henry's chief minister Roger bishop of Salisbury. He had been in origin a poor Norman priest whom, according to one story, Henry first of all made a chaplain to his soldiers because he could say Mass so fast. Through such practical applications of clerical skills to secular life Roger became indispensable to Henry and was described as his *procurator* or 'manager'. His main function was to call the sheriffs and other royal officers to account and to ensure that every possible source of revenue was tapped. This job was judicial as much as administrative because the crown's demands were repeatedly challenged by prelates and lay barons who claimed exemption by custom or charter. Rufus's chief minister Ranulf Flambard had likewise been described as *procurator*, and also as *judex* and *justiciarius*, meaning 'judge'.[10] Although Henry made a great show of dismissing Ranulf on his accession, he in fact governed in the same way through Roger, and furthermore Henry restored Ranulf to his bishopric at Durham in 1101. Like Roger, Ranulf was of humble origin. He had first been known as 'Passeflambard' meaning a 'torch-bearer' or 'link-boy'. Like Roger too, he was a Norman.

The government of England was administered by these two Norman clerics for half a century. Nevertheless Ranulf and Roger were not irresponsible favourites who squandered the king's resources but managers and guardians, as the term *procurator* implied. In Richard I's reign, when Hubert Walter exercised similar powers, he was known as the 'chief justiciar' and the origins of this office can be traced back to Ranulf and Roger. Their greatest achievement was to expand the sources of royal revenue and bring them under strict control through the Exchequer. As England was renowned especially for its wealth, it is appropriate that the most elaborate financial instrument in Europe should have been created there. But this was not intended to benefit the English, as it was devised by the Normans. Where the first generation of conquerors had taken wealth from the country in the form of looted treasure, Rufus's and Henry I's more sophisticated ministers did it through bureaucracy.

The Exchequer

In origin the Exchequer was not a government department but an object. 'It is', says Richard Fitz Nigel, 'a rectangular table measuring 10 feet by 5 feet.'[11] Similarly Gerald of Wales describes it as 'a sort of square table in London where royal dues are collected and accounted for.'[12] The table was covered with a cloth on which lines were ruled, giving it the appearance of a section of a huge chess-board (hence the Latin name *scaccarium* meaning chess or chequers). At one end of the table sat the king's highest officials (the justiciar, the chancellor, the constable, the marshal and so on) and at the opposite end by himself, or at best with the support of a clerk, sat the sheriff whose accounts were being examined. The strange appearance of the table and the high rank of those around it should have been enough to impress upon most sheriffs the hazard of defrauding the king of his revenues. The table served as a simplified gigantic abacus on which the king's *calculator* or accountant, who stood at one of the wider sides of the table, did sums by moving counters from square to square like a croupier. As the accountant set out the counters he called out the numbers, so that everyone could understand what was going on. The great officials sat round the table to resolve disputes about the accounts as they arose. As Fitz Nigel explains, 'The highest skill at the Exchequer does not lie in calculations but in judgments of all kinds, for it is easy to set down the sum due and to set underneath for comparison the sums paid and to find by subtraction if anything is still due.'[13] The way it worked is best illustrated by a diagram:

	£1000	£100	£20	£1
Sum due £2381	• •	• • •	• • • •	•
Sum received £2160	• •	•	• • • •	

The accountant first of all set out on the table in counters the sum due from the sheriff in columns representing tens of thousands of pounds, thousands, hundreds, scores, single pounds and shillings and pence. (For simplicity's sake tens of thousands and shillings and pence have been omitted in the example in the diagram.) Beneath the sum due, the accountant set out a similar representation of the sum so far received, and a glance at the difference between the top set of counters and the lower one told him that £221 were still owing. In essence the Exchequer was a way of doing elementary addition and subtraction. If that is the case, why was it such an important step forward in financial administration? The answer is twofold. First, elementary arithmetic was harder to do with Roman numerals than modern ones. The calculation in the example above is very simple but anything involving shillings and pence was made easier by moving counters from one column to another. The abacus also converted sums into convenient multiples of ten and used a nought by leaving a space blank. Secondly, the Exchequer table ensured that accounts were not only done but seen to be done, step by step, by all those who sat round the table.

As important as doing the calculations in the presence of witnesses was converting the results into a lasting form of record, since the counters on the Exchequer table were impermanent. The principal records were of two sorts, tallies and pipe rolls. Tallies were pieces of wood (rather like a ruler) which served as receipts. Sums were represented on them by incisions of different sizes and shapes using the same notation of units, scores and hundreds as on the Exchequer table. The pipe rolls were sheets of parchment, looking like pipes when rolled up, on which the treasurer's scribe recorded the accounts in detail. Both tallies and pipe rolls were written records. Tallies were only useful if they had inscribed on them the name of the county and the date and purpose of the payment. The sums of money were recorded by incisions with a knife instead of pen and ink in order to prevent fraud, as the incisions were made before the stick was split down its length, one part being retained by the treasury and the other given to the sheriff as his receipt. Receipts could of course have been produced in a purely parchment form from the start. The wooden format of the tally may have been preferred because sheriffs on the threshold of literacy found them easier to hold on to and store and they seemed foolproof. Tallies were in keeping with the basic purpose of the Exchequer to make accountancy visible and tangible. The pipe rolls on the other hand were for the treasury's own use and could therefore be in a more elaborate written form. Both the tally cutter and the treasurer's scribe sat at the Exchequer table to make the record on the spot.

The Exchequer therefore involved interlocking techniques which were simple enough for people with limited education to operate and which could be repeated and expanded. It had three essential components: a method of making calculations (the Exchequer table), a standard form of receipt for payers in of revenue (the tally sticks), and a more detailed form of record for the treasury (the pipe rolls). In being simple, interlocking and expandable the Exchequer system was the foundation of bureaucracy in medieval England. When Fitz Nigel came to write the *Dialogue of the Exchequer* in the 1170s he described the system with pride. Bureaucratic procedure was a peculiar subject for a medieval author to have chosen to write about, instead of theology or history, for example. Fitz Nigel knew this and in his prologue he justifies himself in the face of Aristotelian and Christian traditions: 'We are of course aware that kingdoms are governed and laws maintained primarily by prudence, fortitude, temperance, justice and the other virtues, for which reasons the rulers of the world must practise them with all their might. But there are occasions on which sound and wise policies take effect rather quicker through the agency of money.'[14] The Exchequer ensured that the king's money was duly collected and spent in the right place, at the right time by the right people. There was no value, in Fitz Nigel's opinion, in hoarding up treasure for its own sake; money is not piles of gold and silver but a commodity which smooths over difficulties in both peace and war.

Although he had a great respect for custom and an interest in tradition, Fitz Nigel was unsure about the origins of the Exchequer. Some said it had been imported from Normandy by William the Conqueror, while others believed it had existed under the Anglo-Saxon kings because the rates of county taxes were known from before 1066. 'But', as Fitz Nigel observes, 'this is a cogent proof of the payment of the farm but not of the session of the Exchequer.'[15] Although tally sticks and the abacus may well have been used in Anglo-Saxon administration, the 'session of the Exchequer' (that is, the practice of making financial judgements at its table) was a post-Conquest development, which can be proved to have existed in Henry I's reign but no earlier. The 'lords of the Exchequer' (*barones de scaccario*) are first mentioned in a writ dating from 1110 and the earliest pipe roll dates from 1130.[16] An attractive hypothesis for the Exchequer's beginnings was put forward by R.L. Poole. He pointed out that at Laon in northern France there taught in the first decade of the twelfth century Master Anselm (he is a different Anselm from the archbishop of Canterbury) and his brother Ralph. These two ran the most successful school of their time, Anselm being famed for his biblical teaching and Ralph for arithmetic. Many clerics from England went to this school, among them Adelard

of Bath, who wrote a treatise on the abacus, and two nephews of
Roger bishop of Salisbury. One of these nephews, Nigel bishop of Ely,
subsequently became treasurer and his son wrote the *Dialogue of the
Exchequer.* These and other connections with Laon led Poole to the
conclusion that 'the Exchequer is a system of account rendered possible
by a simple mathematical apparatus which Englishmen learned in
France' in the first decade of Henry I's reign.[17] Although this is an
over-simplification, it perhaps was Roger bishop of Salisbury, on the
advice of masters from Laon, who combined the techniques of abacus,
tallies and pipe rolls into the sessions of the Exchequer and thus created
a new institution.

Sir Richard Southern has argued that 'Henry I was not a creator of
institutions; he contributed nothing to the theory of kingship or to
the philosophy of government; he created men.'[18] The contrasts
between men and institutions and theory and practice in this statement
are difficult to substantiate. Certainly Henry brought in new men,
both as barons and as clerks, but it is also likely that the greatest of
England's medieval institutions, the Exchequer, was created in his
reign. Furthermore Chancery writs for litigation likewise begin to take
a set form at this time. Their peremptory tone – 'Unless you do this,
my sheriff shall have it done so that I hear no further complaint for
lack of justice' – may echo Henry's own voice and is certainly consistent with his reputation for stern justice. Although bureaucracy covered
up all sorts of weaknesses, both the Exchequer and the Chancery contributed to the theory of kingship and the philosophy of government
by making royal orders accountable, repeatable and widespread. Such
orders moreover went out in the form of personal letters from the king
to his men. Although the king would not have known the contents of
every writ sent out in his name, each one bore his seal as a token of
his approval. As the number of such writs increased (annual output
probably doubled between the reigns of Rufus and Henry I), the
king's commands began to reach every village. Henry was certainly
no philosopher but through his ministers like Roger bishop of
Salisbury, on the foundations already laid by Ranulf Flambard, he
put the monarchy's theoretical claims into practice.

Medieval rulers had no difficulty in elaborating political theories,
as the controversy between the papacy and the empire which was
raging at this time demonstrates. Their problem lay in giving substance
to their claims. Being ordained by God and the heir to ancient Rome

did not cause either the pope or the emperor to ride any faster around his domains. The Norman kings of England overcame this disability by establishing bureaucratic procedures which automated royal commands and kept checks on those who disobeyed. In this light Fitz Nigel's *Dialogue of the Exchequer*, with its emphasis on the efficacy of money rather than virtue, looks like the first work by a British empiricist.

Feudalism

The concept of feudalism has been left to the last in this discussion because many of its problems disappear once the bureaucratic and empirical tradition in Anglo-Norman government is understood. For a century or more controversy has raged among historians about whether the Normans introduced feudalism into England and, if they did, whether this demonstrates their superiority over the Anglo-Saxons. Difficulties arise because feudalism is used in different senses. Roughly there is a wide definition favoured by French and German historians and a narrow one preferred by some historians of the Norman Conquest. The classic formulation of the wide definition is Marc Bloch's in *Feudal Society*: 'A subject peasantry; widespread use of the service tenement instead of a salary; the supremacy of a class of specialized warriors; ties of obedience and protection which bind man to man . . . and in the midst of all this the survival of other forms of association, family and state; such then seem to be the fundamental features of European feudalism.'[19] Feudalism in this wide sense thus embraces all medieval societies between the ninth century and the twelfth, as Bloch intended. Consequently late Anglo-Saxon society is broadly feudal, as F.W. Maitland pointed out long ago in *Domesday Book and Beyond* when discussing Oswald of Worcester's memorandum to King Edgar about riding duties and other services owed for land.

Sir Frank Stenton's criticism of Maitland in *The First Century of English Feudalism 1066–1166* is the best introduction to the narrow definition. Stenton's title itself, implying that there was no feudalism before 1066, is significant. He compared Oswald of Worcester's memorandum (dating from the 960s) with twelfth-century charters of feoffment and argued that the differences between them represent 'the habits of thought of two races, and to suggest, as Maitland suggested, that the services described in the memorandum are all the more feudal because they are miscellaneous and indefinite is to give "feudalism" so wide an extension that the word becomes almost meaningless'.[20] In Stenton's view services must be exactly defined in order to be feudal and 'this new precision which governed relationships throughout the higher ranks of post-Conquest society is the most obvious illustration of the difference between the Old English social order and the feudalism which replaced it'.[21] Feudal precision in Stenton's opinion was a product of the habits of thought of the Norman 'race'.

A sufficient explanation for the greater precision found in twelfth-century charters is that more was being written down in 1150 than in 950. Theories about race and even about feudalism are irrelevant in this context. Norman charters of the twelfth century are no more nor less precise on average than those from other parts of western Europe. The move towards greater precision in charters was associated with an increase in the number of people who could read and write and a more professional interest in legal documents. The 'Twelfth-century Renaissance' is a more appropriate general term for this development than 'feudalism'. Nor in the eleventh century can it be convincingly shown that the Normans defined relationships more precisely than the Anglo-Saxons. Norman charters dating from before 1066 do not usually specify the services for which land is held and they rarely even call the land in question a fief. There is insufficient evidence for J.H. Round's thesis that William the Conqueror introduced knight service into England by specifying quotas of knights from each tenant in accordance with Norman practice. Certainly such quotas existed in the twelfth century but they were probably made the rule in both England and Normandy by Henry I rather than William the Con-queror. The quotas being in multiples of five and ten suggests an association with the Exchequer's practice of decimal computing, although there was a precedent in a writ of William the Conqueror to the abbot of Evesham concerning five knights. The kind of preci-sion involved in fixing numbers of knights and in specifying their services is characteristically twelfth-century rather than characteristi-cally Norman.

Where a narrow definition of feudalism does make sense in the context of the Norman Conquest is in the proposition that knights and castles were introduced by the Normans, provided these words are restrictively defined. The Normans did not introduce the 'knight' by that name as the Anglo-Saxon 'cniht' already existed, nor did they introduce the concept of noble service as the 'thegn' was an honoured retainer. If, however, a knight is defined as 'a warrior trained to fight on horseback with a lance', then it can be argued that the phalanxes of such men depicted in the Bayeux Tapestry were a novelty at the battle of Hastings. Nevertheless knights did not invariably fight on horseback (Henry I's barons were on foot when they won the battle of Tinchebrai) and their training and equipment underwent large changes in the twelfth century (most knights in the Bayeux Tapestry do not hold their lances steady at the hip but brandish them around their heads like light spears).

A comparable case can be made for the Norman introduction of castles, provided castle is restrictively defined to mean 'a fort designed to overawe the surrounding town or countryside'. Orderic Vitalis comments that the type of fortifications which the French called *castella* were uncommon in England and that is why the English were weakened in their resistance to the Normans despite being warlike and brave. Similarly the first words of the Anglo-Saxon Chronicle's obituary for William the Conqueror are that 'he had castles built and poor men hard oppressed'.[22] Such castles were built in county towns in particular as strongholds for the first Norman garrisons and then as centres of government. Houses were cleared away and the local population organized into piling up a great mass of earth, the 'motte', on top of which a wooden stockade was constructed. Mottes like this can still be seen in Norwich and Oxford and at Clifford's Tower in York. The building of stone keeps on the top of such earthworks took a longer time, although William the Conqueror had established the pattern for them in the Tower of London. The Anglo-Saxons had boroughs and fortified camps to defend the population but not these strongholds garrisoned by knights, which were designed as concentrations of power in a hostile land. The four or five castles recorded in England before 1066 were the work of the 'Frenchmen' introduced by Edward the Confessor, as the Anglo-Saxon Chronicle complained.

If knights and castles (as restrictively defined as in the preceding paragraph) are the essential characteristics of feudalism, then it would be true to say that feudalism was introduced by the Norman Conquest. But such a statement comes near to being a tautology, since knights and castles were the necessary instruments of conquest and appear in this clear-cut form only in those countries which were subjected to conquest. In this sense the Norman kingdoms of England and Sicily and the crusading lands in Spain, the Mediterranean and eastern Germany are the perfect feudal states. Feudal society is best exemplified in these places because the process of conquest provided a need and an opportunity to sharpen and reinforce relationships. This occurred in the physical sense that the natives faced the sharp end of the knight's lance and the force of his castle and also in the theoretical sense that the rights of lords and the duties of their men were defined and fixed in written surveys, of which the most ambitious is Domesday Book. Definition was essential because war had inevitable destroyed trust and customary practice. Specifying services was an attempt to hold the process of conquest at a fixed point and it might therefore be a sign of weakness rather than strength. The stipulation, for example, that a tenant owed his lord one and a half knights or that he would serve for only forty days does not express the generous spirit in which the heroes of the *chansons des gestes* serve their lords and companions until death.

Feudalism is an all-embracing term, which includes the large world of knightly heroes as well as the restrictive legalism of twelfth-century charters. In English history the different definitions can be built up on top of each other to mark chronological stages. Before 1066 England was a feudal society in the broad terms used by Marc Bloch. As a consequence of the Norman Conquest it became more rigorously militarized by the building of castles and the introduction of specialized knights. With William Rufus, 'that celebrated man, vigorous in knighthood', chivalric values are displayed for the first time. Then in the reign of Henry I the king's clerks and other drafters of documents begin to define services more exactly. This is when the term *feodum* meaning a 'fief' begins to be used consistently. As a consequence feudalism became institutionalized in the twelfth century as a system of holding property and raising revenue. Building on the powerful traditions of the Anglo-Saxon monarchy, the Norman kings thus consolidated their hold on England by heading a hierarchy of lords controlling knights and castles. Nevertheless even this was a fragile edifice, as the civil wars of Stephen's reign were to show. Despite the development of institutions, the king still needed the personal loyalty which a knight pledged to his lord.

4

Church Reform

The Anglo-Saxon church

Through its church a medieval community expressed both its own identity and its relationship with other communities. This was as true of the village centred on its little structure of wood or occasionally of rough-hewn stone as it was of the English people as a whole, whose church as a spiritual entity was headed by the archbishops of Canterbury and York. Ever since Bede had written his *Ecclesiastical History of the 'English People'* (the *gens Anglorum* in Latin, the 'race of the English'), Christianity in England had been the strongest agent of national identity. Because they transcended local rivalries, Christian missionaries and the bishops and reforming abbots who followed them contributed to making England one kingdom. (Following William the Conqueror's Harrying of the North, Lanfranc took this tendency further and claimed to be primate of all Britain, citing Bede to the pope as his authority.) Ideally all Englishmen, regardless of class or regional differences, were united in leading a Christian life which distinguished them from pagan invaders. The Anglo-Saxon kings from Alfred to Cnut in unison with the bishops had promulgated decrees regulating the Christian life down to the requirement (in Wulfstan's redaction of Cnut's laws) that everyone should learn the Lord's Prayer and the Creed. It is impossible to know whether everyone did, as the lives of peasants are unrecorded. Nevertheless in the unique biography of Godric of Finchale, who was born of poor parents in Norfolk at the time of the Norman Conquest, the writer mentions in passing as a commonplace that Godric had learned the Lord's Prayer and Creed from the cradle and often pondered them.

The best evidence of popular piety comes from the building of churches. Although very few Anglo-Saxon churches survive to the present day, as they have been rebuilt, both archaeological evidence and contemporary comment agree that they were numerous. In 1050 Bishop Herman of Ramsbury (who was not English by origin but Lotharingian) boasted in Rome that England was replete with churches and that new ones were being added in new places every day. These churches were in towns as well as in the countryside. At the time of the Domesday survey Norwich had nearly fifty churches, and a similar number has been estimated for Winchester. Such churches were tiny and architecturally unimpressive, but they can be viewed as better evidence of Christian values at the grass roots than the great basilicas built by the Normans. Liturgical practices in these room-sized churches were presumably as unelaborate, if not crude, as their construction. But a priest who preached in English and could expound the gospel from a stock of traditional homilies might have a more profound effect on his community than a foreign bishop who was learned in Latin and canon law.

It is a mistake, however, to regard the Anglo-Saxon church as having purely vernacular and peasant virtues. Its links with the papacy were direct and of long standing. Bede's *Ecclesiastical History* had shown the superiority of Gregory the Great and Roman practice, through Augustine of Canterbury's mission in 597, over the Celtic traditions of the west and north. The special relationship of England with the papacy was brought to everyone's attention each year on St Peter's day by the payment of Peter's Pence. No other kingdom paid such a tax to the papacy. Its names, 'Rome penny' and 'hearth penny', emphasize its purpose and how widely it was levied. There were many other ties with Rome and Italy, as well as with the monasteries of France and Lorraine. Although the best documented links are the formal ones (archbishops going to the pope to receive the pallium, bishops going to ecclesiastical councils, monks experiencing the discipline of other monasteries), the majority of those treading the roads were pilgrims journeying to points as distant as Rome, Santiago and Jerusalem. Even those who never went abroad were made aware of the larger Christian community through relics and images of the saints. The great miracle-working crucifix over the altar of St Peter at Bury St Edmunds was said to be exactly modelled on the Holy Face of Lucca, which Abbot Leofstan had venerated on his journey to Rome. William Rufus later adopted 'By the Holy Face of Lucca' as his distinctive personal oath; his knowledge of this may have derived from Bury rather than Italy.

Like the Anglo-Saxons, William the Conqueror had strong ties with the papacy. Indeed, because they were more recent and personal, they proved to be more effective. Lanfranc, who had been prior of Bec and was abbot of Caen in 1066, was known personally to the pope, Alexander II, and had taught the pope's relatives if not Alexander himself at the school of Bec. Anselm, another immigrant to Normandy and scholar of international reputation, had succeeded Lanfranc as prior of Bec in 1063. The Normans thus possessed the two most influential scholars of their day, who in turn became archbishops of Canterbury. They had perhaps been attracted to Normandy because of its previous generosity to Italian clerics like William of Volpiano and John of Ravenna. Normandy was an open and adventurous society for clergy as well as knights. The pope also knew of the Normans through the exploits of Robert Guiscard, who was well established by the 1060s as the 'vassal of St Peter' and the military protector of the holy see. Through this network of connections William won papal approval for his invasion of England and was presented by the pope with a banner, which headed his troops at the battle of Hastings and is depicted in the Bayeux Tapestry. The pope may have understood this banner to signify that William was now a vassal of St Peter like Robert Guiscard and that he too was to conduct a holy war. For William the banner was perhaps no more than a sign of approval which everyone could see. From his experience of Guiscard the pope may also have estimated on a worldly level that William would win because he was a Norman. The pope's credit would have suffered if his banner had been captured, just as English credit suffered by Harold's banner being sent as a thank-offering to Rome by William.

Although William came to England as the pope's crusader, he took no immediate steps to reform the church. Archbishop Stigand of Canterbury, of whom successive popes had complained for nearly twenty years, was recognized as metropolitan (chief bishop) and assisted at William's coronation, although the archbishop of York anointed the king. Stigand and two other bishops were deposed in 1070 after the spate of rebellions had made William nervous of their loyalty. Stigand was condemned on ecclesiastical charges which were correct in canon law: his appointment to Canterbury had been irregular and he held it in plurality with Winchester. Nevertheless these charges could have been made in 1066, or even in 1062 when the same papal legate, Ermenfrid of Sion, had been on a mission to England. The facts that nothing was done until 1070, that Ermenfrid had already removed an archbishop of Rouen for Duke William in similar circumstances, and that the only prelates to be deposed were those suspected of disloyalty, all suggest that the depositions were primarily political. Henceforward William chose only foreigners to be bishops in England. It may have been at this time that he asked Hugh abbot of Cluny, the most prestigious monastery in Christendom, to send him half a dozen monks to make into bishops and abbots. Hugh refused despite, or perhaps because of, William's offer of £100 of silver per monk per year.

Lanfranc and Norman control

William's instrument for controlling the church in England was a prestigious monk of his own, Lanfranc, who was appointed archbishop of Canterbury in 1070 by papal authority. Superficially he did not look a promising choice for this crucial post upon which the future of Norman rule depended. He was an elderly scholar, wishing to retire from the world, and he was not a Norman. About two years after his appointment he wrote to Alexander II begging to be allowed to return to the monastic life. He explained that there was so much unrest and distress in England that things seemed to be going from bad to worse: 'While the king lives we have peace of a kind, but after his death we expect to have neither peace nor any other benefit.'[1] Nevertheless Lanfranc overcame his understandable nervousness about the future of Norman rule and up until his death in 1089 he set about enforcing discipline among the clergy. His strength came from his grounding in law and logic and his integrity as a monk. Although he was unworldly he had years of political and administrative experience behind him, as he had been responsible for building up the school at Bec and then, as head of the Abbaye-aux-Hommes at Caen, he was William's family counsellor.

Lanfranc's opponents were as often his fellow Norman prelates as English ones. Thus he wrote to Herfast bishop of Thetford, who had been William the Conqueror's chaplain: 'Give up dicing (to mention nothing worse) and the world's amusements, in which you are said to idle away the entire day; read holy scripture and above all set yourself to master the decretals of the Roman pontiffs and the sacred canons.'[2] Enforcement of canon law was the key to Lanfranc's approach. First it was necessary to ensure that the clergy possessed correct and up-to-date copies of the laws. The book of decretals which Lanfranc purchased from Bec and presented to the library at Christ Church Canterbury still exists. His lawyerly approach to problems is best illustrated by the decree of the council of London in 1075, which removed bishoprics to the cities of Salisbury, Chichester and Chester among other acts. Each decree cites an authority or precedent for the action from the early church; thus the councils of Sardis and Laodicaea prohibited bishoprics in villages. The revival of canon law in this learned way was intended to restore the Roman church to its pristine perfection in the days of St Benedict and St Gregory the Great.

The same aim of reviving the splendour of the early church through Roman order and uniformity is displayed in the basilicas which the Normans built in place of Anglo-Saxon cathedrals and abbeys. The size and number of these buildings, together with the speed with which they were erected, is extraordinary. As William of Malmesbury commented on Lanfranc's rebuilding of Canterbury: 'You do not know which to admire more, the beauty or the speed.'[3] The cathedrals of Canterbury and York, Lincoln, Old St Paul's, Old Sarum, Rochester, Winchester and Worcester were all rebuilt (though not necessarily completed) during Lanfranc's pontificate; as were the abbey churches of Battle, Bury St Edmunds, St Albans, St Augustine's at Canterbury, and Tewkesbury. In the next generation work continued with the abbeys of Gloucester, St Mary's York and the cathedrals of Chester, Chichester, Durham, Ely and Norwich. Of the bishops only Osbern of Exeter had not remodelled his cathedral. These buildings were the achievement of numerous and mostly anonymous men and they were not entirely a consequence of the Conquest, as Westminster abbey had been rebuilt in the same style by Norman architects in Edward the Confessor's last years. Nevertheless the common features of the great churches (both abbeys and cathedrals) built in Normandy and England between about 1060 and 1100 suggest common values. In their starkness, repetitiveness and huge proportions they can be seen as buildings typical of conquerors in a hurry to make their mark. The north transept of Winchester cathedral, for example, may be felt to lack the intimate prayerfulness which can be sensed in the Anglo-Saxon church at Bradford-on-Avon. But this is not comparing like with like and furthermore Norman interiors now look stark only because they have lost their paint and metalwork and are no longer lit by lamps and candles. Even so, it is probably right to see a uniform ideology reflected in the design of these buildings. They demonstrate not so much the conquest of England as the triumph of the stone mason and of the clarity and order which the Rome of the Christian emperors and Gregory the Great evoked.

This style of building is appropriately described as Romanesque and in its most rigorous and monumental form is distinctively Norman. Although Lanfranc was not its originator, he was responsible for building the Abbaye-aux-Hommes at Caen in the 1060s which, in its proportions and method of construction, became the model for the great Norman churches in England starting with Lanfranc's own cathedral at Canterbury. For some of these churches the building stone itself was brought from Caen. In accommodating hundreds of worshippers in one congregation, these huge basilicas proclaimed the power of one faith and one liturgy by contrast with local cults and little parish churches. At the dedication of the new cathedral at Canterbury in 1077 there was no ceremonial translation of the church's relics, as was customary on such an occasion, but a procession of the consecrated Eucharist. Christ himself was to be the cult and treasure of the church and not some local bones. Such Roman unity and uniformity was presumably Lanfranc's. His abbey church at Caen and cathedral at Canterbury may have evoked for him the imperial splendour of the sacred palace of Theodoric and Otto III at Pavia, where he had first practised as a lawyer and a Christian. Lanfranc came from a larger and older world than his fellow Norman prelates.

Lanfranc's revival of canon law and Roman idealism was characteristic of the movement which is now called 'Gregorian reform' after Gregory VII, who was pope from 1073 to 1085, throughout the greater part of Lanfranc's time at Canterbury. He did not, however, get his ideas direct from Gregory, as they both shared ideals which had been developing for fifty years or more in France and Italy. Lanfranc was more 'Gregorian' in his devotion to Pope Gregory the Great, the last of the fathers of the church who had been responsible for the conversion of England, than to Gregory VII. Indeed Gregory VII in 1080 accused Lanfranc of disloyalty to the Roman church because he did not succeed in persuading William the Conqueror that he owed fealty to the pope. The demand for fealty from William, on the grounds that he rendered the service of Peter's Pence (and perhaps also because of the papal banner given him in 1066), was characteristic of Gregory VII's methods rather than those of the reformers in general. Lanfranc was able to reconcile the deference he owed the holy see, in accordance with canon law, with the fealty he owed the king. He demonstrated this in Rufus's reign when William of St Carilef bishop of Durham was suspected of treason. When the bishop in accordance with strict 'Gregorian' principles claimed that his trial by laymen violated canon law and was a disgrace to the church, Lanfranc rejected his plea. 'Well spoken, old bloodhound!' a Norman baron shouted.[4]

Lanfranc was the Normans' bloodhound not only in the pursuit of disloyal vassals but in his attitude to English sentiment. The most generous comments were Eadmer's (Anselm's biographer) who described him as 'somewhat unfinished as an Englishman' and 'a novice citizen of England'.[5] In this context he described Lanfranc's attitude to the English hero Archbishop Elphege, who had been killed by the Danes and was venerated as a martyr at Canterbury. Lanfranc had his feast day, together with St Dunstan's, removed from the calendar, although he later relented when Anselm persuaded him that Elphege might be said to have died for truth and justice if not explicitly for Christ. Lanfranc was not gratuitously anti-English like some Normans, but he would not at first allow local sentiment to stand in the way of canonical regulations and the emphasis reformers were putting on the unity of the faith. Furthermore, although he described himself in 1071 as a 'novice Englishman', he was too old and isolated by his office to adopt England in the way he had adopted Normandy thirty years before. This sense of alienation is suggested by Eadmer's record of Lanfranc telling Anselm how 'these Englishmen among whom we spend our time' have set up saints for themselves.[6]

Lanfranc had not come to England by choice and he could not be other than the Norman king's faithful hound. The fact that no Englishman was made a bishop during his time at Canterbury shows that he approved of this policy, even if he were not its initiator. Not every Englishman was removed, as Wulfstan II lived on as bishop of Worcester until 1095, but further appointments were excluded not only in Lanfranc's time but throughout the period of Norman rule. J. Le Patourel has demonstrated that between 1070 and 1140 only one cleric who was definitely English, Aethelwulf of Carlisle, was appointed to an English see, and Carlisle was as much Scottish as English. Not all the bishops were Norman, as some like Lanfranc came from elsewhere in Europe, but they were all aliens in England.

Not only bishops but many abbots and even some of the monks (at Christ Church Canterbury, for example) were brought in from abroad. At Glastonbury Thurstan, a monk from Lanfranc's former abbey of Caen, was appointed abbot and brought bowmen into the church to compel the monks to abandon their English tradition of chant. Although Lanfranc disapproved of this violence, Thurstan was not deposed and the aim of making English monastic practice conform with foreign models had Lanfranc's support, as he based his reformed rule for Christ Church on Cluniac customs. He provoked comparable violence in 1088 in Canterbury itself at St Augustine's when he, together with Odo of Bayeux, imposed a second Norman abbot on the monks. The English prior of the abbey had to be removed to Christ Church, other monks were imprisoned in chains in the castle, and one was made an example of by being publicly flogged at the abbey's gates. 'Thus did Lanfranc enforce obedience by terror' is the contemporary comment of his colleagues on this.[7]

These events reveal the ugly side of Norman rule, which was as real and ever-present as the spaciousness of the new churches and the elegance of Lanfranc's manuscripts. Ideals of reform were inevitably distorted by the violence of the time, and this was compounded in England by the Normans being alien conquerors. Although Lanfranc laid down regulations for his monks at Canterbury as well as for the English clergy as a whole, he did not necessarily benefit the church in the larger sense of the Christian community. Normanization isolated the higher clergy from the rest of the population. This was in a way a 'Gregorian' ideal, as the leaders were to be kept pure and separate. But, when combined with Normanization, 'Gregorian reform' primarily meant that the higher clergy became a privileged class for whom the scriptures and canon law were titles to privilege. Like Gregory VII's dispute with the Emperor Henry IV, the long-term effect of Lanfranc's pontificate in England was to engender scandalous and uncontrollable disputes about clerical jurisdiction. This occurred on a national scale in the dispute about the primacy of Canterbury over York, which Lanfranc started, and locally in the rivalry between St Augustine's Canterbury and Lanfranc's new foundation of St

Gregory's. In each case the participants forged documents and publicly abused each other.

By focusing on rights and law, Norman monks and bishops lost much of the evangelical fervour which had once inspired Anglo-Saxon missionaries and lived on through the episcopate of Wulfstan II of Worcester (1062–95). No new collections of vernacular prayers, homilies or penitential manuals were made by Lanfranc or other Norman prelates because there was too large a gulf in language and culture between them and the native English. A bishop's duty as pastor of his flock was not effectively revived in England until the episcopate of Robert Grosseteste of Lincoln 150 years later. Lanfranc was most effective over the things he could control and best understood. Thus his achievement in assembling good texts of the Latin church fathers and of canon law for the library at Christ Church, as distinct from more popular works in English, cannot be questioned. Likewise the encouragement he gave to the building and furnishing of churches and monastic buildings made its mark. His example in both book collecting and building was followed most spectacularly at Durham by Bishop William of St Carilef. But in the more amorphous area of inspiring parish priests, as distinct from promulgating regulations about them, and reaching down to the mass of believers, Lanfranc cannot be shown to have achieved much because he had to rule through fear. 'He was a good shepherd to everyone, insofar as he was allowed to be,' is how Eadmer sums up his career.[8]

Anselm and religious perfection

Anselm's career before his appointment to Canterbury in 1093 was remarkably similar to Lanfranc's and it might have been expected to continue to follow a similar course. He was an immigrant to Normandy, from Aosta on the Italian side of the Alps, who had succeeded Lanfranc as prior of Bec and then became abbot in 1078. Like Lanfranc he was a scholar and a devoted monk. As he had been prior and abbot at Bec for thirty years before he came to Canterbury, he was accustomed to worldly business and effective at it. Eadmer, his biographer, describes how at meetings he would refuse to intrigue but discoursed on the scriptures instead and, if no one listened, he went to sleep but would wake up and demolish his opponents' arguments in a moment. Anselm was the most intelligent and high-minded prelate of his time and this set him apart from his clerical colleagues as much as from the king and his barons. When he went into exile in 1097 to seek Pope Urban II's advice in his dispute with William Rufus, the bishops chided him (according to Eadmer at least) for not coming down to their level: they had their family and material interests to consider, whereas he already dwelt in heaven. 'If you choose to continue to hold fast to God and to him alone, then, so far as we are concerned, you will have to travel alone. We will not withdraw the fealty we owe the king.'[9]

Anselm's stance differed from Lanfranc's over the crucial question of obedience. At the trial of William of St Carilef, Lanfranc had insisted that the bishop answer Rufus's accusations and not shield himself behind canon law (see page 69 above). At Rockingham in 1095 the roles were reversed. William of St Carilef spoke on Rufus's behalf against Anselm's claim that his first loyalty was to Urban II as pope. Anselm uncompromisingly spelt out the logic of his position. The pope was the successor of St Peter, to whom Christ had given the keys of the kingdom of heaven. This divine charge had been given to the pope and not to any emperor, king, duke or earl whatsoever. As none of the assembled prelates dared repeat Anselm's words to the king, he went and told Rufus this himself. This meeting at Rockingham marks the point where 'Gregorian reform', in the strict sense of the ideology of Gregory VII himself, enters England. Anselm's argument accorded with Gregory's claim against the Emperor Henry IV in 1081 that the authority of kings and dukes, so far from being divinely ordained, originated from the devil and was based on greed, pride, violence, treachery and murder. Moreover Rufus, in the opinion of his clerical opponents, lived up to this image of the prince of darkness by his seizure of church property and the arrogance of his knights.

At the time of his appointment to Canterbury Anselm had likened the attempt to cooperate with Rufus to yoking together a wild bull with a feeble old sheep. This evoked the traditional image of archbishop and king (church and state in later parlance) working together at the plough of God's husbandry. There had never been in the Anglo-Saxon church or in Lanfranc's time fundamental dispute between the king and the bishops because they shared the same ideas about government. But Anselm's image of the plough team failed to mention that there had been a change of driver. In place of the quiescent popes of the tenth century there had been Gregory VII, who tried to destroy the Emperor Henry IV, and now Urban II (1088–99), who took over the leadership of Europe by launching the First Crusade in 1095, the same year as the meeting at Rockingham. By going into exile in 1097 and being in daily contact with Urban II, Anselm was in the forefront of the new papal idealism and a powerful figure in his own right. It was he, for example, who argued the case for the Roman church against the Greeks at the council of Bari in 1098. He was mentally as active as ever. During his disputes with Rufus, which would have distracted any lesser man, he began his *Cur Deus Homo* ('Why was God made Man?'), which revolutionized the theology of the redemption, and he followed this in the last decade of his life with works on original sin, free will and the trinity. Unlike later medieval thinkers, Anselm combined profundity with a clear and attractive style.

Because of Anselm's reputation and the insecurity of his own position, Henry I had no option but to recall him from exile in 1100, although he proved to be more uncompromising than ever. The dispute now centred on the question of royal investiture of bishops with the crozier and ring, symbolizing their pastoral and apostolic office, and the homage which they did to the king. In 1093 Anselm had been invested by Rufus in the traditional manner and had probably also done him homage. Nevertheless, on Henry I's accession Anselm refused to receive investiture from him or to do homage because Urban II's council of Rome in 1099 had prohibited these practices. This is another example of Anselm belatedly introducing 'Gregorian reform' in the strict sense into England, as Gregory VII had banned royal investiture in his struggle with Henry IV in order to clarify the difference between the spiritual eminence of a bishop and the worldly rule of a layman. From a royal point of view the problem was that a bishop, too, exercised worldly rule, as he was a landlord, who in England owed knight-service to the king. At one point in the investiture controversy Pope Paschal II (1099–1118) proposed to follow Gregory VII's logic to the point of divesting the church of all its property, so that it would be truly spiritual, but his clerical colleagues took fright. In England, as elsewhere in Europe, the controversy was settled by uneasy compromises, which kept Anselm once more in exile between 1101 and 1107. Henry I surrendered the right of investiture but bishops continued to do homage.

Superficially Anselm's pontificate achieved less than Lanfranc's, as it was torn by disputes and he was in exile half the time. Real power remained with the king and with the worldly clergy who had told

Anselm in 1097 that he must travel alone on his high-minded road. After his death in 1109 contact with the papacy almost ceased and no new archbishop of Canterbury was appointed until 1114. Henry I seems to have decided to have only one archbishop at a time and he was content with Thomas II archbishop of York. He came from a more traditional ecclesiastical milieu than Lanfranc or Anselm, being the son of Samson bishop of Worcester (who had succeeded Wulfstan in 1096), the brother of Richard bishop of Bayeux, and the nephew of Thomas I archbishop of York (1070–1100). This family of clergy were all associated with the church of Bayeux, of which William the Conqueror's half-brother, the warrior prelate Odo, had been bishop. When Thomas II of York died of overeating in 1114, Henry I wanted to appoint Faricius, the reforming abbot of Abingdon (a native of Arezzo and Henry's physician), as archbishop of Canterbury, but he agreed after protests from the other bishops to have a Norman instead. Thurstan, another clerk with Bayeux connections, succeeded as archbishop of York. His father was a canon of St Paul's who had settled in London with his wife, and his brother was a bishop. These Norman prelates were not reformers in their attitude to clerical celibacy. Eadmer's allegation that they told Anselm that they had their family and material interest to consider rings true.

As archbishop, Anselm had taken an increasingly strict 'Gregorian reform' view of clerical marriage as of his other duties. At the council of London in 1102 priests, deacons and canons were ordered to put away their wives; priests living with women were forbidden to celebrate Mass and their Masses were not to be heard by the faithful; the sons of priests were not to inherit the churches of their fathers. Similar legislation was repeated in 1108 after Anselm had returned from exile. The ban on clerical marriage was intended to reduce simony (the buying and selling of ecclesiastical offices) and it also emphasized that the clergy were the *kleros* (the elect) by contrast with the laity or *laos* (the crowd). Furthermore Gregory VII had emphasized the sacramental function of celibacy: just as Christ had been born of a virgin, so the Eucharist must be consecrated at Mass by a priest dedicated to chastity.

There was nothing new in principle in the idea that the clergy should be chaste. Anglo-Saxon bishops had legislated and preached against clerical marriage, as had Lanfranc. Anselm's legislation differed only in its uncompromising nature. As with the questions of obedience to the pope and investiture, he took his stand on absolute principles, whereas his colleagues acknowledged the world as they found it. The total prohibition of the marriage of priests might cause the collapse of parish life, Herbert Losinga bishop of Norwich warned Anselm, because most priests lived with women and many aimed to pass on their churches to their children or at least to provide for them within the clerical order. The children of priests were not necessarily corrupt. Some of the most distinguished monks of the twelfth century were the sons of priests, like Orderic Vitalis and Ailred of Rievaulx, and they owed their education to that fact. Heredity and family interest had the same advantages and disadvantages for churchmen as for knights. The gains of stability and continuity were counterbalanced by the risks of complacency and incompetence. In the opinion of moderate churchmen celibacy was a counsel of perfection. It was for the truly religious, for monks like Anselm who already dwelt in heaven, and not for the secular clergy who lived in the world. To be 'converted to religion' in the twelfth century meant to become a monk.

Monastic expansion

Strict 'Gregorian reform' aimed to make the life of religious perfection led by monks into the norm for all the clergy. As a whole this policy failed, since the clergy remained predominantly worldly throughout the Middle Ages, though some learned to be more discreet about their women if not their wealth. Nevertheless failure was not total. Although Anselm's and Lanfranc's legislation had little effect, the monastic ideals by which they lived gave an example to both clergy and laity. In the period 1066–1135 the number of religious of all sorts (both monks and nuns), as distinct from the secular clergy, is estimated to have increased from about 1000 persons at the time of the Norman Conquest to 4000 or 5000. Similarly the number of religious houses increased from about 60 to 250 or 300. (The figures are imprecise because the number of inmates is not exactly recorded and the dates of foundation and separate status of some houses is in doubt.) This four- or fivefold increase in the number of religious in seventy years shows that the ideals of the reformers took root among an elite at least. On the other hand even 5000 people 'converted to religion' was pitifully few in a population of one and a half million or more.

Monks were the aristocracy of the church just as knights were of the state. The number of religious in this period was approximately the same as the number of knights. If 2000 or so knights could effect the Norman Conquest (see page 45 above), a similar cohort of monks through prayer and example might overcome the devil. 'In your country there is a prize of my Lord's and yours,' Bernard of Clairvaux wrote to Henry I in 1132 in support of the Cistercian monks who brought Fountains abbey into their order, 'which I am resolved to seize by sending our force of knights. For this purpose I have sent forward these men to reconnoitre. Assist them therefore as officers of your Lord and fulfil through them your feudal service.'[10] Bernard was doing more here than adapting his language to Norman feudalism and Henry I's military fame, as monastic life itself was becoming increasingly military in its organization through religious orders like the Cistercians.

In Anglo-Saxon England as elsewhere in Europe the great monasteries (like Bury St Edmunds, Glastonbury, or St Albans) had been independent of each other and followed their own customs, although they all subscribed to the Rule of St Benedict and were subject to outside reforming movements. Instead of these individual houses, monasteries in the period 1066–1135 were being organized into orders, which took directions from the mother house and followed a common rule in every detail. The Burgundian abbey of Cluny had been the forerunner of such huge and tight organization under its abbot, Hugh the Great (1049–1109), at the time of the Norman Conquest. Although he had refused to send monks to William the Conqueror, even for £100 each (see page 66 above), and was reluctant to extend his jurisdiction across the English Channel, the first Cluniac house was founded at Lewes in 1077 by the Norman baron William de Warenne, and by 1135 there were twenty-four such houses including dependencies. A significant influence here was William the Conqueror's daughter Adela countess of Blois, who became a Cluniac nun in her widowhood. She encouraged her brother, Henry I, to found Reading abbey in 1121 and had her son, Henry of Blois (King Stephen's brother), educated at Cluny. In 1130 Cluny penetrated into the heartland of English nationalism when its abbot, Peter the Venerable, visited Peterborough with a view to bringing it under his rule. 'May God Almighty destroy these wicked plans,' prayed the Anglo-Saxon Chronicle, 'for the wretched monks of Peterborough stand in need of the help of Christ and of all Christian people!'[11] What was reforming severity to Peter the Venerable seemed religious persecution to the Peterborough monks.

The monastic order which made the greatest impact was the Cistercians through the voice of Bernard, who was abbot of Clairvaux from 1115 to 1153. Nevertheless the Cistercian rule, which gave them such an effective organization, may have been the work of an Englishman, Stephen Harding, who became abbot of Cîteaux in 1110. Despite Harding, however, the Cistercians were essentially Burgundians like the Cluniacs who were their rivals. To distinguish themselves from the Cluniacs, they wore white habits instead of black, and Bernard spread it about with effective exaggeration that the Cluniacs were worldly whereas they were pure. The powerful draw of the Cistercians is well described in the account of how Ailred of Rievaulx first heard of them in 1134. He was told by a friend of some wonderful monks who had come to Yorkshire from across the sea. Their habits of undyed wool symbolized their angelic purity. They were all subject to one rule and 'for them everything is fixed by weight, measure and number'.[12] Their house at Rievaulx was set in a wooded valley which seemed like a new garden of Eden. Ailred accordingly rushed to join. By the time Bernard of Clairvaux died in 1153 there were at least three hundred Cistercian houses in Europe and fifty of these were in England.

The Cluniac and Cistercian orders were as much an aristocracy, in both an ecclesiastical and a social sense, as the traditional Benedictines (or Black monks) whom they claimed to reform. Their leaders, like Peter the Venerable and Bernard of Clairvaux, came from Burgundian noble families and their patrons were magnates, like William de Warenne at Lewes and Walter Espec at Rievaulx. The monastic virtues of poverty, chastity and obedience were attractive only to aristocrats. Peasants already lived in poverty, they could not afford chastity (children were needed to assist their labours and support them in old age), and they already owed obedience to their lords. Walter Daniel, the biographer of Ailred of Rievaulx, is careful to explain that the Cistercians cultivate poverty and not the penury of the negligent and idle. This divine poverty is a *voluntaria necessitas* ('voluntary necessity').[13] In this paradox the biographer identifies the contradiction at the root of monastic life, which undid the work of every reformer from St Benedict to St Francis, as real or involuntary poverty was not a virtue in medieval eyes but a common disgrace. Hence the poor could not be fully fledged monks, although the Cistercians did take the unusual step of giving them a place as 'converts' or 'lay' brothers who volunteered their labour. These 'converts' in place of serfs were the gardeners of Eden, who first made Rievaulx, Fountains and Tintern abbeys into the earthly paradises they are today.

Less spectacular but more numerous than Cluniac and Cistercian monasteries were the houses which began to describe themselves as Augustinian in Henry I's reign. About sixty English houses recognized the Augustinian rule by 1135. They were not a centralized organization, taking their instructions from Burgundy, like the Cluniacs and Cistercians. Nor was their rule, for which they claimed the authority of St Augustine, standardized and detailed like that of the other religious orders. Augustinians described themselves as 'canons', who led the communal and celibate life laid down for the clergy by canon law and the fathers of the church. The title 'Augustinian canon' gave a respected name and an air of legality to a variety of usually small groups of monks and nuns. Many, though not all of them, were concerned with pastoral work in teaching, caring for the sick, and preaching. They were 'Gregorian reform' in action, as the canonical life provided a way for clergy to be celibate and yet continue with a pastoral ministry. Whereas the Cistercians claimed to be poor and humble while being collectively rich and powerful, some Augustinian groups really were poor, as they demanded less from their founders. Instead of withdrawing to huge estates like Fountains and Rievaulx, the Augustinians brought the religious life to the laity.

The risk run by Augustinian canons was that they would be contaminated by the world in which they worked. This is why monks in the Benedictine tradition, like Cluniacs and Cistercians, insisted on vast lands to make them independent of the laity. They withdrew from the world and prayed for themselves and their noble patrons because there was no hope of salvation in daily life. A good example of a house of canons being contaminated almost as soon as it started is Lanfranc's own foundation of St Gregory's at Canterbury in 1087. This community acknowledged the Augustinian rule by the 1120s and was typical in its size and purpose. Lanfranc had provided for six priests and twelve clerks, who would conduct a grammar and music school and look after the poor in a hospital. As he had little wealth of his own with which to endow this foundation, Lanfranc transferred to it bits and pieces of Canterbury property within his jurisdiction. Among these was the miracle-working corpse of St Mildred. Lanfranc's disapproval of

Anglo-Saxon saints was well known, but he may have softened in his attitude to English superstitions in his old age and St Mildred would have been useful to his canons, as her cult brought in money from offerings. The dedication of the church to Pope Gregory the Great, 'patron of us and of all England' (as Lanfranc called him in the foundation charter), was too idealistic for the average churchgoer and so Lanfranc had also provided the more immediate attractions of the relics of St Mildred and two other Anglo-Saxon ladies, Sts Eadburga and Ethelburga.[14]

The flaw in Lanfranc's endowment was that the neighbouring abbey of St Augustine's, whose monks Lanfranc had imprisoned and flogged in 1088 (see page 70 above), also claimed to have the corpse of St Mildred and they commissioned the hagiographer and polemicist Goscelin of St Bertin in the 1090s to write 'against the inane usurpers of St Mildred the Virgin'.[15] Goscelin's arguments reveal more about ordinary beliefs at the time than about the idealism of Lanfranc and other reformers. He starts with some strong arguments to a modern ear: St Gregory's is insolently encouraging superstition among the masses and its historical evidence is shaky. But these rational arguments are given less emphasis than the miracles which Goscelin uses to prove his case. He tells how St Mildred once stood up in her tomb at St Augustine's and hit the abbey's janitor, because he was asleep; and on another occasion she hit a man who feel asleep while praying at her tomb. Moreover, when the rival claimants used the ordeal of water to establish the truth, the trussed-up child they used would not sink into the consecrated water, even when the canons of St Gregory's pushed him. Goscelin's most recent evidence was that on St Mildred's last feast day one of the young monks at St Augustine's had foretold rain, because Mildred brought them annual fertility, and it had duly rained.

Remote as fertility cults, sacrificial children and animated corpses are from modern Anglicanism, they were all familiar parts of Lanfranc's and Anselm's world. The gulf which separated Anselm's theology from daily religious life was huge. He even had to reprove Eadmer, his biographer, for wanting a larger piece of the skull of St Prisca than the bishop of Paris had given him. (The bishop had allowed Eadmer as much of the bone as he could break off at one try.) Nevertheless the intellectuals and reformers, although they were a minute group, exercised a disproportionate influence because they were at the top of the ecclesiastical hierarchy at Canterbury as much as at Rome. The Normans reinforced the already strong links between the English church and the papacy, and in Lanfranc and Anselm, who were not Normans, they gave England the greatest spiritual lords of their day. At the bottom of the ecclesiastical pyramid, however, among the English-speaking village priests, nothing perhaps changed for better or worse.

5

The Creation of Wealth

Although England stood on the edge of the civilized world, it was famed for its wealth: in its productive lands and sea coasts, and above all in its sound money (the coinage begins to be described as 'sterling' in the twelfth century). Its merchants went into France and Flanders and down the Rhine to Cologne, and at Rome the English paid the pope an annual cash offering in silver in the form of Peter's Pence. William the Conqueror, as a symbol of what he had acquired, sent to the pope as a thank-offering the banner of King Harold, representing an armed warrior woven in the purest gold thread (an English speciality). According to Norman sources Harold's mother, Gytha, had offered William the weight of her son's corpse in gold in order to give him an honourable burial. William refused. The ability of Gytha to produce so much gold at short notice was not in doubt, as Anglo-Saxon rulers were used to making massive cash payments to invaders. From Harold's own foundation of Waltham abbey alone there might have been enough gold from the gifts he had made to ransom his body. Contrary to the Norman accounts, Waltham claimed that it had recovered his body without any payment through the two monks whom it had sent to the battle of Hastings.

In 1067 William the Conqueror and his followers caused astonishment and envy in France, when they displayed themselves in the jewelled fabrics and cloth of gold from the English royal treasury. Nothing survives of all this magnificence apart from a few finger-rings, pins and brooches. The largest accumulations of conspicuous wealth were amassed in the reliquaries of saints, such as the shrines of St Etheldreda at Ely, St Edmund at Bury and many others. The Ely shrine in the

1100s displayed about three hundred crystals and precious stones as well as gold and silver images. Much of this treasure had been given to these churches as thank-offerings for cures by their saints. The most valuable assets were therefore the relics themselves. Reading abbey, which was founded by Henry I in the 1120s, had acquired 242 relics by 1190, including Christ's shoe, Mary's bed, the rods of Moses and Aaron, and some bread from Christ's feeding of the five thousand, though none of these was believed to be as effective as the hand of St James.

The devout public, as they prayed at saints' shrines, came into direct and intimate contact with all these spiritual and material riches. A person cured at a shrine, who might be of any social class including the desperately poor, became a participator in this wealth and an advertisement for it, if only for a day. Among the miracles recorded at Reading abbey in about 1155 is that of a local woman whose stomach was dangerously swollen. She arrived on Christmas Eve and prostrated herself on the floor by the shrine of St James, defecating and vomiting throughout the night. She was declared cured, and the great crowd which had assembled in the abbey church for Christmas praised and glorified God. At the new cathedral at Norwich (started in 1096) a stone pipe is still in place behind the bishop's throne, which conveyed the sanctified aura from the relics and the high altar down to the crowd of worshippers at ground level.

Competition between churches and towns

The building of Norwich cathedral illustrates how the Norman Conquest stimulated competition. It was one of the largest churches in Europe, as long as St Peter's in Rome, but still not quite as long as its competitor, the abbey church at Bury St Edmunds only fifty miles away. Construction on this scale, and to a very high standard, required in Norwich's case the shipping of stone from Quarr in the Isle of Wight and Caen in Normandy. Competition to resite the bishopric of East Anglia had started with William the Conqueror's appointment of his chancellor, Herfast, as bishop in 1070. He tried to appropriate the wealth of the abbey of Bury for his bishopric, but he met his match in Bury's Abbot Baldwin, whose rebuilding of his own abbey church on a massive scale between 1081 and 1095 looks like a bid to see off

Herfast and make Bury the capital of East Anglia. Baldwin's church was the longest in Europe, though it would soon be overtaken by Winchester cathedral and the abbey of Cluny. Such a building required the assembling of hundreds of workers – skilled and unskilled – which may have been the stimulus accounting for the Domesday survey's description in 1086 of the town of Bury St Edmunds having 342 new houses. Houses constructed of wood could be put up quickly and also removed to another site when required.

Between 1066 and 1086, within the period when Baldwin was abbot, the town of Bury had doubled in value, and so had the number of its houses. Exceptionally, Domesday Book gives further details about this development: a large circuit of new land had been enclosed, which was formerly ploughed and sown; this is where the new houses were presumably situated. Here there now resided thirty priests, deacons and clergy (these were not the monks of the abbey of Bury) and twenty-eight nuns who prayed daily for the king and all Christian people. For the material needs of the town, there were seventy-five tradespeople: bakers, brewers, tailors, washerwomen, shoemakers, clothmakers (or possibly robe-makers), cooks, porters and stock controllers (*dispensers*). To manage the surrounding farms, thirteen reeves lived in the town and there were also thirty-four knights, both Norman and English, who were responsible for guarding it. The detail about the farm managers living in the town emphasizes how towns and their lords controlled the surrounding countryside. Indeed one of the functions of a medieval town was to extract money from the countryside and redistribute it in the town.

A town, as described in Domesday Book, was a concentration of people of different trades and skills, who had been massed together by their lords for their own safety and to ensure that their work could be controlled. Domesday Book describes around 112 towns. All of them were subject to lords, most frequently the king, to whom they rendered dues in money. Probably fewer than twenty of these towns had populations of more than 2000. The two biggest cities, London and Winchester, were not included in Domesday Book, presumably because they required special surveys. Their predominance is indicated in the Exchequer pipe roll of 1130, where the largest contributions to taxation were made by London (180 marks), Winchester (120), Lincoln (90), York (60) and Norwich (45). In addition to these cities, Thetford, Bury St Edmunds, Dunwich and Colchester (all in East Anglia) probably had populations above 2000, together with Canterbury, Sandwich and Lewes (on the south-east coast) and Wallingford, Oxford, Huntingdon, Stamford, Nottingham and Leicester (in the midlands). The only substantial towns in the west were Chester, Gloucester and Exeter. Judging by this distribution, England looked to the south and east with London as its hub. Although there were fewer towns in East Anglia than in the midlands and the west of England, they were markedly bigger, and many of them were seaports or linked with ports.

Most of the major towns in England had developed as part of an Anglo-Saxon system of national defence created to fight the Vikings. Safety necessarily preceded commerce, as there could be no trade or industry without it. If William the Conqueror and Henry I made England a safer place to live in, as the Anglo-Saxon Chronicle states, this must have helped economic activity, even though the Normans governed arbitrarily. There was nothing spontaneous or democratic about town development. The farm managers of Bury St Edmunds would have gone out daily to the villages they controlled, much as workers in the countryside went from their nucleated villages to labour in the surrounding fields. All of them were organized like this for protection.

The practice of grouping houses in lines in streets, whether in villages or towns, indicates that the inhabitants had been institutionalized ('manorialized' is the term applied to the countryside) and brought under the control of lords, whether ecclesiastical or lay. 'All these people daily serve the saint and the abbot and brethren', Domesday Book says of Bury St Edmunds.[1] At the time of the Peasants' Revolt three centuries later the people of Bury and Norwich fiercely resented their ecclesiastical lords. Perhaps they resented Abbot Baldwin of Bury and Bishop Herbert Losinga likewise in the Norman period, but the difference was that they desperately needed the combination of protection and massive capital investment which these ecclesiastical princes could provide. In the entries in Domesday Book for Norfolk and Suffolk the lands belonging to 'St Edmund' take many pages to enumerate, culminating in 'the town where St Edmund, king and glorious martyr, lies buried'.[2] The abbey's property was credited to its patron saint, which gave it the advantage of being an undying corporation, although it was taxed whenever an abbot died.

In 1100 monasteries and cathedrals were the closest medieval equivalents to capitalist corporations. According to Domesday Book, the major churches possessed about a quarter of all the land. Pope Gregory VII's insistence that bishoprics and abbacies must not become hereditary had the perverse effect of increasing the king's influence over ecclesiastical appointments, as he could claim to be opposing local vested interests. This was demonstrated especially by William Rufus's sale of bishoprics and abbacies. In 1091 Herbert Losinga paid 1000 marks (over £666) for the bishopric of East Anglia for himself and the abbey of Newminster at Winchester for his father. Herbert had been appointed abbot of Ramsey by William Rufus in 1087, and he presumably used Ramsey's money to advance himself. In economic terms £666 was not an extortionate amount to pay, as it represented one or two years' income from these benefices. In 1099 William Rufus sold the bishopric of Durham for £1000 to his chief minister, Ranulf Flambard. This was a sound decision in material terms, as Durham was rich and the king needed a bishop whom he could rely on to defend the Scottish frontier. During an episcopate lasting nearly thirty years (1099–1128) Ranulf built at Durham cathedral the most innovative and impressive of all the Norman churches.

The decisive difference an ecclesiastical lord could make to the prosperity of a town is demonstrated by Herbert Losinga's removal of his see of East Anglia from Thetford to Norwich in 1094 or 1095. This was done partly for personal reasons, as two of Bishop Herfast's sons were still entrenched at Thetford, and Herbert had no hope of appropriating Bury now that it had triumphed with its new abbey church. In Domesday Book Thetford and Norwich are both described as big towns (Thetford had 943 burgesses and Norwich 1320), but both also are noted to have declined in 1086 by comparison with 1066. In Norwich 480 men were recorded as being so poor that they no longer paid any taxes. William of Malmesbury describes Herbert Losinga removing his see 'to a town called Norwich, famous for its trade and its populousness'.[3] But William may have been showing wisdom after the event here, as Norwich was not prosperous immediately before its bishop arrived, and without him it might have gone into decline like Thetford.

Quoting the Roman poet Lucan, William of Malmesbury called Herbert 'an accelerator and transformer of business'.[4] He seems to have been an entrepreneur of large vision, with the money, political skill and time to make it a reality, as he lived until 1119. His new cathedral was placed on a specially cleared site, requiring the demolition of houses and even of churches. The huge cathedral precinct stands on a bend of the river Wensum, which is navigable down to Yarmouth. This outlet to the sea was essential, as ships could discharge their cargo in the heart of the town. Norwich's prosperity may have originated in the unglamorous but profitable herring trade with Yarmouth: Norwich bought the herrings, smoked them and sold them on. At the same time in 1096 as Herbert was building the cathedral – along with its precinct, episcopal palace and monastic quarters – the king and the sheriff paid for the new castle keep across the way from the cathedral precinct. The two projects were linked: the castle, like the cathedral, uses Caen stone which has been worked by masons making the same identifying marks on the stones they worked. Like the castles at Oxford and York, the Norwich keep stands on an artificial mound (a 'motte' technically) which would have taken 3000 labourers a year or more to complete. (The building work is entirely undocumented, so numbers like these are only estimates.) Unskilled digging labour was probably enforced from the local villages. Harder to get would have been the masons, whose pillared arcades and elegant windows made this keep look more like a palace than a fortress. Here Henry I celebrated Christmas in 1121.

Foreign merchants who saw Norwich castle and cathedral glistening in their newly cut limestone would have been impressed by their size, which was equalled only in Rome, Kiev and Constantinople. (Some of the merchants visiting Norwich would have known Russia and Byzantium, as England was linked to the Baltic–Black Sea trade route. There were Anglo-Saxons in the Varangian guard in Constantinople, and King Harold's daughter had married Vladimir prince of Kiev.) Another feature of Norwich which linked it to the major trading centres on the continent was the size and shape of its new market-place. Usually markets in medieval towns were held in streets which were cleared for business on specific days, such as the Cornmarket and Broad Street in Oxford. In Norwich, on the other hand, the market-place was permanently cleared of houses and made rectangular in shape (measuring 500 feet × 300 feet) in order to accommodate hundreds of livestock and streets of stalls. Placed close to the castle and within easy reach of the river, the market was both protected and accessible, which was exactly what was required. Taken together, the creation of the cathedral, castle and market-place meant that Herbert Losinga had literally laid new foundations for Norwich.

Markets and money

Because of the Conquest, the Normans could force through reconstruction and public works on an unprecedented scale. Bishop Losinga's
remaking of Norwich has been described as 'colonial domination'
rather than the creation of wealth.[5] Certainly the castle was intended
to frighten people, as this gave security to the market below its walls.
Domesday Book describes some markets being held actually inside
castles, for example at Launceston in Cornwall and Eye in Suffolk.
At Tutbury near Derby Henry de Ferrers had the castle and 'in the
borough around the castle are forty-two men living solely from his
market [*de mercato suo*]'.[6] The meaning is ambiguous, as *mercatum*
describes both a 'market' and the business of 'trading'. If the latter
meaning were intended, Domesday Book is declaring that forty-two
men get a living in Tutbury solely by trading. This seems a high
number, until it is remembered that Henry de Ferrers had made
Tutbury the administrative centre of his estates and hence the hub
of a hundred or more surrounding villages and farms. In these circumstances it is possible that forty-two families and their dependants
(totalling about 250 people altogether) did indeed get a living from
this new 'borough around the castle'.

Markets like Tutbury provided the numerous items which could not
be bought or easily made in the villages: pots and pans (whether of
clay and metal), clothing, footwear, tools, medicines, pins and combs,
salt, candles, and similar requisites of domestic life. The experience of
one merchant, Godric, is known in outline because he was reputed a
saint and has a biography. He was born in a Norfolk village around
1070 and began his career as a pedlar, hawking small wares locally.
This is how he acquired working capital and 'first learned to gain in
small bargains'.[7] Then he travelled further afield in partnership with
other tradesmen to boroughs and castles where there were regular
markets. Finally he advanced to being a seagoing merchant – and
pilgrim – who had visited Santiago, Rome and Jerusalem. Shrines and
markets were linked because shrines provided large crowds and a
secure environment for sales. At one point Godric returned to Norfolk,
where he was employed as the steward of an estate, but he got into
difficulties by accusing colleagues of pilfering. At Norwich, however,
he could presumably hold his own with the international merchants
in the market.

England's principal exports in 1100 were processed food and animal products: cow, sheep and goat cheeses; ham, salt meat, smoked herrings; wool and leather. All these items needed to travel well and be stored. There were also minerals in some areas: lead, iron, coal, salt and – most famously – tin in Cornwall. In return, manufactured luxury objects were imported, particularly into London: gold, silverware and enamels; clothing, carpets and tapestries; oriental spices (especially pepper), and – most importantly perhaps – arms and armour (swords of tempered steel from Spain, coats of mail from Germany). The Normans' contempt for English ale, which kept only for a few days, gave a boost to wine imports, even though England had vineyards of its own. A list of the household expenses of Henry I shows his officers, including the waiters and marshals, getting a daily allowance of wine; the best wine – *vinum clarum* or 'claret' – was reserved for the chaplain (this is the earliest reference to this name for fine French wine).

Henry of Huntingdon in the 1130s emphasized that England's largest import was German silver, which accumulated through an advantageous balance of trade. This surplus had motivated the Viking invasions and likewise the Normans in 1066. As the Anglo-Saxon government had regulated its silver coinage with meticulous thoroughness for centuries, William the Conqueror took over the system without altering it. Numismatists estimate that at the time of Domesday Book at least six million silver pennies were in circulation, an average of twenty-five coins per household. Probably many households did indeed have at least this number of silver pennies, as one sheep was valued at five pennies; savings amounting to the value of five sheep cannot have been large for a single family.

By 1066, and probably much earlier, the number of coins in circulation had reached a critical mass, which caused them to be used for an increasing number of transactions. They were readily available throughout the country because the minting was done locally by licensed moneyers. About seventy towns had mints where moneyers had the equipment to melt and test defective coins and issue new ones. Every coin carried the moneyer's name as a check on its authenticity. Domesday Book shows that no market in England was much more than fifteen miles from a mint. Because the moneyers had access to bullion, they acted as bankers, as they were able to conceal their profits through the process of melting and reminting the coins. An interesting archaeological find (dated around 1112) is a brass brooch showing the reverse side of a penny bearing the name of the moneyer, Godwine of Glouces-ter. Perhaps he made these brooches as novelties for sale. The largest concentration of moneyers was in London. Here around 1140 Thomas Becket got his first job as an accountant and secretary to a moneyer, Osbert Huitdeniers (Eightpence).

To prevent hoarding, forgery and coin clipping, the currency was reissued at frequent intervals. This involved all the moneyers in melting down the existing coins (including any foreign ones) and making new ones. The moneyers and the king might both profit from this process by giving short measure or debasing the silver content. Distrust of the quality of the coinage was consequently very common, despite all the checks on it. The Anglo-Saxon Chronicle reported in 1125, with characteristic exaggeration, that 'a man who had a pound could not get a pennyworth at a market' (there were 240 pennies in a pound).[8] The value of a coin was itself negotiable. Recipients insisted on weigh-ing coins or discounting their face value. Payment by the ounce, for example, meant counting every twenty coins received as sixteen in weight; the payer therefore had to find an extra forty-eight pennies in every pound. As weights themselves varied, a recipient might also insist on 'king's weight' instead of the local moneyer's weight. The most drastic test was to melt the coins down and check their content. Tested money was described as 'blanched' or white because of its high silver content. Some payments in Domesday Book specify this 'blanched' coinage. Demanding to see 'the colour of your money' is still a current expression in English.

The coinage had developed as a unit of taxation; the king's pennies were standardized and readily countable. Only gradually did money become a common means of exchange for business transactions. Domesday Book lists many payments in kind, in the form of renders of food or materials: at Wisbech two fishermen owed 14,000 eels to the abbot of Ely ('the eel place'); at Whitestaunton (Somerset) Ansgar owed four ingots of iron to the count of Mortain. The annual tax in silver pennies due to the sheriff of Wiltshire is converted in Domesday Book into a payment in kind producing 130 pigs, 32 sides of bacon, various measures of wheat, malt, oats and honey, 480 hens, 1600 eggs, 100 cheeses, 52 lambs and 240 fleeces. Conversely, payments in kind were convertible into money values, and this is a commonplace throughout Domesday Book. At Norwich, for example, the render of a bear with six dogs to bait it had been commuted to cash: the money was to be paid in pounds by 'king's weight' and in shillings for the queen 'by tale' (by 'telling' or counting out the silver pennies).

Payments in kind were best suited to the highest ranks of society and rendering them was a sign of servility. The king and the aristocracy perambulated around their estates claiming their food rents throughout the Middle Ages. St Anselm archbishop of Canterbury (1093–1109) admitted that he disliked the system, but it was the only way to feed the enormous retinue he was obliged to have. If he stayed at Canterbury all the time, he explained, 'his men would have been burdened with bringing food to the town'.[9] If in Kent, with its many ports and markets, Anselm felt that he could not forgo the nuisance of perambulation, lords in less economically advanced parts of England could not either. The sheriff of Wiltshire no doubt appreciated the supplies delivered to his castle; they are not so huge, if they are calculated on a weekly basis: he was due two or three dozen eggs a week for example.

The commonest form of renders in kind were services of one sort or another, ranging from knight service down to the millions of agricultural duties exacted from villagers. Domesday Book only has the space to list the numbers of labourers of different sorts in each village and not the particular services they performed. (We are only informed of the latter by landlords' own surveys, among the earliest of which are the cartulary of Burton abbey and the Black Book of Peterborough abbey, both dating from the 1120s.) At its crudest, wealth meant power over the labour of others: the oxherd must provide his plough for the lord; this man gives all the fish he catches; that one does harvesting in August along with his wife; this man must provide a cart to move the corn; that one must thresh it in the barn. By this measure, as by any other, the king was by far the richest individual.

What was wealth?

One Latin word for 'wealth' was *pecunia*, which had originally meant 'livestock', but came to mean 'money' once the Roman Empire had developed a universal coinage. In the Middle Ages this semantic change occurred all over again. In Domesday Book *pecunia* describes a man's 'stock' in the form of cattle, pigs, sheep or goats. At Irish Hill in Berkshire, for example, Hugolin the Steersman was reported by the county court to have 'transported the hall and other houses and the stock [*pecunia*] to another manor'.[10] Because these buildings were made of wood, they could be moved from one place to another. In the *Laws of Henry I*, some forty years after Domesday Book, *pecunia* is used in different contexts to mean either 'money' or 'livestock'. By the time of the *Dialogue of the Exchequer*, a century after Domesday Book, *pecunia* has become the usual term for money. Where greater clarity is required, coin is described as *pecunia numerata* – 'numbered money'.[11] As far as the Exchequer was concerned, food rents were obsolete. The only sort of payment in kind which it continued to accept were 'royal birds', meaning hawks and falcons. The *Dialogue of the Exchequer* discusses the hazards of summoning a hawk when it is moulting, or when there is no falconer on duty at the treasury to receive it. Hawks were hooded and relatively tame. Fortunately for the clerks of the Exchequer, they were not obliged to receive other royal beasts like stags or swans.

Domesday Book reckons wealth primarily in money, despite listing numerous payments in kind and labourers owing services. Every entry counts things and values them in terms of annual income:

> Hugolin the Steersman has held Irish Hill up to now . . . 4 villagers and 4 smallholders have 3 ploughs. There are 3 slaves and a mill rendering 30 shillings. [There are] 3 acres of meadow and woodland for fencing. [The manor] was worth £4; now £3.[12]

Living on the Berkshire Downs far from the sea, Hugolin may have retired with his gains from maritime commerce like Godric in Norfolk. Pounds and shillings existed only as a money of account and not as coins, though moneyers kept silver weights of these denominations in order to test suspect pennies. The makers of the Domesday survey, together with the thousands of local jurors who supplied the information, thought in abstract financial terms about values, incomes, profits and losses. This was nothing new, as villagers must have been calculating rents and taxes for centuries. In this sense there was a money economy long before the Norman Conquest.

The money of account in pounds and shillings which Domesday Book calculates on every page bears no direct relation to the actual number of coins in circulation. Coin finds and later minting practice suggest that silver pennies were issued in hundreds of thousands. The description of Godric's early career confirms this. An itinerant pedlar had to deal primarily in cash because he could not afford to be encumbered by payments, in the form of livestock or food, in addition to his own wares for sale. A miracle story from Oxford in the 1080s describes a worshipper at the shrine of St Ecgwin offering the saint a penny from his purse with each prayer he made, without noticing that a pickpocket was extracting his money at the same time, until the saint caused the pickpocket's hand to stick in the purse. The monks who kept shrines preferred cash to offerings in kind, as they could use the silver to embellish the church or pay for the French wine at their next feast. Abingdon abbey had about eighty feasts a year.

Domesday Book gives an overview of the economic resources of England and in this way it describes its wealth: in land of different sorts (arable fields, gardens and orchards, meadows and pastures, woods and marshes), in waterways (fisheries and power-driven mills), in minerals and manufactures (iron, lead, pottery, salt, stone, tin), and in domestic animals (bees, cows, draught oxen for plough teams, goats, hens, horses, mules and donkeys, pigs and sheep). A similar picture emerges from the rules about paying tithes in *The Laws of Edward the Confessor*: one-tenth of all produce is due to the church, meaning every tenth sheaf at harvest, every tenth foal and calf, every tenth cheese and portion of butter, and every tenth lamb and piglet. Tithes are due likewise from woods and meadows, waters, mills, parks, fish ponds, fisheries, copses, gardens and commerce (literally *negotiationibus*, 'business transactions').[13]

Above all, wealth consisted of workers of different ranks and skills – from bishops and earls down to cottagers and slaves – grouped in their villages, towns and counties. Throughout Domesday Book it is only male workers who are mentioned, with the implication that they support families. Women are referred to only if they have independent status: the queen, a few great ladies (Lady Godiva for instance and the Countess Judith), nuns, and one or two washerwomen and brewers. It is easy to show that Domesday Book does not include even every male worker. There are 6000 mills, for example, but only eight millers. Similarly there are only about seventy blacksmiths, yet a smith would have been needed in any village where ploughing or carting was done or where there was a mill. It is odd too that there are numerous swineherds but only ten shepherds. Sheep were the commonest domestic animal (perhaps there were a million of them in 1086), yet there are only three references to wool in Domesday Book. It is possible, however, that England's export business in wool had not got under way by 1086.

The easiest statistics to extract from Domesday Book concern the wealth of the richest people because that is what the book was organized to show. All of them were Normans. Similarly the counties producing the largest incomes can be computed. They are Yorkshire and Lincolnshire, but all that tells us is that these were the largest counties. Norfolk and Suffolk had populations two or three times larger than Yorkshire's. The consequence of proportionately larger populations in East Anglia was that Norfolk and Suffolk harboured many of the poorest people as well as more freemen. In general, the distribution of wealth was very unequal. More than a third of the population had insufficient land to give them a subsistence and they served as labourers for their lords. 'The real wealth of a country should be measured not by the amount of silver issued by its mints', Christopher Dyer concludes in *Making a Living in the Middle Ages*, 'but by its ability to produce sufficient goods to give its people an adequate living.'[14]

Did the Normans make a difference?

Whether the Norman Conquest gave people an adequate living has been much debated. The lowest social class was the slaves. Domesday Book counts about 28,000 of them in 1086, markedly less than in 1066; in Essex the reduction was 20 per cent. St Anselm's council at Westminster in 1102 had condemned the English slave trade as barbaric; in the past, prisoners of war and their families had been enslaved and sold. Nevertheless, in the *Laws of Henry I* there are some references to slaves, and nowhere is slavery as such declared illegal or immoral. The number of slaves came down not primarily for moral reasons, but because lords no longer wanted to maintain labourers as their total dependants producing no revenue of their own.

It was in the landlord's interest to be ambivalent about the legal status of his workers, and some incoming Normans never understood the complexities of the Anglo-Saxon social system anyway. The *Laws of Henry I* says that many powerful landlords, 'if they can get away with it, want to claim their own men sometimes as slaves and sometimes as freemen, depending on which may be the easier to do at the time'.[15] Bracton's lawbook recalls how the Normans had compelled formerly free tenants to do labour services. (The Normans thought themselves entitled to do this because England and its people were theirs by right of conquest.) The largest group listed in Domesday Book are the 109,000 villagers or 'villeins' (*villani*). This was a new category of person, not recognized in Anglo-Saxon law nor in the *Laws of Henry I*. Consequently the Norman lords could force labour services on them with impunity, as they had no protection in the king's courts. In *Domesday Book and Beyond* the Victorian liberal historian F.W. Maitland concluded that 'Domesday Book is full of evidence that the tillers of the soil are being depressed'.[16] This is true, yet we cannot con-clude that the population in general was worse off in 1086 than 1066, as the Anglo-Saxon evidence is so different from Domesday Book's. The belief that everything got worse with the Normans is itself a historical myth engendered at the time of the Conquest.

There are examples of Norman improvers, though the distinction between improvement and profiteering is a fine one. If Beccles in Suffolk rendered 60,000 herrings to St Edmund in 1086 instead of 30,000, was this an increase in productivity, or did Abbot Baldwin of Bury have the power to double his demands? Richard Fitz Gilbert increased the number of sheep at Clare in Suffolk from 60 to 480 and the number of pigs from 12 to 60; but the number of better-off villagers had fallen. The Domesday commissioners routinely asked: 'Can more be got from this than is got now?' This was the question that every ambitious landlord asked. The village of Aldwinkle St Peter answered the question directly: 'This was worth 20 shillings [and it is] 30 shillings now. If it were well worked, it would be worth 100 shillings.'[17] According to the Anglo-Saxon Chronicle, William the Conqueror always insisted on the highest bidder regardless of the interests of the tenants. William of Malmesbury described the Norman magnate Ernulf de Hesdin as 'a marvel in his skill in agriculture and a marvel too in the wealth which he gave so generously to the poor'.[18] William probably knew Ernulf, as he had stayed at Malmesbury when he came for a cure at St Aldhelm's shrine. Domesday Book shows that Ernulf had indeed increased the profits of his estates. Whether he benefited his poorer tenants, as distinct from the monks of Malmesbury, cannot be known. In 1095 he was accused of treason and disgraced; he died at Antioch on the First Crusade.

One form of Norman improvement which is undeniable is investment in new buildings. Eric Fernie has shown that 'no English cathedral or large monastic church is known to retain within its fabric *any* standing masonry of Anglo–Saxon date'.[19] Did this radical reconstruction – not just of churches, but of castles and bridges – create new wealth? This is a question which will continue to be debated, as we have no statistics for productivity and relatively few economic figures at all in the century after Domesday Book. Major pilgrimage churches, whether cathedrals or abbeys, stimulated trade by attracting visitors and also by providing medical services. Common sense suggests too that Herbert Losinga's remaking of Norwich, or the development of Tutbury castle and borough by Henry de Ferrers, had long-term benefits. Likewise new or restored bridges, such as Robert d'Oilly's Grandpont in Oxford and Ranulf Flambard's stone bridge at Durham, led in each case directly to the market-place.

Beyond the accumulation of treasure, the creation of wealth depends primarily on the provision of security for people and their domestic animals on the roads, in the fields and woods, and in workshops and market-places whether in town or country. Perhaps by the time of Domesday Book in 1086 the Norman Conquest was beginning to produce economic security for the producers, as well as profits for the conquerors. The Normans were no more economically advanced than the English. They had new artistic values in Romanesque art, but they had nothing to teach the conquered people about coinage, water mills, ploughs, fishing, shipping or animal husbandry. Possibly, however, they introduced new techniques in their vineyards, and later in the twelfth century they brought in rabbits. Certainly too they linked England further with the economy of France and the Mediterranean, rather than with Scandinavia and the Baltic.

PART II

The Angevins (1135–99)

The connection between England and Anjou originated in 1128 with the marriage of Matilda, Henry I's daughter and heiress, to Geoffrey Plantagenet, heir of the count of Anjou. Through this alliance Henry hoped to bring Norman and Angevin rivalries to an end and to leave Matilda with a stronger power-base than he had had on his accession. As events turned out, however, the Angevin alliance was a disaster for Matilda because it caused twenty years of civil war in England and bitter campaigns at the same time in France between Angevins and Normans. In the longer term Henry II (1154–89) succeeded in holding together his diverse possessions by his own determination, and Richard I (1189–99) pursued the logic of his great inheritance in the crusade against Saladin (Richard had a claim to the kingdom of Jerusalem through his great-grandfather, Fulk of Anjou) and in war against Philip Augustus of France. Nevertheless the Angevin connection had overstretched the capacities of even these energetic rulers, as they never succeeded in giving a sense of common purpose to their diverse lands. In the words of Sir James Holt:

> The Plantagenet lands were not designed as an 'empire', as a great centralized administrative structure, which was ultimately broken down by rebellion and French attack. On the contrary these lands were simply cobbled together. They were founded, and continued to survive, on an unholy combination of princely greed and genealogical accident.[1]

Historians since the nineteenth century have for convenience described these lands as the Angevin Empire. Contemporaries, on the other hand, although they acknowledged that Henry II's dominions stretched from the Northern Ocean (that is, from Scotland) to the Pyrenees, never used the term 'Angevin Empire' because they looked on Henry's lands as the lucky acquisition of a quarrelsome family and not as an institution.

Henry II's father, Geoffrey count of Anjou, had neither the ability nor the inclination to unite England and Normandy with Anjou. Although his marriage to Matilda designated him as king on Henry I's death, he never set foot in England and Henry I even obstructed him from obtaining the castles in Normandy which were Matilda's dower. Geoffrey's conduct contrasts with that of his father, Fulk, who likewise married the heiress to a kingdom, Melisende of Jerusalem, in 1129. Fulk immediately went to Palestine and ruled there as king from 1131 to 1143, whereas Geoffrey in 1131 forfeited his chance to be king of England by allowing Matilda to cross the Channel without him and accept the oath of allegiance of the English barons at Northampton on her own. Geoffrey had only succeeded to Anjou in 1129 and he may have felt that he could not abandon it, as his father had just done, by crossing over to his wife's kingdom. Furthermore he would probably not have been welcome, either in England or in Normandy.

Contemporaries give no satisfactory explanation for Geoffrey's indifferent career. The chronicler of Anjou, Jean de Marmoutier, characterizes him in much the same way as his son Henry II would later be eulogized as 'admirable in probity, outstanding in justice, dedicated to acts of knighthood, and excellently educated'.[2] Orderic Vitalis in Normandy, on the other hand, describes the failure of Geoffrey's four successive invasions between 1135 and 1138 and records that the Angevins made themselves hated by their brutality, although Geoffrey did get himself accepted as duke of Normandy in 1144. He had also faced rebellions in his native Anjou which obstructed effective action in Normandy. As for England, it was entirely foreign to him and he had problems with Matilda as well. She was the widow of the Emperor Henry V and persisted in calling herself 'Empress' throughout her life, as if her marriage to Geoffrey was of no significance. Geoffrey retaliated by staying put in France. William of Malmesbury reports that when in 1142 Matilda appealed to Geoffrey to do his duty by coming to defend his wife's and his children's inheritance in England, he replied that he knew none of her ambassadors and would deal only with Robert earl of Gloucester. When Robert crossed the Channel at considerable personal risk, Geoffrey made excuses but, as a great favour, he did allow the future Henry II (who was then aged nine) to be taken to England as the rallying point for Matilda's cause. In this oblique way the Angevins came to England.

Geoffrey's lack of success in the decade following his marriage to Matilda contrasts with the future Henry II's vigour in his early years. In 1149 he was knighted at the age of sixteen by David I of Scotland. In that year or in 1150 he was inaugurated as duke of Normandy. In 1151 he succeeded his father as count of Anjou and in 1152 he married Eleanor of Aquitaine. 'It is astonishing', comments a contemporary, 'how such great good fortune came to him so fast and so suddenly that within a short time without expecting it, he was called duke of Normandy and count of Anjou.'[3] Although Henry owed his sudden elevation to the unexpected death of his father (at the age of forty) and to his father's belated pacification of Anjou and Normandy, he managed – by contrast with his father – to establish his authority immediately in his new dominions. Furthermore in 1153, by the treaty of Winchester, Henry's title to the kingdom of England was recognized by Stephen, who disinherited his own surviving son. Henry was now twenty years old, the same age as Geoffrey had been in 1131 when he had first forfeited his chance to be king of England.

Henry II's success, when compared with his father's career, suggests that his dominance depended on personal qualities rather than on luck or on inherited institutions. He created the illusion of an Angevin Empire by grasping opportunities and by hard riding. Herbert of Bosham (one of Becket's biographers) likened government to a human chariot, of which the king is both driver and marksman, dragging everyone along in fear and excitement. Walter Map recorded that Henry was constantly travelling, 'moving by intolerable stages like a courier . . . Impatient of repose, he did not hesitate to disturb almost half Christendom.'[4] There was little that was specifically Angevin in all this. It is true that Henry's methods were similar to those of his ancestors, Fulk the Black and Geoffrey Martel who had made Anjou into a distinct and great lordship, but the dukes of Normandy and the counts of Poitou – indeed all successful feudal lords – had done likewise. Henry looks more Angevin in the circumstances of his birth and death, as he was born at Le Mans (the counts of Anjou had recently tightened their hold on the county of Maine) and he died at Chinon. He also visited these two towns more frequently than any others in his Angevin lands because Le Mans stood at the pivot of Brittany, Normandy and Anjou, and at Chinon was the treasury of the region. Nevertheless, if Henry's long reign from 1154 to 1189 is looked at as a whole, the more striking fact is that he spent only half as long in Anjou as he did in England or in Normandy. All in all London, Winchester and Woodstock – and Rouen, Caen and other towns in Normandy – were more frequently and regularly visited than Henry's patrimony in Anjou.

Henry II could not – and perhaps did not wish to – prevent his continental possessions from centring on France. 'Five duchies has the French crown and, if you count them up, there are three of them missing,' wrote the troubadour Bertran de Born.[5] He meant that Normandy, Brittany and his own Aquitaine were under the lordship of Henry II and his sons, and he exhorted King Philip of France not to make a dishonourable peace with the English king. It is significant also in this context that Bertran calls Henry *il reis engles* (the English king) who bribes those in France with English money. To a Poitevin chronicler similarly Henry seemed an alien and cruel figure: 'the king of the North'. The French kingdom, on the other hand, through its associations with Charlemagne and heroes of epic like Roland and Raoul de Cambrai, was a stronger centre of unity than the Angevin Empire which modern historians have reconstructed out of theories of feudalism. 'The Angevin Empire', writes Jacques Boussard, 'was conceived as an extremely strong state, but within the framework of the feudal system.'[6] This feudal proviso fundamentally weakens the concept of a strong Angevin state. Certainly Henry II strengthened government within his various lordships both in Britain and in France, but the unity of his French lands could be no more than personal because each of their components already owed allegiance to the French crown.

Ironically Henry's energetic rule strengthened the French monarchy rather than his own in the long term. Thus when he distributed his lands among his sons in his will in 1170, he allowed them to do homage to the French king. Moreover in 1183 Henry himself did liege homage to King Philip for all his continental lands. Previous dukes of Normandy had acknowledged the French king's overlordship but they had never humbled themselves to the point of doing liege homage (by which a vassal became the loyal man of his lord). Duke Rollo's warriors had allegedly tipped the French king off his throne for demanding as much (see page 23 above).

England was not dominated by Angevins in the twelfth century in the way that Normans had mastered it in the eleventh or Poitevins were prominent at court in the thirteenth. Contemporary chroniclers do not complain of Angevins in the way that the Anglo-Saxon Chronicle laments the Norman Conquest or Matthew Paris attacks Poitevins. Nor was Henry II seen as an Angevin interloper. His paternal inheritance from the counts of Anjou was played down in England, while his descent through Matilda from the Anglo-Saxon kings was emphasized. Nor had Matilda described herself as countess of Anjou: on her seal she is 'Queen of the Romans' and in charters she is 'Empress' and 'Lady of the English'. Only her opponents called her 'countess of Anjou' or 'Lady of the Angevins' to emphasize that she was an alien interloper. She had become Empress through her marriage to the holy Roman emperor Henry V who had died in 1125. Henry II's imperial associations derived from his being Matilda's son, and hence 'Fitz Empress', rather than from the lordship of a hypothetical Angevin Empire. Nevertheless 'Angevin' is useful as a general rather than specific term for the widening circle of the king of England's interests and influence which stemmed from the Angevin marriage of 1128. England's rulers were no longer narrowly Norman: Stephen came from the house of Blois; Matilda called herself Empress; of Henry II's eight great-grandparents only one (William the Conqueror) was a Norman; Richard I ruled his mother's lands of Poitou and Aquitaine, which were two or three times the size of Normandy, and his troubadour ancestor William IX (who died in 1127) had proudly declared that he had never had a Norman or a Frenchman in his house.

The style of government and culture in the years 1135–99 was therefore cosmopolitan rather than being exclusively English, Norman or Angevin. It is typified by King Stephen's brother, Henry of Blois bishop of Winchester (1129–71), who commissioned the Winchester Bible and bought antique statues in Rome for his episcopal palace, or by John of Salisbury, the greatest Latinist of his age, who (as he tells us) in the year of Henry I's death was beginning his studies with Abelard in Paris. John became bishop of Chartres and his compatriot Nicholas Breakspear was elected pope as Adrian IV (1154–9). How shocked John was when Walkelin archdeacon of Suffolk named his bastard son Adrian in honour of the only English pope and proposed to call a daughter Adriana. There was now a two-way traffic in talent between England and the continent instead of the Normans importing experts, like Lanfranc and Roger bishop of Salisbury, as they had done in the period 1066–1135. In increasing numbers in Henry II's reign in particular, men who had been born in England began to hold high office, but they were not little Englanders or the vanguard of an Anglo-Saxon revival. On the contrary they were the products of a competitive and cosmopolitan education, exemplifying the ideals of French chivalry like William the Marshal or the clerical superiority of the schools of Paris and Bologna like Thomas Becket. Latin and French were therefore the languages in which they excelled, and not English. The two most prolific and original writers moreover, Walter Map and Gerald of Wales, drew their inspiration (as Geoffrey of Monmouth did likewise) from Celtic Britain rather than Anglo-Saxon England. Furthermore, although Marshal and Becket were Englishmen in the sense that they had been born in England, they were the descendants of Normans.

On Becket's suggestion Henry II recalled Englishmen who had been living in France as clerics or masters in the schools and gave them offices. Henry also invited Master Thomas Brown to return from the kingdom of Sicily, where he had been Roger II's secretary, to a seat at the Exchequer to watch over the king's special interests. London, as the seat of Henry II's government as well as of commerce, was becoming a cosmopolitan capital; it was the most famous city in the world in the opinion of William Fitz Stephen (see page 13 above). Looking down over the Thames from his turret window in the Tower of London in the 1170s, Richard Fitz Nigel conceived a new sort of book which epitomizes the distinctive style of Henry II's court. Although his *Dialogue of the Exchequer* is in the classical form of a didactic dialogue, it concerns (as he explains) not the scholastic technicalities (*subtilia*) of Aristotle and Plato but useful information (*utilia*) about government. The law book attributed to Henry II's justiciar Ranulf Glanvill is a similar amalgam of a classical form (recalling Justinian's *Institutes*) and practical modern information. Taking pride in their classical education, these authors flatter Henry by describing his power in terms of a Roman and not of an Angevin empire. Fitz Nigel writes that 'he has extended his power [*imperium*] over large tracts of land in victorious triumph', and Glanvill says that the praise of Henry's victories 'has gone out to all the earth and his mighty works to all the borders of the world'.[7]

These authors did not consider Henry's *imperium* to be particularly Angevin but neither was it distinctively English, because it extended so far over the medieval world. For lack of any better term to describe this distinctive but passing phenomenon, the 'Angevin Empire' stands as a necessary historical convenience rather than a precise twelfth-century reality. Nevertheless, although there was no 'empire' in the sense of uniform institutions, the power of the Angevin family of Henry II was real enough. Through it educated Englishmen, Anglo-Normans and Welshmen extended their horizons and made, most notably through their Latin writings, a considerable and distinctive contribution to the Europe of the Twelfth-century Renaissance.

6

Struggles for the Kingdom (1135–99)

The death of Henry I in 1135 was seen by contemporaries as a calamity. With the wisdom of hindsight they looked back on his reign as a time of tranquillity: 'England, once the seat of justice, the home of peace, the height of piety, the mirror of religion, became thereafter a place of perversity, a haunt of strife, a school of disorder, and the teacher of every kind of rebellion,' wrote the author of the *Gesta Stephani* (*The Deeds of King Stephen*).[1] What was most surprising in the opinion of this author was that even wild animals suffered. Formerly huge herds of them (deer are presumably meant) overflowed the whole land, whereas henceforward a man was lucky to see even one because they had been indiscriminately killed. The miseries caused by robber barons are described in such similar terms by different chroniclers that the catalogue of atrocities becomes trite. Both William of Malmesbury and the Anglo-Saxon Chronicle describe the building of castles and how knights went out from them to plunder the countryside, dragging off anyone with money to their dungeons.

What particularly shocked monastic writers was the lack of respect for churches and churchyards. Because they were vulnerable, these writers looked at war from the point of view of those who suffered from it, particularly peasants (the 'men of the land') in the case of the Anglo-Saxon Chronicle. The knights who committed these atrocities considered themselves entitled to booty and they used arson and robbery as weapons against their opponents. Thus the author of *Gesta Stephani* describes how in 1149 King Stephen and his counsellors decided that the only way to compel their opponents to surrender was to burn crops and destroy all means of sustaining life. Consequently

Stephen's son Eustace, who is described elsewhere in the book as a gentle and affable knight, went to Devizes with his men and killed everyone they came across, 'committing indiscriminately every cruelty they could think of'.[2] By having to generalize, chroniclers exaggerated both the state of peace which had existed before 1135 and the chaos which followed. The idea of England and its ancient institutions – 'the noblest nurse of peace, the special home of tranquillity' (in William of Malmesbury's words) – survived the nineteen winters of Stephen's reign, so that Henry II on his accession could ignore them and claim that he was returning directly to the good rule of his grandfather, Henry I. The chroniclers' contrast between the good old days and the present thus became enshrined in Henry II's propaganda and reinforced in further chroniclers' narratives like that of William of Newburgh.

Property and inheritance

The barons of Stephen's reign can be seen as family men ensuring their own property, rather than as robbers. Because central authority was in dispute, they had to reinforce their local power in order to survive against their rivals. The Norman Conquest had temporarily weakened regional lordships, but they had begun to re-establish themselves in Henry I's reign. Stephen and Matilda were coming to terms with realities in recognizing local principalities. The number of earldoms trebled between 1135 and 1154 and furthermore the earls looked upon the counties from which they took their titles as their family property; sheriffs therefore became earls' deputies rather than royal officers answerable directly to the king. In Latin charters earls are described as *comites* (that is, 'counts' or heads of counties) and sheriffs are *vice-comites* ('viscounts'). As R.H.C. Davis has demonstrated, there were only five counties which had no earl in Stephen's reign and (apart from Shropshire) the omissions can be explained by special circumstances, such as Henry of Blois's jurisdiction as bishop of Winchester in Hampshire or Geoffrey de Mandeville's authority in Middlesex as keeper of the Tower of London.

Royal offices had a strong tendency to become hereditary and the extension of the idea of family property to them could be seen as a force making for stability rather than disorder. As kingship was hereditary (though not necessarily by strict primogeniture), why should not earldoms and sheriffdoms likewise be inherited? Counts and viscounts were hereditary in France; why not in England? The political importance of the reigns of Stephen and Henry II is that they established which offices should be hereditary in England and which should not. The outcome was a compromise. Earldoms, baronies and knights' fees were acknowledged to be hereditary, whereas sheriffdoms and justiceships were not (except in isolated cases like the Beauchamp sheriffdom of Worcestershire). Earldoms, baronies and knights' fees had thus started on the road which would make them titles of honour rather than governmental jurisdictions. Nevertheless, because Henry II successfully reversed the tendencies of Stephen's reign, England never developed a nobility with powers of life and death over their tenants, and neither did the privileges of noble birth extend equally to all members of a family.

There was so much strife in twelfth-century England because this outcome was essentially contradictory. Stephen, with a poor hereditary claim to the throne, granted away royal offices as inheritances whereas Henry II, who insisted on his own hereditary right, deprived the barons of these inheritances. The most revealing of Stephen's grants is his charter to Geoffrey de Mandeville, made in 1141 after Stephen had been humiliated by being captured at the battle of Lincoln. He concedes to Geoffrey the keepership of the Tower of London and the offices of justice and sheriff in London, Middlesex, Essex and Hertfordshire, 'wherefore', Stephen's charter declares, 'I wish and firmly order that he *and his heirs after him* shall have and hold all such holdings and grants as freely and quietly and honourably as any earl in the whole of England.'[3] In reality no earl at this time did hold his lands 'freely and quietly', and Geoffrey would have to fight to maintain his privileges. Nevertheless, if the English monarchy had permanently lost the Tower and the counties immediately north of London, it would have ceased to exist as an effective government. Barons like Geoffrey de Mandeville, who had been granted financial power as sheriffs, judicial power as justices and military power as castellans (in Geoffrey's case with the right to build and maintain castles wherever he wished), would have become independent rulers like the nobility in France and Germany.

In resisting this tendency Henry II was opposing the normal form of aristocratic government in his time, going against the precedents established by his mother the Empress Matilda (like Stephen she had made grants of hereditary sheriffdoms), and contradicting the hereditary principle upon which his own claim to rule depended. Henry described himself even before he came to England in 1142 as the 'rightful heir of England and Normandy' and he attempted to reinforce the principle of hereditary monarchy by copying French and imperial practice in having his eldest son, Henry the Young King, crowned in 1170. In the same year as this coronation attempted to buttress his own family's hold on England, Henry launched the Inquest of Sheriffs, which challenged the hereditary and traditional rights of everyone else. This inquiry extended beyond the conduct of sheriffs themselves to 'archbishops, bishops, abbots, earls, barons, sub-tenants, knights, citizens and burgesses, and their stewards and officers'.[4] As the surviving records from Norfolk and Suffolk show, a detailed scrutiny was made of baronial and bishops' officials as well as the king's. The assumption behind the Inquest was that all authority stemmed from the king. In 1170 the challenge to the clergy was the most provocative part of the Inquest (the king's justices were to inquire into the conduct of archdeacons and deans) and the year ended with the murder of Becket. Under his leadership the clergy had proved more obdurate than the lay nobility in surrendering the privileges which they had gained during Stephen's reign, when Henry of Blois bishop of Winchester had for a time held the balance of power.

Because of the contradiction in his attitude to hereditary and traditional jurisdictions Henry II could not develop a coherent ideology justifying his rule. To his opponents he appeared capricious and tyrannical. Consequently he and his sons, Richard I and John, had to insist on their own will power as the ultimate justification for their actions. *Vis et voluntas* (force and will) and *ira et malevolentia* (anger and prejudice) were the keynotes of Angevin kingship. As J.E.A. Jolliffe has argued: 'The king rules by his passions more than by his kingship, and is ready to advance them, if not as a moral or political, at least as a natural justification.'[5] Henry II's wilful anger was seen at its most formidable on the occasion of Becket's murder. But, as the consequences of that crime and the rebellion of Henry's sons against him in 1173 showed, wilfulness was a double-edged weapon. On the other hand, lack of will power brought worse consequences. Contemporaries were agreed that it was because King Stephen was a 'mild man who was soft and good' (in the words of the Anglo-Saxon Chronicle) that he did no justice.[6]

Stephen and Matilda

It is ironical that Stephen, the classic weak king of English history, should have won the throne by determined action whereas Henry II, the strong king, inherited it with less apparent effort. The author of the *Gesta Stephani* could see in Stephen's changing circumstances only the revolutions of Fortune's wheel; he and his opponents were engaged in 'doleful games of chance'.[7] The circumstances of his accession to the throne were not very different from those of William Rufus and Henry I, who had each excluded a nearer heir, their elder brother Robert. Like Rufus, Stephen claimed that he had been designated as successor by the king on his deathbed. Like Henry I, he rushed to seize the treasury on the death of his predecessor and then presented his rivals with a fait accompli, as he had been accepted as king by the Londoners, by his brother, Henry of Blois bishop of Winchester, and by Roger bishop of Salisbury who had headed Henry I's administration. Stephen could not have succeeded without the support of his brother who rallied the bishops behind him.

Stephen became king for lack of any better candidate. Although Matilda had been designated as Henry I's heiress in 1126 and Stephen had been prominent in swearing loyalty to her, her position had been compromised in 1128 by her marriage to Geoffrey of Anjou. He was not acceptable to the Norman barons and therefore was rejected by their fellows in England. Conversely the Norman barons favoured Theobald count of Blois and Chartres, who was Stephen's elder brother and the closest legitimate male heir, but he seems to have had no wish to add Normandy and England to his considerable domains, which extended from Blois through Chartres to Reims and Champagne. The Normans therefore shifted their allegiance to Stephen. If Theobald had accepted the English crown, historians might have written of a Chartrean empire instead of an Angevin one. Another candidate for the throne (who subsequently became Matilda's principal supporter) was Robert earl of Gloucester, Henry I's bastard son. Bastards might become kings and there could be no stronger precedent than William the Conqueror, the bastard duke of Normandy. But Robert was compromised, like Stephen, by having sworn loyalty to Matilda and furthermore the church was beginning to disapprove of bastards as it developed its laws about Christian marriage. By moving fast and by default Stephen thus came out as the winner and, once he had been crowned, he should have been very difficult to budge. As he declared in his charter of 1136, he had been elected into the kingdom by the clergy and people, consecrated by the archbishop of Canterbury, and confirmed by the pope. Furthermore his rival, Robert earl of Gloucester, was among the magnates who witnessed this charter at Oxford and therefore acknowledged Stephen as king.

Having acquired the throne with dazzling assurance and with as much legality as any of his predecessors, particularly the three Norman kings, Stephen began to lose his hold. Why this happened is a matter of opinion. Contemporary opponents attributed Stephen's lack of success to his failure to support the church; his disasters demonstrated that he was a usurper and a perjurer. His supporters, on the other hand, saw blind chance and his kindness as the causes of his misfortunes; his enemies took advantage of his sense of honour. For example, the author of the *Gesta Stephani* recounts how in 1147, when the future Henry II could no longer pay his troops in England and neither Matilda nor Robert earl of Gloucester would help him, Stephen who 'was always full of pity and compassion' sent him money because he was his kinsman.[8] Thus Stephen 'childishly' helped his most formidable opponent to power.

The problem with all such retrospective assessments, whether they are made by twelfth-century chroniclers or modern historians, is that they are no more than wisdom after the event. Whether it was Stephen's 'weak' acts or his 'strong' ones which brought him down is debatable. By the 'weak' act of aiding the future Henry II in 1147 he may have won his goodwill, which was an advantage to Stephen when he came to negotiate the treaty of Winchester with Henry in 1153. Certainly the author of *Gesta Stephani* thought that Stephen had acted sensibly in this. His 'weakness' or kindness is most vividly illustrated in the biography of William the Marshal. As a child William had been handed over as a hostage to Stephen by his father who repudiated the boy, saying that he had the equipment to make more sons. Stephen should have hanged the boy, but instead he took him from the place of execution to his tent. There they were found playing 'knights' with plantain stalks; Stephen had given William the first turn in the game and he had cut off the head of the king's 'knight'. Stephen's kindness had, as so often, brought him a further humiliation instead of success.

On the other hand Stephen's 'strong' acts also had disastrous consequences. In 1138 Theobald of Bec and not Stephen's brother, Henry of Blois, was elected archbishop of Canterbury. Although the circumstances are obscure, there is little doubt that Henry expected to be elected and it is possible that Stephen excluded him because he thought he was getting too powerful. Nevertheless the principal effect of Stephen's action was not to weaken his brother, as he got a papal legateship instead, but to bring his own support into doubt. In 1139 Stephen took an even more radical action by arresting Roger bishop of Salisbury and his nephews, Alexander bishop of Lincoln and Nigel bishop of Ely. This should have won Stephen control of the administration, as Roger and his nephews had been the principal officers in the Exchequer and Chancery since Henry I's reign. But this resolute action merely enabled Henry of Blois to demonstrate his new powers as papal legate by summoning Stephen to Winchester to answer for the crime of imprisoning bishops. Henry reminded his brother that it was the favour of the church and not the prowess of knights which had raised him to the throne.

These were the circumstances in which Robert earl of Gloucester brought Matilda to England to claim the throne in the autumn of 1139. William of Malmesbury, who favoured Matilda's cause though not the lady herself, compared Robert's arrival with Julius Caesar's crossing of the Rubicon, with this difference: that, where Caesar had only Fortune and his legions to support him, Robert had the strength of the Holy Spirit and the Virgin Mary. Certainly in each case this was the start of a long and bitter civil war. For the next fourteen years (1139–53) the fortunes of each side waxed and waned without much purpose or pattern until the future Henry II, having gained military and political superiority (particularly through his acquisition of Normandy in 1150) and benefiting from the sudden death of Stephen's eldest son Eustace, was able to negotiate the treaty of Winchester: Stephen's second son William surrendered his claim to the English throne in exchange for the right to keep his lands; Stephen himself acknowledged Henry to be his heir and lawful successor.

Of the years of warfare the most important had been 1141. In February Stephen had been captured by Robert earl of Gloucester at the battle of Lincoln and the way was clear for Henry of Blois, as papal legate, to declare that his brother's capture was a judgement of God for his wrongdoing and that Matilda should be chosen in his place. But her supporters had not allowed for the attitude and power of the Londoners. They had formed themselves into what they called a 'commune', the first reference to this type of revolutionary association in England (see page 121 below), and they demanded Stephen's release. Matilda underestimated their strength and, instead of being crowned in midsummer, she was chased out of Westminster by the Londoners. As in later years, the commune proved itself to be 'a tumult of the people and a terror of the realm'.[9] Henry of Blois changed back to supporting his imprisoned brother's cause and turned Matilda's attack on him at Winchester in September 1141 into a rout of her supporters. Robert earl of Gloucester was captured and this enabled the two sides to exchange their prisoners, Stephen being exchanged for Robert. In the years that followed, Stephen was never able to overturn this balance of power. His contradictory qualities are best summed up by William of Malmesbury: 'He was a man of energy but little judgement; active in war, of extraordinary spirit in undertaking any difficult task, he was lenient to his enemies and easily appeased.'[10]

Henry II's ancestral rights

The coronation of Henry II in 1154 symbolized the return of peace. For the first few years everything went well. When Henry left England in the summer of 1158 he was at the height of his power, and he did not return until the beginning of the Becket dispute in 1163. His success enabled him to make a reality of the idea that Stephen was a usurper who had let anarchy loose on the land, and that now Henry II had arrived providentially to restore the good rule of Henry I. This was propaganda rather than simple fact because Henry II came to the throne as Stephen's lawful successor and heir (as negotiated by the treaty of Winchester), and Stephen likewise had been the lawful successor of Henry I (as he had been duly elected into the kingdom and consecrated). Nevertheless Henry's actions in the years 1154–8 made sense of his interpretation of history, as he demonstrated that he had restored the tranquillity of the kingdom which Stephen's contemporaries had described as disappearing on the death of Henry I. 'Stephen's manifest failure, no less than Henry I's excellence, was part of Henry II's title to rule,' as Edmund King has observed.[11] Henry II remained conscious of this role. 'When by God's favour I attained the kingdom of England,' he declared in a charter from the last years of his reign, 'I resumed many things which had been dispersed and alienated from the royal demesne in the time of Stephen my usurper.'[12] Some historians of the reign like Roger of Howden and Walter Map were Henry II's partisans, but even those who were more impartial, notably William of New-burgh, followed suit and described the king restoring order.

Henry's first action after his coronation was to banish William of Ypres and his Flemish mercenaries who had served as a standing army for Stephen. Next Henry ordered all castles which had been built during Stephen's reign to be demolished or surrendered. Similarly he revived the laws of his grandfather, Henry I, and appointed new judges. Most importantly he reclaimed crown lands and restored the Ex-chequer to collect royal dues. The difference between Henry's attempt at strong government and Stephen's was that Henry's worked. He demonstrated his power in 1155 by taking Scarborough castle from William of Aumale, who had been the real king of northern England in Stephen's reign (William of Newburgh remarks), and by taking Bridgnorth from Hugh Mortimer. In 1157 Henry pursued his advan-tage by making Malcolm IV of Scotland surrender Northumberland, Cumberland and Westmorland, the northernmost counties which David I had held and which for geographical and cultural reasons might just as well have been incorporated into Scotland as into England. Henry had less success in his attempt in the same year to subjugate Wales, although his attack on Gwynedd and Anglesey reveals him as a forerunner of Edward I in his strategy.

Henry seems to have aimed from his accession at an overlordship over the whole 'British Isles', as he obtained in 1155 a papal bull autho-rizing him to conquer Ireland. This was issued by the English pope, Adrian IV, and obtained by John of Salisbury. Even so it is surprising that the papacy, which had produced a scheme of reform for the Irish church in 1152, should only three years later in the bull of 1155 have described the Irish as vicious barbarians ignorant of the Christian faith. Furthermore when Henry II at last went to Ireland in 1171, partly to avoid public obloquy for the murder of Becket, his establishment of royal jurisdiction there was likewise welcomed by the papacy. Pope Alexander III's first sign of favour after forgiving Becket's murder was to issue letters in 1172 to Henry and to the Irish bishops and nobility, which reiterated papal disapproval of the Irish in unequivocal terms. Henry was described as the pope's dearest son in Christ, a man of majesty and a devoted son of the church, who through his power would bring peace and tranquillity to Ireland. The Irish, on the other hand, were barbarous and uncouth with bestial sexual practices, and furthermore they all ate meat during Lent. These papal justifications for Anglo-Norman rule in Ireland show the influence of English diplomats in Rome and the need the pope felt to rewin Henry's confidence. The Irish became the scapegoats for Becket's murder.

The dispute with Becket (which lasted from 1163 to 1170) is not only the most dramatic and copiously documented episode of Henry's reign, it is also its crisis point because it concerned both the past and the future. It went back to what Henry claimed were the customs of his grandfather and his Norman ancestors before 1135 and it cast a long shadow forward over the two decades of the reign after 1170. The king had been taken by surprise in 1163 because he had previously worked successfully with Becket in asserting royal authority over churchmen. This is best shown by the case of Hilary bishop of Chichester against Walter abbot of Battle, which was heard in 1157 when Becket was still proud to be the king's chancellor and Theobald was archbishop of Canterbury. Walter claimed that Battle abbey had been exempted from the authority of its diocesan, the bishop of Chichester, by charters of William the Conqueror and his successors. Hilary replied that this was contrary to canon law and he obtained a letter from Pope Adrian IV ordering Abbot Walter to obey his bishop. When Walter appealed to Henry II, Hilary put forward the papalist argument of there being two powers in the world, spiritual and material, clerical and lay; it was therefore illegal for any layman, even if he were king, to grant ecclesiastical exemptions without the authority of Rome and the pope.

At the mention of Rome, according to the Battle abbey chronicler, the king grew angry and accused Hilary of betraying his oath of fealty by slandering the majesty of the crown. Becket as chancellor likewise reminded Hilary of his oath of fealty. The king claimed that Hilary wanted to destroy his prerogatives, which had been handed down to him through God's grace by his royal ancestors in hereditary right. This statement rings true, as it is consistent with Henry's frequent insistence that his mission was to restore the law and order of the Norman kings. That regime was especially symbolized, Battle's advocates argued, by their abbey which was built on the field of Hastings. Once Hilary had angered the king his case lost credibility, despite its basis in canon law, and Becket gave it the *coup de grâce* by revealing that Hilary had a letter from the pope. On hearing this the king's expression changed and Hilary was so frightened that he denied ever having asked for the letter. This case throws more light on the background to the Becket dispute than any other because it shows Henry's power and Becket's loyalty to him. In the face of the king's anger the ecclesiastical arguments were abandoned. Archbishop Theobald could not even persuade Henry to adjourn a decision to the bishops alone. Hilary made his submission to the abbot of Battle before the king and in the presence of bishops and lay magnates, as had been the practice under the Norman kings.

In his dealings with the clergy, as with the lay barons, Henry's authority rested on the alleged good customs of his grandfather, Henry I, which had been justified and reinforced by his own victorious power. If that power were to fail, the justification of these customs was brought into doubt, as they were obscure and inconsistent in themselves. Over the lay barons Henry II had been spectacularly successful in the 1150s in demonstrating the validity of these customs by compelling them to surrender their castles and usurpations of royal authority. He had been equally successful in intimidating churchmen. Shortly before his murder, Becket wrote to the pope citing all the attacks (including that on Hilary of Chichester) which Henry had made in the 1150s on ecclesiastical privileges by virtue of his alleged hereditary right as king. Becket's purpose had been to show that Henry was not taking a new line when he demanded that the clergy acknowledge the Constitutions of Clarendon in 1164. Becket was right; it was he who had changed and not Henry. On being consecrated archbishop in 1162, he transferred his allegiance to God, who was a higher lord than the king. In feudal terms this was not a betrayal of Henry because God was the liege lord of them both. Because Becket actually believed in the superior power of his new lord, he was able to withstand his old one.

Henry therefore found himself resisted from an entirely unexpected quarter: not by a baron with a castle to be assaulted but by the man whom he had created and equipped with the church's weapons. This was indeed a struggle of material versus spiritual power. Becket proved to be Henry's most formidable opponent because he knew the king well enough to withstand his anger. The conventions of the time made it difficult for the king to use physical force against churchmen. He therefore depended on his capacity to terrify them into submission. With the important exception of the council of Clarendon in 1164, when Becket nearly surrendered without consulting the bishops, he stood up to the king and thus deprived Henry of his power of intimi-

dation. Although a reasoned case can be made in terms of modern
political theory for the superiority of the state over the church, neither
Henry nor his defenders like Gilbert Foliot bishop of London were
equipped with such arguments. Henry simply reiterated that he stood
by the customs of his grandfather and that Becket had betrayed him.
As Beryl Smalley concludes, 'It emerged from the muddle of anti-
Becket propaganda that Henry II had no coherent theory of royal
power to oppose to Becket's defence of the church, or preferred not
to state it, if he had one.'[13] Becket's various biographers tended to
idealize him and, like other medieval chroniclers, they use dramatic
dialogue to enliven their narrative. Provided allowances are made for
these forms of bias, the following exchange between Becket and Henry
in 1163 expresses the essence of their different points of view. Becket
explains that he has not betrayed his lord because:

> In the dread Judgement day we shall both be judged as servants of one
> Lord. For temporal lords should be obeyed, but not against God: as St
> Peter says, 'We ought to obey God rather than men.'[14]

To this Henry replies:

> I don't want a sermon from you. Are you not the son of one of my
> peasants?

Becket reacts to this attempt at intimidation by striking at the pivot
of Henry's policies and propaganda:

> Indeed I am not 'sprung from royal ancestors'; neither was St Peter,
> prince of the apostles, on whom the Lord deigned to confer the keys
> of the kingdom of heaven and the primacy of the whole church.

To this Henry replies that Peter died for his lord, which gives Becket
the opportunity to prophesy that he will die likewise. Although this
last exchange was perhaps wisdom after the event on the biographer's
part, the previous ones have a greater ring of plausibility and are consistent with other reports. Whether or not Henry intended it, it was
appropriate that Becket should have been killed at the altar of his own
cathedral because the king's anger – and hence his power – could not
reach his archbishop in any other way.

Henry II and his sons

Becket's death in 1170 was a greater threat to Henry than his being alive. The king's misfortunes in the next two decades were attributed by hostile critics to divine judgement on Becket's murderer. Stories began to circulate of Henry's descent from a demon countess of Anjou and (according to Gerald of Wales) St Bernard had prophesied, when he had met Henry as a boy, that he came from the devil and would return to the devil. The wheel of Fortune, Gerald adds, began to carry Henry down to his doom. Although the pope pardoned him in 1172, Christendom at large did not. Louis VII of France and Theobald count of Blois demanded unprecedented punishment for what the archbishop of Sens described as the greatest crime in history – exceeding Nero, Julian the Apostate and even Judas. When Henry the Young King (whose coronation in 1170 by the archbishop of York had accelerated the final stage of the Becket crisis) rebelled against his father in 1173, Louis and Theobald supported him because Becket's murder had deprived Henry II of his right to rule. It was also of course a God-given political opportunity.

The rebellion affected all Henry's dominions from the Scottish border to Aquitaine. 'Aquitaine exulted and Poitou was jubilant,' wrote a Poitevin chronicler; 'the king of the North' was being judged for the enormity of his crimes.[15] Henry was now compelled to do the public penance from which the pope's legates had excused him in 1172. At Canterbury in 1174 he at last acknowledged Becket's superiority by walking barefoot to the martyr's shrine submitting to a flogging from the clergy and monks. Much to Henry's surprise this humiliation paid immediate dividends in military victory. William the Lion king of Scots was taken prisoner on the same day at Alnwick in Northumberland and this broke the rebellion. Henry had survived in a trial of strength. If he had been killed, his lands would presumably have been split up among his sons, and the Young King's inheritance of England, Normandy and Anjou might have returned to the chaos of Stephen's reign.

Among the aristocracy war was still a test of manhood rather than an instrument of policy. To the troubadour Bertran de Born it was a pleasure and not an evil: fighting was the greatest joy of the springtime; hearing cries for help and seeing the dead with lances through them was even better than eating, drinking or sleeping: 'Barons, mortgage your castles, towns and cities sooner than not wage war among your-selves!'[16] Against such attitudes (even if Bertran intended his song to be ironical), not even Henry II's combination of power and legalism could make much headway. He pardoned the Young King and gave him and his brothers the opportunity to fight another day, just as Stephen had helped him when he had been his young and inexperi-enced opponent in 1147. The Young King rebelled again in 1182, in an attempt to win control over Aquitaine from Richard (his brother), and he died in the Dordogne of a fever. Bertran de Born composed a lament in the Young King's honour, describing him as a model of chivalry, and rumours began to circulate of miracles at his tomb in Rouen. But English chroniclers gave the Young King less enthusiastic obituaries: he was Absalom who had betrayed his father and, though he was loved by his knights, he had brought ruin.

An unsympathetic picture of Henry II and his sons is given in the *Anticlaudianus* of Alan of Lille, where they are depicted as sad ghosts from the ancient world. Henry is the emperor Nero, the Young King is Midas, Richard is Ajax, the unmanly Geoffrey of Brittany is Paris and the unfortunate John is Davus. The decadence of the Angevin family is perhaps intended to contrast in this work with the youthful promise of Philip Augustus of France, who succeeded Louis VII in 1180. Although Henry was described as a tyrant by the French and by Gerald of Wales, he was praised by others in equally extravagant terms, even after the murder of Becket, for example by the pope in his letters concerning Ireland in 1172 and by Jordan Fantosme in his verse history of the war with the Scots in 1173–4. Extravagance was appropriate to the heroic genre of Jordan's poem (Henry is described as the best king that ever lived), as it was likewise to the rhetoric of papal letters. Assessments of Henry II's character and intentions tended to be taken to extremes by contemporaries because his rule was on such a huge scale and his actions, particularly the murder of Becket and his wars with his sons, were unusually dramatic.

Gerald of Wales reported that Henry told his intimates that one strong man might rule the world. Gerald associated this with Henry's diplomatic moves against Frederick Barbarossa and his support of Henry the Lion of Saxony (who had married Henry II's daughter Matilda) against Barbarossa. Henry II extended his influence into Italy by marrying his daughter Joan to William II of Sicily in 1177 and he had proposed in 1173 to marry John to the heiress of Maurienne and

Savoy, the controller of the Alpine passes. This proposal came to nothing, although Henry III would take up these strategies in the 1240s. Unlike Henry III, however, Henry II seems to have had a prudent sense of the limitations of his power, despite the flattery of those courtiers who wanted him to act an imperial role. His caution is shown by his refusal to accept the throne of Jerusalem in 1185, even though the crusader kingdom was in desperate straits and there were strong pressures on Henry to go, both to atone for the death of Becket by dying in Jerusalem and because the kingdom was an Angevin inheritance. When he died at Chinon in 1189, Henry was again at war with his sons, this time with Richard. Henry's reputation has increased with the distancing of time and this phenomenon was noticed by William of Newburgh in the 1190s. He records Henry's contradictory qualities and concludes that 'the experience of present evils has revived the memory of his good points, and the man who in his own day was hated by almost everybody is now declared to have been an excellent and useful prince.'[17]

Richard I

By going on crusade only three months after his coronation Richard I tested the resilience of Anglo-Norman government to its uttermost. Since 1066 England's kings, with the exception of Stephen, had spent less than half their reigns in England. Richard went further and spent only six months of his ten-year reign on the English side of the Channel: four months in 1189 for his coronation and preparation for the crusade, and two months in 1194 for a second coronation and preparation for war with Philip Augustus. At first sight neither Richard's government of England, nor his reign as a whole, look successful. He sold offices to raise money and joked that he would have sold London if he could have found a buyer. He failed to take Jerusalem in the Third Crusade, though the crusaders did succeed in re-establishing a base in Palestine at Acre in 1191. But Richard was now on such bad terms with Philip Augustus of France and Count Raymond of Toulouse that he had to make the return journey in disguise through the Alps and was taken prisoner by Duke Leopold of Austria in 1193, who handed him over to the Emperor Henry VI. A ransom of 150,000 marks was demanded, a sum so large that both clerics and laymen were taxed at a quarter of their rents and goods. Furthermore England was surrendered to the emperor as a fief. On his release in 1194 Richard was therefore a vassal of Henry VI for England and a vassal of Philip Augustus for his lands in France. Richard's career at this point is comparable to Stephen's: initial success had been followed by the humiliation of captivity and release on unfavourable terms; in each case the captors admired the chivalry and personal bravery of their prisoner.

Unlike Stephen's, however, Richard's captivity had not weakened his government in England. On the contrary, the effort needed to raise his ransom had strengthened the administration. Hubert Walter was chief justiciar from 1193 to 1198 and combined that office with the archbishopric of Canterbury. Richard I had therefore achieved without stress Henry II's ambition of having the head of his government at the head of the English church. Hubert was moreover an administrator of exceptional competence. His school had been the Exchequer, as Gerald of Wales contemptuously complained to the pope, and in the five years of his justiciarship the main forms of judicial records took shape: the plea rolls, the coroners' rolls, and the final concords (copies of property agreements). In the ecclesiastical courts of Canterbury likewise Hubert initiated systematic record-keeping. Paradoxically therefore Richard I, who seems to have taken no interest in England except as a source of revenue, did more than any other king to give English government that central capability and continuity through record-keeping which made it such a formidable institution. Hubert was moreover not a deskbound bureaucrat but a politician and a man of the world who had accompanied Richard on his crusade, negotiated with Saladin, and led the English crusaders without their king back through the diplomatic minefields of Italy and Germany. Richard's reign needs to be seen in the light of the effectiveness of his government in England and of his successes in France in the years between 1194 and his death by the bolt of a crossbow at the siege of Chalus-Chabrol in the Limousin in 1199. In these years he tightened the grip of royal government in England, primarily in order to raise revenue for the war against Philip Augustus, and in France he came near to getting the better of Philip militarily. Richard could not know that his efforts would fail and that, through forces larger than his own personal bravery and military experience, the Capetian monarchy would triumph in thirteenth-century France and the Moslems in Palestine.

Although some contemporaries criticized Richard's war taxation and his character, no one thought that Jerusalem had been lost forever or that its loss was a matter of no importance. Ralph Niger was unique in voicing objections, and his doubts were not about the rewinning of Jerusalem as such, but about the means of doing so and the motives of true crusaders. More typical is Gerald of Wales who took part in the preaching of the Third Crusade in Wales. Although he wrote of Richard I that he was a tyrant who took pleasure in the spilling of blood, he nevertheless approved of the crusade in principle. When Henry II had remarked that the patriarch of Jerusalem had come to England in 1185 only to seek his own advantage in asking for help, Gerald was shocked: 'I immediately lost all the hope which I had conceived with such great desire; for I had hoped that Israel would be redeemed in our days.'[18] When the True Cross and Jerusalem were captured by Saladin in 1187, neither Henry II nor Philip Augustus could do other than take the cross as crusaders themselves.

Richard I's departure for Jerusalem so shortly after his coronation was therefore not an irresponsible whim on his part but the fulfilment of his sworn duty. He had been the first of Europe's rulers to take the cross and he should therefore be the first to go. In 1185 Henry II's counsellors had advised him to think of his subjects at home and not go in person to Jerusalem. But Richard's position in 1189 was different because Jerusalem had fallen. It was moreover a good opportunity to get the better of Philip Augustus and to settle old scores. The Third Crusade like its predecessors was a mixture of religious inspiration and political calculation. The provisions which Richard made for the government of England in his absence were not neglectful, though they turned out to be ill-judged. His dismissal of his father's officials in 1189 and the fines he levied from them were the usual practice on the accession of a new king and were not unpopular nor necessarily undeserved. The appointment of William Longchamp turned out to be misjudged but Richard recognized his mistake and provided for his replacement by Walter of Coutances, who had been a Chancery officer of Henry II. Similarly Richard could not exclude his brother John from power, particularly not in his absence, and he acquiesced in his being the 'rector' of the kingdom in 1191.

Just as the necessity of raising Richard's ransom reinforced the English governmental machine, so his absence in 1191 had the paradoxical effect of strengthening a common sense of English identity centred on London. Longchamp was removed by the authority of two communal meetings: the first was held in the chapter house of St Paul's cathedral and the second, which took place in the open air near the Tower, was attended by ten thousand people according to Richard of Devizes. Emphasis was put on Longchamp's being a foreigner, who had insulted the English nation and was ignorant of the English language. All England, wrote the bishop of Coventry in his propaganda letter against him, had to bend its knee to his French pride. Although the meetings in London had been headed by John and the magnates, they were backed by the citizens of London who formed themselves into a commune (as they had done in 1141 against Matilda). As in 1141 and likewise later in the formation of the commune of England in 1258, the magnates and bishops were compelled to become sworn members of this revolutionary association. The removal of Longchamp by an association which claimed to speak for the English people and the Londoners in particular is therefore a significant step towards the articulation of public opinion as a political force. Although the baronial part of the association did not remain in being, London was henceforward a commune with its own elected mayor. The terminology and forms of the new community politics, which were borrowed form France and Italy, took another seventy years or so to establish themselves as norms in England.

Richard I's reign marks the point at which the power of the monarchy and not its weakness becomes the focal point of politics. The king's government, with its Chancery and its Exchequer, its sheriffs and its judges, was now the paramount power, whereas in Stephen's reign fifty years earlier its survival had been at stake. Stephen had been unable to restrain the barons even by energetic campaigning up and down England, whereas Richard ruled in absence through Hubert Walter's masterly bureaucracy. Henceforward the question was: 'How should royal power be used?' and no longer 'What could be done to strengthen it in the face of baronial separatism?' Should government be conducted purely for the personal profit of the king and at his whim, as Henry II had assumed, or should it consider the public interest? The barons who imposed Magna Carta on King John in 1215 and the Provisions of Oxford on Henry III in 1258 provided the answers to such questions. Richard I himself looked back in time for his ideals: to the crusade, to the troubadours of the Languedoc, and to international chivalry. These all turned out to be lost causes and so he became a hero of romance. Nevertheless he had also been a man of business and through his choice of officials he proved an able as well as a heroic king. In the concluding words of his modern biographer John Gillingham, 'he was a highly competent ruler, unusually effective across the whole range of a king's business, administrative, diplomatic and political as well as military'.[19] Similarly his Islamic contemporary, the historian Ibn al-Athir, considered Richard the most remarkble man of his time.

7

Law and Order

English law in Henry II's reign was based on two fundamental principles, in civil and criminal cases respectively, which might have surprised a lord or baron in France or Germany. The first principle (as
stated in the book attributed to the chief justiciar, Ranulf Glanvill)
was that 'no one is bound to answer in his lord's court for any free
tenement of his without an order from the king or his chief justiciar'.[1]
In other words a tenant's title could only be questioned in his lord's
court by the king's authority, because he was the overlord of all
freemen and freehold property. The second principle was that in criminal cases the king had sole jurisdiction over everybody, that is, not
only over freemen (as in civil cases) but over serfs as well. This principle is not succinctly stated in a single rule by Glanvill, but it is
exemplified in the many particulars of the assize of Clarendon of 1166,
which gave royal officers like sheriffs and judges exclusive power to
hunt down killers and robbers. For example chapter 9 of this assize
(an 'assize' is the forerunner of an act of Parliament) warns: 'Let there
not be anyone whether within a castle or outside one, not even in the
honour of Wallingford, who shall forbid the sheriffs from entering his
court or his land.'[2]

These two principles were not novelties. Glanvill states that the first
one was a custom of the realm; it was perhaps one of those good old
rules which Henry II claimed were the customs of his grandfather.
The second principle appears in the *Laws of Henry I* where 'the rights
which the king of England has solely and over all men' for keeping
the peace are listed.[3] (This is not an official compilation, but its list of
crimes is reliable and is based on Anglo-Saxon sources.) Murder, arson,

premeditated assault, robbery, rape and other serious offences are included in this list.

The law and feudalism

Neither of these principles was necessarily anti-feudal. The first one recognized the legitimacy of the lord's court while bringing the higher authority of the king to bear upon it. Any feudal society involved a hierarchy of tenants, lords and overlords. Furthermore the king claimed only to be the protector of titles to freehold property; he was not making himself the owner of the land in question. The landlords of medieval England exploited their estates for their own profit as effectively as their counterparts anywhere in Europe. The king granted his protection in property cases only to freemen; serfs had no recourse beyond their lord's court. That 'freemen' essentially still meant the Norman lords in Henry II's reign is suggested by a writ of his protecting the monks of Winchester from being sued 'for any tenement by the claim of an Englishman' unless that Englishman could show possession from the reign of Henry I.[4] An 'Englishman' was a 'native' and hence he was normally a serf.

The second principle might have given a baron in France or Germany more surprise than the first. For example the troubadour Bertran de Born would not have tolerated an officer of the duke of Aquitaine, let alone the king of France, entering his castle of Hautefort in the Dordogne in pursuit of a criminal. Nor would he have accepted that his court had no authority over crimes carrying the death penalty such as murder, robbery and rape. Nevertheless even this principle in English law did not undermine feudal hierarchy as such. It simply stated that the king of England as overlord had greater powers than rulers elsewhere. His jurisdiction over life and death was his inherited right and part of the customs of his kingdom, just as labour services from serfs were the rights of other lords and part of the customs of the manor. Henry II's contemporaries, the Emperor Frederick Barbarossa and Philip Augustus of France, aspired to comparable authority as the heirs of the Ottonian emperors and Charlemagne, but they had fewer means of making monarchical rule a reality. Moreover it was only in England, because of the reinforcement of royal power by the late Anglo-Saxon monarchy and William the Conqueror, that Henry II insisted on such far-reaching powers. In England he believed them to be the customs of his grandfather, Henry I, whereas in Anjou he had a different inheritance and in Aquitaine things differed again. In each place Henry II, like any lord of his time, aimed to rule in accordance with the custom and tradition of the locality.

Most historians now agree that Henry II was not explicitly anti-feudal in his attitude to law. His biographer W. L. Warren writes: 'Henry could not be anti-feudal without destroying the society in which he lived; fief holding and the mutual obligations of lord and man appear to have seemed to him, as to other men, the natural framework of the social order.'[5] The importance of feudal law is clearly shown in Henry II's use of it in his struggle with Thomas Becket as archbishop. Henry was the first king to be entitled *dominus rex* – 'lord king'. The addition of *dominus* emphasized that the traditional monarchical authority of the English king was now reinforced by his being the feudal lord of his tenants, including the bishops. The Constitutions of Clarendon in 1164 insisted that 'the archbishops, bishops and prelates of the kingdom, who hold from the king in chief, have their possessions from the lord king as a barony'.[6] This is the new technical language of feudalism: a tenant 'in chief', at the top of the hierarchy of knights and their men, holds a 'barony', meaning a high office of service. Feudal law obliges Archbishop Thomas Becket, like the other barons, to counsel his lord the king and participate in the judgements of his court. In Henry II's opinion, this baronial duty of loyalty and solidarity overrode Becket's obligations to the church and the pope. The thinking here is comparable with that in the *Song of Roland*, where Charlemagne's high court is made up of the lords and barons who serve him. Henry II's new title of 'lord king' emphasized that feudalism and monarchy acted in unison.

If the struggle between feudalism and monarchy in medieval societies is overemphasized, a third element – the strength of community action and the customs which governed it – gets lost sight of. Without a police force, either royal or seignorial, law enforcement depended upon community action. The most common penalty for crime was outlawry, that is, expulsion from the community. In much of England every adult male was supposed to be in a tithing (a group of ten), which was collectively responsible for its members' behaviour. A hierarchy of communities and courts extended upwards from manor and village through the hundred (a group of villages) to the county court and ultimately to the *curia regis*, where king and barons gave judgements through 'parliament' (meaning 'discussion'). Both

Henry II in his enforcement of law and rebel barons in Stephen's reign aimed at using communal powers to the advantage of their cause. Thus Henry's administration largely depended on local juries, both to identify criminals and to decide property cases. Ultimately it was jurors of the neighbourhood, and not royal judges or feudal lords, who decided the fates of men and property by their verdicts of 'Guilty' or 'Not guilty'. Just like the king in his kingdom, lords on their estates had to come to terms with the custom of the manor in order to get their land worked and their tenants disciplined. Nevertheless, collective decisions should not be confused with democracy. Royal officers and landlords herded people into groups in order to control them.

Monarchical authority (the 'tremendous power of the royal majesty' as the *Laws of Henry I* called it; see page 53 above), feudal authority (a hierarchy of lords and tenants), and communal authority (collectivities like tithings and hundreds taking decisions binding on their groups) all interlocked. Whether a particular development or rule is monarchical, feudal or communal in essence is often impossible to say because these three forms of authority overlapped; sometimes they are no more than different ways of looking at the same person or thing. For example the king is the crowned monarch of all his subjects, the feudal overlord of his barons and knights, an immediate lord of serfs on the royal demesne, and the head of the community of the English nation. Similarly a freeman is a member of various communities in his county, hundred and village; he is also the tenant of a lord as well as being, like all freeholders, a privileged subject of the king with the duty to bear arms in his service. Furthermore this tripartite analysis takes no account of other forms of lawful authority, most notably that of the church. Another important general point is that, because courts were community meetings and legal experts were educated through them and not by book learning, knowledge of the law was more widely diffused than in modern societies. Neither Henry II nor anybody else therefore aimed at sweeping changes because everybody's rights and duties were part of a nexus of custom and dependence.

The system described by Glanvill

The main elements of the legal system need to be described before Henry II's contribution to it can be assessed. This can best be done from the book attributed to Glanvill which was completed in the last years of the reign (1187–9). But Glanvill's warning in his prologue must be borne in mind that it is 'utterly impossible for the laws and legal rules of the realm to be wholly reduced to writing in our time, both because of the ignorance of scribes and because of the confused multiplicity of those same laws and rules'.[7] Glanvill's book overcomes these difficulties by being structured around the forms of royal writs and expounding with clarity the rules of procedure pertaining to each of them. The material is also arranged in a logical order, distinguishing between civil and criminal business, and starting with claims of right to land before proceeding to churches, status, dower and so on.

The great majority of writs cited by Glanvill are in the form of letters by the king to the sheriff of a county. Their tone is peremptory: 'Command N. to render to R. justly and without delay one hide of land in such-and-such a village' or 'Summon N. by good summoners to be before me or my justices at Westminster on the third Sunday after Easter to show why he did not do so-and-so'.[8] The emphasis throughout is on effective enforcement of the law by giving orders that are unambiguous and specific: sheriffs are to be promptly obeyed; recalcitrant defendants will suffer if they make undue delays or excuses; as soon as a decision is reached, it is to be executed by the sheriff's officers. Nowhere does Glanvill suggest that the king is opposed to feudal lordship or ancient custom, but the book does give the impression that royal authority is rigorously applied in order to overcome the indecision and confusion caused by conflicting jurisdictions and uncertainties about procedure. In prescribing decisiveness through his writs Henry II was certainly acting in the spirit of his grandfather, Henry I, and evoking the majestic powers of William the Conqueror and the Anglo-Saxon kings.

Glanvill does admit however that there have been some innovations, particularly in the making of 'assizes', which he describes as 'a royal benefit granted to the people by the goodness of the king acting on the advice of his magnates' and as a 'constitution of the realm'.[9] These legislative acts provided trial by jury in various forms of property disputes. Thus the 'grand assize' of twelve knights replaced trial by battle in actions of right, and 'petty assizes' of twelve freemen decided disputes about recent possession, most notably in claims of inheritance ('mort d'ancestor') and unlawful seizure ('novel disseisin'). Jurors acted like witnesses who were expected to know the facts about a case because they were men of standing in their locality. Glanvill is troubled about whether twelve men will always be found who know the facts and whether they will speak the truth, but jury trial is assumed to be better than the doubtful outcome of a duel. The use of juries is a good example of how English law contained monarchical, feudal and communal elements and drew on customary procedures. Juries had been used by William the Conqueror to make Domesday Book, the knights of the 'grand assize' were a feudal element, their collective neighbourhood decisions emphasized the communal element, and their verdicts expressed local custom and belief.

A peculiar feature of Glanvill's book from a modern lawyer's point of view is that although it gives rules of procedure in civil and criminal cases and discusses the effects of Henry II's assizes, it nowhere ascribes this legislation to particular years or places. We depend upon chroniclers of Henry II's reign, particularly Roger of Howden (who was also a royal judge), for texts of the assizes of Clarendon in 1166, Northampton in 1176 and Woodstock in 1184. Glanvill omits these texts for two reasons perhaps. First, he aims to explain current procedural rules and he is not very concerned about how these came into being. Secondly, he cannot include everything (as he explains in his prologue) and he may not have thought piece-meal regulations, which is what these assizes essentially are, had any permanent standing. Roger of Howden rightly recorded them because he was a chronicler concerned with how history came about. Glanvill as rightly omitted them because he was concerned with permanent general rules.

The effect of Henry II's reign on the criminal law, as on civil, was to standardize procedure and make enforcement more likely. The assizes of Clarendon and Northampton had insisted that jurors in every hundred and every village should name those of their neighbours whom they suspected of murder, robbery or other serious offences and that the accused should be brought to trial before the king's justices. These assizes also indicate Henry II's impatience with some traditional features of the law, as he insisted that persons of ill repute who were acquitted should go into exile nevertheless: 'Within eight days they shall cross the sea unless the wind detains them; and with the first wind they shall have afterwards they shall cross the sea, and they shall not return to England again except by the mercy of the lord king, and they are outlawed both now and if they return.'[10] The realm of England was to be cleared of malefactors at a stroke. Nevertheless these draconian measures were less than successful. Henceforward jurors made many accusations, and trials proceeded before royal judges, but most of the accused were never caught. They became the outlaws and desperadoes of legend and fact in the greenwoods of England.

Henry II's intentions

Henry II has been credited since the nineteenth century at least with being the founder of England's common law. (By 'common law' is meant the royal law that was common to the whole country.) R.C. van Caenegem in *The Birth of the English Common Law* describes him as 'that man of genius – the word is not too strong – who was by instinct a lawyer', and Lady Stenton in her description of what she calls 'The Angevin Leap Forward' in legal development agrees that 'genius was at work'.[11] The problems with this point of view are twofold. First, these modern assessments of Henry II are at variance with contemporaries who emphasize his deliberate dilatoriness in settling lawsuits and the notorious corruption of his judges. Secondly, if he had been a legislative genius, one would have expected to find an 'Angevin Leap Forward' in Anjou and Normandy as well as in England, which is not the case. Another generalization often made is that Henry II introduced his legal reforms, like the 'grand assize' and the 'petty assizes', in order to restore law and order after Stephen's reign. But the difficulty with this is the chronological gap. There is no evidence that the assize of novel disseisin was introduced as a regular procedure until 1166 at the earliest (twelve years after Stephen's reign) and no evidence of the assize of mort d'ancestor until 1176. If these changes are to be related to political events, the Becket crisis is a better explanation for the year 1166 and the aftermath of the rebellion of Henry's sons for the year 1176.

Henry II's intentions were an enigma to his contemporaries and they must therefore remain an enigma to us. The assize of Clarendon and the procedures in civil pleas described by Glanvill suggest that he wished cases to be resolved speedily and with consistency, even if that meant overriding traditional rights. In this light Henry was 'the subtle discoverer of unusual and hidden judicial procedure', as Walter Map described him.[12] The same point is made in a less complimentary way by Ralph Niger, who says that Henry produced new laws which he called 'assizes' every year. Royal judges were certainly seen by some contemporaries as a public nuisance, rather than as the paragons whom Glanvill describes dispensing equal justice to rich and poor: they were extortioners rather than judges in John of Salisbury's opinion, and the 'wandering judges' (that is, the justices in eyre who went from county to county) 'wandered from the path of equity in order to plunder the people'.[13] Both Ralph Niger and John of Salisbury were partisans of Becket and were therefore prejudiced against Henry II. But even the chronicle belonging to Benedict of Peterborough, which is generally favourable to Henry, criticizes his judges when it describes him in 1178 agreeing to reduce their number from eighteen to five because of their oppression.

Although some of this criticism of Henry II arose from prejudice or misunderstanding, the aspect of his rule which is hardest to reconcile with his being a legislative genius is the deliberate way in which he delayed decisions. Gerald of Wales accuses Henry of thinking only of his own advantage in the selling and delaying of justice. Benedict of Peterborough's chronicle describes him postponing things from day to day in accordance with his custom, and Walter Map alleges that Henry was so dilatory that many people died before bringing their suits to a conclusion. Richard of Anstey's graphic account of how it took him seven years, considerable expense (in gifts of gold, silver and horses), and numerous journeys around England and France in order to get possession of his uncle's land suggests that Walter Map may have been right, although Richard survived to tell the tale.

Henry II, or any other king for that matter, was in a difficult position when petitioners asked him for justice because what they usually meant was that the case should be settled in their favour. The king could often not afford to alienate either party in a dispute because both were his loyal subjects. For example, the chronicler of Battle abbey describes his abbot going to Westminster at dawn to catch the king at Mass. Henry was in the process of granting the abbot's request when the bishop of Chichester came running up to complain. Henry learned from experiences like this to avoid irrevocable decisions. Indeed Walter Map says that Henry's mother, the Empress Matilda, advised him to protract everybody's business: men should be tamed like hawks by giving them a sight of the raw meat and then snatching it away.

The contradiction between Henry's deliberate dilatoriness and the speed and decisiveness of the writ system described by Glanvill is obvious. It suggests that Henry II was speaking the truth when he insisted that he was doing no more than enforcing the customs of his grandfather, as the peremptory tone of Glanvill's writs is that of Henry I and earlier kings (see pages 53 and 58 above). Henry II perhaps remained content with this as a policy until the controversy with Becket compelled him to define in writing what the customs of his grandfather were. The constitutions of Clarendon of 1164 mark the starting point of what a modern lawyer would call 'law reform' or 'legislation', although Henry claimed that they were no more than a 'record' (*recordatio* in Latin) of part of the acknowledged customs and dignities of the kingdom.[14] The canon lawyers whom Henry opposed in the Becket controversy had built up an impressive system of written law. Becket as former royal chancellor knew that the king had nothing to match this and he used his learned counsellors, like John of Salisbury and Herbert of Bosham, to create a coherent clerical ideology. This seems to have been the stimulus for Henry, who was highly educated, to make his court likewise a place where there was school every day (as Peter of Blois described it) and to attempt from 1164 onwards to reinforce the customary law of England by written instructions to judges and other royal officials. Hence the constitutions of Clarendon were followed by the assize of Clarendon of 1166, the inquest of Sheriffs of 1170, the assize of Northampton of 1176, the assize of Arms of 1181 and the assize of Woodstock of 1184. The author of 'Glanvill' likewise aimed (as we have seen) to reduce law to writing in Henry II's last years.

Bureaucracy

Glanvill's book and Henry II's assizes looked greater achievements in retrospect than they did in the twelfth century because the use of writing gave them permanence. Henry II may have done no more to invigorate the law than his grandfather, Henry I, but the difference was that from Henry II's reign onwards the legal system had a fixed identity because of its set procedures. Bureaucracy set in fast and the forms of the possessory assizes and the main elements of the criminal law remained in being until the nineteenth century. Victorian historians of the law, looking back over the centuries, understandably enough credited Henry II with being the founder of the system. In reality, however, more was probably due to the effects of writing as a technology than to Henry himself or any other individual. The impressive legal monument left by Henry II was the product of fossilization rather than deliberate policy. Writing preserved and hardened the old forms in much the same way as the flora and fauna of the primeval forest were fossilized. Writing proved to be a more powerful and intractable force than anyone had bargained for.

This is best illustrated by considering the effects of the writs in set forms described by Glanvill. The rule that 'no one is bound to answer in his lord's court for any free tenement of his without an *order* from the king or his chief justiciar' was probably customary as Glanvill says. But Glanvill also gives this rule in a significantly different form in another part of his book, where he says that no one can sue for a free tenement 'without a *writ* from the king or his justices'.[15] The crucial difference here is between 'an order' (*preceptum*) in the first version and 'a writ' (*brevis*) in the second. Before writs became a routine part of legal procedure a litigant needing 'an order from the king or his chief justiciar' depended on the word of the king or the justiciar, delivered either in person or through an accredited messenger. In these circumstances royal intervention in a lord's court must have been a rare event. Not even a fast-riding king like Henry II could hope to patrol all his dominions in person (even with the aid of his chief justiciar), particularly when they extended from Scotland to the Pyrenees. The use of writs, on the other hand, meant that the king's authority extended as far and as fast as his Chancery officials could write them out, as aggrieved litigants could fetch and carry them, and as sheriffs and bailiffs in the localities were willing and able to enforce them.

Through the technology of writing, therefore, the king's right as overlord of all freemen to redress the wrongs of undertenants could be effectively enforced for the first time. The use of writs as a method of defining and extending royal instructions to remote areas was Anglo-Saxon in origin. The innovation of Henry II's reign lay in providing writs in standardized and replicable forms. Perhaps from the time of King Alfred and certainly since the tenth century the king had given protection to complainants through his writs. But the complainant was expected to draft and sometimes also to write out the complaint for himself, as well as delivering it to his opponent, which might be a hazardous undertaking. Henry II's writs given in Glanvill's book, on the other hand, are in set forms and the great majority of them are addressed to the sheriff and not to the other party in the dispute. The sheriff is to provide a jury, or whatever the writ requires, and he is also to return the writ to the king's justices as evidence of its execution. Where earlier kings had granted petitioners writs against their opponents and then just hoped for the best, the system from Henry II's reign onwards provided well-defined bureaucratic machinery for enforcing royal orders.

The assizes of novel disseisin and mort d'ancestor and similar routine procedures automated the legal system. Complaints were expressed in standard forms, they were written out by Chancery clerks in fast cursive script, the king's will was expressed by impressing his seal on the writs, and his sheriffs enforced them in accordance with their standing orders. The result was that an obscure freeman, provided he could pay the fees and bribes demanded by officials, could obtain a portentous document against his lord announcing the intervention of 'Henry king of the English and duke of the Normans and Aquitainians and count of the Angevins' in his cause. As a consequence the royal courts became flooded with cases and a quantitative change became a qualitative one. Henry II had not probably intended to undermine relations between lords and tenants but this was an inevitable result of making it easier to litigate in the king's court. Without being aware of it, Henry had achieved what Max Weber describes as 'the routinization of charisma'. The majestic power of the king, symbolized by his seal showing him seated crowned on his throne, was disseminated throughout the kingdom in thousands of royal writs containing his orders.

From the point of view of making society more just and law-abiding this 'routinization' of royal authority was not necessarily a change for the better. The king's court raised expectations which it could not satisfy; hence the bitterness of contemporary comments against the corruption of judges and officials. Although more grievances were brought into the king's court and a larger proportion of crimes were reported to royal judges, their powers to do justice were vitiated not only by corruption and incompetence but also by the fact that ultimately everything depended on local opinion. In both civil and criminal cases the essential decisions were made by the verdicts of jurors from the neighbourhood and not by the judges from Westminster. English law gave the appearance of being a centralized system emanating from the royal majesty, whereas in reality it was rooted in local opinion. Had it not been acceptable to local interests, and to the land-lords in particular, it could not have worked at all.

Why did England develop a system of its own?

The Flemish historian R.C. van Caenegem, from his study of both English and continental medieval law, poses a paradoxical question about the changes of Henry II's reign. Why did English law enter upon its distinctive course in the twelfth century, precisely at the time when cultural and political contacts between England and the continent were at their closest?

> English scholars studied then in continental universities, John of Salisbury was bishop of Chartres and Nicholas Breakspear became Pope Adrian IV, the English church was ruled by clerics of contin-ental extraction and very attentive to papal directives. The knightly class that colonized England was of continental extraction and owned land on both sides of the Channel. Kings, prelates and knights spoke French and the kingdom itself was no more than an acquisition first of the Norman and then of the Angevin family.[16]

Van Caenegem discusses various explanations for this paradox. First, English historians of a nationalist temperament cannot see that there is a problem: English law is different because England has always been wonderfully different. But what was so different: the climate; the economy; the tradition of government? Manors and landlords were a commonplace of medieval Europe, and even the English climate was less distinctive in the twelfth century as it was warmer. Van Caenegem concedes that the Anglo-Saxons had built up a unified state, but he puts more emphasis on the Norman conquerors who brought in their own kind of controlled and constructive feudalism. He argues that 'the precision, briskness and sharpness of the common law procedure and its whole atmosphere are quite unlike the traditional qualities of the English of Anglo-Saxon times, who are depicted as warm and gentle . . . If the common law started geographically as an Anglo-Norman phenomenon, its tone in that initial phase was over-whelmingly Norman.'[17]

The 'precision, briskness and sharpness' of the system is accurately characterized here and is borne out both in the arrangement and in the tone of Glanvill's book and the writs it contains. But the contrast van Caenegem makes between Anglo-Saxon and Norman characteristics is overgeneralized. The peremptory tone of Henry II's writs echoes those of Henry I and they in their turn derive from Anglo-Saxon precedents. Briskness and sharpness are arguably Anglo-Saxon characteristics as much as Norman, but there is little point in attributing such general characteristics to whole peoples. Other historians have therefore attributed the briskness and sharpness to Henry II himself, though the difficulty with this is that some contemporaries characterized him as dilatory and evasive, as we have seen. A sufficient explanation for the briskness and sharpness of royal writs is that these qualities result from the use of writing and from the scholastic training of their original drafters.

The distinctive style of English common law derived from many sources and traditions: Anglo-Saxon, Norman, ecclesiastical, Roman and scholastic. The system took the form it did because it developed in the period of the Twelfth-century Renaissance and it retained that form for centuries thereafter because bureaucracy perpetuated it. Hence later lawyers and historians praised as peculiarly English something that was really peculiarly twelfth-century and cosmopolitan. The Latin learning of the schools epitomized by John of Salisbury, the ecclesiastical and canonical world of Nicholas Breakspear and the papacy, the values of French courtly and feudal society, and the eclectic political dominance of Henry II, were all strands in the formation of the common law. Its distinctive form was therefore a product of England's close contacts with the continent at the time and not in opposition to them. All these strands moreover were woven into an existing fabric of custom and organization which was Anglo-Saxon in origin. Without the sheriffs, counties and hundreds, and without the habit of thinking of the king as the lord of all freemen (barons and knights, cleric and lay) and of all England, there could have been no common law.

Ultimately the common law system was shaped by the individuals who drafted in Latin the forms of the first returnable writs and the king's instructions to judges and sheriffs. Although we cannot know precisely who these individuals were, there is no reason to think that they were newcomers from Normandy or the Angevin lands. The two most prominent names associated with the law in this formative stage are Ranulf Glanvill, Henry II's chief justiciar from 1180 to 1189, and Hubert Walter, who was Richard I's justiciar from 1193 to 1198 and

King John's chancellor from 1199 to 1205. Both Ranulf and Hubert were of East Anglian origin. Although Ranulf claimed Norman ancestors, he was not a newcomer to England. If he were the author of the book attributed to him, he was evidently proud of England's ancient laws, and the best manuscript of Roger of Howden's chronicle states that 'by his wisdom the laws which we call English were established.'[18] Ranulf would have learned law in the first place by attending local courts and listening to debate, rather than by specific instruction. He may have been the author of an account of how his father Hervey Glanvill during Stephen's reign gave evidence in the court at Bury St Edmunds of the wisdom he had gained there by fifty years of attendance.

Both the oral lore of these customary courts and academic learning in Latin were important in the formation of legal experts like Ranulf and Hubert. If Ranulf were the author of 'Glanvill', he was an accomplished Latinist with some knowledge of Roman and canon law. He was also described as the 'master' or tutor of King John when a boy; he may therefore have been a master in the scholastic sense. Hubert likewise, who was brought up in Ranulf's household, knew some Latin as he was archbishop of Canterbury, although Richard I corrected his grammar on one occasion. But Hubert was probably not a graduate of Bologna, as has sometimes been suggested. Gerald of Wales says his school had been the Exchequer; in other words he was educated in administration. Nevertheless that would have required both Latin and intelligence, as the *Dialogue of the Exchequer* demonstrates.

Conflict between book learning and oral learning, and between an academic approach and a practical one, seems to be resolved in the achievements of Ranulf and Hubert. The author of 'Glanvill' explains that the laws and customs of England have their origin in reason and he intends to describe them in a form of Latin which is appropriate to business practice: *in verbis curialibus* is the term he uses, meaning 'in the language of the court'.[19] The court (*curia*) that the author has in mind here is the court of Henry II, which is the hub of political and aristocratic life as well as being a court of justice. The adjective *curialibus* might be translated as 'courtly', but that would be misleading because of its associations with courtly romance. The 'courtiers' (*curiales*) of Henry II were men of business rather than romancers. They were also men of action. Ranulf Glanvill captured the king of Scots at the battle of Alnwick in 1174, and he died accompanying

Richard I on crusade. Hubert Walter likewise came to prominence in this crusade as a diplomat and war leader before being appointed chief justiciar.

The careers of Ranulf and Hubert are outstanding, but they are probably also typical of the men who shaped the common law in its formative period. They crossed and intercrossed the conventional divisions of medieval society, combining clerical with lay expertise and the oral traditions of England with the Latin learning of Roman and canon law. Likewise they were men of action as much as being men of ideas, who were as proud of England as of their Norman descent. Such a mixture of talents and influences best explains why the law was neither exclusively monarchical nor feudal nor communal, but included all these elements; and it also explains why the law embodied ancient custom and yet looked modern in its logical procedures and dependence on writing. The common law of England is a monument to a brilliant time in western Europe, rather than to any single individual (whether Ranulf Glanvill, Hubert Walter or even Henry II himself) or to any exclusively national characteristics (whether English, Norman or French). And the law became a monument because it used writing, in the form of Latin writs, as its special instrument.

8

The Twelfth-century Renaissance

The idea of the Twelfth-century Renaissance was given currency in the 1920s by the American medievalist C.H. Haskins, in order to draw attention to the achievements of the period and to challenge the assumption that everything stagnated between the fall of the Roman Empire and the Italian Renaissance of the fifteenth century. To keep his arguments as parallel as possible to those of Italian Renaissance historians, Haskins concentrated on the influence of the Latin classics, the development of original Latin prose and verse composition, the awakening interest in Greek science, and the revival of Roman jurisprudence and Aristotelian logic. Seen in this light, the schoolmen of the twelfth century like Abelard and Gratian – and the universities of Paris and Bologna which originated in this time – became, like the humanists of the fifteenth and sixteenth centuries, the harbingers of a new learning instead of obscurantist purveyors of superstition. Drawing on the best of classical tradition and at the same time adapting it to their own needs, the men of the twelfth century created a new art which developed from Romanesque into Gothic, a new literature in both Latin and vernaculars (notably the *Carmina Burana* and the romances of Chrétien de Troyes), and a new system of education centred on the teaching of theology and law at universities.

To carry conviction the term 'renaissance' has to be broadly, and even vaguely, interpreted as a convenient way of describing a renewal of creativity and expertise. Like the 'Angevin Empire', the 'Twelfth-century Renaissance' is not so much a precise reality as a cluster of ideas which cannot be better described in any other way. Strictly speaking there was not a 'rebirth' (*renaissance* in French) of classical learning in the twelfth century because regard for the classics had never died. (The metaphor of 'rebirth' looks like nonsense anyway, as it is impossible in the physical world.) Latin was the dominant language of literacy and literature in the west in the twelfth century just as it had been a thousand years before. John of Salisbury described in *Metalogicon* how the best Latin teaching was done by training boys to imitate the Roman poets and orators and grounding them in grammar. Medieval letters and chronicles are consequently full of quotations and allusions to ancient authors, though their range of emphasis differs from post-Italian Renaissance Latin writing as it includes the Bible and the church fathers. Considering the paucity of resources, the extent and accuracy of medieval knowledge of Latin is more cause for astonishment than its supposed lapses from classical purity.

The attitude of twelfth-century writers to their classical heritage was ambivalent. Ambivalence is the keynote of the remark of Bernard of Chartres (reported by John of Salisbury) that 'we are like dwarfs perched on the shoulders of giants'.[1] The giants are the pagan philosophers and writers, both Greek and Latin (notably Plato and Aristotle, Cicero and Virgil), and their Christian counterparts (the prophets and evangelists of the Old and New Testaments, and the church fathers like Jerome and Augustine). The dwarfs are inferior to them, in both intellect and appearance, but they can see further because they stand on their shoulders. This image therefore conveys a theory of progress. Bolder spirits among the schoolmen voiced impatience with the giants and the authority of antiquity. They coined a new Latin word to describe themselves: they were the 'men of now' (the *moderni*) as distinct from the 'ancients' (*antiqui*). In an often quoted passage Chrétien de Troyes in the 1160s or 1170s proudly repudiated the dominance of ancient Greece and Rome:

> Our books have taught us that Greece once had pre-eminence in chivalry and learning. Then chivalry passed to Rome, together with the highest learning which now has come to France. God grant that it remain here, and that it find the place so pleasing that it never departs from France. The honour which stops here, God had but lent to the others. For of the Greeks and Romans no more is said; their word has ceased, their glowing embers are extinguished.[2]

Chrétien is expressing here the idea of a *translatio studii*, of a transfer of culture from the ancient world to the modern one. He claims this inheritance for France whereas at about the same time the Romans, in their revival of the republic under Arnold of Brescia, were claiming it for themselves while the Emperor Frederick Barbarossa replied that he and his Germans had inherited Roman power and now bore the club of Hercules. The Greeks of the twelfth century likewise asserted with equal conviction, notably in the *Alexiad* of Anna Comnena, that 'chivalry' (that is, political and social leadership) and learning had never passed away from Byzantium.

Chrétien de Troyes makes a witty and combative bid for the pre-eminence of French culture in his time. Although he claims that this is God-given, he is aware of the fragility of the flame which has come to rest in France. In saying that 'chivalry' (*chevalerie*) is now French, Chrétien presumably has in mind the knights of epic and romance (in the *Song of Roland* and his own works) as well as the reality of French (including Norman) knights dominating Palestine, southern Italy and Britain. The crusades certainly belonged more to France than to any other nation. Learning (*clergie* in Chrétien's terms, that is, clerical knowledge) had likewise taken root in France, in the schools of Paris, Orleans, Chartres and Laon among others, and in the persons of such masters as Abelard and Hugh of St Victor. France likewise dominated in a more strictly clerical sense with its monastic reform movements, above all with the Cistercian order and St Bernard. Although Chrétien may not have been thinking of the visual arts, a comparable French pre-eminence is evident in Abbot Suger's rebuilding of St Denis (consecrated in 1144) and the first Gothic cathedrals which grew up in much the same places as the schools. Like the schoolmen and the composers of romances, the Gothic artists performed subtle variations on the themes of ancient and modern, and in the brilliance of stained glass and manuscript illumination they revived the 'glowing embers' of past greatness.

England's place in this Renaissance

At first sight England's place in all this looks undistinguished. 'Culturally the most obvious thing about England in the twelfth century is its dependence on France,' Sir Richard Southern argued; 'it was a colony of the French intellectual empire, important in its way and quite productive, but still subordinate.'[3] As generalizations these statements are a useful corrective to the chauvinism of some nineteenth-century critics and historians, who wrote of twelfth-century art and literature in England without appreciating its continental context. The best example of this narrow approach is the use of the term 'Early English' to describe the first phase of Gothic architecture, a term still favoured in descriptions of parish churches. It goes back to Thomas Rickman's *Attempt to Discriminate the Styles of Architecture in England* in 1819. Rickman's analysis of the different styles was excellent, but his naive nationalism led him to argue that the purest form of Gothic architecture was the 'Early English' type. Foreign examples, he suggested, such as Chartres cathedral, were spoiled by Italian features. The gradual transition from 'Norman' (Rickman's term for Romanesque) architecture to 'Early English' convinced him that these 'styles were the product of the gradual operation of a general improvement, guided by the hand of genius, and not a foreign importation'.[4]

Rickman stands to the architectural history of the Middle Ages much as Stubbs does to constitutional history. For such nationalists England's great churches, like her parliament and legal system, had to be purely English. They were the products of native 'improvement' (a favourite Victorian concept) uncontaminated by Rome or France. There is some truth in such views, of course. In art and literature, as in law and politics, Anglo-Saxon traditions influenced the imported forms and produced works which were distinctively English even though they belong to the mainstream of medieval culture emanating from France. The choir and stained glass of Canterbury cathedral, the illuminated books of the Bible associated with Henry of Blois bishop of Winchester, and the works of Latinists like Walter Map and Gerald of Wales are identifiably English (or rather, British in the cases of Walter and Gerald with their Welsh associations). Nevertheless these writers and artists worked in the most sophisticated idioms of their time and they addressed a wider audience than the English.

To describe England as 'a colony of the French intellectual empire' is, however, a simplification, as Southern points out at the end of his essay. French culture was indeed pre-eminent but it was not as dominant as the metaphor of colonization suggests. Writers and artists in England drew their inspiration from many sources. Their approach was cosmopolitan rather than exclusively French, which is not surprising considering the eclectic nature of Henry II's dominions, the diverse legacies of the Norman Conquest, and the close links between English churchmen and Rome. After 1066 the educated class in England were distanced from their own culture and encouraged to prefer Latin and French to their native English. That this was a largely voluntary process is suggested by the speed with which the property-owning inhabitants of Winchester and Canterbury adopted foreign personal names in the twelfth century (see page 39 above). The bright young men, like John of Salisbury and Gerald of Wales who were sent to France for their education, were attracted to a rootless life, searching for the best masters and the most generous patrons who might employ them as letter writers or even as entertainers. Many of the wandering scholars were Englishmen whose education had made them strangers in their own country, although they were at home at a bishop's court or a scholar's desk in any part of western Europe. The distinct vein of satire which runs through the works of Walter Map, Gerald of Wales and even John of Salisbury may have been a product of ambivalence about their identity (which was compounded in the case of the Welshmen). Experience had made them citizens of the world and they looked on it with a cynical eye.

A notable work in this cosmopolitan satirical genre is *A Mirror for Fools* (*Speculum Stultorum*) by Nigel Whiteacre, who was resident in Canterbury in the 1190s. He tells the story in Latin elegiac couplets of how Burnel the Ass (echoing the *Golden Ass* of Apuleius) goes to the medical school at Salerno to seek a longer tail, then to Paris where he joins the English students (in the hope of becoming a bishop by mastering theology and law), before deciding in despair to be a monk; but this project also fails because Burnel is dissatisfied with all existing religious orders. The English at Paris are described as clever, charming and elegant, but they drink without restraint: 'Wassail' and 'Drink Hail' are their favourite toasts; Burnel hopes to become an honorary Englishman. In both its style and content this work mirrors the cosmopolitan world of the rootless Englishmen of the time. Polished Latin, invective against religious hypocrisy and the sycophancy of courtiers, moralizing anecdotes, and a jumble of incidents symbolizing the absurdity of life are features not only of *A Mirror for Fools* but of other works by Latinists in England, notably John of Salisbury's *Policraticus* and Walter Map's *De Nugis Curialium*. In real life moreover John of Salisbury and Gerald of Wales recount going from school to school for many years before ending up as bishops, or only bishop elect in Gerald's case. Burnel the Ass described the ambitions and frustrations of many others:

> To Paris then my way I'll make,
> A ten years' course in Arts to take;
> I'll start at once. Then, if God will,
> I'll come back home, and learning still,
> Become well versed in all the rules,
> By studying in Bologna's schools
> Of civil law: the Sacred Page
> And the Decreta will engage
> My final labours, if I live.
> Then, then at last I shall receive
> The title and reality
> Of Master; Master shall I be,
> And 'Master' shall precede my name.[5]

Curiales and Latinists

Nigel Whiteacre also wrote a tract 'Against Courtiers and Clerical Officials'. The word he uses for 'courtier' is *curialis*, and the *curialis* is the anti-hero of the English Latinists of the twelfth century. John of Salisbury gave to his *Policraticus* ('Statesman's Book') the alternative title 'Courtiers' Trifles [*De Nugis Curialium*] and Footsteps of Philosophers'. The same title of 'Courtiers' Trifles' was given likewise to Walter Map's book, perhaps because he began with the thought, 'I am in the court and speak of the court but what the court is God alone knows, I do not.'[6] As characterized by these authors, the *curialis* is a cleric who leads a worldly life at court; his is a bewildering life because he is at the beck and call of princes instead of living in the scholarly decorum befitting a university 'Master'. The contrast between the lofty aspirations of the *curialis* and the realities of being a hanger-on at court gave him a taste for the absurd. 'Courtiers' Trifles' were jests both for and about *curiales* and the vanity of human wishes. *Policraticus* was dedicated to Thomas Becket, in his worldly phase when he was Henry II's chancellor, and Walter Map likewise served Henry as an official, as did Peter of Blois who wrote about court life. Like Burnel the Ass these writers were torn between the plain and single-minded life of scholarship and the variegated demands of worldly advancement.

The prominence of the *curialis* theme among Latin writers in England may also be explained by the nature of Henry II's court. Unlike Eleanor of Aquitaine, Henry was no patron of letters or learning for its own sake. He was clever and highly educated (the great master, William of Conches, had been among his tutors), but his interests were in running the monarchy as a day-to-day business. From his court therefore emanated Fitz Nigel's *Dialogue of the Exchequer* and Glanvill's lawbook, containing *utilia* (useful information) and not *subtilia* (see page 102 above). As Southern has emphasized, 'these books were not simply manuals or textbooks for office use like the contemporary collections of decretals [papal and other letters illustrating canon law]: they aspired in some degree to invest the routine of government with an intellectual generality. They were all written in England, and they provide a glittering testimony to the growing claims of secular government such as we could find nowhere else in Europe.'[7] Thus Fitz Nigel composed his work in the form of a classical dialogue, and Glanvill presented English custom in terms of Roman law. They aspired like the other *curiales* to Latin scholarship and an audience larger than English officialdom.

The mastery of Latin displayed by twelfth-century writers in England is remarkable. John of Salisbury is the most eminent of all medieval Latinists and the principal textbook for writing verse, the *Poetria Nova*, was also written by an Englishman, Geoffrey, sometimes surnamed 'de Vinsauf'. Like John, Geoffrey had presumably acquired his advanced knowledge in France and Italy. 'England sent me to Rome as from earth to heaven, it sent me to you as from darkness to light,' he wrote when dedicating his work to Innocent III.[8] Like the *curiales*, Geoffrey is both flattering and facetious towards authority, beginning his work with: 'Holy Father, wonder of the world, if I say Pope Nocent I shall give you a name without a head; but if I add the head, your name will be at odds with the metre.'[9] Such word-play is tiresome to a modern reader, and perhaps it was also to the pope, yet it is fundamental to these Latinists because they were writing in a painfully learned foreign language. Hence they delighted in showing off their varied accomplishments. Fine writing was not restricted to professional rhetoricians. Most twelfth-century historical writers display it (for example William of Malmesbury, Ralph Diceto and William of Newburgh) and none has a finer style by the standards of the time than Richard of Devizes in his chronicle of Richard I. He may have learned his exotic Latin in the school of Winchester while Henry of Blois was bishop.

Writing good Latin meant much more than imitating the Romans, as the language had to remain alive. Numerous new words were therefore coined for medieval needs. Walter Map gives a lively example of this process when he describes St Hugh of Lincoln visiting Henry II at a hunting lodge in the 1180s. When the guards barred his entrance, Hugh demanded their identity and received in Latin the answer, 'We are foresters' (*Forestarii sumus*).[10] (They may have answered Hugh in Latin because he was a Frenchman and they perhaps knew only English and some smatterings of Latin.) This answer gave Hugh the opportunity to make a pun: *Forestarii foris stent* ('Foresters should stand outside'). The king heard this and came out to greet Hugh with laughter. This story illustrates not only Henry II's grasp of Latin but the way that a new word, *forestarius*, was received. Particularly at the level of practical business, for composing writs and charters, for example, or keeping accounts, it was essential that Latin vocabulary should be kept up to date. The text of Magna Carta is an excellent example of the clarity and precision of this living Latin.

The legacy of the classics could be a burden, as Walter Map was ready to admit: 'The industriousness of the ancients is in our hands; they even make their past present in our times and we are struck dumb; their memory lives in us and we are without memorials of our own. What a miracle! The dead are alive and the living are buried by them.'[11] Walter does not feel here like a dwarf perched on the shoulders of a giant. Instead the giants are going to bury him and his age in oblivion. Writers of Latin were in a dilemma. They could not hope to better the giants of the ancient world, and yet they wished to excel. Chrétien de Troyes had one answer: the Greeks and Romans were finished; modern authors should follow his example and write in French. But Walter felt that this solution was humiliating and impermanent. 'Caesar lives in the praises of Lucan, and Aeneas in those of Virgil,' he writes, 'but only the trifling of mummers in vulgar rhymes' celebrates the achievements of Charlemagne.'[12] This is presumably Walter's opinion of the *Song of Roland* and other verse in the vernacular. Nevertheless his attitude is ambivalent, as it is so often, because he is credited in medieval manuscripts with composing Arthurian romance (like Chrétien de Troyes) and even with writing in French. Walter's literary achievements are as enigmatic as his view of life, and perhaps that is what he intended. It was difficult to create an acceptable convention of fiction. 'I am not the only one who knows the art of lying,' wrote the romancer Hue de Rotelande, 'Walter Map is very good at it too.'[13]

The Owl and the Nightingale

The most brilliant literary work composed in England in the twelfth century, the debate between the owl and the nightingale, was written in English. Judging from its contents, it is the work of an author who was familiar with Latin and French learning and culture as well as the folklore and natural history of his own country. If the author is the Master Nicholas of Guildford who is described in the poem as a writer of much wisdom, and as good a judge of a song as of right and wrong, he takes shape as a scholastic and a man of the world like the English Latinists. But, unlike John of Salisbury or Walter Map, Nicholas is not alienated from his native environment.

The Owl and the Nightingale has all the polish and wit of contemporary Latin works without being weighed down by their irrelevance and citations from the classics. It is set not in the hectic and artificial world of the court but in the southern English countryside, in a hidden nook of a summer dale. This is a real environment (the vegetation and the physical characteristics of the owl and the nightingale are precisely described), though it is also the ideal medieval world of the secret garden where birds sing sweetly and maidens are courted.

The owl and the nightingale decide to conduct their debate with courtesy ('with fair words'), with each protagonist pleading her case by reasoning ('with skill') as in a law court or in the disputations of the schools. Because he is a 'master', presumably of the schools and also of canon and secular law, Nicholas is fitted to be their judge and, unlike Burnel the Ass, he has learned wisdom from experience. The owl says that although Nicholas spent an ardent youth delighting in the nightingale, he is not such a fool now and is set on the road of righteousness. The owl stands for seriousness and the nightingale for frivolity, though their positions are more subtle than that. They are worked out in the course of the poem with such sympathy by the author that it is impossible to know which side he prefers. Having reached the high point in the argument when both protagonists are to appear before Master Nicholas, the poem unexpectedly concludes with the author saying: 'How they fared in that judgement I cannot tell, for there is no more of this story.'[14]

The lack of a final decision for one side or the other is in keeping with the ambivalence of much twelfth-century writing. The reader is left poised between truth and falsehood and even uncertain as to which is which. John of Salisbury achieved a comparable effect in *Policraticus* by citing a bogus Roman authority (Plutarch's letter of instruction to the Emperor Trajan) for his image of the body politic with the prince at its head. As John invented this authority, we cannot be sure whether he meant us to take his image seriously; but only a handful of experts in the classics would have been able to recognize this dilemma. *The Owl and the Nightingale* is similarly thought-provoking in its ambivalence and different levels of meaning. The owl is ugly and execrated and yet she is Christ-like and wise. The nightingale is frivolous and yet she can speak seriously and convincingly about love. To the owl's conventional diatribe against lust she replies that the sins of pride and malice, which are sins of the spirit, are worse than bodily sins. Sex cannot be evil in itself and it is usually men who cause the trouble anyway. The nightingale seems familiar with the argument of Abelard's *Ethics* that only an evil intention makes an act sinful. One need not assume however that the author had read this work specifically, as he shows a general familiarity with a range of ideas current in the schools and courts of the time.

The author's most original and inscrutable achievement was to write in English. This was more difficult than composing in Latin or French because he had to adapt the form and diction of his poem from these languages. Master Nicholas, if he were the author, was probably helped by his grounding in grammar and rhetoric in the schools. At about the same time the bishop's clerk and master of the schools in Winchester, Jordan Fantosme, wrote his chronicle of Henry II's war of 1173–4 in French verse instead of Latin prose. Like *The Owl and the Nightingale*, this was a daring and successful experiment. But Jordan at least had Gaimar's *Estoire des Engleis* and other works like Wace's history to follow, whereas Master Nicholas had nothing. Or rather, Nicholas had no model which has survived. He must have written in the hope of pleasing a patron and hence there was evidently some demand for courtly literature in English, as Layamon's version of Arthurian history (the *Brut*) likewise suggests.

Among the rulers of twelfth-century England different languages were appropriate to different occasions and calling. In their written forms, and perhaps in speech too, they all had to be deliberately learned and polished. Thus Jocelin of Brakelond, the biographer of Abbot Samson of Bury St Edmunds (1182–1211), describes his linguistic skills: 'in French and Latin he was eloquent', speaking plainly rather than using ornaments of speech.[15] In other words, at the schools of Paris Samson had learned to speak French correctly, and in Latin he rejected the flowery style of rhetoricians like John of Salisbury. Jocelin similarly distinguishes between different kinds of English: Samson 'knew how to read literature written in English most elegantly and he used to preach in English to the people, but in the speech of Norfolk where he was born and bred'. The distinction here is between written English, which demanded elegance like any literary language, and the colloquial diction of each locality. These distinctions emphasize the complexity of twelfth-century English culture. There was no simple dichotomy between French dominance and English dependence, because French culture was itself part of a larger world of Latin scholarship and cosmopolitan courtly life, and conversely English culture subsumed different regional traditions.

Artists and patrons

The visual arts present a comparable picture of a variety of influences which cannot simply be described as French. This has been specifically demonstrated in the parallels between the full-page painting of the death of the Virgin Mary in the Winchester Psalter and representations of the same scene at Palermo and Mount Sinai. The psalter was probably made for Henry of Blois bishop of Winchester (who died in 1171) and it used to be surmised that he had brought in a Byzantine artist from Sicily to do the painting. An alternative hypothesis is that an artist from England had seen the mosaics of the church of the Matorana in Palermo and copied the scene. English artists might well have visited Palermo, as there were numerous contacts between the Norman kingdoms of England and Sicily. Henry II recalled Thomas Brown from Sicily to a seat at the Exchequer, Robert of Selby had been chancellor of Roger II of Sicily, Englishmen were archbishops of Messina and Palermo, and these contacts were reinforced by the marriage of Henry II's daughter Joan to William II of Sicily in 1177.

Nevertheless it is difficult to see how an artist sketching the mosaics at Palermo would have achieved as close a copy as the painting in the Winchester Psalter. Francis Wormald has therefore suggested that the painting in the psalter was done in England from a Byzantine icon, like the one of this scene still extant at Mount Sinai. Such an icon could easily have been acquired on behalf of Henry of Blois in southern Italy, as John of Salisbury describes him transporting antique statues from Rome to Winchester. Alternatively the icon might have been acquired at Constantinople, or even at Mount Sinai itself, as the crusades provided many points of access between east and west. A significant feature noticed by Wormald is some characteristically English details in the painting which echo the conventions of the Bury and Winchester Bibles. The best explanation is therefore that this painting was done by an English artist imitating a Byzantine icon. In the Winchester Bible (like the psalter, this is thought to have been made under the patronage of Henry of Blois) there are other Byzantine-inspired paintings, particularly the figure of Christ the Pantocrator at folio 169, which echoes the mosaic dominating the apse of Roger II of Sicily's cathedral at Cefalù. But in this case the links in the transmission between Sicily and England cannot be traced.

Numerous other examples could be given of the use of imported motifs by twelfth-century English artists. Although it is possible to interpret these as subservience to foreign masters, a deliberate process of absorption and selection makes better sense. In Romanesque art in England a favourite motif is arcading formed by interlaced round arches. This seems to have first been systematically used to ornament the aisle walls of Durham cathedral (completed by the 1130s), and in the course of the twelfth century it makes its way into country churches; for example, interlaced arches ornament fonts at Alphington (Devonshire), Avebury (Wiltshire) and Foxton (Leicestershire). Such motifs were presumably transmitted by artists' pattern books and manuscript illuminations rather than by direct observation. The motif of interlaced arches is Islamic in origin and appears in Spain and southern

Italy. The artists who used it in England may have known nothing of these associations, however; they may merely have thought it to be fashionable.

Country churches were not as remote from cosmopolitan culture as they appear today. They were built by the well-travelled lords who were their patrons, rather than by the parish community. The richness of the imagery of the Herefordshire school of stone carving (especially in the churches at Kilpeck, Brinsop, Stretton Sugwas and the ruins of Shobdon, together with the fonts at Eardisley and Castle Frome) is best explained in this way, as T.S.R. Boase and G. Zarnecki have argued. Celtic, Anglo-Saxon and Viking motifs can be discerned which may be of local and traditional origin (probably transmitted by metalwork), but in addition to them there is imagery associated with the abbey of Cluny, the pilgrimage churches of Poitou, and the baptisteries of Italy. The echoes of Cluny can be explained by the building close by of Leominster priory, a daughter house of Reading abbey, which had been founded by Henry I in association with Cluny. Poitevin motifs may have been the idea of the builder of Shobdon, Oliver de Merlemond, who made the pilgrimage to Santiago by the land route in the late 1130s. The font at Castle Frome mounted on crouching figures as in Italy is harder to explain, but there were all sorts of contacts with Italy (Zarnecki argues for instance that the west front of Lincoln cathedral built in the 1140s was inspired by that at Modena).

The mistaken assumption is to think of Herefordshire as a backwater. Among its bishops were the schoolmen Gilbert Foliot (in 1148–63), and Robert of Melun (1163–7). It was the home of Walter Map and Hue de Rotelande, the romancer, and Worcestershire (where Layamon wrote the *Brut*) was its neighbour. A more appropriate metaphor for such regional centres is that of a transmitter or transformer. Herefordshire was a meeting place of languages (Welsh, English, French and Latin) and of cultures (Celtic, Anglo-Saxon, Anglo-Norman and cosmopolitan). The great Jerusalem-centred world map, drawn in the thirteenth century and still kept at Hereford cathedral, may have had a twelfth-century predecessor. Roger of Hereford compiled a set of astronomical tables for the meridian of the city in 1178. Simon du Fresne, who also wrote in French, composed a polished Latin poem in the 1190s describing Hereford as a centre of the numerate arts in particular. Gerald of Wales called it a place of joy for philosophers. There were a dozen or more such regional centres in

England, associated with cathedrals (for example Lincoln, Chichester, Exeter, York) or abbeys (Bury St Edmunds, Malmesbury, Peterborough, St Albans) or both (Canterbury, Winchester, Durham).

The variety of achievement round a relatively small centre like Hereford helps explain the brilliance of the best work from twelfth-century England: Durham's great cathedral and its library of manuscripts; the Winchester illuminated books of the Bible associated with Henry of Blois; the choir and stained glass of Canterbury cathedral. In each case local traditions and expertise were married to the latest ideas from continental Europe. For example the line drawings in Henry of Blois's books may have been as fundamentally influenced by Anglo-Saxon manuscripts (such as the Benedictional of St Aethelwold) as they were by Byzantine and Sicilian exemplars. The results are works of daunting quality and confidence which nevertheless have an individual feeling of their own, despite being the product of many hands and diverse influences. The designers of Durham cathedral cannot be identified, and their work had been completed by the beginning of the period 1135–1200. The Durham style, presumably transmitted by its masons, was carried as far north as Kirkwall cathedral and also to the south, to Waltham abbey in Essex. By the latter half of the twelfth century, however, Durham's Romanesque was beginning to look old-fashioned. When the choir of Canterbury cathedral had to be rebuilt after a fire in 1174, it was done in what we now call 'Gothic' (Rickman's 'Early English').

Canterbury is well documented for a twelfth-century building because the chronicler Gervase recorded its construction, pillar by pillar, and commented on what struck him as novel. He was particularly interested in the new type of vaulting centring on prominent key-stones. To describe this effect he used the image of a 'canopy'. Thus William the Englishman, who had taken over as architect when William of Sens fell from the scaffolding, in the summer of 1179 'turned the canopy which is over the high altar' (that is, he completed the great vault over the crossing).[16] Stone vaulting as such was not new, as it had been conspicuously used at Durham. What impressed Gervase was the elegance of the new work with its Sicilian marble double columns, acanthus leaf capitals, and rib vaults forming canopies. Surprisingly Gervase does not describe the stained glass which perfects the design at Canterbury. It too, though, dates from the same time (as M.H. Caviness has demonstrated) and reflects, particularly in the work of the Methuselah master, a classicism that is distinctly English. As Gervase records, the Canterbury monks had consulted French and English architects and brought in William of Sens as their master of works. But the resulting east end at Canterbury is not dominated by any one particular previous building. It draws, like all the best English work of the twelfth century, on many techniques and traditions both native and foreign, new and old. In these ways the masters of art and language of the Twelfth-century Renaissance revived the 'glowing embers' of the past.

9

The Matter of Britain

In one manuscript dating from 1200 of the *Topography of Ireland* by Gerald of Wales a map is included which shows Scotland, Wales and Ireland by their Latin names – *Scotia*, *Wallia* and *Hybernia*. The principal rivers and cities are indicated in red and the proportions and relationships of the lands depicted are approximately correct. However, the area we now call England is designated *Britannia* and not *Anglia*. This manuscript, with its map and illustrations, may have been made under Gerald's own direction. In describing 'England' as 'Britain', the map maker was either reiterating ancient Welsh claims to the whole of Britain or he was assuming that 'England' and 'Britain' were interchangeable terms. By 1200 the latter possibility is the more likely, as England had grown so powerful that it now subsumed Britain: 'the whole monarchy of the entire kingdom of Britain is now called the kingdom of the English', a London legal commentator explained.[1] This island, Henry of Huntingdon declared in his *History of the English*, was once called 'Albion', then 'Britain' and now 'England'. In historical writing, this English sense of overarching superiority reached back to Bede and forward to Bishop Stubbs and the Victorians. The meaning of 'Britain' was consequently a highly controversial matter.

In the twelfth century the Latin words *Scotia* and *Wallia*, which were not the names by which the native populations of Scotland and Wales described their lands, began to be used on all sides – and especially by the English – as descriptions of these newly defined territories and political allegiances. For the first time Ireland too was brought within the political ambit of the 'British Isles' by Henry II's assertion of overlordship there in the winter of 1171–2. Seventeen kings submitted to him, headed by the high king Ruaidrí Ua Conchobair of Connacht. The terms of this submission were formalized in the treaty of Windsor in 1175: the territory of Ireland was partitioned between the invaders and the natives. This was the fateful 'Arrival of the English' as chroniclers called it: 'the English came into Ireland and Ireland was destroyed by them' is how an Irish-language entry in the Book of Leinster sums up the shock of their arrival.[2] Certainly the kingdom of Leinster bore the brunt of the invasion and, furthermore, the centuries-old artistic culture of Ireland was showing irreversible signs of decay. One of the last manuscripts to be illuminated in the Insular style of the Book of Kells was the Psalter of Cormac, which dates from the time of the invasion. English propagandists persuaded the papacy that the Irish, rather than being heroic pioneers of Christian conversion, were little better than pagans.

The contested kingship of Stephen (1135–54) was a turning point in Britain as much as in England because it undermined the Anglo-Norman domination of Wales and fractured the English frontier with Scotland. So powerful had Henry I been in Wales in his last years that the Welsh-language *Chronicle of the Princes* stated that there was nothing worth recording for the years 1132–5; in other words, the chronicler left his pages blank because the English king had instilled such fear in the native princes that they suspended their dynastic struggles for the time being. On Henry I's death the Welsh and the Scots were quick to take advantage of the renewed strife in England. David I king of Scots (1124–53) invaded the newly established Norman fortress towns of Carlisle and Newcastle, and his son Henry became earl of Northumbria. It was at Carlisle in 1149 that David knighted the future Henry II and made him acknowledge that Cumbria and Northumbria henceforward belonged to Scotland.

Nevertheless, once Henry II (1154–89) got control of the immense resources of the English monarchy and his French lands he easily humiliated the Scottish kings. In a reversal of Henry's own knighting at Carlisle in 1149, David I's successor, Malcolm IV, came to Toulouse (the southern limit of Henry II's power) to be knighted in 1159, even though this submission cost Malcolm rebellions on his return to Scotland. In 1174 his successor, William I (1165–1214), suffered the humiliation of being taken prisoner by the justiciar of England in a skirmish at Alnwick. His captured helmet, lance and saddle were exhibited at York Minster as proof of his defeat and a warning to the

Scots for the future. By then the Scots were hated in northern England because of the reputation of their armies for cruelty and pillaging, or at least this is what Yorkshire monastic chroniclers reported.

With the native rulers of Wales Henry II was less spectacularly successful, as his armies experienced a series of setbacks and stalemates. The mountains gave an advantage to small groups of guerrilla fighters as against conventional armies. On the death of Owain Gwynedd in 1170 leadership of the Welsh passed to Rhys ap Gruffudd (the Lord Rhys) and remained with him; in 1197 he was described in a Welsh annal as the unconquered head of all Wales. Henry II recognized him as his justiciar throughout South Wales. Thus Henry conceded that Welsh rulers could indeed do justice, but Rhys had to acknowledge by the same token that his power stemmed from his overlord, the king of England. This recognition by Rhys allowed Henry to use South Wales as his base for invading Ireland in 1171. That invasion was not originally aimed directly at the Irish, but at checking the independence of the Norman lords of the Welsh March who had taken lands in Ireland. 'Divide and rule' had to be Henry II's guiding principle across his huge dominions and among his diverse peoples, as he had no standing army nor uniform administrative system.

Gerald of Wales, who had experience as an envoy of Henry II in Ireland in 1185–6 and aspired to be his confidential adviser and military strategist, hoped to win his favour by praising his victories: 'You, our western Alexander, have stretched your hand from the mountains of the Pyrenees as far as the furthest western limits of the northern ocean'.[3] Gerald similarly claimed that Henry II had exceeded the achievements of Claudius, the Roman conqueror of Britain. By comparing Henry with Alexander the Great and the Emperor Claudius, Gerald gave him a place within the historical process of the 'Matter of Rome', which included both Greek and Roman history.

Court poets and story-tellers divided their historical narratives into three great 'Matters': the 'Matter of Rome', the 'Matter of France' (meaning Charlemagne and the *Song of Roland*) and the 'Matter of Britain' (tales of King Arthur and his knights). All three 'Matters' mixed up history and myth, while giving their audiences an imaginative sense of the awesome length and scale of the past. Part of the fascination of these narratives was that they crossed and recrossed the boundary between fact and fiction; indeed it was not clear where that boundary lay. These 'Matters' were more than aristocratic entertainment or ancient history, however, because they matched the aspirations of the three most powerful rulers of the latter half of the twelfth century: Frederick Barbarossa the Roman Emperor (1152–90), Philip Augustus king of France (1180–1223), and Henry II king of England – or was it to be Britain?

Arthur and Merlin

Tales about King Arthur burgeoned in popularity from the 1130s onwards. Ailred of Rievaulx describes a novice monk recalling how he had wept over fabulous tales which he had heard sung or recited about Arthur. The significance of this is that Ailred is writing about Yorkshire and not Wales or Cornwall or Brittany, where Gaelic oral traditions about Arthur had a long history. By the 1130s Arthur is also associated with Scotland, through Arthur's Seat in Edinburgh and his mythical palace further north in the land of the Picts. Arthur's multiplicity of personages and places of residence seems to have reinforced his myth rather than weakened it. The poet Wace, writing in French in a book dedicated to Eleanor of Aquitaine in 1155, says the adventures of Arthur are recounted so often that they have been turned into the stuff of fiction: 'not all lies, not all truth, not all foolish, not all knowledgeable'.[4] The Arthurian romances of Chrétien de Troyes originate in the 1160s. In the first of them, *Erec and Enide*, he describes Arthur's court and the kings and dukes who come to it from many different countries, including the Irish, Scots and Welsh. According to Chrétien, Alexander and Caesar were poor compared with King Arthur, who crowns Erec and Enide with diadems of gold.

Enide is escorted to her coronation by Sir Gawain and the king of Galloway. In reality in 1160 the actual king of Galloway, Fergus, had been taken prisoner by Malcolm IV of Scotland and compelled to become a monk. For Chrétien and his French audience, Galloway was a faraway country of which they knew nothing. Nevertheless, by this time the reputation of Arthur and the 'Matter of Britain' had been put on a surer footing by Geoffrey of Monmouth's *History of the Kings of Britain*, which was completed around 1138. He gave solidity to the story of Arthur by writing in Latin, the language of academics and intellectuals. Although Geoffrey described his style as rustic, he knew his achievement was comparable with that of the great Roman historians, as well as with his own contemporaries William of Malmesbury and Henry of Huntingdon. Indeed he warned these two historians of England to say nothing about the kings of Britain, since they had no access to the book in the British language which was Geoffrey's authority.

Gaimar in his *History of the English* likewise claimed to have used this 'good book of Oxford', but it has never been identified and perhaps it was no more than a literary fiction. Nevertheless, Geoffrey and Gaimar vouched that they had obtained this very ancient book from Walter archdeacon of Oxford, who had got it from Wales or Brittany. As archdeacon and head of St George's college in Oxford, Walter was a reputable person who may have been connected with the early university. Geoffrey was probably his colleague at St George's and he witnessed charters there as 'Master Geoffrey'. In the 1130s 'Master' was still an unusual and coveted title, which in the context of Oxford suggests that Geoffrey was a teacher (of Latin literature perhaps) in the university. The schoolmen were experts in language and they were therefore well placed to pioneer new forms of literature, so it may not be strange that the 'Matter of Britain' and Arthurian literature first took authoritative shape in the Oxford schools, as this is where the 'Matter of France', in the form of the earliest manuscript of the *Song of Roland*, was probably being written at the same time. When later in the century Gerald of Wales wanted to publicize his *Topography of Ireland*, he chose Oxford as the best place to give a series of readings.

Geoffrey of Monmouth's *History of the Kings of Britain* brought together the 'Matter of Rome' and the 'Matter of Britain' by linking the origins of Britain with the Trojans, who had been promised a new home by the goddess Diana. Geoffrey's Arthur is not a romantic knight, however, but a conqueror who unites Europe by force. The Round Table, 'famous throughout the world', was first documented by the poet Wace in 1155, not by Geoffrey. Its purpose was to make the knights equal regardless of where they came from, 'whether Scot, Briton, Frenchman, Norman, or Angevin', whereas Geoffrey's Arthur is an autocrat.[5] Both Wace and Geoffrey modernize names in order to give their narrative topicality. To Arthur's court come the rulers of all the lands he has conquered: the king of Alba, which 'is now called Scotland' (Geoffrey explains); the kings of the Venedoti, 'now the North Welsh'; and the Demetae, 'now the South Welsh'.[6] According to Geoffrey, Sir Bedevere the Cup-Bearer was duke of Normandy and Sir Kay the Seneschal was duke of Anjou. Kay dies at Chinon, as Henry II was to do in 1189.

Geoffrey's insight into political trends at the time he was writing his *History* in the 1130s enabled him to anticipate, through the exploits of Arthur, events in the Angevin Empire of Henry II a generation later. There was nothing miraculous about this, but it was perspicacious. Oxford was a good vantage point for political intelligence, as it was at the centre of England and travellers (including the royal court) repeatedly passed through. Geoffrey's description of Arthur's conquest of Ireland has many features in common with Henry II's invasion in 1171. The Irish are rapidly defeated, despite their more numerous forces, because they have inadequate armour. Once the high king Gilmaurius submits, the other Irish rulers follow suit because an invasion on this scale is completely unexpected. Geoffrey could have learned about masses of Gaelic warriors being no match for men equipped with modern armour from the battle of the Standard in 1138, when English knights had put to flight the men of Galloway. Once Arthur had conquered the Irish, Geoffrey says, he was free to wipe out the Scots. This conflict too needed no foreknowledge on Geoffrey's part, as David I had invaded England in 1135.

Geoffrey's attitude to the Welsh, who were the natural heirs to Arthur's Britain, is complex. He situates Arthur's coronation (after his victories in Britain) at the City of the Legions, which is identified with Caerleon-on-Usk in Geoffrey's native Monmouthshire. The archbishop of this city is described as the primate of all Britain and hence the superior of the English archbishops. This was an allusion to the bid for the independence of the Welsh church from the authority of Canterbury, which Bernard bishop of St David's (1115–48) was making repeated efforts to obtain. Fifty years later this allusion was used by Gerald of Wales for the same purpose. Gerald likewise used Geoffrey's account of Arthur's conquest of Ireland to justify Henry II's invasion of 1171. In the earliest version of the *Topography of Ireland* in 1186 Gerald had given only two justifications for the invasion (the Irish kings had lawfully surrendered and the pope had supported Henry II), whereas in the *Conquest of Ireland* he added three extra reasons which were all taken from Geoffrey. Gerald turned to Geoffrey's *History* for support when it suited him, even though he described it elsewhere as fictitious and mendacious.

Geoffrey's greatest success was to highlight the magician and sooth-sayer Merlin in his *History*. The prophecies of Merlin, he claimed, began to be talked about even before he had finished the *History* and so he published them as a separate book. Subsequently he also wrote a brilliantly imaginative life of Merlin in Latin hexameters. It was Merlin who foretold that Arthur would return from the dead, a proph-ecy which was already well known in twelfth-century Wales. Proph-ecies about the fates of kings were dangerous; King John had a man hanged who foretold his death. Wace, in his account of Arthur's death, was very careful to avoid its political implications:

> Arthur, if the story is true, received a mortal wound to his body. He had himself carried to Avalon to heal his wounds. He is still there, awaited by the Britons, as they say and understand, and he will return and live again. Master Wace, who made this book, will say no more of his end than the prophet Merlin did. Merlin said of Arthur, if it is right, that his death would be doubtful.[7]

Gerald of Wales claimed that Henry II had urgently asked for an explanation of the prophecies of Merlin. Likewise, according to Gerald, it was Henry himself who had initiated the excavations at Glastonbury which led to the discovery of the bodies of Arthur and Guinevere in 1191. This alleged discovery demonstrated – in English eyes at least – that Arthur's final resting place was in a great English abbey, even if it did have Celtic associations. He could not therefore be claimed by the Welsh or the Scots; nor by the Bretons, whose heir to the duchy had recently been christened Arthur. By the 1190s the English appro-priation of Arthur can be seen, as he begins to be described as king of the English instead of king of the Britons; the chronicler Roger of Howden, for example, amended his text in this way. In Layamon's English-language version of Geoffrey's *History*, written in the early 1200s, the return of Arthur is promised first to the Britons and then a few lines later to the English, as if the author hoped to please both Welsh and English readers (Layamon came from the English side of the Welsh frontier by the river Severn):

> Who knows how to say any more about the truth concerning Arthur.
> Yet once there was a prophet and his name was Merlin:

He spoke his predictions, and his sayings were the truth,
Of how an Arthur once again would come to aid the English.[8]

Wales – defining an allegiance

'Wales' was an English word which in its Latin form *Wallia* began
to be used in the twelfth century, even by Welsh rulers themselves,
as a description of their country. 'Cambria is called Wales nowadays',
Gerald of Wales explained; 'this has become the most used name,
although it is foreign and not really appropriate'.[9] Owain Gwynedd
(1137–70) is described in documents as *Walliarum rex* (king of the
Welsh) and *Walliae rex* (king of Wales). His father, Gruffudd ap Cynan,
had been addressed as 'king of the kings of Wales'.[10] These ambitious
kings of Gwynedd perhaps hoped to appropriate the idea of 'Wales'
for themselves because it was unifying for them and acceptable to the
English. But Owain's kingdom did not include the southern half of
modern Wales, where his rival Rhys of Deheubarth (1155–97) – the
Lord Rhys as he is generally known – was likewise described as 'prince
of Wales' and 'the acknowledged king of Wales'.[11]

Old local loyalties ran deep; Wales had no focus for a single
monarchy such as England had recently created at Westminster, with
its great hall, abbey and palace. Gruffudd ap Cynan was buried in the
heart of Gwynedd in the cathedral he had built at Bangor, looking on
to Anglesey (*Môn* in Welsh) 'the mother of Wales', while the Lord
Rhys, like previous kings of Deheubarth, was buried by St David's
shrine. These two cathedral sites, at the northern and southern extrem-
ities of the Welsh peninsula, faced on to the Atlantic Ocean and the
Irish Sea. They recalled an earlier Celtic world of seafaring and mis-
sionizing, as if the Welsh rulers of the twelfth century wanted – in
death at least – to turn their backs on the new threat from the east.
Rhigyfarch of St Davids, in his eloquent Latin lament for the days
before the coming of the Normans, asks: 'Why have the blind fates
not let us die? Why does the earth not consume us or the sea swallow
us up? . . . The people and the priest are despised by the word, heart
and conduct of the French.'[12]

Wales presented a paradox. It was more united than any other region
of medieval Britain in its culture and language, and yet it lacked political unity. Gerald of Wales ascribed this to national character. 'Obsti-

nately and arrogantly', he wrote, 'the Welsh people refuse to accept the rule and lordship of a single king.'[13] The power of a 'king of the kings of Wales' like Gruffudd ap Cynan was personal and did not survive his death. There were no nationwide institutions through which a single king could rule, despite the extraordinary unity of Welsh culture. When making the case for a Welsh archbishopric, which was the first step towards international and papal recognition of nationhood, Bernard bishop of St Davids, who was a Norman incomer himself, insisted that the Welsh differed fundamentally from the English 'in nation, language, laws and habits [and] judgements and customs'.[14]

Unity in 'judgements and customs' is most evident in the law code attributed to Hywel the Good. (Hywel, who died in 949 or 950, was the king who had come closest to uniting Wales, at much the same time as Aethelstan was uniting England.) The earliest extant form of this code dates from more than two centuries after Hywel's death, however. Its author is associated with the Lord Rhys, who may have been the patron of the project. The book states that it was intended for all Wales, as the author drew on 'the best books that he found in Gwynedd and Powys and Deheubarth' (that is, in the three principal kingdoms).[15] In coherence of exposition Hywel's code surpasses its English equivalents, the *Laws of Edward the Confessor* and the *Laws of Henry I*, though all three of these codes are antiquarian compilations, containing rules which must already have been archaic curiosities. For example, the money values which Hywel's code puts on hundreds of commodities, ranging from swords to sieves, cannot reflect twelfth-century prices.

The most powerful uniter of the Welsh people was their language (*Cymraeg*), which gave them their identity as *Cymry*, a word implying compatriots or people of the same region. By the twelfth century the territory of the *Cymry* was becoming restricted to modern Wales; that is, it no longer included Cumbria and Strathclyde which David I had incorporated into Scotland. Likewise, in the twelfth century Welsh intellectuals stopped describing themselves as 'Britons'. In the *Chronicle of the Princes*, which was compiled in Welsh year by year, the change of name occurs in 1135 (the year in which Henry I of England died); from then on the Welsh are called the *Cymry*. Much the same distinction is made in the biography of Gruffudd ap Cynan, where Arthur is described as king of the kings of *Brydein*

(Britain), while Gruffudd is king of the kings of *Kemry* (*Cymru* – Wales).

Despite some differences between northern and southern speech (Gerald of Wales says the northern language was 'more charming' – *delicatior*), Welsh was essentially a single language.[16] Bards and story-tellers moved without difficulty from one princely court to another. In 1176 at Cardigan the Lord Rhys had held a competition for bards (the first recorded Eisteddfod) from across Wales, which had been won by poets from the competing kingdom of Gwynedd. The stories in Welsh in the *Mabinogion* – stories of magic, intrigue, dreams, heroism and mystery – 'assume an audience [in Rees Davies's words] that can move freely in its imagination across the whole of Wales'.[17] The audience learned of the glorious past, when their kings had been crowned in London and ruled all the Island of the Mighty. Hywel's law code gives the dimensions of Britain, nine hundred miles from Pictland to Cornwall, 'before the crown of London and the sceptre were taken by the English'.[18]

The memory of the Anglo-Saxon conquest, six or seven hundred years earlier, was the most formative element in Welsh ideology. 'When the British were faced with extermination by the incoming English', explains the Yorkshire chronicler William of Newburgh, 'those who could escape took refuge in Wales. They were protected from enemy attacks by the beneficence of nature and there this nation subsists up to the present day.'[19] Gerald of Wales enlarges on this 'beneficence of nature' protecting Wales, which is 'very well fortified by high mountains, deep valleys and immense forests, waterways and marshes'.[20] Gerald reports that the Lord Rhys told him that the Welsh constantly feed on the hope of recovering all the territory which the English have taken from them. If there was to be a miraculous Welsh revival, the prophecies of Merlin about King Arthur took on a distinct political dimension. As early as the 1130s (according to Gaimar's history) the Welsh were saying openly that they would get everything back through Arthur. This must have been after the death of Henry I in 1135, when the weakness of King Stephen allowed Welsh rulers to recover lost ground.

Nor were these beliefs simply the fantasies of chroniclers and story-tellers, as they were matched by numerous individual family traditions. The genealogy of Gruffudd ap Cynan for example reached back a hundred generations to the legendary founders of Rome, Ascanius and

Aeneas, and to Brutus the Trojan. When Gruffudd ap Llywelyn, the greatest Welsh ruler of the eleventh century, confronted Edward the Confessor of England as the two kings stood in their robes of state on opposite sides of the river Severn, Gruffudd shouted across the water that he was 'heir in the most direct descent' from the men who had conquered the whole of England, together with Scotland, Cornwall and Wales, from giants.[21]

Before the Norman Conquest, Welsh rulers could make such grandiose claims with conviction. But all this was threatened by William the Conqueror, who came in person with an army to the western extremity of Wales at St Davids in 1081. The extraordinary success of the Normans strengthened England, while exposing Wales to invasion on many fronts. The southern route into Wales, from Gloucester through Glamorgan and Gower to St Davids, avoided the mountains, and it could be reinforced by English sea power in the Bristol Channel. When King Rhys ap Tewdwr was killed in this southern sector in 1093, a Welsh annalist understandably commented: 'And then fell the kingdom of the Britons.'[22] This was the 'French' victory which had sparked off Rhigyfarch's lament and brought the Norman adventurer Gerald of Windsor (Gerald of Wales's grandfather) to Pembroke. 'From that day', wrote the Worcester chronicler, 'kings ceased to rule in Wales.'[23] This was a pardonable exaggeration, though it is certainly true that the English did not respect Welsh kings. Writing in Winchester in 1175, Jordan Fantosme remarked that every one of Henry II's knights in his battle armour thought himself the equal of a Welsh king.

Harder for the Normans to penetrate than the southern coastline was the mountainous eastern frontier along Offa's Dyke. Here William the Conqueror had created three great earldoms at Chester, Shrewsbury and Hereford. The Domesday survey in 1086 recorded a line of newly constructed castles, some of which would have been of wood rather than stone, from Rhuddlan in the north down through Montgomery (the family name of the Norman earls of Shrewsbury) and Wigmore to Chepstow and Caerleon. This was the Welsh March, a designated war zone. The 'barons of the March' (says Gerald of Wales) confront the Welsh continuously and bring in their wake the 'English race' (*Anglorum gens*) as colonists.[24] (Hence 'Anglo-Norman', describing the combination of English and Norman, is an appropriate word for these incomers.) The word 'March' is first recorded in

Domesday Book, where ploughlands in Herefordshire are described as unproductive because they lie on 'the marches of Wales'.[25] Gerald included his own family of the Geraldines among the barons of the March, even though their castles were in Pembrokeshire and not on the eastern frontier. In his book on the conquest of Ireland, Gerald widened the meaning of 'marchers' (*marchiones*) even further, as he uses it as a general laudatory term for the Anglo-Norman frontiersmen, like his cousin Raymond le Gros, whom he credits with victories across southern Ireland.

Gerald's own loyalties varied in accordance with his fortunes, which is why he can be so revealing about attitudes to nationality. His mother, Angharad, was Welsh (she was the granddaughter of Rhys ap Tewdwr), but he does not seem to have learned Welsh as his mother tongue. He says he was brought up 'among the English'.[26] He dedicated his *Topography of Ireland* in 1186 to Henry II, 'the invincible king of the English', and his *Description of Wales* in 1194 to Hubert Walter, Richard I's justiciar and viceroy in England. In it he described how Wales might be conquered: surround the land with castles, blockade the coasts to stop imports of essential commodities (iron, salt, corn), attack in winter when the trees provide no cover, use lightly armed infantry, and so on. He even proposed that the Welsh should all be deported, leaving the whole country as a 'forest' in the Norman sense of a game preserve. Instead of rewarding Gerald for this advice, however, Hubert accused him of being of Welsh birth and therefore unfit to be a bishop. He was connected by blood and affinity, Hubert said, to many of the great men of Wales. Obviously Hubert was not referring here to the Anglo-Norman Geraldines, but to Gerald's cousins on his mother's side, such as the Lord Rhys.

Gerald's *Description of Wales* is overtly ambiguous. After failing to win Hubert Walter's favour, he altered the passage about deporting the Welsh and attributed this policy to the English instead. In Wales today the best known part of Gerald's book is an anecdote at its conclusion. A Welshman who was fighting on the English side, as many did for pay or for personal reasons, was asked by Henry II who would win the war. He replied that, however strong the king's army might be, only the Welsh would answer on the Day of Judgement for 'this little corner of the earth'.[27] Like many of Gerald's anecdotes, this one is double-edged: while it acknowledges that the English would never eradicate the Welsh, it concedes that their claim to the whole of Britain was finally extinct. In political terms the king of England was now the sole heir to Arthur's greatness and the Island of the Mighty.

Modernization in Scotland

The king of England was as formidable a presence in Scotland as in Wales. In 1072 William the Conqueror had marched north as far as the river Tay, in the heartland of the Scottish kingdom, and compelled Malcolm III to submit to him. Further south, on the Anglo-Scottish border the ruins of castles scattered over the hills demonstrate to this day how this frontier was as fiercely contested as the Welsh March. Scotland reached its maximum southerly extent under David I, who for a while controlled Lancaster in the west and Newcastle upon Tyne in the east; in 1149 he had attempted to take York. When he knighted the future Henry II of England at Carlisle in the same year, he secured an undertaking from him never to deprive the Scottish kings of Northumbria and Cumbria. Once he became king Henry repudiated this. David I's successor, Malcolm IV, surrendered these territories in 1157. In the words of the Yorkshire chronicler William of Newburgh, he 'prudently considered that the king of England showed the merit of his cause through the power of force'.[28] Through the same 'power of force' Henry II made Malcolm come to Toulouse to be knighted, a journey of two thousand miles which nearly cost Malcolm his throne. When he got back to Perth in 1160, he faced a rebellion from six of the earls.

The experience of Malcolm's successor William I, known as 'William the Lion' from the thirteenth century, underlined the rule that the king of England was too strong to confront. As a child in 1152 (in David I's reign), William had been inaugurated at Newcastle as earl of Northumbria. To rewin this inheritance, he joined the rebellion against Henry II in 1174, but he was taken prisoner. Jordan Fantosme describes in his verse account of the war how he witnessed the king's disgrace with his own eyes: he saw William being disarmed and led away on a palfrey, a woman's saddle-horse. He surrendered all the key castles in lowland Scotland: Roxburgh, Berwick-upon-Tweed, Jedburgh, Edinburgh and Stirling. He was taken to Normandy to the formidable castle of Falaise, where he agreed to do homage to Henry II 'just as other men are accustomed to do'.[29] This was not total humiliation, however. William was not blinded and castrated, nor forced to become a monk, because Henry II needed a king of Scots to control the north and support him in the conquest of Ireland.

In military terms the history of Anglo-Scottish relations in the twelfth century comprises a series of humiliations for the Scottish kings. Nevertheless, although they lost the war, they succeeded in winning the peace. Richard I in 1189 released William I from all his undertakings to Henry II and returned the Scottish castles; Richard dared not leave a hostile Scotland at his back as he was departing on crusade. Fifty years earlier in 1139, King Stephen had confirmed the Scottish king in possession of Cumbria and Northumbria, even though David I had been crushingly defeated in the preceding year at the battle of the Standard. In reality there was an uneasy balance of power between Scots and English. David I had shown in 1139 how large and intimidating an army he could bring as far south as Yorkshire, including contingents from Galloway and Moray, while the English believed that they had won their victory through the Yorkshire saints, who had duly punished the atrocities of the Scots. Again, in 1141 at the Rout of Winchester, David I had to escape in humiliating circumstances, yet he held on to his English lands.

The king of Scots looked weak when viewed from London, but in his own kingdom he was a growing force. David I was as active in the north of what is now Scotland as in the south, particularly in the earldom of Moray, which he began to colonize with knights. He encountered an extraordinary opponent in Wimund, a monk of Furness abbey, who became bishop of the Isles under Norwegian patronage in the 1130s. His bishopric comprised the isles of Skye, Iona and Man and much else on the western seaboard. Wimund also claimed the earldom of Moray and a right to the Scottish throne as a descendant of Lulach, the stepson of Macbeth (1040–57). With Norwegian support, he threatened the Scottish kingdom across the whole of the north and west. Sometime in the late 1140s he was captured by treachery. 'For the sake of the peace of the kingdom of the Scots', reports William of Newburgh, he was blinded and castrated and ended his days in Byland abbey, where William saw him and heard his story.[30]

Malcolm IV, who was so powerless in the face of Henry II, pursued his rivals in Scotland as energetically as David I did. In 1160 he captured Fergus king of Galloway and compelled him to become a monk at Holyrood in Edinburgh. Malcolm's most significant victory was in

1164 when Somerled king of Argyll and the Hebrides was killed at Renfrew. This was the fortress in the Clyde estuary which defended Glasgow; it had recently been established by Walter Fitz Alan. He was one of the Anglo-Norman warlords, like Hugh de Moreville and Robert Bruce, who had been brought into Scotland by David I and given further responsibilities by Malcolm IV. Somerled (the name means 'summer voyager' in Norse) had probably been driven to attack by the incursions of Walter's knights in the Clyde region. He was typical of the sea-borne rulers, heirs to the Vikings, who levied tributes of slaves and foodstuffs on the people of the Highlands and Islands. Whether such rulers were essentially Norse, Irish or Scots is difficult to determine. In 1164 Somerled may have mustered as many as 160 ships from the Hebrides and Ireland as well as the Scottish mainland.

According to one account, Somerled was honourably buried with the kings of Scots at Iona. But a Latin poem written in Glasgow says his head was cut off by a priest and presented as a trophy to the bishop, who gave thanks to the Scottish saints (*sancti Scotticani*) and particularly to Kentigern, the patron of Glasgow. 'The whole kingdom with loud voices praised Kentigern', the poem says, without making any mention of Walter Fitz Alan or the royal forces.[31] The poet's purpose was to promote the miraculous powers of Kentigern as a patron saint for Scotland as against his better-known rivals Andrew, Columba, Cuthbert and Ninian. In addition to Kentigern, whose holy well and shrine are still preserved in Glasgow cathedral, 665 saints lay buried in its precinct according to the twelfth-century life of Kentigern. A patron saint, such as Denis in France and Edward the Confessor in England, gave unity to a medieval nation. By the thirteenth century Andrew the Apostle performed this function in Scotland, rather than Kentigern or Columba. This was a victory for the east coast over the west (that is, for the bishopric of St Andrews over Glasgow) and for the new Anglo-Norman elite in Scotland over the indigenous Celts. Malcolm IV was the last king to have a Gaelic name (*maol-Columb*, meaning 'servant of Columba'). His brother and successor, William I, had been given the name of the Norman conqueror perhaps because, as a younger son, he might need to ingratiate himself with the Anglo-Normans as David I had done as a young man.

The bishops of Glasgow praised Kentigern because this stressed the special status of their diocese. Kentigern's life story claimed that he had been given the kingdom of Strathclyde as well as the bishopric; the Glasgow diocese was therefore coterminous with the kingdom of Strathclyde, which extended into Cumbria. But in 1133 Henry I had established a new bishopric at Carlisle, forming an English diocese in Cumbria, and he refortified the city as a bastion against the Scots. Despite this setback, the bishops of Glasgow soon recovered their power in the west of Scotland and reinforced the cult of St Kentigern at their cathedral. Even the concession which William I had to make in 1174, when he was a prisoner of Henry II, that the Scottish church should be subject to the English one, did not prevent the bishop of Glasgow from obtaining a bull in 1175 declaring his bishopric a 'special daughter' of the Roman church.[32] By 1192 this privilege was extended to Scotland as a whole. Papal recognition of the Scottish church as a 'special daughter' was the foundation of Scotland's independence from England in international law.

Equally with the church and the nation, the Scottish kings gained from special recognition by the papacy. In 1182 Lucius III presented William I with a golden rose, which was the highest honour the pope could bestow. Good relations between the monarchy and the papacy had been established by St Margaret, the second wife of Malcolm III (she probably married him in 1068), who had introduced papal reform. The reformers' ideals of canonical marriage, clerical celibacy and inheritance by primogeniture had the potential to establish a new system of monarchical succession. These ideals are evident in the eulogy of St Margaret, written by Turgot bishop of St Andrews (1107–15). She taught her six sons to line up in order of age and defer to their seniors. In real life this duly happened, at least with the three younger sons. The older ones were not so fortunate, however: Edward was killed in battle along with his father in 1093, Edmund made an attempt to be king in 1094 but was forced into a monastery, and Ethelred became abbot of Dunkeld whether willingly or not. David I, on the other hand, who was the youngest son, inherited the throne in 1124 in due succession from his brothers Edgar (1097–1107) and Alexander I (1107–24).

David in his turn ensured that his eldest grandson Malcolm IV succeeded him in 1153, even though he was only twelve years old. The continuity of the monarchy is displayed in a document from 1159 depicting David and Malcolm as an old man and a young one, seated on thrones alongside each other, as if recalling David and Solomon in the Old Testament. The rule of canonical marriage was as important a principle as primogeniture, as it justified the exclusion of claimants who were deemed illegitimate by the church's laws. The awkward fact for David I and his descendants was that his father Malcolm III had a son, King Duncan II (1094), by his first wife. Duncan's descendants continued to trouble the Scottish kings well into the thirteenth century. One of the last claimants, a baby girl, was publicly battered to death against the market cross at Forfar in 1230. When describing the beheading in 1212 of Guthred, another of Duncan's descendants, the Barnwell chronicler (in Cambridge) explained that he and his ancestors had long been enemies of the 'modern' kings of Scotland.[33]

The modernity of the Scottish kings is linked by the Barnwell chronicler with their being French in language and culture. This makes sense when French styles in building, warfare, learning and literature led Europe. As Chrétien de Troyes famously observed, the French now carried the flame of the ancient Greeks and Romans. David I had been educated at the court of Henry I, where French was the language of culture and business. When he became king in 1124, he appointed to the highest offices in Scotland his trusted officials from the earldom of Huntingdon and Northampton: Walter Fitz Alan became the steward, Hugh de Morville the constable and Ranulf de Soules the butler. These men brought in their wake many more Anglo-Norman and Flemish knights and townsmen, who settled wherever there was royal land. Because David's successors (Malcolm IV and William I) reinforced this policy, the incomers established their families at the head of Scottish society. Of the twenty-one magnates whom William I surrendered as hostages to Henry II in 1174, three-quarters were descended from incomers and only two had Gaelic names (Earl Duncan and Ness MacWilliam).

The Barnwell chronicler accuses the Scottish kings of reducing the Scots to utter servitude. This paradox is revealing. By 'Scots' the chronicler probably meant the Gaelic speakers of the ancient kingdom of Alba. There was a fissure in Scotland between the peoples of the Highland north and west, who were Gaelic in culture, and those of the south and east, who spoke a northern form of English and had the best arable land and seaports. Queen Margaret, in an action which must have been deliberate and controversial, gave none of her sons the Gaelic names of the Scottish royal family: the first four were named after English kings of Wessex, the fifth was called Alexander (probably after Alexander the Great) and the sixth David. Some Gaelic learned culture persisted even in the east, however: at the inauguration of Alexander III in 1249 his genealogy was recited in Gaelic by the king's poet, possibly from sources preserved at Scone abbey.

Although the Scottish kings of the twelfth century became French in culture and were historically Gaelic, their first language was probably English. English in its northern form replaced Gaelic as the principal language of the rulers of Scotland for a number of reasons. It was the mother tongue of Queen Margaret, who influenced her sons so strongly, and also of the people of Lothian where much of Scotland's wealth lay. Here in the south-east were most of the religious houses which David I endowed or refounded: Coldingham, Dryburgh, Holyrood, Jedburgh, Kelso, Melrose, Newbattle and Selkirk. At Melrose abbey David I's son Earl Henry addressed his men as 'French and English of the whole kingdom of the Scots'.[34] In the 1180s Adam abbot of Dryburgh described his situation in Lothian as living 'in the land of the English and in the kingdom of the Scots'.[35] He persisted in making this distinction between peoples even though Lothian had been part of the Scottish kingdom since the eleventh century.

Scotland contrasts with Wales in the politics of its language and culture. Whereas Wales was relatively unified in language but divided politically, Scotland contained within a single kingdom a diversity of peoples and languages: there were descendants of Britons, Picts, Irish, Cumbrians, Welsh, Norse, the English of Lothian, Anglo-Normans, Flemings and the Scots themselves – whoever they now were (originally they had come from Ireland). A description of Scotland in the 1180s argues that *Scotia* is not the correct name for the kingdom anyway, as the Gaelic name is *Alba* (*Albania* in Latin). But the twelfth-century kings never describe themselves in charters as kings of Alba. Why they preferred the terms 'Scots' and 'Scotland' is unclear, as the name *Scotia* was as strongly associated with Gaelic culture as *Alba*. Jordan Fantosme, in his account in French verse of the capture of William I in 1174, uses *Albanie* and *Escoce* indifferently depending on what suits his verse. At one point he declares that 'the Scots (*Escot*) who are in *Albanie* have no faith in God, the son of Mary'.[36] Possibly he excepted the English of Lothian from this accusation of paganism.

David I is rightly credited with transforming this assemblage of peoples into a nascent nation state. He founded and reformed abbeys and bishoprics; he extended the powers of sheriffs and justiciars; he promoted trade through the first Scottish coinage and the privileging of towns and markets; and, most controversially, he introduced Anglo-Normans as warlords, managers and settlers. Nevertheless, the range and originality of David's achievements may have been exaggerated by the surviving historical records, as it is only from his reign that continuous evidence survives. The most revealing documents are the royal writs, which show a hierarchical structure of bishops, abbots, earls, barons, justices, sheriffs and lesser officials. This structure was not all new in David's reign. There had been bishops for centuries, for example, and sheriffs had long existed in Lothian because it had been part of the Anglo-Saxon kingdom of Northumbria.

The Scottish kings built on habits of obedience reaching back to the beginnings of the kingdom of Alba in the ninth century. The core of that kingdom incorporated the rich land on the eastern seaboard, extending northwards from the Firth of Forth (the 'Scot Water') to the Moray Firth, with Scone as its ancient centre. There the Scottish kings – and probably the Picts before them – were inaugurated in ceremonies reaching back into the pagan past. Like their predecessors, the 'modern' kings of Scots of the twelfth century were frequently in this heartland. The surviving writs of William I indicate that Perth (2 miles from Scone) and Forfar (25 miles from Scone) were the most visited places; next comes Stirling which was the gateway to Alba from the south. Queen Margaret had established an additional crossing point from Alba to Lothian at the Queensferry (where the modern Forth road and rail bridges are). This made Edinburgh more accessible; William I is recorded as being there thirty-four times. The twelfth-century kings were frequently in Lothian because of its wealth and strategic importance on the English frontier.

The Barnwell chronicler, as we have seen, complained that the modern kings of Scotland had become French in manners, language and culture. At the exalted level of the king and his court, the chronicler's observation is undoubtedly correct. William of Malmesbury commented that David I had 'rubbed off the tarnish of Scottish barbarity by his living in familiarity with us from boyhood'.[37] By 'us' William meant the Anglo-Norman courtiers and ecclesiastics of Henry I. William added that David had offered exemption from taxation for three years to all Scots who 'wanted to live in a more civilized way, dress more elegantly and eat with more refinement'. This is credible, as David's mother Queen Margaret had similarly aimed to improve the appearance of the Scottish court by dressing the nobility in imported fabrics and silks. Along with better dress went better conduct, her biographer explained, as the king's bodyguard in their new uniforms ceased robbing people and despoiling the countryside.

John Gillingham has pointed out that William of Malmesbury's contrast between the 'civilized' English and the 'barbarous' Celts was novel and very significant; here were the beginnings of English imperialism.[38] The English or Anglo-Norman perception of 'otherness' made the Gaelic-speaking Scots, Irish and Welsh into enemy aliens. The author of *The Deeds of King Stephen* for example described the Scots as 'barbarous and filthy . . . surpassing all other foreigners in cruelty' and Jordan Fantosme characterized the country as *Escoce la salvage* – 'Scotland the savage'.[39] The Barnwell chronicler implied that the Scottish kings had been mistaken to make themselves French. Perhaps, to the contrary, they had to do this in order to survive. David I and his successors, together with their Anglo-Norman nobility and French reformed clergy, were men with whom the international powers of Latin Christendom could do business. Even when William I was Henry II's prisoner in 1174, the integrity of the Scottish kingdom was preserved in the treaty of Falaise and the pope protected the independence of the Scottish church. The twelfth-century kings of Scots saved their kingdom from the English by becoming English themselves – or at least Anglo-Normans.

Civilization in Ireland

Henry II's treaty of Windsor in 1175 with the high king of Ireland, Ruadrí Ua Conchobair, is comparable in form with the treaty of Falaise of the preceding year; but its terms are strikingly different, as it partitions Ireland. Henry and his barons were confirmed in their titles to the lordships they had taken in Dublin, Meath, Wexford, Leinster, Waterford and Munster; this amounted to the richest parts of Ireland to the east and south. Ruadrí, who was king of Connacht in the west, may have mistakenly thought that he could save his own kingdom by making this compromise. Henry knew he could exact such harsh terms because he had the support of Pope Alexander III, who had already condemned the Irish in 1172 as barbarians and abjurers of the Christian faith. He congratulated Henry on 'assembling a mighty force by land and sea to subject this people to your rule in order to extirpate the foulness of their abominations'.[40] Henry himself was described as 'a devoted son of the Church . . . this Catholic and most Christian king'. This was an extraordinary volte-face by the pope, as Henry had been accused of the murder of Becket in Canterbury cathedral only eighteen months earlier. One Irish source blamed the invasion on raiders in Munster who had robbed a cardinal legate of his horses and mules: 'this is why the successor of St Peter sold the tax and tribute of Ireland to the Saxons'.[41] Certainly Alexander III expressed concern to Henry II about the payment of tithes from Ireland.

At the time the pope wrote these letters, he was being threatened by the Emperor Frederick Barbarossa in Lombardy and he could not afford to alienate Henry II as well. In the political map of Christendom Ireland could only be of secondary importance. The missions of Columba and Columbanus were long past and they had never been liked in Rome anyway. Suspicions were rekindled in the 1140s by St Bernard, who was the chief propagandist for the reformed papacy and the Cistercian order, which had experienced difficulties getting established in Ireland. As in his preaching of the Second Crusade in 1146, Bernard justified the invasion of Ireland by describing the natives as filthy barbarians: Christians in name but pagans in reality. Papal rhetoric repeated these slanders. In 1155 the English pope, Adrian IV, took the radical step of authorizing Henry II to rule Ireland. John of Salisbury brought back from Rome a gold ring set with an emerald as evidence of this. Certainly there was talk of invading Ireland in 1155; a charter from Winchester attests this, as does the chronicler Robert of Torigny. But Henry II, still at the start of his reign, was more concerned in 1155 with defending his possessions in France. Furthermore, he was not yet in a logistical position to attack Ireland, as this required safe passage through Wales to an embarkation point on the west coast.

These circumstances had changed to Henry II's advantage when he returned to this unfinished business in 1171. With the aid of the Lord Rhys, the ruler of south Wales, he crossed from St David's to Waterford with a force of about 500 knights and up to 4000 archers (many of them Welsh perhaps) together with siege engines and other supporting forces and supplies. The annalist of Loch Cé, who usually wrote in Irish, turned to Latin to record this portentous event: *Henricus potentissimus rex Angliae* – 'Henry the very powerful king of England' – landed in Ireland.[42] Latin was appropriate because he was doing something which even the Roman emperors had never achieved, as the pope explained in his congratulatory letter. Henry needed such large forces because his main quarry was not the Irish themselves, but his own Anglo-Norman warlords from Wales who were crossing to Ireland in the wake of King Diarmait Mac Murchada's call for military assistance in 1167. The most distinguished of the incomers was Richard Fitz Gilbert (known in Ireland as Strongbow), who took up Diarmait's offer to marry his daughter and become king of Leinster. In 1171 he captured Dublin by defeating the Irish high king Ruaidrí Ua Conchobair and the Norwegians who had controlled the eastern seaports since Viking times.

Henry II could not allow one of his barons to become king of Ireland and monopolize the Irish Sea. He therefore had no option but to invade Ireland himself. He launched his expedition at the onset of winter, in October 1171, because speed was essential. He stayed until April 1172, taking the submissions of his own barons and the Irish kings, when he left at short notice because of threats in France. Gerald of Wales says Henry very much regretted having to leave Ireland before 'establishing a firm and stable peace through castle-building and getting it all back into shape'.[43] The phrase 'getting it all back into shape' (*in formam omnino redigere*) is revealing, as this is the language of imperialism. The Irish needed getting back into shape because they had deteriorated into barbarism, according to the pope and English ecclesiastical chroniclers.

These writers were proud of the peacefulness of England. The author of *The Deeds of King Stephen* described how one of the Anglo-Norman lords made his part of Wales 'so abundant in peace and all sorts of productivity that it might very easily have been thought a second England'.[44] His contemporary, Geoffrey of Monmouth, had concluded his Arthurian history by contrasting English peace and prosperity with the Welsh, who had allegedly declined into barbarity. In his English-language version of Geoffrey's history in the 1200s Layamon enlarged on this. The defeated king of the Britons, Cadwalader, is told how Aethelstan of England has established counties and hundreds, shire courts and manor courts, deer parks and villages, and he has named them all in English. When Cadwalader hears this,

he wishes he were dead. Naming, as Layamon understood, is an essential part of control. Most place names in England are indeed Anglo-
Saxon and not British. In Ireland and other conquered territories,
personal and place names were Anglicized in ways which are still being
unscrambled.

The beginnings of the British Empire may be seen as unintentional
and coming about almost by default. Ireland is the earliest example of
this. Henry II was compelled to invade it in pursuit of his own barons
and to satisfy the pope. At first he tried indirect rule and partition.
The treaty of Windsor required the high king Ruadrí Ua Conchobair
to collect an annual tribute (in the form of animal hides) from the
lesser kings throughout Ireland, but he was forbidden to interfere in
any way with the English king's lands or with those of his barons. This
left Ruadrí in an impossible position: he had insufficient authority to
collect all the tribute and yet he got no help from Henry II either
against recalcitrant Irish kings or the foreign invaders. Henry's power
too was limited. He could not have expelled the Anglo-Normans, even
if he had wished to. His invasion of 1171 at least asserted his overlordship and secured him the largest share of the spoils.

In future those who profited most from Ireland would be royal
nominees. The best example is William the Marshal, who by gift of
Richard I in 1189 married Strongbow's heiress, though it took him
some years to bring this inheritance together. In 1207 the Marshal
crossed over to Leinster and got 'wide lands for himself by butchery
and burning'.[45] These are the words of the usually pro-English chronicler Matthew Paris. He was writing in 1245 after the Marshal's five
sons had all come to premature deaths, which Matthew attributed to
the curse of the bishop of Ferns (the capital of Leinster). In 1220 or
1221 when the bishop was already an old man, he crossed to London,
went to the Marshal's grave, and damned him as a despoiler of the
church. Ailbe Ua Máel Muaid had been appointed bishop of Ferns in
1186, before Archbishop Hubert Walter (1193–1205) banned natives as
bishops in English dominions (just as he had banned Gerald of Wales
from the bishopric of St Davids). Hubert had this authority because
the synod of Cashel of 1172 had agreed that the Irish church should
follow the observances of the English church.

By 1200 the king's title was established as *Dominus Hibernie* – 'Lord
of Ireland'. There had been talk in the 1180s of making John, Henry II's
youngest son, king of Ireland. A crown of gold and peacock feathers

was sent by Pope Urban III in 1185. It was probably Henry II himself who best understood the dangers of this. A crown granted by the pope might by the same authority be taken away. It was also hazardous to give any of his sons the title of king, as the rebellion of Henry the Young King in 1173–4 had demonstrated. Furthermore, if John were made high king in accordance with Irish custom it would concede that the Irish had rights which should be respected. It was therefore safer for Henry II simply to insist that the Irish kings had become his lawful subjects by submitting to him. Their surrender was allegedly spontaneous and voluntary. This was the point emphasized by Gerald of Wales in his *Topography of Ireland* in 1186. (Gerald was one of the advisers commissioned by Henry II to accompany John to Ireland in 1185.) By being 'Lord of Ireland' and nothing grander, Henry II could do whatever he pleased there because that was a lord's prerogative.

In fact, a replica of the English state was established in Dublin with its own judiciary, Chancery and Exchequer. For men like William the Marshal, Ireland was a land of opportunity which needed getting 'back into shape'. In the name of civilizing the Irish, the new lords took away their lands, turned pastures into cornfields and brought in English farmers and townsmen. These changes can be seen either as 'an extremely progressive policy' (in the words of the Marshal's biographer, Sidney Painter) or as 'butchery and burning' (in the words of Matthew Paris).[46] Capitalist development and war were not really contradictory, as change was made easier by displacing the native population. Thirteenth-century Ireland became divided between the incomers, protected by English law and the government in Dublin castle, and the 'mere Irish' (as the English called them) without enforceable rights.

Geoffrey of Monmouth's *History of the Kings of Britain* had imagined the invasion of Ireland thirty years before it occurred (see p. 158 above). According to Geoffrey, King Arthur went on – after conquering Ireland – to the City of the Legions to celebrate his victories. From the island of Britain there came to him the kings of Scotland, Moray, North Wales, South Wales and Cornwall. (No king of England attended because Arthur and his Britons had just defeated and scattered the Anglo-Saxons at the battles of Bath and Thanet.) From across the northern seas came the kings of Ireland, Iceland, the Orkneys, Norway, Denmark and Gotland, and from across the Channel the princes of Flanders and Gaul. Writing in Oxford in Stephen's reign during a time

of civil war in England, Geoffrey created a brilliant fantasy of monarchy which was both nostalgic and futuristic. Medieval kings did indeed
hold crown-wearing assemblies of this sort in order to cement their
authority, and the kings of England did become extraordinarily
powerful.

Geoffrey is too subtle a story-teller to conclude his history with the
triumph of Arthur. His fate remains uncertain, and so he goes on to
become the once and future king, the greatest mythological figure in
literature. In reality it was the kings of England, and not Arthur of
Britain, who asserted their power in Ireland, Wales and Scotland. The
Celtic peoples experienced for the first time the new force of the
English monarchy. This is why their chroniclers generally described
the invaders as 'the English': the leaders were Anglo-Normans and
some of the soldiers were Flemings or native mercenaries, but the
colonists themselves were predominantly English. Furthermore, it was
the organization of the English monarchy – its Exchequer, Chancery
and lawcourts – which gave permanence to these invasions. The monarchy of England (embodying political power) and the Matter of
Britain (signifying Arthurian literature) went their separate ways.

PART III

The Poitevins (1199–1272)

In 1204 Philip Augustus of France took over Normandy and thus brought a formal end to what has misleadingly been called the 'Norman empire' or the 'Anglo-Norman state'. Henceforward, the argument runs, England stood on its own. This argument has been repeated by numerous historians and derives from Stubbs: 'From the year 1203 [*recte* 1204] the king stood before the English people face to face; over them alone he could tyrannize, none but they were amenable to his exactions: and he stood alone against them, no longer the lord of half of France, or of a host of strong knights who would share with him the spoils of England.'[1] Apart from its narrowly English bias (the king could still 'tyrannize' over Ireland, Wales and Scotland, as the thirteenth century demonstrated), Stubbs's statement exaggerates the effects of the loss of Normandy. After 1204 King John remained, in his capacity as count of Poitou and duke of Aquitaine, lord of the area south of the river Loire. Although these lands do not constitute half of modern France, they are at least a quarter and possibly a third of it.

More important than size is the fact that John did not accept the events of 1204 as final. He was determined to hold on to Aquitaine and he hoped to restore his influence north of the Loire in Brittany, Anjou and Touraine, if not in Normandy and Maine (see the map on page xii). It had been relatively simple for Philip Augustus to win control of Rouen, the capital of Normandy, which is only 85 miles over easy terrain from Paris; controlling Poitiers (200 miles from Paris) or Bordeaux (350 miles) was much more difficult. Normandy, Maine, Anjou and Poitou were not irrevocably conceded to France until the treaty of Paris in 1259 and even then the king of England remained duke of Aquitaine. The bitterness of Anglo-French relations in the reigns of John and Henry III only makes sense when it is understood that the king of England was still a threat to the king of France and that conversely the kings of England did not accept the loss of their overseas inheritance with equanimity.

Where Stubbs's statement is most misleading is in the assumption that the king of England 'stood alone' and that he could no longer bring in 'strong knights who would share with him the spoils of England'. This is an oversight on Stubbs's part, since in other passages in his *Constitutional History* he is vituperative about John's alien captains like Fawkes de Breauté, who was sheriff of six counties, and the Poitevin favourites of Henry III. The consequence of the loss of Normandy was not to confine the English political system within its own shores but to widen the circle to include the king's vassals south of the Loire. Since 1066 this circle had steadily widened beyond England and Normandy: first with the struggle between Stephen and the Empress Matilda, then with the accession of Henry II count of Anjou, and now with Richard I and John, counts of Poitou and dukes of Aquitaine. Henry III attempted to widen the circle even further to include the Provençal and Savoyard kinsmen of his wife as well as the Poitevins and Lusignans on his own side of the family. This widening reached bursting point in 1258 with the 'Sicilian business', the attempt by Henry III to win the Hohenstaufen inheritance in Italy for his son Edmund as well as having his brother Richard of Cornwall as emperor in Germany. In this network of alliances extending from Spain to Germany and from Scotland to Sicily the king of England stood very far from alone. That was why the barons rebelled in 1258 and that was also why they were defeated.

The aliens to whom the rebel barons most objected in 1258 were the Poitevins, particularly Henry III's half-brothers, William and Aymer, who had landed at Dover as refugees rather than adventurers in 1247. William had been made lord of Pembroke, and Aymer was given the rich bishopric of Winchester. Resentment against them seems to have been so strong because it was felt that Henry III already relied too much upon Poitevins such as Peter Chaceporc and Peter des Rivaux who managed the king's finances. The appointment of Peter des Rivaux went back to 1232, the year in which Henry dismissed Hubert de Burgh and attempted to restore royal authority to what it

had been before Magna Carta. The Poitevins were therefore associated
with the growth of royal power and with the king's distrust of the
native English. The description 'Poitevin', applied by the St Albans
chroniclers to the king's unpopular friends, did not mean that these
incomers had all been born within the county of Poitou. It was a
generic term describing a new sort of acquisitive and unwelcome
Frenchman, just as 'Norman' had been a century earlier. (Some
of William the Conqueror's 'Normans' had come from Brittany,
Ponthieu, Boulogne and Flanders and not from the duchy of
Normandy itself.)

The term 'Poitevin' distinguished King John's and Henry III's
favourites from their 'Norman' predecessors. Poitou had first entered
England's orbit with Henry II's marriage to Eleanor of Aquitaine in
1152. 'Poitevins' – as opposed to 'Normans' – came from the sunnier,
wine-growing part of France extending south from the Loire valley.
They spoke and wrote a different sort of French, the Occitan of the
troubadours, and to the beer-drinking English they were not readily
distinguishable from Provençals, Italians and other incomers from the
Roman and Mediterranean world. The most virulent critic of the
'Poitevins' in England, the St Albans chronicler Matthew Paris, had
probably been educated in Paris (as his name suggests) and he wrote
French verse for great ladies in England. To Anglo-Norman monks
and aristocrats, now settled in England for over 150 years, Henry III's
'Poitevins' were alien newcomers. This distinction between 'Normans'
and 'Poitevins' helps explain how Simon de Montfort, a Frenchman
who did not arrive in England until 1231, could become the leader of
the English baronial movement opposed to foreigners in 1258–65. He
came from northern France (Montfort l'Amaury is between Paris and
Rouen) and he readily identified with his Anglo-Norman counterparts
in England, as distinct from the 'Poitevins' favoured by Henry III.

The most prominent of all the 'Poitevins' was Peter des Roches, a
sketch of whose career best illustrates the dominant role played by
aliens in the governments of John and Henry III and the range of their
cosmopolitan European experience. Peter originated from the Touraine
in the Loire valley. He had been a member of Richard I's household,
treasurer of the great Romanesque church of St Hilary at Poitiers, dean
of Angers and prior of Loches. He came to England in 1200 and was
appointed bishop of Winchester in 1205 through the influence of King
John. He had experience in war as well as in the administration of the

Exchequer, with its pipe and memoranda rolls, and is depicted by an anonymous satirist of the time as:

Wintoniensis armiger Presidet ad Scaccarium/Ad computandum impiger Piger ad Evangelium Regis revolvens rotulum . . .

[The warrior of Winchester, Up at the Exchequer, Sharp at accounting, Slack at Scripture, Revolving the royal roll . . .][2]

Des Roches remained loyal to John throughout and was temporarily appointed to the highest office in the realm, that of chief justiciar, in 1213 or 1214. When John died, it was Peter and not the archbishop of Canterbury who crowned the young king Henry III in 1216 and who was confirmed in office as the boy's tutor and protector. He was there-fore in a position to exercise more personal influence than anyone else over the growing king. Shortly before Henry declared himself of age in 1227 Peter departed for the crusade, where he commanded an army and entered Jerusalem with the Emperor Frederick II in 1229. The next year he was in Italy as one of the negotiators of the peace of Ceperano between Frederick II and Pope Gregory IX. Returning to Winchester, he organized the coup d'état in 1232 which removed Hubert de Burgh. But this time Peter had overreached himself and in 1234 he was obliged to withdraw. Nothing daunted, he went back to Italy to command Gregory IX's army and suppressed a rebellion in the papal states. Having won a victory at Viterbo, Peter returned once more to England and died at his castle at Farnham in 1238.

Peter des Roches had exercised more influence over English politics than any other individual of his time apart from King John. Further-more in the coup d'état of 1232 he had made sure that his influence would continue by having his nephew (Roger Wendover says he was his son), Peter des Rivaux, appointed royal treasurer and titular sheriff of twenty-one counties. The younger Peter's is also an instructive career. The title accorded him in English royal documents is *capicerius Pictavensis*, 'the Poitevin sacrist'; possibly he held some office in the church of St Hilary at Poitiers like his putative father. The high point of his career was the years 1232–4 when, according to Matthew Paris, 'the whole of England lay under his regulations'.[3] Peter des Rivaux used his authority to reform the Exchequer's system of accounting so that it came under direct royal control. Although he had temporarily to withdraw in 1234 (indeed he was imprisoned), he reappeared as keeper of the Wardrobe in 1236 and thereafter he held various offices concerned with the control of finance until the revolution of 1258 when he was dismissed by the barons. He retained the king's favour, however, until his death in 1262.

The careers of the Poitevins Peter des Roches and Peter des Rivaux span the reigns of John and Henry III. Although Peter des Rivaux was less flamboyant than Peter des Roches, he was as influential as his father behind the scenes. Where the elder Peter had influenced high policy through his wide experience in Poitou, England and Italy the younger Peter concentrated on improving the financial machine. Without the advice of the elder and the expertise of the younger, Henry III might never have successfully re-established a personal monarchy after Magna Carta and the minority. Nor were the two Peters an isolated phenomenon. Aliens dominated much of the royal administration and court life of both John and Henry III because they were not aliens to them but familiar friends; the aliens were the English speakers. The alien character of the court was reinforced in the case of Henry III by his Poitevin mother and his upbringing by Peter des Roches. It is not therefore surprising that Henry preferred Poitevin officials and welcomed his half-brothers in 1247. Poitevins were as prominent and powerful in England in the first half of the thirteenth century as Normans had been in the eleventh century or the Angevin connection was in the twelfth. Partly in reaction to them and partly by assimilating their contribution to government, England developed as a distinctive nation.

King John and the Minority of Henry III (1199–1227)

The Poitevin connection

The critical events of John's reign originated south of the river Loire. Richard I (as we have seen in chapter 6) was killed in April 1199 at Chalus in the Limousin, the strategic area controlling access to south-western France. John had to fight for his own succession against the supporters of his nephew Arthur duke of Brittany. The question in law was whether this son of John's deceased elder brother was next in line or whether John himself should succeed (see the genealogical table on page 323). The decision turned in reality on force. Arthur had the support of Philip Augustus and of the area approximately between Normandy and the Loire. John had the support of Eleanor of Aquitaine and the southerners. The crucial points in this struggle were the castles of Chinon and Loches south of the Loire (see the map on page xii). They remained loyal to John and thus by the summer of 1200 he had secured his inheritance – for the time being – from the Cheviots to the Dordogne. That same summer he married Isabella the heiress of Angoulême, which lies west of the Limousin. The purpose behind this marriage (apart from John's reported passion for Isabella) was to secure this strategic area, just as Richard I had been trying to do when he was killed. Both kings recognized this southern extremity of Poitou as a key area in which Philip Augustus must be resisted by diplomacy and war.

The risk in John's marriage, which he underestimated, was the offence it caused to another great lord of Poitou, Hugh de Lusignan, to whom Isabella had been betrothed. After being harassed instead of conciliated by John, Hugh appealed to the overlord of them both, Philip Augustus of France. Hugh based his appeal on the principle of judgement by his peers in France (the principle later incorporated into Magna Carta as clause 39) and not by John's court in England. This appeal gave Philip the opportunity in the spring of 1202 to declare John a contumacious vassal and all his lordships in France forfeit. John's nephew Arthur was allocated Aquitaine, Maine and Anjou, and Philip took over Normandy himself.

It is often said that Philip Augustus, unlike John, acted with scrupulous regard for feudal law and won Normandy because he presented himself as the champion of righteousness. This is certainly the impression Philip wished to give but it is not strictly true. It was not as duke of Normandy that John had offended but as duke of Aquitaine (Hugh de Lusignan had nothing to do with Normandy). Even if Philip were entitled to confiscate Normandy in order to coerce John in Aquitaine, he should have restored Normandy to the next heir after a year and a day. Pope Innocent III, when asked by the Norman bishops how they should act, prudently expressed himself ignorant of the rights and wrongs of the dispute. The takeover of Normandy illustrates how strict feudal law did not apply to instances of what would later be called *raison d'état*. Philip Augustus is admired by historians as the founder of the French state precisely because he had the nerve to override traditional law and ecclesiastical sanctions. His proof of legitimacy was success. In a way that too was a traditional idea which Philip turned against John, as it was by conquest that the descendants of the Normans claimed their lands in England. Success in medieval war showed that God was on the victor's side.

At the beginning of the struggle, however, it looked as if it might be John rather than Philip who would succeed. The critical area at first was Poitou. In the summer of 1202 at Mirebeau (just north of Poitiers) John overcame all his enemies except Philip: 'We have captured our nephew Arthur, Geoffrey de Lusignan, Hugh le Brun, Andrew de Chauvigni, the viscount de Châtellerault . . . and all our other Poitevin enemies who were there, about 200 knights or more, so that not one of them escaped,' John wrote back to England, asking people to 'give thanks to God and rejoice in our successes'.[1] But the benefits of this victory soon evaporated because John was suspected of ordering Arthur's murder in captivity, and that gave the Bretons a cause for war and Philip a further opportunity to demonstrate his righteousness. Moreover, Philip directed his main force in the winter of 1203–4 not at Poitou but at Normandy. John is accused by the chronicler Roger Wendover of inertia in failing to defend Normandy, whereas his government records show constant activity. Whatever the cause, the fact remains that John proved unable to defend Normandy, and there may be something in Wendover's allegation that he did not consider it of crucial importance.

Wendover certainly gives a convincing explanation of how Philip used a combination of persuasion and terror to win over the Normans. He went in force from town to town and castle to castle on a hearts-and-minds exercise, telling the Normans that they had been deserted by their lord John and that he, Philip, was therefore taking over as overlord; he begged them in friendship to receive him as their lord since they had no other; anyone who was unwilling would be hanged or flayed alive. This policy worked and Philip entered Rouen in triumph in 1204. The totality of the English withdrawal was shown by the arrival at Shoreham in May 1204 of Peter de Leon with the Norman government archives, which were transported to London where they have remained ever since in the royal archives. It is often suggested that John lost Normandy because its inhabitants had grown progressively more French in culture and sympathies since 1066. Although a good case can be made for this, the extent of Philip's force was the immediately critical factor at the time. This is shown by the way the Channel Islands (*Iles Anglo-Normandes*, as the French call them) were in a strong enough position to refuse to acknowledge Philip as their duke: they remained loyal to the English crown. (Nevertheless, French forces did take control of the islands in 1204–5 and again in 1216–17 after the death of King John, but they were repelled by the defeat of the French Channel fleet.)

The loss of Normandy did not mean the end of the king of England's involvement in France. Whether wisely or not, John persisted with the strategy he had pursued since the beginning of his reign of concentrating on Poitou and threatening Brittany and France from the south instead of from the English Channel. There was some sense in this, as south of the Loire he commanded more loyalty and he had a secure land base from which to conduct operations. (This was later to be the strategy of the Black Prince in the Hundred Years War.) John therefore conducted two expeditions to Poitou, in 1206 and 1214, each time landing at La Rochelle. It was in pursuit of the same policy,

together with family obligations towards his queen, that he brought
Poitevins like Peter des Roches and Savari de Mauléon to England.
Such men served a dual purpose: they maintained contacts between
John and Poitou, and in England itself, because they were dependent
on the king, they made useful royal officers, much as they were hated
by the English. Similarly the few Englishmen whom John trusted, like
the justiciar Hubert de Burgh who was governor of Chinon, had seen
service in Poitou.

The Poitevin connection, which by Hugh de Lusignan's appeal to
Philip Augustus had occasioned the loss of Normandy, may also be
seen as the cause of the greatest crisis of John's reign: the battle of
Bouvines in 1214 and the baronial rebellion leading to Magna Carta
in 1215. John's expedition to Poitou in 1206 had been a failure, and
when in 1213 he demanded a scutage (a tax on knights' fees) for a
further expedition, barons in the north of England argued that they
were not obliged to serve overseas and certainly not as far south as
Poitou. The scutage of Poitou and the other quasilegal methods, particularly charging excessive sums for inheritances, which John used to
raise money for his expedition, were the chief causes of the rebellion
against him. Finally, John's concentration on Poitou meant that he was
in the wrong place at the wrong time when the decisive opportunity
to defeat Philip presented itself. In 1214 John was initially successful
in Poitou in defeating the Lusignans and in penetrating north of the
Loire by capturing Nantes and Angers. He had written back to England
in triumph in May: 'Now by God's grace an opportunity is given us
to advance beyond Poitou at our chief enemy, the French king.'[2] The
decisive battle in July 1214 was indeed fought 'beyond Poitou'; it took
place in Flanders at Bouvines, and John, who was 400 miles away at
La Rochelle, had no time nor means to get there. His nephew and ally
the Emperor Otto of Brunswick and his general William Longespee
earl of Salisbury were routed by Philip. The battle of Bouvines, which
ensured the succession of the Hohenstaufen Frederick II as emperor
and secured the northern coast of France for Philip, is generally considered one of the few decisive battles in medieval European history.

John's strategy had failed. Instead of rewinning Normandy from
Poitou, he had weakened his position throughout all his lands. Nevertheless this did not prevent either John or Henry III after him from
preferring the company of men who came from south of the Loire.
Normandy had been lost, but Peter des Roches and the alien captains

remained to impress upon the English that they were still a subject people.

The record of King John

Any person in the public eye acquires a mixed reputation. In the Middle Ages diverse opinions about public figures were conveyed to posterity by monastic chroniclers, whose works developed from mere lists of rulers and public events into comment and narrative. A common practice was for the chronicler to write a succinct obituary notice when recording the death of a well-known person. Thus the Barnwell chronicler writes of King John in elegant Latin antitheses which are difficult to render in English:

> He was indeed a great prince but less than successful; like Marius he met with both kinds of luck. He was generous and liberal to outsiders but a despoiler of the inhabitants. Since he trusted more in foreigners than in them, he had been abandoned before the end by his people, and in his own end he was little mourned.[3]

Depending on their experience and knowledge, contemporaries would have differed as to how far they thought this an accurate summary of John's career. By and large, however, the contemporary chroniclers' opinions which have come down to us agree that John was formidable, partial to foreigners and unsuccessful. The disasters of his last years shaped his obituary notices. Not even a partisan could argue that a king was successful who in 1213 had made England a vassal of the pope, in 1214 was defeated by Philip Augustus, in 1215 submitted to Magna Carta, and who died in 1216 with his treasure lost and the French occupying London.

The question arises whether John's failure was due to bad luck (as the Barnwell chronicler suggests) or to some other cause. After his death the belief was given currency by the St Albans chroniclers Roger Wendover and Matthew Paris that John had failed because he was evil and he had therefore received his just deserts: 'Foul as it is, Hell itself is defiled by the foulness of John,' as Matthew Paris expressed it.[4] Victorian historians and their public enjoyed such extravagance, and Matthew's comment (which he had cited not as his own opinion but as that of a reprobate versifier) was stated in J.R. Green's best-selling *Short History of the English People* in 1875 to be the sober judgement of history. In the same year Stubbs published his *Constitutional History*. Although this was a more cautious work than Green's, when Stubbs reached the death of John he let himself go. Like the audience in a court room, his readers had patiently endured many pages of evidence all duly footnoted; now they should have their reward and hear the judge send down the prisoner to exemplary punishment with some fitting words: 'the very worst of all our kings . . . a faithless son, a treacherous brother . . . polluted with every crime . . . false to every obligation . . . not devoid of natural ability . . . in the whole view there is no redeeming trait'.[5]

Because the works of Stubbs, who was Regius Professor of Modern History at Oxford, were prescribed reading for all British history students until well into the twentieth century, his condemnation of John caused a reaction. Furthermore, because Stubbs had purportedly based his work on chronicle evidence, medieval chroniclers began to be suspected by the next generation of historians; they hoped to find a less biased source of information in government records. Partly by coincidence and partly because John was so distrustful of people, the great series of copies of government letters (the charter, close, patent and liberate rolls of the Chancery) begin in his reign. Hence it is possible to compare their circumstantial details of daily life with the reports of the chroniclers.

At first sight records seem more reliable than chronicles, as they are free from prejudice and do not depend on hearsay. The Chancery letters, the pipe rolls of the Exchequer and the plea rolls of the royal courts seem to record events just as they were, intriguingly preserved like flies in amber. On closer acquaintance, however, record sources present as many problems of interpretation as chronicles. What is the significance, for example, of the following entry in the pipe roll for 1209: Peter des Roches is fined a cask of good wine 'because he did not remind the king to give a belt to the countess of Aumale'?[6] What was John's relationship with this lady? Why should Peter have remembered? Was the fine a serious punishment or a joke? These and other questions arising from this single enrolment show how intriguing the records are, but they do not lead to some incontrovertible truth about John's policy or character. Ideally every type of evidence needs to be used up to the limit of its value, whereas the preference of recent historians for records has caused them to exaggerate the shortcomings of chroniclers. It was not the chroniclers who should have been the first target of critical historians but Stubbs, who had misrepresented them. His condemnation of John is a product of Victorian culture and has no more in common with medieval realities than a Victorian history painting. The difference in quality and subtlety between the Barnwell chronicler's assessment of John and Stubbs's one is self-evident.

Recent historians have expected too much of chroniclers. Of course chroniclers make mistakes of detail and show bias, just as reporters do today. Moreover the fullest monastic chronicles, like those of Roger Wendover and Matthew Paris, were not written to report mundane events for their own sake but to justify the ways of God to men. Wendover in particular has been the butt of unjustified criticism. The two best works on John's reign (W.L. Warren's *King John* and Sir James Holt's *Magna Carta*) are sometimes overcritical of Wendover. Warren illustrates Wendover's unreliability by considering his report of how John had Geoffrey archdeacon of Norwich crushed to death in prison by starving him and making him wear a cope of lead. Warren states that in no other chronicle is there any hint of the alleged horrific torture. But the annals of Bury St Edmunds report that Geoffrey of Norwich, 'a noble cleric', was arrested at Nottingham and 'dressed in so much iron that he died'.[7] As crushing prisoners with metal weights while starving them, the *peine forte et dure*, became a customary English punishment, these chroniclers may be correct in this respect, although Wendover did misidentify the Geoffrey of Norwich concerned. The chroniclers were probably shocked not by the penalty as such but by 'a noble cleric' being punished in this way.

Holt is over-critical of Wendover's account of how the barons first developed the idea of using the coronation charter of Henry I as the legal form through which to express their grievances. This charter provided the basis for Magna Carta, as has often been pointed out. Wendover ascribes this crucial initiative to Stephen Langton, the archbishop of Canterbury. He reports that in 1213, when Langton attended a meeting at St Paul's about ending the papal interdict, he took 'certain barons on one side and told them in secret' that a charter of Henry I had been found at Winchester (the site of the first royal archives) by which they could recover their liberties.[8] Holt criticizes Wendover's report on the grounds that there is no supporting evidence for it and that the text of the public sermon which Langton preached on this occasion gives no indication at all that the archbishop was ready to partake in a baronial conspiracy. This criticism is a good example of how too much is expected of chroniclers. There is no supporting evidence because Langton's remarks were secret and Wendover depended here on hearsay, as he points out. The fact that the sermon does not record Langton's remarks supports Wendover; if it had let out the secret, Wendover's account would be invalid. We know moreover that at least one hearer of this sermon thought Langton to be two-faced, as the Waverley chronicler reports that when Langton opened with the text 'My heart hath trusted in God', someone in the congregation shouted 'You lie, your heart never trusted in God' and temporarily silenced Langton.[9]

Chronicles, like records, provide intriguing details and lead to unanswerable questions. It is the wealth of such material, in both chronicles and records, which gives John's reign its interest. No previous medieval ruler is so well documented anywhere in Europe. This rich material makes it possible for a diversity of opinions about John to coexist. Such diversity, which medieval chroniclers expressed in antithesis and contradiction, is likely to be nearer historical truth than uniformity. A new determination to put things in writing motivated John's Chancery officials with their letters, Peter des Roches 'revolving the royal roll' at the Exchequer (see p. 181 above), the monastic chroniclers and many others. It was this determination too which made the rebellion against John in 1215 different from its predecessors, as it produced a record of its own in Magna Carta.

Magna Carta

Magna Carta is one of the best known documents in the English-speaking world. Its fame is primarily due, however, not to its intrinsic merits but to the use parliamentarians made of it in their struggle with the Stuarts in the seventeenth century and the export of this myth to New England by the early settlers; Shakespeare's *King John* had made no mention of Magna Carta. Closer acquaintance with the charter is inevitably a disappointment except to specialists. For a start the physical appearance of the earliest copy, preserved in the British Library, is unimpressive. The actual original sealed by John is lost; nor was any copy kept on the Chancery rolls, because John had no wish to be reminded of it and Pope Innocent III soon annulled it. Although Magna Carta contains at least one eloquent declaration of principle – 'no freeman shall be arrested, or imprisoned, or dispossessed, or outlawed, or exiled, or in any way ruined, except by lawful judgement of his peers or by the law of the land' (clause 39) – most of its clauses concern detailed points of law and administration, some of which are of purely local or temporary interest. The removal of fish traps from the Thames and the Medway (clause 33) and the undertaking to dismiss from royal service Gerard d'Athée, Engelard de Cigogné and other named alien officers (clause 50) are extreme examples of how Magna Carta is rooted in its own time and place. Nevertheless the charter is impressive as legislation precisely because it concerns specific grievances, which are clearly defined and systematically listed. From the point of view of legal drafting, Magna Carta contains hardly a redundant word or an ambiguous phrase, although it has frequently been misunderstood by later commentators with insufficient knowledge of the administrative practice of the period.

Sir James Holt comments that in the Europe of its time 'Magna Carta was far from unique, either in content or in form.'[10] This is too large a devaluation of its originality. Certainly rulers before John had made concessions to corporations and barons, as the Emperor Frederick Barbarossa did in 1183 when he made peace with the Lombard cities, or as Alfonso VII of León (in northern Spain) did in 1188 when he undertook not to make war without consulting his magnates. The ideas that rulers must make concessions when defeated in war and have the support of their leading men in major decisions were commonplaces of medieval politics. Nevertheless, compared with earlier grants by rulers to their vassals, Magna Carta is original in being so comprehensive and specific in the range of its regulations, which cover the church, family law, contracts, taxation, legal procedure, penalties, duties of royal officers, weights and measures, merchants, forests and so on. Furthermore Magna Carta is uncompromising in its security provision (clause 61) which entitled a committee of twenty-five barons together 'with the commune of the whole land to distrain and distress us in every way they can', if the king should fail to remedy grievances within forty days. The ideas here expressed, of the country being a 'commune' and of the constituted group being entitled to coerce the king as an individual, may have been implicit in traditional medieval custom but never before had they been given clear expression. Furthermore, like the rest of the common law, Magna Carta applied to all freemen and not only to the little group of barons who had coerced the king.

Pope Innocent III had no doubts about the radical nature of Magna Carta. He based his annulment of it first of all on international principles of feudal law: the barons had made themselves both judges and executors of judgement in their own suit; they were conspirators, rebellious as vassals against their lord and as knights against their king. In addition to this feudal condemnation, which Innocent was entitled to make as John's lord (since England had been surrendered to him as a fief in 1213), he condemned Magna Carta from the plenitude of papal power as a dishonour to the apostolic see, an injury to the king and a reproach to the English people. To emphasize the authority of papal monarchy Innocent cited the text from Jeremiah, 'I have set thee over the nations and over the kingdoms, to root out and to destroy, to build and to plant.' Impressive as all this sounds, the dilemma of the papacy in its dealings with monarchies was the gulf which separated the uncompromising rhetoric of its public letters from the realities of politics. Although Innocent publicly condemned Magna Carta, the fact remained that his personal agent in England, Pandulf, had been one of its signatories. Furthermore when Innocent and John both died in 1216, the legate Guala set his seal to a revised text of Magna Carta within fifteen months of the pope's perpetual annulment of it. The papacy could do this without total loss of credibility because its claim to plenitude of power and its view of events in the light of eternity placed it above mundane considerations of verbal consistency.

The event which assured the future of Magna Carta was John's sudden death in October 1216. Up until April 1216 he had looked like winning the civil war which his repudiation of Magna Carta had caused. Then the tide had turned against him with the invasion of England by Louis of France (the son of Philip Augustus), who claimed that John had forfeited the kingdom and that he was the next lawful heir. Louis's claim won the support of the rebel barons who at the time of John's death once more had the upper hand. The future of Magna Carta had therefore lain in the balance. But now that John was dead, his supporters, whether from political expediency or from genuine commitment, reissued the charter in order to win over the rebels. During Henry III's minority Magna Carta was reissued three times in different versions (in 1216, 1217 and 1225), each of the reissues being a concession by the government to its opponents. The contractual nature of the arrangement is made clearest in the reissue of 1225, which states that the king has made this concession of liberties to all the people of his realm in return for a fifteenth part of their movable goods. The 1225 reissue is the version of the charter which became established as the law of the land and constituted the first document in books of statutes. Such books were themselves a product of the struggle for Magna Carta, as they were formed by knights and lawyers in the shires on the basis of the texts of the charter which were issued officially to every shire court.

England was thus – for better or worse – the first country in Europe to have a written constitution, whereby people's rights were enshrined in an official document disseminated and recited throughout the land. Like all written constitutions, however, Magna Carta had severe limitations when it came to practice and it disregarded those who were unfree (apart from clause 20), just as the American Declaration of Independence disregarded slaves. Continuing the American analogy, the weakness of Magna Carta as a basis for civil rights was that there was no Supreme Court to judge violations of it. The clause already cited prohibiting imprisonment without trial and the undertaking appended to it that 'to no one will we sell, to no one will we deny or delay right or justice' (combined as clause 29 in the reissue of 1225) had no enforceable meaning against the crown because the judges were the king's personal servants. Furthermore they continued to be corrupt. Justice was bought and sold, denied and delayed as much in England after Magna Carta as it had been before it because winning their cases was more important to litigants than upholding abstract ideals of justice. Nevertheless these ideals persisted in the minds of both judges and litigants and Magna Carta became associated with them. It thus lived on as a myth after its use as a practical remedy for specific grievances had disappeared.

Saying that Magna Carta lived on as a myth is not to undervalue its importance. Myths are the cultural beliefs which give a sense of identity to societies and sustain them over time. The repeated demands for Magna Carta to be publicly confirmed, notably by Henry III in 1237 and 1258 and Edward I in 1297 and 1300, are manifestations of widely held beliefs that government at all levels, from palace to village, should be subject to the rule of law and communal sanction. The rebel barons demonstrated in 1258 that the king's councillors could lawfully restrain him and remove his officers. Such attempts to limit the powers of the executive rarely succeeded for long. Nevertheless, over the centuries the belief persisted and grew in the expanding English-speaking world that Magna Carta was the foundation of just government. Today, in the courts of the United Kingdom as much as in the United States, the detail in the clauses of Magna Carta no longer has legal force, as it has been superseded by later legislation. Magna Carta, as a statement of law, is now restricted to its historical context in the thirteenth century. As a sustaining myth of justice, on the other hand, it remains a fundamental formulation of belief in the rule of law. The first decade of Magna Carta's existence, following the death of King John, was crucial in establishing its unique authority in English law.

The regency of William the Marshal

John's sudden death in 1216 might have brought the end of his dynasty and a second conquest from across the Channel. Louis of France and the rebel barons who supported his claim to be king of England controlled the crucial south-east of the country: the ports of London, Southampton and Portchester and the castles of Guildford, Farnham and Winchester. It is true that access to the midlands was blocked by John's foreign captains, Fawkes de Breauté and Engelard de Cigogné, and that the justiciar Hubert de Burgh was holding out in Dover castle. But now that John was dead, the French 'were confident' (in Wendover's words) 'that they had the kingdom of England in their power'.[11] Even before John's death French soldiers had been boasting that England was theirs and that the English had no right in the land. In principle this boast was a riposte to the English claim still to be entitled to Normandy. The French were going to redress the balance: William the Conqueror after all had taken England with a small army in 1066. Because of the power of armed knights a battle involving few troops could have decisive results, as Philip Augustus's victory at Bouvines in 1214 and the Spanish crusaders' victory at Las Navas de Tolosa in 1212 had recently shown. Louis's invasion might even be seen as another Norman conquest. Certainly the Norman branches of families who had lost their English lands in 1204 took part in it, as they were excepted from the peace terms in 1217.

Louis had favourable conditions for victory: control of the centres of government, support of the rebel barons who claimed to be upholding Magna Carta, and a just cause in terms of avenging the disinherited Normans. That 'hammer of kings', Hugh bishop of Lincoln, had supposedly prophesied on his deathbed in 1200 that 'this Frenchman, Philip, will wipe out the English royal stock, just as an ox plucks up grass by its roots, for already three of the sons [Henry the Young King, Geoffrey duke of Brittany, Richard I] have been eliminated and the fourth one [John] will only have a short respite'.[12] Hugh thought this to be appropriate vengeance on the adulterous Eleanor of Aquitaine, who had insulted Louis VII of France by marrying Henry II with such alacrity. Prophecies are not facts, of course, but medieval ones often expressed significant points of view and they were much regarded in a culture which considered divine or devilish intervention a common experience in life.

The answer to the French threat in 1216 was to rely on William the Marshal. He became the hero of the hour, or at least that is the story in his biography which was written in romantic verse (that is, in French) in the 1220s. The Marshal had led an exciting and dangerous life from the time he had been handed over to King Stephen as a hostage in 1152 at the age of five or six. Reality and chivalrous romance blend in his actual life and in his verse biography in a way which it is impossible to disentangle. His recorded career is a model of chivalry: he was trained as a squire in the Tancarville family who were the master chamberlains of Normandy; as a knight he was ransomed by Eleanor of Aquitaine; he himself knighted the Young King (Henry II's son) and fought in France with him against his father. After a pilgrimage to Jerusalem the Marshal returned to the allegiance of Henry II and saved him from defeat by killing a horse under the future Richard I. Yet he won Richard's favour, just as he had won Henry II's. To King John he behaved in a similarly firm way, refusing to give up his homage to Philip Augustus after 1204 and yet supporting John against the rebel barons in 1215. When John died so suddenly the next year, his will named William the Marshal first among his lay executors. The verse biography elaborates this and has John say with his last gasp: 'Sirs, for God's sake beg the Marshal to forgive me, and because I am surer of his loyalty than that of any one else, I beg you to entrust to him the guardianship of my son, for the land will never be held by anyone except with his help.'[13] The Marshal was reluctant to take on an almost hopeless cause but at last he was persuaded by the sight of the helpless child, the future Henry III, and by his sense of honour.

John's men buried him at Worcester and went to Gloucester where the pathetic dignity of the future king, then aged nine, caused them to burst into tears. The boy seemed, as a poet put it with pardonable exaggeration, a 'tiny spark of minute beauty, the sole hope of the torn kingdom', like the star of Bethlehem.[14] With dubious legality John's men immediately crowned their little king as Henry III in Gloucester abbey with an improvised gold circlet, for they had no archbishop of Canterbury (Langton was in Rome and has been thought a traitor by John), no Westminster abbey (Louis held London), and no regalia (some of it had been lost in John's disaster crossing the Wash and the rest was inaccessible in Westminster abbey). During the coronation dinner a messenger rushed in to say that the Marshal's castle at Goodrich only twelve miles away was being attacked by Louis's partisans.

The Marshal confided to his knights that he seemed to be embarking on a sea without bottom or shore. They replied that even if the worst happened and Louis took the whole of England, there was still an honourable course open to them by seeking refuge in Ireland. Heartened by this, the Marshal told his men that he would carry the little king on his shoulders from island to island and country to country and would not fail him even if he had to beg for his bread. The sentiments expressed here in the verse biography are not so much those of the Dunkirk spirit as of the knights errant in contemporary romances who pledge themselves to superhuman quests. The Marshal's motives in upholding Henry III were presumably more complex than this. Nevertheless, as the verse biography argues, Henry's cause might have foundered at the start if it had not been championed by the Marshal with his reputation as one of the best knights in Europe. This gave the regime prestige, and the Marshal stood as a focus of loyalty in terms of European chivalry as well as of English custom and feudal law.

Support for the boy king, however, did not depend as exclusively on the Marshal as his biography suggests. Like other apparently simple medieval narratives, the biography is a work of art which skilfully presents its author's and hero's point of view. Other elements favouring Henry can readily be cited. First of all, John's death deprived his opponents of the personal cause of their rebellion. Instead of a tyrant they were now resisting a helpless boy, who was as entitled to his inheritance as any other heir. Magna Carta (clauses 2–6) had shown the importance the barons attached to laws of inheritance by specifying the rights of heirs immediately after the claims of the church. Secondly, the boy had the official backing of the new pope, Honorius III, through the legate Guala. He had added papal authority to the make-shift coronation ceremony at Gloucester by presiding at it, and fur-thermore within a month of John's death he set his seal along with the Marshal's to the revised text of Magna Carta, which was issued by the new government to all magnates and royal officials. This reversal of Innocent III's condemnation deprived the rebels of another of their grievances, yet it did not release them from excommunication. On the contrary, Guala made the struggle against Louis into a holy war. The royalist forces wore the white cross of crusaders, they were absolved of all their sins before going into battle, and recruits were described as converts. The precedent for launching a crusade against fellow Christians had been established eight years earlier by Innocent III when he authorized the Albigensian crusade against the Cathar heretics of southern France. That was a frightening precedent, as a crusade meant that the enemy were considered infidels and were therefore given no quarter. Henry III's troops were to show that this was what they too meant by a crusade when they sacked Lincoln and committed other atrocities in 1217.

A third element favouring the royalists in 1216 was the character of the men they had on their side in addition to the Marshal and the papal legate. They were few but formidable. First there were John's foreign captains of whom the two most important – the Norman exile Fawkes de Breauté and the Poitevin aristocrat and troubadour Savari de Mauléon – had been named among John's eight lay executors. Of great experience and the king's personal tutor was the Poitevin bishop of Winchester, Peter des Roches. Then there was the justiciar Hubert de Burgh, who independently of the Marshal had refused to surrender to Louis at Dover when told of John's death. Thirdly, there were loyal English nobles like Ranulf earl of Chester, and John's agents of long standing such as William Brewer. The king's side lacked numbers but not prestige nor experience.

Decisive victory for Henry III came in 1217 in the land battle at Lincoln in May and the sea battle off Dover in August. Battle was joined at Lincoln to prevent the French, who had won control of East Anglia, from penetrating northwards. It was an overwhelming victory for Henry's side despite their inferior numbers: the count de Perche, the French commander, was killed and numerous knights were taken prisoner. The captain responsible for the surprise stratagem of attacking from within Lincoln castle was Fawkers de Breauté. The sea battle off Dover was thought even more crucial than Lincoln by both Louis and his opponents because it lost the French their access to Kent and London. Matthew Paris has Hubert de Burgh, the justiciar and castellan of Dover, say, 'I beseech you by the blood of Christ to allow me to hang rather than give up the castle to any Frenchmen, for it is the key of England.'[15] Despite the nationalist bias of Matthew Paris (and of his predecessor Roger Wendover), these events should not be seen in simplistic terms as victories of the English over the French. This would be absurd, since the most effective of Henry III's captains, Fawkes de Breauté, was a Norman, and the Marshal himself was Norman by upbringing and remained throughout his life – in his opinion at least – a true vassal of Philip Augustus as well as of the English king. Nevertheless this hard-fought struggle with Louis of France, coming on top of the loss of Normandy, polarized the difference between English and French interests and encouraged a sense of apartness on both sides of the Channel. Such apartness was foreign to the whole life experience of international knights like the Marshal and it was foreign too to the Poitevin and papal influences which shaped the education of the new king, Henry III. He could not have felt that his throne had been saved for him by the English, still less by the French of Paris, but primarily by people of southern (technically Occitan) speech who had come like his mother from south of the Loire or like Guala from Italy.

Although in the autumn of 1217 a formal peace was made with Louis, and another revised issue of Magna Carta (together with a new Charter of the Forest) symbolized settlement at home, the Marshal did not think that anything permanent had been achieved. The only solution he could see when he lay dying in 1219 was to entrust the kingdom to the pope in the person of his new legate, Pandulf:

Car n'a tele gent en nule terre
Comment il a dedenz Engleterre
De divers corages chascuns . . .

[Because there are no people in any land
like those in England,
where each person has his own opinion . . .][16]

That comment came from a man whose memory of strife extended back to Stephen's reign, but it would apply equally well to the next fifty years and the struggles of Henry III with his barons.

Every Christian knight wished to die in Jerusalem. To the Holy Sepulchre the Marshal had borne the cloak of the Young King in accordance with his oath more than thirty years before. He himself was appropriately buried in that evocation of the Holy Land in England, the round church of the London Temple, which had been dedicated by the patriarch Heraclius of Jerusalem in 1185. The Marshal's biographer gives Philip Augustus the last word: 'The Marshal was truly the most loyal man I ever knew in any place where I have been.'[17] Such praise was possible from the king of France because the Marshal, through his conduct as a knight, stood above national rivalries. The Marshal symbolized old-fashioned idealism.

Implications of the minority

Despite the Marshal's pessimism it was evident at the time of his death in 1219 that the beleaguered group who had improvised the coronation of Henry III at Gloucester two and a half years earlier had succeeded. Their success was made manifest in the king's second coronation in 1220. This time he was crowned in accordance with tradition: at Westminster by the archbishop of Canterbury with St Edward's crown. Beneath the surface a strong element of improvisation persisted, however, as the loss of the Marshal's authority brought intrigue and rebellion. To counter this Honorius III in 1223, acting in his capacity as overlord of England (in accordance with John's submission to the papacy), declared Henry III to be sufficiently grown up to control the kingdom; he was sixteen years old. Royal letters henceforward bear the significant attestation *Teste me ipso* ('witness, myself'); the word of the king, unlike that of lesser mortals, required no other witnesses' names to uphold it. Nevertheless this formal change did not mean that Henry's tutelage had come to an end in political terms. He was dependent in particular on the justiciar Hubert de Burgh to overcome a rebellion by Fawkes de Breauté in 1224.

Also accredited to Hubert is Henry's proclamation in 1227 that henceforward all charters would be issued under his own seal and that all persons enjoying royal grants must show by what warrant (*quo waranto*) they claimed them. The end of Henry's minority is usually dated from this ominous proclamation, which questioned the validity of all previous acts done in his name or in that of his predecessors. The thinking behind the *quo waranto* proclamation may not have been inspired by Hubert de Burgh, however, to whom it was a potential threat, but by a greater authority. The most recent precedent for resuming grants retrospectively in this way after a minority was that of the Emperor Frederick II in Sicily following his coronation in 1220. He shared with Henry III the experience of being a papal ward, and Henry had written to him in 1226 recommending the services of Peter des Roches. That recommendation bore fruit when Peter organized Henry's coup d'état of 1232.

The experience of Henry's minority can be interpreted from opposite points of view. Either it can be seen as a time when the king's incapacity exposed him and his kingdom to foreign influences, notably those of the pope and the Poitevins, which reinforced the Angevin tradition of arbitrary government and in adulthood made Henry III an autocratic ruler repeatedly taking advice from foreigners. Alternatively the king's minority can be seen as a unique opportunity to establish a consensus among the governing class after the excesses of King John. The successive reissues of Magna Carta and the generally moderate terms offered to individual rebels after the civil war of 1216–17 suggest that some reconciliation was achieved. Likewise the re-establishment in 1218 of the justices of the Bench and the procedure of the Exchequer symbolized the restoration of normality and the intention of the government to conduct business as usual. Furthermore the system of justices' circuits or eyres, which was the principal method of enforcing the government's will in the counties and of checking in every village that the law was being obeyed, was re-established in 1218 with unprecedented elaboration. Teams of justices perambulated the counties (half of which had not seen a justice in eyre since 1203) in eight circuits during 1218 and 1219. In 1225 another countrywide visitation was made with the specific purpose of investigating disseisins and clearing gaols, and in 1226–8 a second general eyre was held. Not since the days of Hubert Walter's justiciarship during Richard I's crusade had royal justice been so systematically administered.

The king's absence or incapacity seemed to bring the best out of the judicial system. Indeed from the point of view of legal development the latter years of Henry III's minority are the true age of Bracton, the royal justice to whose authorship the treatise *On the Laws and Customs of England* is attributed. This treatise seems to have been put together in the time of Bracton's predecessor, Martin of Patishall, who was the chief royal judge in the years 1218–29. Patishall and his fellow judges laid down the principles upon which the law was administered for the next fifty years. The treatise attributed to Bracton, which was passed on to him by Patishall's clerk, seems to have been intended as a kind of handbook for the judges which defined the rules system-atically and illustrated them by current cases. Despite – or perhaps because of – its creation during Henry III's minority, the law which this treatise expounds is explicitly English: its author starts by pointing out the differences between English custom and Roman or canonical procedure. This tradition of a distinctive English common law was to prove more resilient over time than either royal absolutism or baronial revoluton.

Business as usual was not as straightforward or uncontroversial a principle for the royal administration as it looked. Restoration of due process of law inevitably meant restoration of the bureaucracy whose routines extended back fifty years or even a century before Magna Carta. All royal officers were first and foremost executors of the king's will and not the servants of the general public or the common good. 'I notice', says the pupil to the master in the *Dialogue of the Exchequer*, 'that with all your regulations you always stick to the king's advantage.'[18]

As far as the principles behind Magna Carta were concerned, the king's officials had learned nothing and forgotten nothing. This is well illustrated by the Exchequer pipe roll for 1219: debts owed to King John for benevolences were still being collected; lists of the northerners who had refused to pay the scutage of Poitou in 1214 were still noted, together with the names of their heirs if they had died. The enrolment for Yorkshire notes that the scutage of Poitou has 'always been in respite from that time until now', but the clerk wrote it down all the same, just in case presumably the ghost of King John should triumph in the end.[19] This attitude of the administration was to be one of Henry III's greatest and most effortless strengths. The king's officials stood poised to do his will – whatever it was – because he was their lord and they were especially his, as was shown by the liveries they wore and the advantages they received in his service. At the end of Henry III's minority in 1227 the monarchy had revived extraordinarily compared with its position in 1216. As 'King of England, lord of Ireland, duke of Normandy and Aquitaine, and count of Anjou', to quote the royal title, Henry had the opportunity to wield as much power as any ruler in Europe, although he would have to fight very hard if he were to regain what he had been taught to believe was his rightful inheritance in England and abroad.

II

The Personal Rule of
Henry III (1227–58)

Henry III lived in a time of new risks and new opportunities for kings and, like his father King John, he met with both kinds of luck. From his own point of view his greatest piece of luck was the success of the coup d'état in 1232 which removed Hubert de Burgh and put the Poitevins Peter des Roches and Peter des Rivaux in power. Potentially this reversed the effects of John's surrender to Magna Carta in 1215, since Hubert had replaced Peter des Roches as justiciar in that year. In 1232–4 the Exchequer was once more under Poitevin management and Peter des Rivaux undertook a sweeping reform which established Henry as master of the central administration and of the sheriffs in the counties for the next twenty-five years. Understandably enough such radical change produced baronial reaction in the rebellion led by Richard the Marshal in 1233, but Henry overcame this and by 1236 he had established himself firmly in power. From then until 1258 he conducted a highly personal government, successfully resisting repeated demands for the offices of justiciar and chancellor to be public appointments under baronial control.

In one way Henry's style of government was gratuitously provocative, as he favoured Poitevins in his household and after 1236 he added the Savoyard and Provençal kinsmen of his wife. But in another way it was Henry who established the distinctive pattern of the English monarchy, as he named his surviving sons after English royal saints and built Westminster abbey and palace as the religious and administrative centre of a settled monarchy. Through the justices in eyre, who were nearly all Englishmen, he maintained contact between the centre and the localities. Through them too he reinforced the tradition of a common law before whose majesty all freemen, even if they were barons or bishops, were equal.

The high point of Henry's personal rule came in 1250 when he addressed all the sheriffs of England at the Exchequer, telling them among other things that no peasant should suffer for the debt of his lord and that they should diligently and righteously inquire into how the magnates were treating their men and correct their transgressions. The year 1250 was also the occasion of Henry's ceremonially taking the cross and promising to go on crusade like St Louis. Thenceforward it became increasingly evident that Henry had overreached himself, both in his attitude to the barons and in his ambitious strategies abroad. Thwarted in recovering his inheritance in France, he hoped to establish his family in the even greater inheritance of the Hohenstaufen Frederick II in Italy and Germany. In 1255 Henry's son Edmund became titular king of Sicily and in 1257 Henry's brother Richard of Cornwall was crowned king of the Romans. This looked like Henry's greatest triumph, but in accepting the Sicilian crown for Edmund from the pope Henry had allowed opportunity to blind him to the risks. He could not fulfil the pope's financial conditions and as a consequence he was threatened, like King John before him, with excommunication. This threat at last brought about a successful combination of the barons, who imposed on Henry in 1258 a radical form of control through public officials and standing committees answerable to parliaments. Seen in the short term, from an English viewpoint, Henry's attempt at personal government had failed and the baronial movement symbolized by Magna Carta had successfully reasserted itself.

Contemporary rulers

If Henry's failure in 1258 is viewed in a European context and in the longer term, however, it does not appear so unusual or so exclusively due to his own misjudgement. Other rulers of his time suffered in similar ways. Most spectacular were the disasters which overcame the Emperor Frederick II (1215–50) after the high point of 1231 when he promulgated the *Liber Augustalis*, the most ambitious and overtly monarchist law book of the Middle Ages. In that same year Frederick faced baronial rebellions in the kingdom of Jerusalem as well as in his Italian kingdom. Thereafter his failure to subdue the Lombard communes in the 1230s gave Pope Innocent IV the opportunity to depose him at the council of Lyons in 1245. At that council another king, Sancho II of Portugal, was likewise deposed. His case was similar in some ways to that of Henry III in 1258. A successful *conquistador*, he had reigned (though first as a minor) since 1223, but he opposed the clergy and gave offices to his wife's family. He was deposed by Innocent IV on the grounds that he had devastated the church and used evil counsel. Charges similar to those against Henry III were directed also against the *conquistador* James I of Aragon (1213–76) by his nobility in 1264 and he was forced to make concessions: honours were to be reserved for nobles by birth and the justiciar of Aragon heard complaints against the crown. Worse happened to Alfonso X of Castile (1252–84), the maker of the *Libro de las Leyes*, which is the Spanish equivalent of Frederick II's *Liber Augustalis*. He faced rebellion in 1272 after twenty years of personal rule and in 1282 an association of nobles and cities declared him incapable of governing.

New power and authority was given to these rebellions by the formation of baronial communes, which claimed to speak for the nation as a whole with the backing of the local church and clergy. Whereas in the twelfth century communes had been associated mainly with rebellious citizens and burghers whom the nobility despised, in the thirteenth century barons joined forces with civic and clerical movements in order to elevate rebellion above family conspiracy and feudal defiance. (These ideas are more fully discussed in chapter 13 on the commune of England.) The important point in the present context is that Henry III was not engaged in an isolated dispute. Indeed, Frederick II, in the manifestos he issued to the other rulers of Europe, claimed that he was neither the first nor the last who would be threatened with deposition and that all rulers suffered from the declared and secret hatred of their peoples and the machinations of the church. After his excommunication in 1239 Frederick made a personal appeal to Henry III as his good neighbour, his brother-in-law (he had married Henry's sister Isabella in 1235), his friend and his kinsman.

Although Henry judged it expedient to ignore this appeal, it would be a mistake to underestimate the range of contacts and sense of common problems which rulers of the time shared. They were interrelated through generations of alliances and sometimes had common physical peculiarities, like the drooping eye which disfigured both Henry III and Frederick II. Henry's three sisters married Alexander II of Scotland, Frederick II and Simon de Montfort respectively (see the genealogical table at page 323). Henry's wife's sisters married Louis IX of France (St Louis), Richard of Cornwall (Henry's brother), and Charles of Anjou king of Sicily (see the genealogical table at page 324). Although Henry's sense of family solidarity grew excessive in the eyes of his enemies when he lavished favours on his wife's Savoyard uncles in the 1230s and 1240s and on his mother's sons by a second marriage, the Lusignans, in the 1250s, obligations of kinship had strong customary backing in the institution of the bloodfeud and aristocratic vendettas. Louis IX was probably not being purely diplomatic when he is reported to have assured Henry III in 1254 that it grieved him how the opposition of his barons prevented the differences between Henry and himself being amicably resolved, considering that they were such close kinsmen. Similarly Joinville reports in his biography of Louis that he allowed Henry to hold on to Aquitaine because their children were first cousins. As traditionalists, Louis and Henry were probably both rather mystified by the changes happening in France, where forces of public opinion made articulate by barons and clergy were causing Henry to lose his Angevin inheritance and Louis to gain it by means which could not be adequately justified by the ordinary rules of family and feudal law.

The common interests and problems of thirteenth-century rulers have tended to be ignored because medieval political history has often been written with a nationalist bias. The development of academic history in the latter half of the nineteenth century coincided with the growth of competitive feeling among the European nations. Conse-quently, instead of examining the similarities between medieval rulers, historians of each nation picked out individual traits in their own kings which they thought revealed incipient national character. Thus Louis IX symbolized French cultural superiority, Alfonso X the Spanish genius for legislating for subject peoples, and Frederick II was the tragic hero of aggrieved German power. By the same token Henry III was the anti-hero against whose futility, 'folly, falseness and foreign pro-clivities' (in Stubbs's words) the English barons rebelled and thus created parliament.[1] In the Oxford History of England Sir Maurice Powicke indicated a similar narrowness of view by asking, 'How was it that in England alone, among the monarchies of the west, the right of the king to select his own advisers became a subject of such bitter controversy?'[2]

In fact in all the European monarchies but particularly in the most westerly ones of Portugal, Castile and Aragon, the king's choice of advisers was fiercely debated. New men in government were always resented by baronial families, however short their own pedigrees were. But there was more than prejudice and snobbery at issue in the thirteenth century. The nobility were up against a new type of royal counsellor, who was typically a graduate from a law school and a specialist in finance or record keeping. John of Salisbury and Walter Map had first identified such peoples as *curiales* in Henry II's reign (see pp. 143–4). By Henry III's reign there were many more of them and they were more assured. Frederick II had founded the university of Naples in 1225 specifically to produce such men to serve in his administration. They deprived traditional counsellors of their influence because they were the masters of the bureaucracy through which advanced monarchies like Frederick II's and Henry III's operated. Decisions no longer had to be made orally at large meetings of counsellors. Instead, little conclaves of experts executed their orders by written instructions to sheriffs and bailiffs in the localities. The key officials therefore became the keepers of privy seals and the accountants of the king's household. Traditional offices like that of steward, justiciar and even chancellor began to wane in importance not only in England but in France, Sicily, Aragon and Castile.

Furthermore the new type of official tended to do things by the book instead of by oral custom. Consequently new law codes and books of statutes become prominent. The largest such collection is the papal decretals which were formed in the 1230s by Pope Gregory IX into the *Corpus Iuris Canonici*. The most comprehensive of such books are Frederick II's *Liber Augustalis* (1231) and Alfonso X's *Libro de las Leyes* (1256–65), which have already been mentioned. Because these works used Roman law textbooks as their models, they also had the added advantage for rulers of encouraging the Roman imperial idea that the prince himself was above the law because he was its maker. Frederick II's *Liber Augustalis* goes so far as to claim that it is blasphemous to dispute royal decisions. The English equivalent of these books is the treatise ascribed to Henry III's judge, Bracton. Comparable work was being done in most parts of Europe, notably the statutes of Alexander II of Scotland, the German *Sachsenspiegel*, the Norwegian and Icelandic law codes, and the *Etablissements* of Louis IX. Although such works appealed to academics both then and now, they were distrusted by traditionalist barons because written law often claimed that rulers were absolute and because knowledge of the law was restricted to experts. This restriction was emphasized in medieval thinking by the similarity in Latin between *lex-legis* meaning 'law' and *legere* meaning 'to read'. Thus the treatise ascribed to Bracton defines 'law' as meaning 'in its broadest sense everything that is read'.[3] Rulers consequently were tending to become readers as much as warriors. Thus Frederick II and Alfonso X, nicknamed *el Sabio* (the Learned), were very highly educated; James I of Aragon was likewise an author in his own right and Louis IX is said to have read devotional works every day. Henry III showed little interest in books except as treasured objects. Nevertheless, because Peter des Roches had been his tutor, he too had a good grasp of administrative procedure.

The return of Peter des Roches

The network of political contacts between England and other European powers is displayed in the coup d'état of 1232, which brought the Poitevins Peter des Roches and Peter des Rivaux to power (see page 181 above). Peter des Roches returned to his bishopric at Winchester in 1231 after an absence of nearly four years during which he had entered Jerusalem with Frederick II in 1229, negotiated the peace of Ceperano between Frederick and Gregory IX in 1230, and on his way back through France in 1231 had participated in the truce between Henry III and Louis IX. Each of these potentates, the Emperor Frederick II, Pope Gregory IX and the French king Louis IX, were involved – directly or indirectly – in Peter's seizure of power in 1232. They are best considered in reverse order, starting with the French. The purpose of the truce of 1231 was to save Henry's face after the failure of his expedition to Brittany in 1230. Henry blamed that failure on the justiciar, Hubert de Burgh, whom he suspected of not wishing to conduct an offensive war in France. Henry is reported to have drawn his sword on Hubert and called him a traitor in 1229, and in 1230 Hubert stopped him accepting an invitation from some of the Norman nobility to invade Normandy. In restraining Henry, Hubert may have been motivated simply by caution and long military experience. Nevertheless Henry's expedition of 1230 seemed to offer the best opportunity ever of rewinning the continental lands, as Louis IX was inexperienced and he faced civil war in France. In replacing Hubert by the Poitevin Peter des Roches, Henry hoped to play a more active and creditable role in French politics.

Hubert was also suspected by Henry of being disloyal to Gregory IX and encouraging an 'England for the English' attitude (in Matthew Paris's words) towards the papacy.[4] In the winter of 1231–2 papal tax collectors in England and religious houses which gave them hospitality received threatening letters, which purported to come from a confederation of knights and magnates dedicated to saving the king and kingdom from Roman oppression. In the name of this confederation masked terrorists held Italian clergy to ransom, burned houses and seized crops. As justiciar Hubert de Burgh was responsible for restoring order but at the same time circumstantial evidence, such as that he was earl of Kent where the trouble started, pointed to his conniving at the confederation if not actually being a member of it. Whatever the truth was, this break-down of law and order gave the king and Peter des Roches the opportunity in 1232 to demand Hubert's resignation. Furthermore he was charged with a mass of offences ranging from financial peculation to poisoning, witchcraft and treason. The financial and administrative accusations were probably accurate by and large, whereas such charges as that he had poisoned William the Marshal in 1219, or that he had given Llywelyn of Wales a talisman which made him invincible, strained credulity. Nevertheless the king and Peter des Roches successfully used these charges to whip up popular hatred against Hubert so that he ran for sanctuary and was totally humiliated. Royal letters were then addressed to all Christians explaining how Hubert had been discovered attacking the Roman church and Italians, and how he had surrendered entirely to the king's will, but the king in his mercy had respited judgement against him in return for the confiscation of everything Hubert had acquired since becoming justiciar in 1215. By this clever move Henry avoided having to substantiate the charges against Hubert, while at the same time he acquired Hubert's huge treasure of gold and silver and − more importantly − Henry moved nearer to establishing a government of his own making.

Henry and Peter des Roches used their triumph to restore royal authority to what it had been in the days of King John by tactics of shock and deliberate confrontation. To emphasize the return to John's policies, his captains and clerks were again given offices. Among the captains the Poitevin Peter de Maulay came back in 1232 and Engelard de Cigogné, who had been banned by name in Magna Carta, was back in 1233. Similarly Robert Passelew, who had been Fawkes de Breauté's loyal clerk, was made deputy treasurer. Henry was careful, however, not to repeat John's mistake of making a foreigner chief justiciar, and Stephen of Seagrave, the senior justice of the Bench, was promoted to Hubert de Burgh's office. Along with Hubert nearly all the sheriffs were dismissed and Peter des Rivaux took control by becoming sheriff of twenty-one counties. In addition to that, he was the keeper of all wardships and escheats (the medieval equivalent of death duties), chief justice of the forests, and had charge of the king's property and houses. Of course Peter des Rivaux could not exercise all these offices himself. The purpose of his holding them was to effect a clean sweep in government by centralizing financial control at the same time as mastering the localities. To enforce Peter des Rivaux's authority throughout England, Flemish and Breton mercenaries were brought in to garrison castles. Roger Wendover says that Peter des Roches filled England with 'legions of Poitevins'.[5] This is an exaggeration, as many of the foreign mercenaries came from places other than Poitou and there were two thousand of them at the most. Nevertheless, in thinking of them as Poitevins, Wendover probably reflected popular opinion, which rightly attributed these changes to Peter des Roches and Peter des Rivaux.

These shock tactics brought about a baronial reaction, which was perhaps what Peter des Roches had been hoping for as a test of strength between the revived monarchy and the champions of Magna Carta. The rebellion was led by Richard the Marshal, a younger son of William the Marshal, who came into his English inheritance on the death of his elder brother in 1231. Richard had earlier inherited the Marshal's Norman lands and he had become a liegeman of Philip Augustus and had perhaps commanded a French royal army. Understandably enough Henry III refused at first to allow him his English inheritance, although the two men were reconciled in 1232. However, Richard began to support Hubert de Burgh after his dismissal and he also resented a judgement in a property dispute, where the claim of the Poitevin Peter de Maulay had been preferred to that of Richard's ally Gilbert Basset. Perhaps it was this dispute which turned Richard into a champion of the English baronage against the Poitevins. It is true that Richard, like Simon de Montfort who had also come to England in 1231 to claim his inheritance, was a Frenchman by prior allegiance, but Frenchmen were as much the enemies of Poitevins as

English patriots were. By 1233 Henry and Richard were openly at war on the Welsh border and in 1234 Richard was killed in Ireland, perhaps on the instructions of Peter des Roches.

The differences between Henry and Richard were on fundamental matters of principle, if Wendover's account (which is the only one extant) is reliable. In reply to Richard's first remonstrations, Peter des Roches provocatively said that the king was entitled to bring in outsiders to reduce his rebellious men to their proper obedience. Later, in 1233, the rebel barons refused to attend the king at Oxford and threatened to make a new king unless the evil advisers were dismissed. Henry reacted by demanding hostages and special oaths of fealty from the barons. This demand and the barons' threat recall the struggle with King John, when the rebels had made Louis of France king of England. In Henry's mind the rebellion of Richard the Marshal was probably associated with what he and Peter des Roches saw as a revival of French baronial ideology. When Henry was accused of condemning Richard without trial by his peers, Peter des Roches answered that there were no peers in England in the way there were in France and that the king was entitled to condemn anyone by judgement of whatever justices he chose to appoint. At issue here was the meaning of clause 39 of Magna Carta (see page 191 above), stating that no freeman should be condemned except by 'judgement of his peers or [vel] by the law of the land'. This clause was ambiguous because the Latin word vel could mean both 'or' and 'and'. What Peter des Roches probably meant by stating that were no peers in England was that, in accordance with the principles of common law established by Henry II, all freemen were equal in the king's court and Richard was not therefore entitled to claim special consideration because he was a baron: judgement by peers meant judgement by other freemen.

English law in Peter des Roches's view was not associated with French aristocratic privilege but with all men being equally humble before the king's majesty. Such a view of English legal development had much to commend it from a historical point of view and it also accorded with the most recent ideas about the powers of rulers emanating from Frederick II's *Liber Augustalis*. This had been promulgated in 1231, shortly after Peter des Roches had left Frederick to return to England. According to Wendover, Richard the Marshal believed that the reason why the Poitevins were so dangerous was that Peter des Roches had given a secret undertaking to Frederick II to make England subject to the emperor. Although Peter had probably never been on such conspiratorial terms with Frederick, it is easy to see how their similar political attitudes gave credence to the idea that Peter was a foreign agent who intended to subdue the barons through Roman law. Ironically enough, Henry III wrote to Frederick II in 1235 that Peter had attributed too much to the plenitude of royal power and he therefore had to dismiss him. Similarly it may not be a coincidence that shortly after Peter's dismissal the teaching of Roman law was prohibited in London. In 1234 Henry was obliged by baronial pressure arising from the killing in Ireland of Richard the Marshal to repudiate Peter des Roches and Peter des Rivaux. But time showed that this was no more than a temporary expedient as Peter des Rivaux, along with Passelew and Seagrave, were given new royal appointments in 1236 and Peter des Rivaux continued to serve Henry until he was removed by the baronial rebellion of 1258.

Henry's style of kingship

The years 1232–4 had established Henry's style and method of government and they also established the lines along which criticism would be repeatedly made for the next twenty-five years. The principal baronial fear continued to be that voiced in 1233 by Richard the Marshal: that the Poitevins were aiming at absolute power. By 1258 this aim had become associated with the second wave of Poitevins, the king's half-brothers, who had come to England in 1247. They were the sons of Isabella of Angoulême's second marriage to Hugh de Lusignan. Of the four younger sons Henry had made William heir by marriage to the Marshal earldom of Pembroke, Aymer bishop of Winchester, and to Guy and Geoffrey de Lusignan he paid large pensions; in addition their sister Alice was married in 1247 to John Warenne earl of Surrey. The rebel barons alleged in 1258 to the pope that the king's brothers 'damnably whispered to him that a prince is not subject to law, thus putting the prince outside the law, and so justice itself was banished beyond the boundaries of the realm'.[6]

To such criticism Henry replied that he was not an unlawful innovator but a restorer of the authority and dignity of the English crown. 'Up until now', he complained of the barons in 1261, 'the kingdom has been governed by three things in particular: by the law of the land, by the seal and by the Exchequer, or rather by the good and wise men who direct these three things.[7] By 'the law of the land' Henry meant the common law system established by Henry II. Henry III's claim to have upheld the law is undeniable, insofar as the administration of royal justice through professional judges was intensified and regularized. But it can of course be argued against him that the judges were often corrupt or partial and that insistence on recovering the rights of the crown conflicted with their duty to be fair to everyone. By 'the seal' Henry meant the Chancery's authority to issue royal letters, which initiated policy of all sorts ranging from international diplomacy to orders to sheriffs to arrest particular individuals. The thousands of copies of such letters of Henry's preserved in the royal archives substantiate his claim to have governed by the seal, although as with the law his critics argued that the keepers of the seal were corrupt or incompetent. By 'the Exchequer' Henry meant financial control. Here again the reforms of Peter des Rivaux improved procedure and made fraud more difficult, but there is no doubt that by modern European or North American standards corruption was still common. The overall impression given by the extant records of Henry III's government for the years 1234–58, which are far too large for any individual historian to master entirely, is of consistent attention to detail and of persistent endeavours to supervise localities.

Henry's government was distrusted by many barons and prelates not primarily because it was incompetent but because it was ideologically distasteful. Henry had learned from Peter des Roches not to apologize for royal power, and throughout the period of his personal rule he repeatedly made provocative statements about the nature of his authority and gave them substance by appointing foreigners and relatives to royal offices. Although he was in no way an intellectual like Frederick II or Alfonso X of Castile, Henry articulated more clearly than any of his predecessors the fundamental principles on which the English monarchy rested. His ideas, as befitted a hereditary monarch, were conservative. He believed that he was God's vicar with a duty to look after his people, under the majesty of 'whose protective wings they breathe' as he put it.[8] Likewise he saw himself as the father of a family or head of a great household with total authority within his domain. These were very old ideas, reaching back to Alfred and Charlemagne and imperial Rome, and they gave little room to the developing political theory of the twelfth and thirteenth centuries which saw rulers as the elected heads of communes, and divine authority as the confine of the pope and clergy.

Identifying his chief opponent and meeting him head on in characteristic fashion, Henry got into dispute with Robert Grosseteste, the greatest English prelate and scholar of his time. The principal dispute was occasioned by Grosseteste's refusal in 1245 to approve the appointment of Robert Passelew to a church in Northampton, which came within Grosseteste's jurisdiction as bishop of Lincoln. Passelew, whom Henry had first brought to prominence in the Poitevin coup of 1232 and whom Grosseteste had already prevented from becoming bishop of Chichester, was a justice of the forests. Grosseteste, as a conscientious pastor, rejected Passelew's candidature because he was a royal justice exercising a worldly jurisdiction. But this dispute raised larger questions than that, as Grosseteste wrote to Henry at the same time that the sacrament of anointing a king 'by no means places the royal dignity above or on a level with the priestly' and warned him of the precedent of Uzziah king of Judah who was struck down with leprosy for usurping the priestly office.[9] That text had also been cited by Grosseteste a few years earlier when he had told Archbishop Edmund of Canterbury that the clergy, who are the gods and angels of scripture, should not be judged by kings as they are beasts of burden like all laymen. Whether or not Henry knew the full extent of Grosseteste's commitment to clerical superiority is obscure. Whatever the circumstances, Henry obliged Grosseteste to make an apology in which Henry is addressed as your 'royal excellence', your 'royal magnificence' and your 'royal serenity'.[10] That was the tone Henry liked to hear from the clergy.

Although Grosseteste's claims seem absurdly scholastic to a modern ear, and Henry's victory a shallow one, this dispute was one of many conducted by Henry with Grosseteste and other prelates and the issues involved were very large. Henry was upholding the traditional prerogative of the king to be God's vicar and lord of all men in the realm whether cleric or lay. Grosseteste, on the other hand, championed the jurisdiction of the clergy, reinforced by the decrees of the Lateran Council of 1215, over the souls of all Christians whether kings or peasants. Ecclesiastical authority had renewed vigour at this time, as the foundation by Innocent III of the Franciscan and Dominican orders of friars and the establishment by Gregory IX of the inquisition against heretics demonstrated. As a progressive churchman and an intellectual,

Grosseteste welcomed the friars and set up an inquisition in his diocese to investigate the sins of laymen. This was prohibited by Henry in 1252 in a letter which clarified the differences between them. The letter describes Grosseteste's inquisition as an unprecedented harassment of the poor and defamation of good Christians, as the inquisitors compel people to give evidence on oath about the private sins of others. As a result of this prohibition no clerical inquisition, like that which persecuted the Albigensians in France, was permitted in England. Henry's reason for banning it was not to protect the freedom of the individual but because it was a public nuisance, as the inquisitors interfered with 'the cultivation of the fields and other necessary temporal duties'.[11] Paradoxically Henry's championing of divine kingship defended secularism by humbling the clergy. 'You prelates and religious', he is reported to have told the master of the Hospitallers in 1252, 'have so many liberties and charters that your superfluous possessions make you proud and from pride drive you to insanity.'[12]

Henry had less success intimidating the lay barons than he had had with the prelates, although here too he used traditional arguments and had the support of lesser men who did not benefit from baronial and clerical privileges. He maintained that the barons should extend the principles of Magna Carta to their own men and that it was wrong for the king to be limited in his power whereas they were not. According to Matthew Paris, Henry told the assembly of barons in 1248 that they were trying to deny him the right which every head of a household had to appoint or remove his officers and that it was contrary to feudal law for vassals to bind their lord to conditions and make him an inferior. Henry was referring here to the baronial proposal, which had perhaps first been made in 1238, to elect conservators of liberties who would be with the king constantly to hear complaints and control expenditure, and that the justiciar and chancellor should be similarly elected by the barons. These were the demands which the barons at last realized in 1258.

The argument that the realm of England was different from a private estate or an ordinary family household and that it should therefore be governed in a different way would not have been understood by Henry. He governed not as an exclusively national monarch but in the tradition of his Angevin predecessors who had amassed a conglomeration of lordships by inheritance and war. Landlords in the thirteenth century were replacing customary leases and fixed rents by a system of direct control through bailiffs rendering accounts. Henry aimed to do the same with the land of England through Peter des Rivaux and reformed Exchequer procedure. Ironically enough a code of rules about how to manage an estate, in the form of advice to the countess of Lincoln, was attributed to Robert Grosseteste. In these rules there is no mention of officials being elected or of open government. On the contrary, the lord commands and the servants obey: 'if any of them complain or grumble, say that you intend to be lord or lady and you intend them to serve you according to your will and pleasure'.[13] The tone of this advice attributed to Grosseteste is identical with that expressed in Henry's speech in 1248, although he put the idea in more legalistic terms as befitted the formality of the occasion. He told the barons that inferiors 'have to be directed at the will of the lord and the wish of the ordinary', who exercises jurisdiction *suo jure*.[14] In Henry's view his critics were simply grumblers, who had to be repeatedly told that he was their lord just as they were lords of their inferiors.

Henry drove home the lesson that he governed according to his own will and pleasure by appointing men of humble origin and foreigners to high office. In doing so he was following the precedents of Henry II and King John, which had been reinforced in Henry III's case by his education by Peter des Roches and the success of the Poitevin coup d'état in 1232. Henry made his distrust of the barons even more explicit than John had done and he favoured foreigners on a scale surpassing any of his predecessors. The extent of Henry's distrust is demonstrated by his ordering to be painted in his washroom at Westminster in 1256 a picture of a king being rescued by his faithful hounds 'from the sedition plotted against him by his own men'.[15] Such distrust was of course self-verifying and Henry was correct in thinking that his numerous enemies conspired against him. Although it is possible that his Poitevin upbringing made him distrust all English people, his attitude seems to be more complex than that. Matthew Paris reports him saying, 'You English want to hurl me from my throne as you did my father,' but he also reports Henry's interest in the old English kings, which is confirmed by Henry's veneration for Edward the Confessor.[16] As well as to Westminster abbey, Henry was devoted to his birthplace at Winchester and it is probably from there that he learned about the pre-Conquest kings buried in the cathedral. Henry does not seem to have objected to English people as such, but to the barons claiming that they spoke for England and had authority over him. Likewise, although it is true that many foreigners were given high offices, as many if not more powerful and loyal royal officials were Englishmen of obscure origins like Henry's secretary John Mansel and his judge Henry de Bracton.

Henry's blend of English and continental traditions is best seen in the works of art which are his greatest memorial, although what survives is only a shadow of what he achieved. His palaces of Westminster and Clarendon have been destroyed, but the choir and transepts of Westminster abbey still stand and the great hall of Winchester castle is impressive even as a shell. Although the design of the new Westminster abbey (started in the 1240s) was influenced by the latest French work at Amiens and Reims, for example in the use of flying buttresses and window tracery, it combined this with distinctively English proportions and craftsmanship in sculpture and tile work. To this and his other buildings Henry devoted huge sums of money, using the unique resources of his government to obtain materials and labour. Consequently the work is well documented from an administrative point of view in the public records. In 1250–1, for instance, 800 men were employed on the building of Westminster abbey and that figure excluded the even larger number servicing and equipping these craftsmen. Henry's delight in buildings is indicated by a French song which has him say that there is a chapel in Paris which he covets so much that he would like to carry it off in a cart to London. This is the Sainte Chapelle, which Henry saw, along with Amiens and Chartres, on his visit to Louis IX in 1254.

It would be a mistake to pigeon-hole Henry's building work as an interest in art separated from life and politics. Through buildings and their furnishings he gave visual expression to his conception of monarchy and of his own place as king. In his palace chambers he had paintings done of the Wheel of Fortune, the exploits of Alexander the Great and the combat of Richard I and Saladin. In his churches, and above all in Westminster abbey, he surrounded his kingship with awe and majesty. He loved liturgical ceremonies, such as processing to Westminster abbey in 1247 with his newly acquired relic of the Precious Blood, or entering Winchester cathedral as though he were a bishop to preach in support of his half-brother Aymer's candidature in 1250. Similarly Henry increased in 1233, the year of his struggle with Richard the Marshal, the number of occasions on which the *Laudes*

Regiae, the ancient liturgy of praise to the ruler, was chanted. Most importantly, Henry promoted the veneration of Edward the Confessor as a popular cult and he had his own tomb in Westminster abbey placed in Edward's aura of sanctity and constructed of identical mosaic materials. Henry is responsible for establishing Westminster abbey as the royal burial place and its palace as the centre of government.

In all these features Henry's style of kingship is comparable with that of his contemporary Louis IX, who like Henry was thought by his critics to spend too long in church and who built Sainte Chapelle to house relics. Louis and Henry too had similar ideas about the rights of monarchy, as Louis's judgement in Henry's favour in 1264 (the Mise of Amiens) made clear to the barons. Yet Louis and Henry differ in their historical reputations. Louis is considered a saint and a hero of France, whereas Henry has often been presented as a foolish and extravagant king who should have reached agreement with his barons. These differences of reputation took shape in the lifetimes of the two kings and are a product of different attitudes towards kingship in England and France. In emphasizing the sacredness of royal authority Henry was up against English tradition, which had Becket as its favourite saint and knew that Henry was not directly descended from Edward the Confessor and an ancient line of legitimate kings but from William the Bastard, the conqueror of 1066. Louis IX on the other hand benefited from more than two centuries of sympathy and admiration for the Capetian monarchy of France where one king had succeeded another in unbroken male succession, thus proving that the dynasty had God's blessing.

Attitudes to the two kings differed in much the same way in nineteenth-century national historiography. English national character was identified with baronial liberty and parliament, which Henry had opposed, whereas Louis was admired because his monarchy had united France. If Louis had reigned in England, 'where each person has his own opinion' (as the biographer of William the Marshal wrote), he might not have found it so easy to be the pattern of justice and goodness.[17] In his style of government Henry modelled himself not on the sweet reason of the Capetians but on the wilfulness of his Plantagenet predecessors Henry II, Richard I and John. Henry was as tough, opinionated and mercurial a politician as any of them and, like them, he suffered from pursuing strategies which were becoming too ambitious for a king of England.

Henry's European strategy

As his palaces and churches showed, Henry had extravagant ideas. Yet they were in keeping with the reputation the kings of England enjoyed of being the richest rulers in Europe. That reputation, which went back to the Norman Conquest, had been reinforced in the generation before Henry's by the immense lands of Henry II and the size of the ransom paid for Richard I. Its firm foundation moreover was the power and thoroughness of the English Exchequer. Seen in this light, it is not so surprising that Henry III himself and many of his contemporaries considered the losses of John's reign a temporary misfortune which better luck and better management would overcome. Henry hoped to rewin his inheritance in France and when those hopes faded after his defeats at Taillebourg and Saintes in 1242, he substituted for them even more ambitious projects in Italy.

In France it is difficult to see what the right policy for Henry might have been. If he had been able to foresee the growth of the French state and had conceded to the inevitable by granting Louis IX all his overseas possessions, Henry would have been so discredited that he might have exposed England itself to invasion. He received an intelligence report in 1227 that the French were planning to invade England in order to restore the dispossessed Normans to their English lands; the memory of Louis of France's successes in England in 1216 was still fresh. The best form of defence was attack and consequently Henry made his expedition to Brittany in 1230. The failure of that expedition exposed his main weakness, which was that he could only attack the French with the aid of magnates like the duke of Brittany whose loyalty could not be relied upon. Henry found himself in much the same dubious position in the greater military fiasco of 1242, when he was encouraged by Hugh de Lusignan to make an expedition to recover Poitou and was then betrayed by him. Nevertheless Henry had been obliged by honour and the fear of losing face to make that expedition. Louis IX in 1241 had invested his brother Alphonse as count of Poitou, which was an explicit challenge to Henry, as his own brother Richard of Cornwall had been titular count of Poitou since 1225. Furthermore Henry's mother Isabella of Angoulême, who had returned to Poitou and married Hugh de Lusignan in 1220, claimed that she had been personally insulted by Louis IX. In addition to that, the troubadours of Languedoc were circulating insulting *sirventes*, calling Henry a coward for not coming to defend his people from French domination. So Henry and Richard of Cornwall had duly come to Poitou in 1242 only to be betrayed and defeated.

On the whole Henry hoped to get the better of the French by diplomacy rather than war, and the failure of his military expeditions in 1230 and 1242 convinced him that the best hope of success lay in his network of international alliances. His strategy here was to use English money to buy supporters and to pay other people to do the fighting. This strategy extended beyond the struggle with France itself to Italy and Germany, although it is probable that it was always the French whom Henry had in mind. If he could not defeat Louis IX within France itself, he could block French ambitions elsewhere in Europe. With this aim in view Henry's interests centred on his marriage in 1236 to Eleanor, the second daughter of Raimond Berenger count of Provence and of Beatrice of Savoy. This was neck-and-neck competition with France, as Louis IX had recently married Eleanor's elder sister; subsequently Richard of Cornwall married the next sister and Charles of Anjou the youngest one (see the genealogical table on page 324). The reason why the royal houses of England and France formed such a close alliance with the relatively minor family of Provence-Savoy was that this prolific family had roots in the most strategic area in western Europe and also acted as international agents linking the papacy and the empire of Frederick II with France and England. The family aimed to control the western Alps and Provence and thus straddle the mountain and coastal routes between what is now France, Switzerland and Italy (see the map on page xiii).

Among her uncles Henry III's queen Eleanor had Amadeus count of Savoy, William bishop-elect of Valence, Thomas count of Flanders and Piedmont, Peter who was made lord of Richmond by Henry III, Boniface who was made archbishop of Canterbury, and Philip archbishop of Lyons (see the genealogical table on page 324). Through the experience and contacts of these men Henry hoped to build a network of alliances extending across southern France into Italy and Germany. As he was in competition with Louis IX, who equally had them all as uncles by marriage, Henry outbid Louis in the lavishness of his gifts. At the time of his marriage in 1236 Henry was constructing the Painted Chamber at Westminster and he had written over its great gable the

motto *Ke ne dune ke ne tine ne prent ke desire* ('He who does not give
what he holds does not receive what he wishes').[18] By playing the traditional lordly role of gift-giving, Henry hoped to win over these new
uncles so that he would be at the centre of their diplomatic web in
Europe.

Henry also hoped to use the expertise of the Savoyards to govern
England in the same way as he had used Peter des Roches. Henry was
first impressed by the abilities of William bishop-elect of Valence and
his clerk, Peter of Aigueblanche. In 1236, when William accompanied
the future queen Eleanor to Henry's court, he was made Henry's chief
counsellor according to some monastic sources. But these reports may
be exaggerated, as William left England in 1237. Monastic commentators attributed such authority to him because their memories of the
Poitevin coup d'état of 1232 were still fresh and they now feared a
Savoyard one. Thus Matthew Paris complained that the king was per-
mitting aliens, 'now Poitevins, now Germans [i.e. Savoyards], now
Provençals, now Romans', to fatten themselves on the goods of
the kingdom.[19] It is certainly true that William's clerk, Peter of
Aigueblanche, was much favoured by Henry and became bishop
of Hereford in 1239. Henry used him on diplomatic missions and
as a financial agent involved with the papacy. Another Savoyard clerk
who proved useful was Henry of Susa, better known as the canon
lawyer Hostiensis, whom Henry made master of St Cross hospital in
Winchester. He acted as the king's proctor in ecclesiastical cases, before
leaving England in 1243 to become a chaplain to the pope.

The Savoyard uncles who were given the most by Henry were Peter,
who was made lord of Richmond in 1240, and Boniface, who was
nominated archbishop of Canterbury in 1241. These were able but
intimidating men who served Henry's interests well, although they frequently differed from him about policy. Peter became known in Savoy
as 'little Charlemagne' because he was such an energetic administrator
and formidable knight. Boniface was particularly useful at the council
of Lyons in 1245 (where the Emperor Frederick II and Sancho II of
Portugal were deposed by sentence of the pope), as Boniface's brother
Philip was archbishop of Lyons and provided the military force for the
council. Boniface became a prelate of the same mould as his elder
brother, William bishop-elect of Valence; proceeding backwards and
forwards between England and the Alps, fighting (Boniface felled the
prior of St Bartholomew in London with one blow of his fist), living

well and intriguing. Although Boniface was far from Robert Grosseteste's ideal of a Christian pastor, he upheld the liberties of his church in the way his contemporaries best understood, that is, by threats and litigiousness.

The characteristic which may have most attracted Henry to the Savoyards was that they had been brought up in a hard country where lordship had constantly to be fought for and power was nakedly displayed. They reminded him perhaps of King John's captains whom he had known in his childhood. Henry even tried to bring English law into line with Savoyard custom, which was a departure from his usual policy of maintaining Englishness in this sphere. When in 1253 the king's baggage train as well as overseas merchants had been robbed by bandits on the Southampton road, Henry introduced the Savoyard custom whereby the residents of the area in which a robbery takes place would be collectively obliged to pay compensation. Matthew Paris reported the objections to this as being that geographical conditions were different in England from Savoy, that people would be punished without sufficient proof and, above all, that such a great change in the law should only be made with baronial consent. This illustrates very well the differences between Henry and his barons. He wished to maintain law and order by the strongest means available, whereas his opponents gave greater emphasis to the importance of consent and tradition. The earls and barons would not change the laws of England.

Although Henry used the Savoyards within England, their main function was in international relations. In the land they dominated, the interests of Frederick II as emperor and king of Arles and of Louis IX as overlord of France converged. Henry aimed to use Provence-Savoy as a wedge between these two great powers and also as a staging post between his lands in southern France and the pope and emperor in Italy. Henry's strategy is illustrated by his sending an expeditionary force in 1238 commanded by Henry de Trubleville, the English governor of Gascony, and William bishop-elect of Valence to aid Frederick II against the Lombard communes. In 1246 following the deposition of Frederick II, Henry made a more ambitious move whereby Amadeus count of Savoy became his vassal and Henry took over responsibility for the Alpine passes. This suggests that Henry was already moving towards the idea of dominating Europe by acquiring the Hohenstaufen inheritance. Although all this seems too much like armchair diplomacy with no grip on reality, Henry's agents like John Mansel and Peter of Aigueblanche went in person on numerous diplomatic missions and Mansel had taken part in the fighting at Milan in 1238 and Saintes in 1242.

The 'Sicilian business'

Henry's ideas grew more ambitious with each decade and by the 1250s they had reached a peak of provocation and stupidity in the opinion of his opponents. The cause of the collapse of Henry's many years of personal rule was the 'Sicilian business' (*negotium regni Siciliae*), the transaction whereby Henry agreed with the pope in 1255 to send money and troops to Italy in exchange for his younger son Edmund being recognized as king of Sicily and Apulia (that is, southern Italy). In itself this was not a stupid idea. The kingdom of Sicily was reputed to be the wealthiest in Europe and the island of Sicily was the key to the Mediterranean just as the Alpine passes were the key to access between northern and southern Europe. After the deposition of Frederick II his kingdom of Sicily might be taken by whoever had the power and formal papal authority to do it. If either the French or the Aragonese got it, they would grow so powerful that Henry's lands in Gascony might be endangered. The best counter move therefore was for Henry to get the kingdom of Sicily for himself.

To nationalist historians like Stubbs, Sicily seemed incredibly remote from England and Henry's plan therefore looked absurd. But to Henry, who viewed Europe through the eyes of the Savoyards and Poitevins, Sicily was not so far away. Matthew Paris in his chronicle included a beautifully illustrated itinerary all the way from London to Apulia. Henry was not the first English king to intervene in Sicily, as Richard I had captured Messina in 1190. In Henry II's reign likewise there had been many contacts between England and Sicily: Henry II's secretary Thomas Brown had been a councillor of Roger II of Sicily and another Englishman, Robert of Selby, was Roger's chancellor. England and Sicily were felt to have close links because they had both been conquered by Normans. In a way, therefore, Henry III was attempting a reconquest by which Sicily would be wrested from its German overlords and returned to the heirs of the Normans. Many barons were familiar with Sicily because of the crusades. Thus Peter des Roches had been there before his return to England in 1232. Similarly after the defeat and death of Simon de Montfort at Evesham in 1265 his disinherited sons went to make their fortunes in the Sicilian kingdom and were given large fiefs by Charles of Anjou. Sicily, like Provence-Savoy, was the kind of multinational lordship which fascinated Henry III because it seemed similar to his own multinational status as overlord of Britain and Ireland and of lands in France extending as far as the Alpine passes.

Henry's mistake was not in buying Sicily for Edmund but in the unfavourable terms of sale which he agreed with the pope. In addition to annual tribute the contract of 1255 specified that Henry was to pay the pope 135,541 marks within eighteen months. If he failed, he personally would be excommunicated and the kingdom of England would be laid under an interdict (as it had been in John's reign before Magna Carta). The huge payment was stated so exactly to the nearest single mark because the pope claimed that these were the costs already expended by the papacy on rewinning Sicily, and Henry must reimburse them. This sum was almost as much as Richard I's ransom, or as a tax on the English clergy for ten successive years. Furthermore this was merely the entrance fee, as Frederick II's son Manfred controlled much of the kingdom and Henry might have to fight him all the way. The offer had been made to Henry's brother Richard of Cornwall before it was accepted for Edmund and (according to Matthew Paris) Richard had replied to the papal nuncio: 'You might as well say, I will sell or give you the moon; go up and take it.'[20]

Why did Henry agree to such unfavourable terms? There are many explanations, though no single one is satisfactory. Henry was used to taking risks and outbidding his rivals: 'He who does not give what he holds does not receive what he wishes.'[21] The Sicilian business was a gamble, just as outfacing Richard the Marshal in 1233 and many other angry prelates and barons since then had been gambles. More than twenty years of unprecedented power for an English king perhaps blinded Henry to the danger he was in. Not having the historian's advantage of hindsight, Henry may have thought that he was still going up on the Wheel of Fortune, that favourite medieval image like the big wheel in a fairground, which he had had painted in 1247 above the chimney-piece at Clarendon. Indeed events in the short term went in his favour. In 1257 Richard of Cornwall was crowned king of the Romans (emperor designate) at Aachen. The Hohenstaufen inheritance seemed within the grasp of the Plantagenets. In that same year Henry presented the twelve-year-old Edmund, dressed in Apulian costume as king of Sicily, to the English barons. He expected them to be impressed and to see in Edmund the new *puer Apuliae*, as the young Frederick II had been known fifty years earlier, the future lord of Europe. Those other images painted on Henry's palace walls, the exploits of Alexander the Great and the combat of Richard I and Saladin, likewise perhaps played a part in Henry's hopes. The greatness of the Plantagenets was about to be restored and recent humiliations in France forgotten. Or, as Pope Alexander IV put it in 1255, 'the royal family of England which we view with special affection and the distinction of our intimate love, we wish to exalt above the other kings and princes of the world'.[22]

If these were Henry's aspirations, he was entering the realm of fantasy. Yet that too is understandable considering the way high politics were conceived at the time. Frederick II in his *Liber Augustalis* created a fantasy of an all-powerful ruler, laying down the law in books while his people rebelled. Frederick also was responsible for inflating the value of his kingdom of Sicily in the rhetorical letters he sent to other rulers. In one medieval tradition, exemplified above all by the papacy, it was words rather than deeds which mattered in politics. Henry's gain from the contract of 1255 was the pope's word that Edmund was the legitimate king of Sicily; Henry could provide the deeds later, or so he thought. Even the huge sum to be paid to the papacy can be partly explained. Henry had undertaken in 1250 to go on crusade and as a consequence the clergy had been taxed. It was legal to tax the clergy for a crusade because it was an ecclesiastical enterprise. An advantage of the Sicilian contract was that Henry's obligation to go on crusade against Islam was commuted by Alexander IV to crusading against the Hohenstaufen in Italy. The prize for Henry to win was the kingdom of Sicily. This was a more realistic objective than Louis IX's attempts to reconquer the kingdom of Jerusalem; compared with Louis, Henry was a realist.

The sum due to the papacy was indeed huge, but Henry calculated that the clergy would be compelled to pay most of it by papal tax collectors, like the Gascon Rostand whom Henry took into his household. The favour Henry showed to Rostand was consistent with his policy over many years of exploiting papal power to humble the English clergy and promote royal interests: Peter des Roches had taught him that lesson when he brought down Hubert de Burgh, allegedly in the name of an outraged pope, in 1232. In this context Henry's agreeing to the penalty of excommunication and interdict makes sense: the clergy would be impressed by that threat and it would oblige them to pay up. Seen in its most optimistic light from Henry's point of view, the Sicilian contract meant that Henry, in Edmund's name, would win control of the most important kingdom in Europe at the expense of the English clergy. But this time Henry had provoked the prelates and barons too far. They produced a succinct list of objections as seen from England, starting with the distance and going on to the cost and the risks. One point to which they gave emphasis, which Matthew Paris confirms, was the risk of a French invasion of England. The French felt so threatened by the combination of Richard of Cornwall in Germany and Edmund in Italy that Louis IX was patrolling Normandy in 1257. The Sicilian business had therefore had the reverse effect for Henry to the one intended. Instead of perfecting his network of alliances, it united all his enemies at home and abroad and isolated him.

This sense of isolation was reinforced by the barons' tactics in 1258. They were determined to avoid the charge of treason and of plunging England into civil war, as the rebellion against King John had done. They therefore treated Henry as if he were a simpleton who had to be taken into wardship like a child. In this way the rebels could claim that they were acting in the king's own interests and they petitioned the pope to abrogate the Sicilian contract. This was a delicate manoeuvre, as Henry had willingly made the contract and it was consistent with his ambitions over many years. Nevertheless the idea that Henry was a simpleton gained wide currency and it is in this guise that he appears in Dante's *Divina Commedia*, in the valley of unsatisfactory kings in Purgatory, along with other rulers involved in Italian politics:

Vedete il re della semplice vita
Seder là solo, Arrigo d'Inghilterra

[See the king of the simple life,
sitting there alone, Henry of England][23]

Henry did not lead a simple life in an ascetic sense, although he might be thought simple in his singlemindedness. Nevertheless Dante has characterized him well in the words '*seder là solo*'. By pursuing sole royal power Henry had come to sit alone by 1258, isolated from people in England.

12

National Identity

.

National feeling in Henry III's reign

The identity of the English as a distinct people had survived the Norman Conquest and been maintained as an ideal by the great Benedictine monasteries with their roots in the Anglo-Saxon past. That identity also existed as a fact of everyday life in the language spoken by the serfs or 'natives', as the landlords called them, of the countryside. There was therefore nothing new in the virulence with which the St Albans chroniclers, Roger Wendover and Matthew Paris, reported Henry III's favours to the Poitevins, Savoyards and other aliens. They were writing in the tradition of English monastic chroniclers. A number of twelfth-century monks had written histories of the English and no one expressed their bitterness more powerfully than William of Malmesbury did in 1125: 'no Englishman today is an earl or bishop or abbot; the newcomers gnaw at the wealth and the guts of England, nor is there any hope of ending this misery.'[1]

The difference between William of Malmesbury's attitude and that of monastic chroniclers a century later is that the latter did see some hope of their humiliation ending. This hope came not from Henry III himself, who pursued the policy of all his predecessors since Edward the Confessor of relying on men from overseas, but from the lay magnates who began to identify themselves with England. In Wendover's report of Richard the Marshal's protest against the Poitevins in 1233 he has Richard complain that they oppress Henry's 'own native men of the kingdom'.[2] The Latin word for 'native' here is *naturalis* meaning 'trueborn'. Wendover avoided the word *nativus* because that described the 'natives' in the sense of 'naifs' or low-born serfs. The word *naturalis* had the added advantage that it meant 'natural' as well, and hence the king could be accused of dismissing his natural counsellors and appointing unnatural aliens instead. The idea that the barons should counsel the king by right of nature, meaning by birthright and by rightness in the order of things, was thus made explicit. Nor was the concept of 'natural' counsellors a private idea of Wendover's, although it may have been a precocious one in 1233, as the barons themselves used comparable language in their petition in 1258 where they demanded that castles should be entrusted to 'faithful men, natives of the kingdom of England'.[3] The word for 'natives' here is *nati* meaning 'born' and this is associated with the barons' demand that ladies shall not be married to men 'who are not of the nation [*natione*] of the kingdom of England'.[4] A 'nation' meant a kindred group and hence by extension it was applied to the people of each distinctive country; for example, students at medieval universities were divided into nations for mutual protection.

The barons' opposition to the aliens in 1258 was exacerbated in the civil war which followed. The *Song of Lewes*, which celebrated their victory in 1264, alleges like Wendover that the king intended to supplant the 'native people' (*viri naturales*) by aliens. The song claims too that the rebels fight for England:

> Now England breathes again hoping for liberty; the English were despised like dogs but now they have raised their heads over their vanquished foes . . . Read this, you Englishmen, about the battle of Lewes for if victory had gone to the vanquished, the memory of the English would have been cheap.[5]

National sentiment is often voiced under stress, when the group is threatened by a powerful neighbour or torn by civil war. Thus the war with Louis of France, culminating in the battle of Lincoln in 1217, was seen by one contemporary poet as a struggle for English survival. 'England' (*Anglia*) is personified in this poem (as it is in the *Song of Lewes*) as 'she grasps her conquering swords' and the tears of the English invoke English strength.[6] The 'English people' (*Angligena gens*) have grown degenerate and suffered from the 'belligerent French', the 'black Scots' and the 'feckless Welsh'. This part of the poem thus identifies the main enemies of England in the later Middle Ages and it also illustrates the tendency of nationalists to associate degeneracy at home with viciousness abroad. Matthew Paris similarly characterizes the different nations in abusive terms: the French are proud, the Welsh are faithless, Poitevins are wily, Flemings are filthy, Greeks are insolent and so on. Matthew too makes Hubert de Burgh into a national hero of the war of 1217 as he defended Dover, 'the key of England', and saved England for the English. According to Wendover likewise the king's side at the battle of Lincoln were fighting 'for their country' (*pro patria*).[7] These texts have been cited in a little detail in order to show that the idea of 'England' as a cause to fight for was familiar to thirteenth-century writers. As the biography of William the Marshal makes clear in its rendering of his harangue to the troops before the battle of Lincoln, to defend one's country is a cause justifying war; the troops fight also for themselves and their women and children and to win honour and protect the church. Such sentiments are not dissimilar from those voiced by military leaders in many later wars.

Familiar elements of later ideology are also evident in a lament for the former greatness of England which was composed in 1265 following the battle of Evesham. The anonymous writer, who is a royalist by contrast with the author of the *Song of Lewes*, reminds England of her qualities starting with her sea power: 'You had the sea for a wall and ports as your gates fortified by strong castles; in your knights, clergy and merchants all flourished.'[8] According to this writer English ships brought spices and treasure from the four quarters of the globe. Furthermore within England there was an abundance of wild and domestic animals, beautiful countryside and numerous birds and fish. Although England was only a small country, the fleeces of its famous sheep warmed the backs of all the nations of the world. But now England had degenerated into civil war because it spurned the heavy yoke of kings. This is an extravagant and tendentious panegyric. Yet it is valuable in showing that the image of England as a sea power, depending on trade and the prosperity of its agriculture, had already been articulated. The baronial wars heightened sentiment for the suffering of England and the English among both royalists and rebels:

Plange plorans Anglia plena iam dolore

[Wail, weeping England, heavy now with woe][9]

The papacy and internationalism

As in the modern world, national pride and exclusiveness existed alongside powerful international organizations. Indeed the growing influence of the papacy encouraged nationalist particularism in reaction to its universal claims. As a consequence of King John's submission to Innocent III and the legations of Guala and Pandulf during Henry III's minority, the papacy had established itself alongside and even inside the English governmental machine. The aspect of papal power which was most resented was the practice of paying papal officials and nominees out of the revenues of English benefices. From the papacy's point of view there were many justifications for this. Its right to appoint to benefices derived from its supervisory authority over all churches to prevent corruption and uphold Christian values. Rich benefices had often been held by royal or baronial favourites as a reward for secular services. The papacy and the higher clergy now needed more revenues to provide for the efficient running of the church. Innocent III had come closer than any of his predecessors to making clerical authority a reality throughout Christendom.

To implement the programme of reforms decreed by the Lateran Council of 1215 required an army of preachers, nuncios, inquisitors, letter writers, accountants and so on. Good government had to be paid for in the church as in the state. The pope, unlike a secular ruler, had few revenues at his disposal and he therefore began to raise funds by taxing the clergy and also by obtaining regular incomes for his officials by requiring churches throughout Christendom to provide benefices for them. In England this was easier than elsewhere because during Henry III's minority papal officials were on the spot. Furthermore the king's government was willing to assist the papacy in exchange for a share of the profits both spiritual and temporal.

The problem for the papacy, as so often in its activities, was the gulf between theory and practice. The most prominent beneficiaries of papal provisions to benefices tended not to be high-minded reformers but the nephews and kinsmen of the pope and cardinals. This was because the pope was expected like any other great man to reward his followers upon whom he depended for protection. Robert Grosseteste was so infuriated by an order from Innocent IV in 1253 to provide for a papal nephew from the endowments of Lincoln cathedral that he refused, arguing ingeniously that the papal plenitude of power could not be used to destroy the church because that was contrary to its purpose. Although Grosseteste was acting here not as an English nationalist but as a conscientious bishop, his resistance fed popular opposition to the papacy just as his controversies with Henry III were used for the secular purpose of attacking the monarchy.

In 1253, the year of Grosseteste's protest, Italians were receiving at least 50,000 marks a year from English benefices according to hostile critics. Moreover Innocent IV himself acknowledged this income to be above 8000 marks, as he offered to restrict it to that sum. It has been estimated that 8000 marks represents about five per cent of the income of the church in England and Wales for taxation purposes at the time. From the papacy's point of view a levy of five per cent on ecclesiastical income was a reasonable charge for its services. But papal tax collectors were more conspicuous than their royal and baronial counterparts because they were foreigners and they had to proceed in accordance with publicly stated rules of canon law. Furthermore, in order to get the money to Italy they depended on Lombard and Tuscan bankers and thus built up in the public mind – and in reality – the connection between the papacy and international finance. The contract with its exchange charges, expense provisions and penalty clauses made in 1255 between Henry III and the pope to promote the Sicilian business shows very well how the pope headed a multinational finance corporation as well as a religious institution.

Resentment against papal provisions in England is best illustrated in the disturbances of 1231–2 which occasioned the fall of Hubert de Burgh (see page 209 above). Threatening letters imitating the tone and style of the papal chancery were sent to prelates in the name of a confederation (*universitas*) 'who would rather die than be oppressed by the Romans'.[10] The letters were sealed with a special seal representing two swords, which traditionally symbolized spiritual and secular authority and for these conspirators symbolized also the use of force. The letters ordered their recipients to pay no more revenues to Roman nominees under penalty of having their produce burned. Italian clergy were held to ransom, papal messengers were attacked and the letters they carried torn up, and houses and crops were seized. The leader of the terrorists was Robert Tweng, a Yorkshire knight who had been deprived of his hereditary right to nominate to a church by a papal provision. He operated under the pseudonym of William Wither ('wither' means 'opponent' in Old English). Tweng alias Wither is a real-life example of a folk hero of the Robin Hood type, who robs fat prelates and fights for English liberties. Instead of being hanged for arson and robbery, Tweng was given a safe-conduct to the pope and subsequently went on crusade. This leniency at the hands of the king and the pope suggests that Tweng had powerful friends in England, as his propaganda maintained. He is last heard of in the baronial wars as an executor of the will of John Mansel, Henry III's secretary.

Tweng's confederation can be interpreted in a number of ways. It was a nationalist movement insofar as the letters it sent out claimed to speak for the laymen and magnates of England against the Romans. The movement also claimed to represent everybody (hence it is a *universitas*) who 'has chosen to resist by common counsel of the magnates'. In these features Tweng's confederation presages the 'commune of England' which was formed to resist Henry III in 1258. But Tweng had a narrower purpose than the rebels of 1258; at his narrowest he is little more than an anti-clerical with a specific grievance. The principal significance of Tweng is that his confederation shows that the anti-Roman prejudices of the St Albans chroniclers were not a private eccentricity of their own but voiced wide resentment against the intrusion of foreigners into the English church. Instead of promoting international understanding and Christian fellowship, the growing power of the papacy from Innocent III onwards united churchmen and laymen in protest and led to the formation of national churches.

The identity of England

England and the English formed a distinct entity not only in their own opinion but in the view of outsiders. For example Innocent III had condemned Magna Carta as a reproach to the English people. Innocent is also reported to have alluded on another occasion to the English reputation for drunkenness. A dispute between Evesham abbey and the bishop of Worcester had been taken on appeal to the Roman court in 1206. The bishop's advocate was imprudent enough to show off what he had learned in the schools about one of the points of ecclesiastical law involved. He was caustically rebuked by the pope: 'You and your masters must have drunk a lot of English beer when you learned that.'[11] Medieval England had a reputation for hard drinking which is now more associated with other northern nations. On Richard I's crusade the natives were astonished at the amount the English consumed and at their custom of draining toasts to the sound of horns and trumpets. Similarly Gerald of Wales in his invective against the English at the court of Rome in 1199 emphasized their reputation for drunkenness and double-dealing. The author of the *Dialogue of the Exchequer* blamed the frequency of crime in England on the innumerable riches of the kingdom and the innate drunkenness of the inhabitants.

England's wealth referred to here is another commonly mentioned national characteristic. The French in particular seem to have felt that England was a much richer country than their own. In his life of Louis VI (1108–37) Suger of St Denis contrasted Louis with William Rufus, who enjoyed the profusion of the treasures of the English, and Louis VII (1137–80) similarly contrasted the wealth of Henry II with his own material poverty: 'We in France have nothing except bread and wine and joy.'[12] Louis meant of course that the French had everything worth having. From these and many other comments a consistent picture emerges of England through foreign eyes: the English were drunken, grasping and untrustworthy. In his style of life and diplomacy Henry III was perhaps attempting to correct this unfavourable image, as he was sober (although he enjoyed a glass of wine), generous and consistent in his affection for his kinsmen. A medieval characteristic of the English which has not survived is that they were reputed to have tails. Thus Simon de Montfort showed that he did not think of himself as an Englishman when he remarked that the English get you into a tight corner and then turn tail. Simon is also reported to have commented that he had been in many lands and different countries both pagan and Christian but 'in no nation have I found such infidelity and deception as great as that which I have experienced in England'.[13] In retrospective report, treachery of that sort explained his death at the battle of Evesham. These opinions of the English, like all generalized opinions about national character, were no more than prejudice constantly repeated. Nevertheless they show that the English possessed distinct characteristics, in the opinion of their enemies, which made them identifiable as a nation.

The identity of England also became clearer in the thirteenth century in more precise ways. Most importantly, England became territorially distinct from Scotland and Wales because they too were developing into nation states (see chapter 9 above). Pope Gregory VII wrote to Archbishop Lanfranc distinguishing the Scots (by whom he meant the Irish) from the 'island of the English' (by which he meant England, Scotland and Wales).[14] Although this was a simplification even in 1073, Gregory was right in assuming that Scotland and Wales were not distinct territorial entities and that the Norman conquerors claimed overlordship over the whole island. In the thirteenth century by contrast, both the kingdom of the Scots and the principality of Wales had set locations and names. The Scots were now recognized for international purposes as the people of Scotland and not of Ireland, and similarly the Welsh now acknowledged that name in Latin instead of calling themselves Britons.

In constitutional terms vis-à-vis the English, the Scottish position was stronger than the Welsh one. In particular from 1192 the papacy recognized the Scottish church as a special daughter of the holy see (see p. 168 above), which meant that it was independent of the arch-bishop of York, whereas Gerald of Wales failed to win similar recogni-tion for the Welsh church's claim to be independent of Canterbury. Nevertheless the papacy did not support Scottish claims to be free of English secular dominion; for example in 1235 Gregory IX wrote to Alexander II reminding him of the homage and fealty due to the king of England. Even in this letter, however, the Scottish cause received one support as the king is addressed as king of 'Scotland' (*Scotia*) instead of king of 'Scots' and is thus acknowledged to rule over a specific ter-ritory. That territory moreover was defined in the Anglo-Scottish treaty of 1237, which settled the border between England and Scotland. The numerous disputes which followed did not contradict the basic principle that the ancient kingdom of Northumbria had been parti-tioned and that henceforward Northumbrians north of the Tweed were Scots, whereas those to the south were English. As on other land frontiers in Europe divisive national identities were thus imposed on people whose language, traditions and way of life were the same.

Welsh status and aspirations were as complex as Scottish ones and they too were most explicit when opposed to the English. In 1212 Llywelyn the Great (1194–1240), describing himself as prince of North Wales and as writing with the assent of all the princes of Wales, made an alliance with Philip Augustus of France to fight their common enemy the English and free the land 'from the yoke of their tyranny'.[15] But Llywelyn's position was not as secure as that of the king of Scots. He was not a king and feudal overlord but a prince in the sense of principal ruler. Nor was Llywelyn prince of the whole of Wales and, even if he had been, he had still to contend with the descendants of the Norman marcher lords who formed a buffer between England proper and Wales. Nevertheless in Wales as in Scotland the thirteenth-century kings of England had to contend with the new force of a sense of national identity (Welshness or Scottishness) being combined with territorial lordship and organization. Llywelyn the Last took the opportunity offered by the baronial wars to establish himself as 'prince of Wales' and to be recognized as such by Henry III in 1267.

The land of the English, 'England' as distinct from the whole island, was thus defined by its apartness from Scottish or Welsh land. At the same time this sense of apartness fed prejudice between the nations. For example Richard of Devizes puts a racy description of the characteristics of different English towns into the mouth of a French Jew: Worcester, Chester and Hereford are to be avoided 'because of the Welsh who are prodigal of life', while York 'abounds with Scots who are filthy and faithless sub-humans',[16] Richard's facetious description (composed in the 1190s) has the merit of giving a bird's-eye view of England and its principal towns. From the middle of the thirteenth century there survives a list of more than a hundred centres of population along with a particular characteristic of each, such as 'school of Oxford', 'plains of Salisbury', 'shipping of Southampton' and 'cod of Grimsby'.[17] A more ambitious depiction of England, in the form of a map, appears in four of Matthew Paris's manuscripts made in the 1250s. This map contains more than 250 geographical names and includes the whole island with north at the top and Scotland and Wales described by those names (*Scotia* and *Wallia*). Although this map is crude by modern standards, its cartographer (who was probably Matthew himself) is well aware of the importance of scale and of directional relationships between one place and another. The achievement of mapping England is itself an indication of how the country was beginning to be conceived in territorial terms on the ground instead of in abstract terms, though it must be emphasized that very few thirteenth-century Englishmen would have understood what a map was.

Unlike Scotland and Wales, England did not have to create a new national identity bounded by the authority of its ruler but to restore that idea from the Anglo-Saxon past. The Norman conquerors had to be absorbed and to identify with England instead of France. Generally speaking by the end of the twelfth century the Normans had been absorbed by intermarriage. This is specifically stated in the *Dialogue of the Exchequer* and it is also indicated by the way charters are no longer addressed to both French and English but simply to all faithful persons. Some residual Norman pride remained however; for example at the battle of Lincoln in 1217 the Normans on Henry III's side claimed their traditional right to strike the first blow but they had to concede this to the earl of Chester when he threatened to withdraw altogether unless he commanded the front line. Although a variety of people fought on both sides in 1217, Louis's defeat was seen in retrospect as a victory for England over France: 'Thus the Lord struck his enemies who had come to destroy the English people,' the chronicler Ralph of Coggeshall commented.[18] This nationalist attitude is explicit even in an official document from 1217, which looks forward to the 'English' (*Anglici*) recovering their lands in Normandy.[19]

This form of national cohesion brought with it both advantages and risks. An advantage was that the ruler's authority to enforce law and order within his realm was strengthened. But there was the risk that massive conflict with other rulers was more likely. Under the feudal convention lords with lands in England and Normandy could go back and forth between them and do their best as individuals to keep the peace. But once Norman lands were thought of as English the risk of war between 'England' and 'France' increased. The polarization of loyalty between England and France also put the English kings in a difficult position because they were the inheritors of lordships on both sides of the Channel. In maintaining his inheritance Henry III inevitably isolated himself from English opinion because he identified with all his lands.

The use of the English language

The point where English national identity seemed weakest was in the way the English language had lost status since the Norman Conquest. A nation does not need to use only one language (for example both English and Gaelic were used in Scotland), nor does the predominant language need to be exclusive to the nation (various modern nations use English or Spanish). Nevertheless one exclusive language is a powerful maker of unity and this is what England had possessed before 1066. Old English was the standard language of government, overcoming differences of English dialect as well as Scandinavian languages. In place of this the Norman conquerors had imposed the standard language of western Europe, Latin. This meant that Latin composition in England improved and that English scholars and clerics could participate in the revival of learning associated with the Twelfth-century Renaissance.

The Normans' effect on the English language is more complex. Old English lost status once it ceased to be the language of government, and by the middle of the twelfth century texts were being written in a variety of English dialects because a common standard was no longer being imposed (see page 40 above). By 1200 original works were being composed in Middle English, of which the best known are *The Owl and the Nightingale* (a debate poem; see pages 146–7 above), Layamon's *Brut* (Arthurian history) and the *Ancrene Riwle* (spiritual guidance for ladies). Although such works owed a great deal to Latin and French models, they absorbed these new styles into English idiom and thus re-created English as a literary language. English was also capable once more of expressing in written form the requirements of administration, as the letters in English sent by the baronial government to all counties in 1258 demonstrate. Nevertheless this experiment was an exception, proving the rule that until the fourteenth century English was a language of low status.

Why did English continue to have a low status despite its literary revival by 1200? The chief reason is that all vernacular languages had a low status compared with Latin. Latin had reached a peak of originality and prestige in the twelfth century with its use by great preachers and polemicists like St Bernard, scholastic masters like Abelard, and the innovative poets of the *Carmina Burana*. In addition Latin had shown itself to be an excellent medium for more mundane legal and business documents. Magna Carta was expressed in Latin because it was easiest to achieve precision and economy in that language. English nationalists, like the anonymous authors of the poem on the battle of Lincoln in 1217 and the lament for England in 1265, used Latin as their medium because of its power as the language of rhetoric for more than a thousand years. Furthermore these authors wished to give dignity and permanence to their work and therefore chose Latin. Writers of English were daring eccentrics whereas Latin was the language of the *literati*, of all those educated in the classics of pagan and Christian Rome. With or without the Norman Conquest it is probable that Latin would have superseded Old English as the language of record in the twelfth century because of the influence of the schools and the church.

The English language also had to compete with French and, as with Latin, it is probable that French literary language would have been introduced into England whether or not there had been a Norman conquest. The fact that the conquerors of England spoke various forms of French obviously helped to promote it, but the Norman Conquest cannot explain why French begins to be used in England as a language of literature and government from the middle of the thirteenth century onwards, as this occurs two centuries after 1066. Like the growth of Latin in the twelfth century, the flourishing of French in the thirteenth was a European phenomenon and was connected with the dominance of French culture. English knights, like their German or Spanish counterparts, learned French because it was in a special way their language, as it was the language of chivalrous romance. Chrétien de Troyes and other writers in French challenged the cultural dominance of classical Greece and Rome and claimed that France was now the centre of Europe and the arbiter of taste. Furthermore Philip Augustus and St Louis, with Notre Dame de Paris and the Sainte Chapelle, existed to prove it. In addition to the dominance of Parisian France, Henry III and his court of Poitevins, Savoyards and Provençals kept alive the Occitan culture of the south. The cosmopolitan royal court was therefore another force discouraging English, as patronage was extended by Henry to native artists and craftsmen but not to writers.

The English language therefore existed close to the ground under the huge shadows of Latin, both classical and modern, and of French, both *langue d'oc* (south of the Loire) and *langue d'oil* (north). In social terms English was the language of the *nativi*, the serfs bound to the soil. By 1200 it was the mother tongue of nearly everyone except the royal family because the nobility and gentry were brought up by local wet nurses. Men of ambition were educated in Latin and French by tutors because these were the languages of lordship. Latin led to a career in the church and French to advancement at court or in a noble household. English was therefore the most common language in every sense of that word: it was the most frequently used (in speech though not in writing) and it was associated with the common people. This ambivalent position of English, being deeply rooted and yet overshadowed, explains why it could flourish so suddenly in the time of Chaucer and Langland when the impediments to its growth had been removed. By the fourteenth century both Latin and French had waned as universal languages of European education and vernaculars could therefore develop.

English as a literary language thus did not contribute to a sense of nationhood among educated people until the fourteenth century. The fiercest nationalists of Henry III's reign, most notably Matthew Paris, wrote in Latin or French. Nevertheless the ordinariness of English speech must have given it a spontaneity which the learned languages of Latin and French lacked and ultimately this brought English out on top. Legal records in Latin and French begin to have pieces of English embedded in them when the clerk is unwilling or unable to abandon his native idiom. An early example of this practice comes from the king's court in 1241 when Henry III's counsellors were so exasperated by his claim for damages of 10,000 marks against Gilbert the Marshal that it is described in the plea roll as *illud nameles fremeles*: something 'nameless' (in the sense of unspecific) and 'pointless'.[20] The English language, like the sense of Englishness, lay just below the surface and it bursts out from time to time when the alien ways of the king and his court become hard to bear. The scarcity of writing in English in this period is misleading, since the language was not declining but growing as it gradually absorbed the literary and scholastic vocabulary of French and Latin and developed through everyday speech into the mother tongue of knights and clergy as well as peasants.

From lordship to nation state

A sense of national consciousness and an awareness of the characteristics of the different nations were not developments confined to England, Scotland and Wales as they occur throughout Europe. For example, when Frederick II wrote in 1241 to the rulers of Europe warning them of the threat of the Mongols, he picked out the qualities of the different powers: Germany 'fervent in arms'; France 'the mother and nurse of chivalry'; Spain 'warlike and bold'; England 'fertile and protected by its fleet'.[21] The lands on the edge of the ocean (that is, at the extremity of the known world) are also distinguished, namely 'bloodstained Ireland, active Wales, watery Scotland and glacial Norway'. The countries named here and the qualities attributed to them have quite a modern ring. Nevertheless they did not exist as sovereign states: Germany was an assortment of principalities; the boundaries of France were undefined; Spain consisted of a variety of kingdoms held together by alliances; England was only beginning to be distinguished in the mind of the king from his overseas lands.

Although medieval nations cannot be equated in terms of political power with the sovereign states of modern Europe, national identity was already in the thirteenth century an important element in a ruler's authority over his own subjects and in the assertion of power over his neighbours. The problem each ruler faced was how to convert his inherited properties and titles into a territorial unit or state. The development of England is a microcosm of Europe in this respect. Henry III had an impressive list of titles as he was king of England, lord of Ireland, duke of Normandy and Aquitaine and count of Anjou. But these titles did not accord with his power. They claimed both too much and too little: too much because Normandy and Anjou had been lost since John's reign; too little because no mention was made of the English claim to overlordship in Wales and Scotland. Henry had either to make these titles into territorial realities or abandon them.

A king could no longer be merely a symbolic overlord, the man on horseback with a conspicuous retinue of nobles and priests who made an appearance from time to time to collect tribute and hear grievances. Instead, a king had to have permanent officials on the spot watching over his interests from day to day. To be lord of the land a king had now to act like a landlord. In Normandy Louis IX was now the ruler on the ground and Henry III was duke merely in name. Furthermore Louis gradually used the force of French common feeling and fear of the English to make Normandy part of his territory.

Conversely within what had once been called the 'island of the English' Henry asserted his rights on the ground vis-à-vis the Welsh and the Scots. Thus in the 1240s and 1250s he asserted royal authority over the lords of the Welsh March and also over individual Welsh princes. This was a piecemeal process – typical of how territorial units were painstakingly built up over time – of claiming authority in individual disputes as they arose. Gradually the two sides polarized so that the issue became one of English or Welsh dominance, rather than the exercise of royal or feudal authority as such. A similar policy of definition village by village was pursued on the Anglo–Scottish frontier and in the parts of Northumberland and Cumberland which had been granted to the king of Scots in 1237. Scottish lords were not deprived of their lands in England in the way the Normans were because the king of Scots did homage to the king of England. Nevertheless the idea, which was foreign to traditional international feudalism, that a man could owe loyalty to the ruler of one country only, was slowly gaining ground. The sons of William the Marshal or the sons of Simon de Montfort (the elder), who inherited lands on both sides of the Channel, had to decide whether they were Englishmen or Frenchmen and they found that difficult. For men at the top the demands of nationalism caused a crisis of personal identity.

In a feudal system it had been normal for various individuals at different levels of the hierarchy to have rights over the same land whereas in a territorial state that could not be tolerated. Each ruler therefore tried to make his inheritance into a uniform territory and in doing so inevitably came into conflict with other rulers who had claims in the same territory. Henry III, for instance, could not avoid disputes on the marches of Wales and with the king of Scots because although some boundaries were regulated by treaty they depended in reality on the variable force at each ruler's command. Furthermore each ruler increased that force by appealing beyond his traditional feudal tenants or kinsmen to his men as a whole.

Taxation for purposes of national defence became increasingly common. Unlike feudal taxes these new ones were levied not on knight's fees but on the movable goods of all subjects. Not only vassals, therefore, but every category and rank of society contributed, and in theory consented, to the tax. For example the writs collecting the aid granted to Henry III in 1232 specify that it is granted by the 'archbishops, bishops, abbots, priors and clerics, earls, barons, knights, freemen and serfs of our kingdom'.[22] Although for the great majority, the serfs and poorer freemen, consent meant no more than tacit assent (they did not actively resist when their goods were taken), a tax of this sort overrode the traditional divisions of cleric and layman and lord and vassal and united everyone in adversity. Furthermore, because such taxes were in theory voluntary gifts to the king for specific purposes, matters of royal policy such as Henry III's 'Sicilian business' became the subject of common discussion. More than anything else, perhaps, taxation shaped a forceful public opinion, articulated at every level of society through institutions which had originally been formed to levy the money. Thus a 'national interest' first at the level of barons and higher clergy, then of knights (in the civil war of the 1260s) and ultimately of peasants (in the revolt of 1381) began to emerge in England.

The most powerful rulers of Europe were ambivalent in their attitude towards this concentration of lordship on particular territories and the identification of rulers with specific local groups or nations. The two greatest rulers by tradition, the pope and the emperor, had titles and aspirations which were too large to confine within a single territory and furthermore they both centred on the same territory, Rome and Italy. Nevertheless they could not avoid competing for territory and using the current methods of tax-raising and constant attention to detail in order to consolidate claims of all sorts. Similarly Louis IX was torn between his determination to uphold the international tradition of the crusade and the need to assert himself as king of France with territorial disputes to settle with the kings of England and Aragon. Henry III too, with his claims to half of France, considered himself to belong to this top league of rulers who stood above local prejudices because of the richness of their inheritances. All such heterogeneous rulers came into conflict with their local subjects when they demanded taxes to pursue ambitions which extended beyond the territory concerned. Henry in particular found himself in difficulties because he was so persistent in giving preference to his overseas inheritance and ambitions rather than to England itself. The strength of the reaction against him is the best evidence that the days of symbolic lordship and chance inheritance were waning and that the nation state, formed out of ancient feelings of common kinship and identity reinforced by concentration on territorial units, had taken shape.

The expulsion of the Poitevins

The strength of national feeling among makers of opinion in England is demonstrated by the terms in which monastic chroniclers, up and down the country and not just at St Albans, reported the rebellion of 1258 and the expulsion of Henry III's Poitevin half-brothers. Writing after the war, the chronicler of St Benet of Hulme in Norfolk attributed the troubles solely to the hatred felt for the Lusignan brothers, 'for true-born men [*naturales homines*] were like the disinherited and the magnates of England grieved very much because no Englishman could get his right or obtain a writ against them'.[23] This chronicler is in fact repeating allegations which were frequently made against the Lusignans in 1258. Thus the Waverley abbey chronicler states that there were so many foreigners of diverse languages in England and they had been so enriched by gifts from the king that they despised the English as inferior beings. This chronicler goes so far as to allege that the foreigners intended to poison the nobility and depose the king and thus bring the whole of England under their sway. He, like other chroniclers, names the Lusignan brothers in particular and reports how they broke the law. 'But at last', the Waverley chronicler concluded, 'the earls and barons, archbishops and bishops, and the rest of the magnates of England, as if miraculously awoken from sleep', united together and expelled the foreigners from England.[24]

Such accounts, like most chronicle reporting, are simplified and exaggerated. The Waverley chronicler borrowed the passage about foreigners of diverse languages from his predecessor who had written of the rebellion against King John in 1215. Foreigners in England in 1258 could not have numbered more than a few hundred and they were not of very diverse languages, as most of them were Poitevins and Provençals speaking Occitan. Nevertheless there is no doubt that Henry III did enrich his four half-brothers when they arrived in 1247. In particular William de Valence, who was made lord of Pembroke, and Aymer, who became bishop of Winchester, were prominent in the king's counsels and received numerous gifts. The two older brothers, Guy and Geoffrey de Lusignan, did not settle in England, though they were granted privileges there. Like the Waverley chronicler, Matthew Paris reported that the king had given his half-brothers protection from being damaged by his writs, a concession which amounted to immunity from prosecution. Although no such orders are recorded on the Chancery rolls, they may have been issued nonetheless, as routine writs of protection for individuals were not always enrolled. A number of cases suggest that the king's half-brothers interpreted his protection to mean that they were above the law.

When the king's half-brothers were driven into exile in 1258, their English officials were left exposed. The most notorious was William de Bussey, the steward of Geoffrey de Lusignan and councillor to William de Valence. In Surrey William de Bussey was accused of extortion so that 'the tenants all came to ruin'.[25] For a steward, the distinction between making a profit for his lord and being extortionate was a fine one. The sheriff of Lincolnshire described William de Bussey as a Poitevin. This is revealing, as he was in fact the younger brother of a Sussex landowner. Hatred of the Poitevins evidently rubbed off on their associates, like William, and this might account for the chroniclers' reports that there were foreigners everywhere. It is also possible that people in Lincolnshire mistook William for a foreigner, despite his family having connections there, because they would not have understood either his Sussex English or his southern French if he had learned to speak Occitan like the Poitevins. Even at their maximum extent, however, the activities of the Lusignan brothers cannot have caused all the havoc which contemporaries attributed to them.

Nevertheless the exaggeration of the chroniclers underlines the importance of national feeling in Henry III's England. In reality the Poitevins were not necessarily above the law, nor did they have the king in their power, and it is unlikely that they conspired to kill the native nobility. Nevertheless these rumours were circulated and constructed by contemporary chroniclers into a recognizably consistent image of a long-suffering England waking miraculously from its sleep. The force of nationalism has always been associated with feeling rather than fact, with prejudice fed by fear and with a sense of identity sharpened by comparison with a minority of aliens. The rebel barons of 1258 expressed to the pope the force of their feeling in a statement of priorities which they claimed Henry III had ignored: 'a prince owes all his duty to God, very much to his country [*patria*], much to his family and neighbours, and nothing whatsoever to aliens'.[26] For better or worse patriotism had become a force in politics.

13

The Commune of England
(1258–72)

Henry III's flamboyant regime crashed in 1258 with a suddenness which only the wisdom of hindsight has made look inevitable. For more than twenty years he had withstood criticism and ignored proposals for change. Now that the opportune moment had come (as well as the demands of the pope, record grain prices and famine for the second year in succession caused by harvest failures contributed to unrest), his opponents were well prepared and they proposed a radical constitution in which the king was to be controlled by committees answerable to the community. Although Henry was obliged to swear to these proposals in 1258, he had outmanoeuvred the barons by 1261 and obtained papal absolution from his oath. Furthermore his more determined opponents, led by Simon de Montfort, were isolated in 1264 by Henry's greatest diplomatic triumph, the Mise of Amiens, whereby Louis IX (whom both sides had accepted as arbiter) came down uncompromisingly in favour of the king.

Henry had brought the weight of European opinion, expressed by the pope and Louis IX, against his opponents in the same way as he and Peter des Roches had discredited Hubert de Burgh in 1232. Instead of running for sanctuary like Hubert, Simon de Montfort decided to stand up and fight and took the king prisoner at the battle of Lewes in 1264. But Simon could not benefit from his victory because the king remained the rightful ruler and retained the loyalty of his family and supporters. In 1265 Simon was defeated and killed by the Lord Edward (the future Edward I) at the battle of Evesham. In the bitter fighting which followed, the king's opponents were hunted down and killed until terms of surrender were published by the king in the

Dictum of Kenilworth of 1266. Henry and Edward had won the most total victory in England's history since the Norman Conquest, so total that Edward succeeded as king on his father's death in 1272 although he was away on crusade until 1274.

The confederates of 1258

Henry III was temporarily brought down in 1258 by a confederation of seven magnates. They took a mutual oath in April to stand by each other against all men, saving their fealty to the king and the crown of England. The document recording this oath, which is preserved only in a copy in the de Montfort archives in France, is careful to avoid the charge of treason and therefore excepts the king and crown from its implications. Nor does the document specify what the confederates propose to do; it simply gives each of them an assurance of the others' loyalty come what may. It was the brief but comprehensive terms of this oath which formed the revolutionary commune of England, as the same formula was sworn to at Oxford in June by everybody present. Those who refused to take the oath and join in the commune, like the Lusignan brothers, fled and were harried out of the kingdom as mortal enemies. This was likewise the oath which Simon de Montfort insisted on upholding for the next seven years, even after it had been declared invalid by the pope and Louis IX. To Simon the backsliders, including Henry III, were traitors.

The seven original confederates formed a powerful and experienced group familiar with European politics. Richard de Clare earl of Gloucester had been on pilgrimages to Pontigny and Santiago and on diplomatic missions to the pope at Lyons, to Alfonso X at Burgos, and to Scotland and Germany; he had also fought in Gascony and frequently on the marches of Wales. John Fitz Geoffrey was a marcher lord like Richard and the son of King John's justiciar, Geoffrey Fitz Peter. Roger Bigod earl of Norfolk had fought in Poitou and Gascony and had headed the English delegation to the council of Lyons in 1245, which aimed to end England's feudal subjection to the papacy. Hugh Bigod, Roger's brother, had taken part in negotiations with France and was chosen as justiciar in 1258. Peter of Savoy, 'little Charlemagne', was the queen's uncle whom he had made lord of Richmond; he was the first of the seven to change sides thereafter. Peter de Montfort (no relation of Simon) had fought in Poitou and Gascony and been on pilgrimages and diplomatic missions to Santiago, Burgos and France; he was keeper of the Welsh march. These six men therefore combined political experience with military power, which was concentrated on the Welsh marches within easy reach of the midlands and south of England.

The seventh man was Simon de Montfort, whom the king with characteristic sharpness identified as his chief opponent: 'I fear thunder and lightning terribly, but by God's head I dread you more than all the thunder and lightning in the world.'[1] These words are reported by Matthew Paris, who had also reported in 1252 that Henry had taunted Simon after complaints about his governorship in Gascony: 'Go back to Gascony, you lover and maker of strife, you will find trouble enough there and reap its fitting reward just as your father did.'[2] Henry was referring here to the ambivalent reputation of Simon de Montfort the elder, who from 1208 until he was killed at Toulouse in 1218 had led the Albigensian crusade, killing and despoiling heretics and innocent alike in southern France. The younger Simon's governorship in Gascony revived his father's arbitrary rule in the opinion of his opponents.

Both the elder and the younger Simon were titular earls of Leicester and both too were chosen as revolutionary rulers of England. The elder Simon had been deprived of his English lands by King John because he remained loyal to Philip Augustus. But his prestige as a crusader was so great that he was rumoured to have been elected king of England by a group of rebel barons at Nottingham in 1210. Whether he or the younger Simon were ever informed of this is unknown. The younger Simon has sometimes been compared with the Poitevins and Savoyards whom Henry favoured, as he (like them) settled in England in the 1230s and he made a profitable marriage in 1238 to Eleanor, the king's sister. Nevertheless Simon felt himself to be in a different class, because he was not a Poitevin but a Frenchman who had come, like Richard the Marshal, to claim his rightful inheritance. Like Richard too, he claimed a hereditary office with wide powers, that of Steward of England, as well as the earldom of Leicester. Simon's coming to England was a family arrangement (again comparable with the Marshal family), whereby his elder brother Amaury took up the French and Norman inheritance and Simon went to England. Although Simon adopted England as his country and in the opinion of his partisans died a martyr for it, he consistently despised the English if the comments of chroniclers are correct.

Because of his father, Simon was unusual among the magnates in being associated with the evangelical Christian movement of his time. His first recorded action in England in 1231–2 was to expel the Jews from his lordship of Leicester. This was done (his charter declares) for the salvation of his own soul and those of his ancestors and successors. Such an action identified Simon with the crusade for an uncompromising and militant Christendom. His mentors in England seem to have been clerics and intellectuals, rather than his fellow lay magnates. Most prominent among them were Robert Grosseteste and Walter Cantilupe, both reforming bishops, and the Franciscan friar Adam Marsh. In 1251 Grosseteste sent Simon a copy of the arguments he had been using at the papal court to distinguish tyrannical from lawful government. This may have been intended to help Simon defend himself against accusations of misgovernment in Gascony. Grosseteste evidently thought Simon would appreciate abstract arguments rooted in Aristotelian logic. Like other younger sons, Simon may have had a scholastic education with a view to his taking up a great ecclesiastical benefice. Certainly he saw to it that his sons like himself were educated in Latin and in the scriptures. When he was killed at Evesham, he was found to be wearing a hair shirt like the most ascetic clergy.

Simon's greatest and most unusual contribution to politics was his moral rectitude. His determination to keep his oath at all costs must have been motivated by deep conviction. As the *Song of Lewes* put it, 'Simon's wholly singular religion' was the cornerstone of the baronial movement; on his faith depended the security and peace of the whole of England.[3] Already in 1258 Simon had the reputation of being a strong man: a trouble-making and proud fanatic in the opinion of his enemies, a passionate upholder of Christian knighthood in the opinion of his friends. Unlike that earlier model of chivalry, William the Marshal, everything that Simon did went wrong: the king hated him although he had married his sister; he was a divisive governor of Gascony; after 1258 he waited to fight until it was too late; he got no advantage from his victory at Lewes in 1264, as the Lord Edward subsequently escaped and caught him unawares at Evesham. But, unlike the Marshal, Simon was never forgotten because he was England's tragic hero. His story was told in ballads long after his death and the Victorians believed him to be the founder of the House of Commons.

The idea of the commune

The original confederation of seven magnates was expanded by progressive stages into the commune of England. The seven had recorded their oath on 12 April 1258. By 30 April other barons and knights had joined them and on that day they confronted the king in Westminster Hall. They had come armed, although those who entered the hall left their swords at the door. According to an eye witness the king said: 'What is this, am I your prisoner?'[4] Henry was perhaps suddenly reminded of the days of his minority when he was the ward of the barons. Roger Bigod reassured him that no harm was meant but that he must dismiss the 'intolerable Poitevins'. Bigod added that he and his companions wished to confess their 'secret' to the king: Henry and the Lord Edward must take an oath on the gospels to abide by their rulings. Having no choice, Henry and Edward took the oath and they too therefore became members of the commune. On 2 May the king published letters announcing that he had sworn that the state of the realm would be reformed and that a meeting would be held at Oxford on 9 June for this purpose. At Oxford the delegates again came armed and more oaths were sworn in the name of *le commun de Engleterre*.

A commune was an association bound together by a common oath of loyalty; whereas a vassal swore an oath of homage to his lord alone, the members of a commune swore to serve each other for their mutual benefit. Communes had come to prominence in the twelfth century as revolutionary associations, particularly in cities, opposed to aristocratic and ecclesiastical power. Thus Richard of Devizes describes the formation in 1191 of the commune of London, 'into which all the magnates and even the bishops were compelled to swear'; hence it was a conspiracy (*conjuratio*).[5] Richard then gives a definition of a commune which emphasizes its revolutionary associations: 'a commune is a tumult of the people, a terror of the realm, a torpor of the clergy'. By 1258 the communal idea had become more familiar. For example John's government had used it to organize the defence of England after the loss of Normandy. In 1205 a commune was formed throughout the whole realm, to which all men over the age of twelve swore loyalty.

This commune like that of 1258 was founded to defend the kingdom against aliens. The communal idea also appears in Magna Carta, where 'the commune of the whole land' is entitled to distrain the king (clause 61).

These precedents show how the conspiratorial nature of a commune as a sworn association could be directed to a public and indeed a national purpose. The king's government increasingly depended on sworn groups of representatives at every level of society, from local jurors speaking for the conduct of each village up to communes defending the realm. In Maitland's words, 'men are drilled and regimented into communities in order that the state may be strong and the land may be at peace'.[6] Although the term 'commune of England' is not used before 1258, the idea of uniting everyone by a common oath was therefore familiar. Nevertheless the communal idea still retained revolutionary potential in its historical association with popular rebellion and in its mechanism. Whereas Henry III claimed power from above by divine right, the 'commune of England' derived its authority from the mutual oath taken by its members; it assumed that people were entitled to form associations and to use their combined force even to overawe the king. The commune stood for everybody. In French it was described as the *commun*, in Latin as the *communitas*, and in the English-language letters of 1258 it was rendered as the *loandes folk* ('the people of the land'), as English lacked a precise equivalent for 'commune'.[7] To counter the king's divine authority the commune pointed to the sanction of the oath taken on the gospels by all its members. Both Henry III and Simon de Montfort understood the fundamental importance of this oath. That is why Henry devoted his diplomatic skills to getting it invalidated while Simon insisted that nothing could alter it.

Simon may also have had another precedent in mind when he took his oath in 1258. In 1241 the baronial commune of the crusader kingdom of Jerusalem, which had rebelled against Frederick II ten years earlier, requested Frederick to approve the appointment of Simon de Montfort as guardian of the kingdom. This request does not necessarily imply that Simon was a partisan of this commune, as his name may have been put forward as a compromise candidate acceptable to both Frederick and the barons. Nevertheless the request does suggest that Simon, who had gone out to Palestine in 1239, was familiar with the issues involved. The historian of the crusader kingdom, Joshua

Prawer, points out that the similarities between the communal oath made at Acre in 1231 and that made at Oxford in 1258 are so close that 'one is almost tempted to look for straightforward links between the two events'.[8] Such links are possible, as Simon de Montfort was not the only English baron in 1258 to have been on crusade, and Jerusalem was an attractive precedent since it was the holy land, which (like England) had been conquered by its barons. They claimed, like the descendants of Normans, that the Conquest had been a cooperative enterprise and that the power of the elected king was therefore limited. Two political philosophies, both with deep medieval roots, were therefore in conflict in 1258. On one side stood sacred authoritarian monarchy, championed by Henry III, and on the other communal custom and baronial rights, championed by Simon de Montfort.

The Provisions of Oxford

The rebellion of 1258 was more far-reaching in its proposals than that against John in 1215. Magna Carta had been intended to remedy specific grievances and to establish fundamental principles of legal practice for the future, but it had not provided an effective mechanism for ensuring that justice was administered in accordance with its principles. In the light of this failure the rebels of 1258 drew up a new list of shortcomings in the law (the Petition of the Barons) as well as appointing Hugh Bigod as justiciar to hear complaints against sheriffs and other royal officers in each county. Out of all this activity came the Provisions of Westminster of 1259, which reformed legal procedure on numerous detailed points in a non-partisan way.

Where the rebellion of 1258 differed fundamentally from that of 1215 was in the so-called 'Provisions of Oxford', the reorganization of the system of government undertaken by the commune at its meeting at Oxford in June 1258. Despite its importance, the details of this reorganization exist only in an informal memorandum copied into the chronicle of Burton abbey. The lack of an official record has never been satisfactorily explained. It may be that, as with John's attitude to Magna Carta, Henry III had it excised from the record. Alternatively it is possible that an official statute never was made because Henry soon grew powerful enough to avoid ratifying it. Certainly the details took a long time to settle, as the king (prompted by the rebels) wrote to the pope on 12 August 1258 telling him that the barons were working hard on the reform of the kingdom: "When we have their ordinance, one most fruitful to us and to our heirs, we beg your serenity with all the affection we can to find it not unworthily pleasing and acceptable."[9] The pope's formal reply came two and a half years later in 1261 when all the ordinances, which 'under the pretext of reforming the state of the realm' had been made by 'some sort of tumult of the magnates', were condemned.[10] But that is to look ahead to Henry's diplomatic victory, whereas in the summer of 1258 he had no option except to go along with the rebels.

The memorandum preserved by the Burton chronicler is of critical importance despite being informal and rather muddled. Under the rubric 'A provision made at Oxford', it gives the Latin text of the arrangements for the justiciar to hear complaints.[11] This is followed by the names of the twenty-four: twelve men from the king's side and twelve from the barons' who are responsible for reform. The king's group actually includes only eleven names, most of whom are his relatives or members of his household, which emphasizes how isolated he had become. The barons' group on the other hand includes six of the seven original confederates (Peter of Savoy has dropped out) together with other magnates. The idea of two groups of twelve may have derived from juries or from town councils. After the names of the twenty-four come texts of oaths in French: the oaths of the commune of England, of the twenty-four, and of the justiciar, chancellor and castellans. As already explained, these solemn oaths of loyalty were the ideological basis of the commune. The names of the new council of fifteen persons follows; this was chosen by electors nominated by the opposing group and then confirmed by majority assent. Such an elaborate system of delegation and election would have been familiar to the barons from arbitrations in legal disputes as well as from the constitutional arrangements of city-states in Mediterranean Europe. Indeed the barons intended England to be governed henceforward rather like a city-state with an elected council, officials answerable to the commune, and regular public meetings. 'It is said that the best ordered state [civitas]', the barons wrote in their defence (recalling Plato's republic), 'is one in which each person puts aside his own interests and this is proved most conspicuously today in the reformation and ordering of our kingdom'.[12]

The latter half of the Provisions of Oxford consists of a list of proposed reforms starting with the church, going on to the control of public officials (justiciar, treasurer and chancellor are to be appointed for a year at a time) and concluding with arrangements for parliaments and the powers of the council of fifteen. This is one of the earliest references to 'parliament' by that name (*parlemenz* in French); what it meant is 'discussion'. Parliament is to be held with automatic regularity at Michaelmas, Candlemas and Midsummer each year. It is not intended to be a large body, as it consists of the council of fifteen together with twelve reliable men elected by the commune. This provision narrowed down the number of representatives who had customarily agreed to taxation. Nevertheless this may not have been intended as an aristocratic measure excluding the commons who might support the king, but as a practical method of limiting regular parliaments to those who were willing and able to attend.

Taken together, the Provisions of Oxford reduced the authority of the king of England to that of a figurehead, directed by the council, which was answerable to the commune. Although such a change was comparable with the way royal power had been reduced in the kingdom of Jerusalem and by the princes and city-states in the Empire, no other kingdom in Europe had gone so far towards a republican constitution. Furthermore the commune in some form was intended to be a permanent part of the constitution. Henry III's incompetence had been the occasion of putting the king in the rebels' power, but the barons of 1258 did not claim (as those against King John had done) that once their grievances were settled the king's power should be restored. On the contrary, in a letter to the pope in August 1258 the ordinance of the barons is described as 'most fruitful to us *and to our heirs*', and in the case put to Louis IX in 1264 the barons explain that castles were to be held by their nominees for a period of twelve years so that their provisions and ordinances 'could pass into law'.[13]

The rebels had a well thought out and long-term plan. They proposed such far-reaching changes because they knew that nothing less would prove adequate. An elected justiciar and chancellor had been demanded without effect for twenty years or more. The king had decades of experience of escaping attempts to control his actions, and one or two of the barons could probably remember how King John had repudiated Magna Carta. The Provisions of Oxford were so elaborately devised in order that not even Henry III could slip out of them. He was to be tied down by the council of fifteen, by the public officials at the centre and in the localities, and by the automatic meetings of parliament.

Henry III's recovery

The councillors, Henry complained, 'strive day in and day out to limit and diminish the king's status against his will, although no advantage comes to anyone from this'.[14] He considered it his duty to release himself from these constraints and he vigorously argued his case. Like any head of a medieval family, Henry was obliged to hand on as much of his inheritance as he could to his children. The outlook was bleak in 1258 but, as at the time of the minority, the king had long-term advantages. The force of inertia would favour his servants and established routines. He could expect the backing of the pope because of the 'Sicilian business'. Most importantly Henry was successful in winning the support of Louis IX. Whereas at the time of the minority the French had intervened on the side of the rebels, Henry succeeded – at the heavy price of surrendering his claims in France north of the Loire and in Poitou (the peace of Paris of 1259) – not only in avoiding a French invasion but ultimately in getting Louis to condemn the rebels. By making concessions in France Henry restored his position in England and thus moved one step further towards the formation of a national monarchy, although that had not been his intention.

Henry broke the rebels' unity in the first instance by absenting himself from England. He was in France from November 1259 to April 1260. The communal government could function to a certain extent in his absence, but the idea of controlling the king himself through the council of fifteen foundered. Henry's tactics are best illustrated by a letter he sent the baronial justiciar, Hugh Bigod, in January 1260. The king explained that he had hoped to return to England immediately after Christmas but Louis was pressing him to stay on because of both a marriage and a funeral. Furthermore delicate negotiations were still in progress about Henry's overseas possessions. In addition to these reasons, Henry used the threat of a Welsh invasion to tell Bigod not to waste time with a parliament but to proceed immediately against the Welsh. The point about parliament is then repeated:

Make no arrangements for a parliament and permit none to be held
before our arrival in England. When we return, we shall arrange to
hold a parliament with your advice and that of the magnates, as will
seem best for us and for our realm.[15]

Henry concludes by telling Bigod that he is proceeding 'by easy stages'
from Paris and that he will await a reply on the French coast.

In this letter Henry seems to have been testing the resolve of his
opponents. Parliament was due to assemble on 2 February in accordance with the provision that it should be held regularly at Candlemas.
Henry's excuse for postponing it (his absence in France and the threat
from the Welsh) could equally well be seen as compelling reasons for
holding it. The commune had been formed so that the magnates could
look after themselves in such emergencies. Moreover the phrase 'as
will seem best for us and for our realm' might be interpreted to mean
that Henry should be the judge of when parliaments were to be held.
Meanwhile he waited in France to see how Bigod would react. Bigod's
submission is best described in the reported words of Simon de
Montfort:

In the common provision made by the king and his council it is provided that three parliaments shall be held every year, of which one is
at Candlemas, and so the earl [Simon de Montfort] – to keep his oath
– came there, along with the honourable men of the council who were
in England, and there in the morning the justiciar came and told them
from the king that they should hold no parliament until the king
came.[16]

This statement emphasizes the clarity of Simon's position: he intended
to stand by his oath whatever the circumstances. He appreciated the
political consequences of compromise. Regular parliaments were an
essential part of the communal constitution. If the least concession
were made to the king, he would take advantage of it. Henry was (as
Matthew Paris had noted in 1258) like Proteus, the classical Houdini,
who needed only one loose knot to escape. Bigod on the other hand
had presumably been impressed by Henry's sense of authority and by
the apparent reasonableness of his requests. Henry's tactics had succeeded in destroying the unity of the barons.

By slow and painful stages from February 1260 onwards Henry
recovered his authority. In doing so he divided his kingdom into

partisans of monarchy and opponents until, as a consequence of Louis IX's Mise of Amiens in 1264, open war was declared. Henry concentrated on winning over international opinion, which was a task that suited him. His first public triumph came in 1261 when, through the diplomacy of John Mansel, Pope Alexander IV absolved the king from his oath to the commune. The pope alleged that the oath had been made under pressure and furthermore a religious oath should not be used to uphold 'depravity and perfidy'.[17] He argued, in other words, that the commune as such was an act of treason: a celestial ordinance placed princes, who are lords of laws, above others and they should not be repressed by their subjects. Such statements from the pope were to be expected, both because of Henry's alliance with the papacy and because it was the most monarchical institution in Europe. Even so, this unequivocal invalidation of the communal oaths was of value to Henry as it justified his stand in international law. The hazard of any papal pronouncement, however, was that a new pope might declare its opposite with equal forthrightness on another occasion. This had happened with Magna Carta and, if one chronicler is to be believed, it now happened again. Alexander's successor, Urban IV, in 1262 allegedly ordered the Provisions of Oxford to be observed. But no such letter from Urban is extant, whereas Urban's bull supporting Henry can still be seen in the royal archives.

Monarchy versus community

Henry's greatest vindication was Louis IX's Mise of Amiens. Both sides, including Simon de Montfort, had sworn to accept Louis's arbitration and be bound by whatever he ordained. Before his court at Amiens the English monarchy was therefore put on trial. Evidence was given by groups and individuals on both sides and their summarized claims survive. Henry's case, which was presented by his chancellor Walter of Merton (the founder of Merton College, Oxford), concentrated on the way councillors and officials had been elected against the king's will; his subjects had betrayed their oath of fealty; the king asked for a fine from the barons of £300,000 and also claimed damages of 200,000 marks. The barons' case was presented by Thomas Cantilupe (venerated after his death as a saint), a canon lawyer and recent chancellor of Oxford university. It rehearsed the main points in the Provisions of Oxford and emphasized that the king had sworn to observe them; it therefore concluded that 'this provision and ordinance is holy and honest and is made for the king's honour and the common benefit of his kingdom'.[18]

Louis's judgement was uncompromising in its support of the king. It reads as if he had never listened to the barons' case, although he claimed to have fully understood the arguments and counter-arguments of each party. He blamed the rebels for everything that had gone wrong in England since 1258 and then declared all the barons' provisions invalid in the name of the Father and of the Son and of the Holy Spirit, as if he were a priest putting a curse on them. Furthermore he ordered that Henry should have 'complete power and free authority in his kingdom' and that everything should be restored to the state it was in before 1258.[19] The only concession made to the barons was that Louis did not uphold Henry's claims for a fine and damages; instead Henry was to give them a full pardon.

Louis had a reputation as a peacemaker but his judgement started a war. Even the royalist chronicler Wykes thought that Louis had acted with less wisdom and foresight than was necessary. Why did he support Henry so uncompromisingly? Answers can only be speculative, as Louis's reasons are not on record. The barons cannot have thought him to be such an absolute monarchist, otherwise they would not have agreed to the arbitration, although they were being pressed so hard by the royalists that their options were limited. A possible explanation for Louis's conduct is that he only learned the full implications of the barons' commune of England as a consequence of the hearing at Amiens. He might have got the impression from the numerous individual disputes leading up to the arbitration that he was being asked to settle wrangles of a familiar sort about property and offended honour. Not perhaps until the masters from Oxford appeared on the scene to argue the case for each side did Louis realize that monarchy itself was on trial and that Henry faced not a revolt but a revolution. At that point Louis took fright and added his total condemnation of insubordination to the pope's.

The Mise of Amiens had a paradoxical effect. It united the forces against the monarchy and brought about their victory at the battle of Lewes but it also deprived them of legitimacy. After his victory Simon de Montfort could no longer govern in accordance with the Provisions of Oxford because he had insufficient support. Instead a new constitution was devised consisting of three wise men (Simon de Montfort, Gilbert de Clare, Stephen bishop of Chichester) who nominated a council of nine. All this was done in the king's name, as he was Simon's prisoner; the new constitution was uncompromisingly monarchist and authoritarian. The demands of war had narrowed the 'commune of England' down to the 'community of prelates and barons', who might be consulted in certain circumstances.[20] Although the battle of Lewes brought about a narrow dictatorship in the king's name, it nevertheless briefly symbolized in wider estimation a triumph of the community over the monarchy. Or at least that is how it was interpreted in chronicles sympathetic to the barons and also in the *Song of Lewes*.

The song, a long and sophisticated Latin poem, expressed the feelings of Simon's partisans who are identified with the people of England. His steadfastness is contrasted with the duplicity of the Lord Edward, who had supported the rebels for a while. The latter half of the song states the arguments for each side, as in a scholastic disputation, or as in the pleadings before Louis IX at Amiens. A significant point is the difficulty the author has in rebutting the royalist arguments, which are stated concisely and fairly: the king wishes to be free and to appoint whomsoever he chooses; the command of the prince has the force of law and the barons of England are not to interfere; every freeman in the country has the right to manage his own affairs, why should the king be more servile than they? This question was difficult to answer because the rebel barons were not democrats; they had no intention of allowing all freemen – still less serfs – to elect the stewards of their estates and to manage them for the common good. Like the sorcerers' apprentice and many other rebels, Simon had released forces which he could not control. The commune of England, which he and his fellow magnates in 1258 had envisaged as an aristocratic body, had enlarged into something approaching a community of the people, or at least an association of the lesser knights and burgesses. The *Song of Lewes* voices these wider feelings:

> If one person chooses, he is easily mistaken, as he does not know who will be useful. Therefore the community of the realm [*communitas regni*] should advise and let it be known what everyone [*universitas*] feels, for their own laws are most familiar to them. Nor are all the people of a country such fools as not to know more than others about the customs of the realm which have been passed down from father to son.[21]

Simon's dilemma was that by the time he had triumphed at Lewes in
1264 partisan feelings had grown too fierce to build on this idealism.
Despite his summoning of knights and burgesses to parliament, his
government was as arbitrary as the king's, indeed it was the king's in
name and form. The Wheel of Fortune had turned full circle and
brought the king up to the top again.

The king and Westminster abbey

The king and the cause of monarchy would have triumphed even if
Simon had not been defeated and killed at Evesham in 1265 because
the seven-year struggle had exhausted the moral and physical resources
of the rebels. Henry had won by diplomacy and persistence. His
triumph at Evesham was hideously celebrated by the dismembering of
Simon's body. The head, arms and feet were cut off and he was castrated. The head was carried on a lance to Wigmore castle (about fifty
miles from Evesham) as a present for Roger de Mortimer's wife. The
Mortimers had once been Simon's supporters; the reason for Maud de
Mortimer's bitterness against Simon is unknown. One chronicler
explains Simon's castration as fitting retribution for his marrying
Eleanor, the king's sister, who had been vowed to chastity. The dishonourable treatment of Simon's body explains why Guy de Montfort,
who survived the battle and made a new career with Charles of Anjou
in Italy, killed Henry of Almain (Richard of Cornwall's heir) in
revenge in 1271. Ironically it was Simon's son and not Henry's whom
the 'Sicilian business' brought south. Guy de Montfort died as a
prisoner of the Aragonese in Sicily.

The image of Simon's severed head contrasts with the elegant scene
Henry enacted in 1269 when the body of Edward the Confessor was
translated to its new resting place in the choir of Westminster abbey.
Among the armorial shields carved in stone in the choir is that of
Simon de Montfort. Henry had at least not had that excised, even
though the remains of Simon's body had been denied honourable
burial. Henry himself made characteristic arrangements for his own
end in 1268. At the centre of the new choir in Westminster abbey was
placed a mosaic pavement. Its enigmatic inscription establishes Henry's
place in space and time. Here, the reader is told, he will find the end
of the *primum mobile*, the prime mover which encircles the universe:

'King Henry III, the city, Ordoricus and the abbot have set here these stones of porphyry.'[22] The city referred to is Rome, Ordoricus is the Roman artist who made the pavement, the abbot is Richard of Westminster, and the stones of porphyry symbolize Henry's impending death and his high status, for emperors were buried in sarcophagi of porphyry. The date is given in the curious form $1000 + 200 + 12 + 60$ (= 1272) $- 4$ (= 1268). Henry died in 1272. By backdating the year to 1268, the designers of the inscription gave the impression that Henry had had foreknowledge of his own death. His special place in time and space was established by this mystery and also by the remarkable disc of porphyry, at the centre of the mosaic, whose fiery, swirling lines seem to evoke the act of creation itself.

All this was an ambitious assessment by Henry of his own importance, but it is consistent with his own grandiose ideas. Moreover he had come through such vicissitudes since his accession in 1216 that he had reason to think that divine providence favoured him. Unlike King John he died at the height of his power and the monastic obituary writers therefore treated him kindly. Because of his ultimate success he was identified with the sharp-sighted lynx in the prophecies of Merlin. Thus the St Albans chronicler summed Henry up:

He was strong and vigorous but precipitous in his actions; but because he brought them to lucky and happy outcomes, many thought him to be the one designated by Merlin as the lynx penetrating all.[23]

The prophecies of Merlin, which had been circulated by Geoffrey of Monmouth in the 1130s along with his *History of the Kings of Britain*, were one of the most popular works of the Middle Ages. They evoked a mythological world of dragons, giants and other ominous creatures whose struggles unlocked the future, provided a key could be found to interpret them. Similarly Henry had had set into his mosaic pavement at Westminster a list of creatures (stag, raven, eagle, sea serpent and others) from the multiple of whose ages the end of the *primum mobile* could be computed. Like Geoffrey of Monmouth he put his own and his kingdom's destiny in a wide frame. His dreams of grandeur seem to have shielded him from a sense of failure and furthermore he had given them reality in Westminster abbey and his other buildings.

Henry III created the impressive theatricality of the monarchy which has lasted until the present day. Fantastic as his sense of destiny was, it gave him an imaginative grasp of England's past. By naming his first-born son Edward and making the shrine of Edward the Confessor the focal point of Westminster abbey, he acknowledged the Anglo-Saxon roots of royal authority. On the other hand the Poitevin favourites and the Sicilian business emphasized equally the foreignness of his family and household. In these contradictions Henry personified the diversity of England's experience since the Norman Conquest. At Westminster with its great hall, palace and abbey the monarchy stood at the centre of a strife-torn but resilient community.

14

Lordship and the Structure
of Society

Lordship was the most enduring and characteristic feature of medieval society. The baronial hall with its high table and heraldic banners, the butler and valets on bended knee offering gilded dishes to the lord and lady, the knights and gentlemen in attendance, the big dogs asleep on the floor: this was once a reality, though all that now survives are ruined castles and empty halls like those from the thirteenth century at Winchester, Oakham and Stokesay castle. 'You yourself should be seated at all times in the middle of the high table, so that your presence as lord or lady is made manifest to everyone.'[1] This is the advice attributed to Bishop Grosseteste which he gave the countess of Lincoln in the 1250s.

Lordship allowed for huge inequalities in social and economic circumstances, extending downwards from the 'lord king' and his court through knights and freemen to the mass of the peasantry. Although many peasant men were unfree, they too had 'lordly power' (*potestas dominica*, a Latin legal term) within the domestic sphere over their wives, children and animals. (In peasant longhouses the farm animals were kept at one end and the family lived at the other.) Women and domestics lived 'under the rod' (*sub virga*, another legal term) of the head of the household. Husbands were entitled – indeed were exhorted – to beat their wives, children and servants, though they must not kill them, as that brought them up against the lordship which the king had over everyone's 'life and members'. Only he and his officers should kill, blind, maim or castrate his enemies.

The ideology of lordship was realistic about power relations, and it legitimated them by creating a reciprocal system of dependence and obligation. 'The bond of trust in lordship must be mutual', Glanvill's lawbook insists, 'so that the lord owes as much to the man by his lordship as the man owes him.'[2] This ideal of reciprocity is exemplified in Langland's poem *Piers Plowman* (dating from the fourteenth century) where Piers makes an offer to an out-of-work knight: 'I shall sweat and sow for us both and labour for you all your life, trusting that you will protect us from wasters and wicked men, and from the boars and bucks that break down my hedges; make your falcons catch the wild fowl which come to my croft and despoil my corn.'[3] Langland has transformed the knight's recreations of hawking and hunting into useful agricultural skills. Judging from the number of robberies (the thirteenth century is when Robin Hood first emerges), peasant farmers did indeed need protection from 'wasters and wicked men'. Ideally the knights, together with the king who was their lord, kept everyone safe and the people reciprocated by paying taxes and doing labour services.

Lordship allowed law and custom, which had developed over time, to mitigate the savagery of relationships which in reality depended on brute force. It invested the knight with moral and social stature: his sword was blessed by Holy Church and the harshness of his armour was softened by the heraldic surcoat stitched by his lady. Clerics and lawyers recognized that law and order was man-made. Because of Adam's sin, there could be neither peace nor natural equality on earth. Furthermore, as Eve had succumbed to temptation before Adam, the female sex was particularly weak. 'God is no respecter of persons, but men are' is the stark explanation which Bracton's lawbook (dating principally from the 1220s) gives for the existence of a hierarchical law of persons.[4] Lordship meant that everyone had a superior, though there was fierce debate (in the light of Magna Carta and the Provisions of Oxford) as to whether the king himself was subject to any earthly constraint. As lordships proliferated, the law concerning them became increasingly complex, but in theory at least it was possible to invoke rules of precedence. In cases of inheritance, for example, Bracton explains that, where there are many 'chief lords' on both the father's and the mother's side, there will nevertheless be one who is 'the first feudatory and liege lord' of the claimant.[5]

The hierarchy of lords should have been all-embracing, including clerics as much as laymen and the poor as well as the rich. Jews were excluded, but this exception proves the rule, as all 'our Jews' were under the king's capricious protection. 'If we have given our peace to a dog, it ought to be inviolably observed', King John wrote in defence of them.[6] In reality, however, the king's peace was far from being inviolably observed, as there was an underclass of vagrants and outlaws who were treated no better than dogs. Outlaws 'bear the wolf's head' (in Bracton's words): they carry their judgement with them and might be killed on sight.[7] Wolves were getting rarer in thirteenth-century England, whereas contemporaries believed that outlaws were increasing. Whether 'wasters and wicked men' (in Piers Plowman's words) had fallen out of lordship through sinfulness or adverse economic circumstances has been much debated. Possibly by 1300 the population had increased to unsustainable levels, causing famine, disease and crime.

Lordship would persist as a social system as long as monetization and commercialization remained relatively restricted. Appropriately enough it was in towns, with their markets and industries, that traditional structures were least evident. Townsmen formed communes and guilds whose officers were elected, instead of accepting the hierarchical bond of lord and tenant. In the countryside, where money transactions were less common and social conditions less volatile, there were obvious advantages for landlords in receiving rents in the form of services (ploughing, carting and harvesting for example) and rewarding serfs with food and beer rather than money. When a tenant died, the landlord might seize his best animals, the contents of his larder and even his cooking pots. As long as lords depended on payments in kind they had to move from place to place to receive them. Bishop Grosseteste advised the countess of Lincoln to plan her itinerary a year in advance, once she had learned from her bailiffs and gamekeepers in the autumn about the corn harvest on her various manors and the availability of meat.

The surplus from the manors was intended to pay in cash for the luxuries which the thirteenth-century aristocracy could not do without: 'your wine, your wax and your wardrobe' in Grosseteste's words.[8] By 'wine' he meant French wines, probably from Bordeaux, as English production had ceased by 1250. 'Wax' meant beeswax for candles, together with smaller amounts for making polishes, sealing-wax and writing-tablets. (Poorer people had foul-smelling candles of animal fat, if they had light at all.) By 'your wardrobe' Grosseteste meant clothing of all sorts (dresses, belts, shoes, pins, jewellery), together with other precious small things such as medicines. He advised the countess to buy these luxuries at the annual fairs at Boston, St Ives near Huntingdon, Bristol and Winchester. Strangely he did not mention London, which was already the main centre for shopping.

At the aristocratic level (meaning some 200 households, cleric and lay, out of a population of four million or more) the money economy was certainly advancing. For example, the accounts of the bishops of Winchester (which had been started by Peter des Roches in 1208) are so detailed that it is possible to see the cost of shoeing horses, repairing ploughs, purchasing rope, buying locks for a barn, making a dovecote, digging the garden, fetching wine from Southampton, and thousands of other transactions. However, although these items were accounted for in shillings and pence, the transactions themselves may not all have been done in money, as the smallest coin in circulation was the silver penny, which was inconveniently high in value.

Payments in kind are mixed in with money payments even at the exalted level of debts due to the king. In 1205 the earl of Warwick died and King John took his widow and children into his guardianship as he was entitled to do. To avoid the arbitrary consequences of the king's lordship, the countess undertook to pay him £1000 and ten palfreys (palfreys were the finest trotting horses, particularly suited to ladies riding side-saddle). The countess did indeed part with some of her palfreys, but most of them were accounted for at the Exchequer as money payments. The commutation of payments in kind into money facilitated a market economy, even though converting services into commercial transactions undermined the personal nature of lordship. In *The Commercialization of English Society* Richard Britnell notes that the meaning of the word *feodum* – 'fief' – changes over the thirteenth century: before 1200 it implied a grant of land, whereas by the 1280s it had come to describe the annual salary or 'fee' paid by a lord to one of his officers.

Personal display

The *Book of Fees*, which records services due to the crown in 1250, is a mixture of the archaic and the modern: the tenant of Hemingstone in Suffolk was obliged on Christmas Day each year to do a leap, a whistle and a fart before the king; likewise on Christmas Day the tenant of Kingston Russell in Dorset had to count the king's chessmen and put them back in the box when the king finished the game. These services emphasize the capricious and arbitrary side of lordship, which makes it so different – in theory at least – from modern employment law. Through his oath of homage (*homagium* in Latin) the tenant became the lord's 'man' (*homo*) for better or worse. If the lord king chose to ridicule his man in the course of the Christmas festivities, the latter had to accept this, though he should refuse to do anything dishonourable. Bracton's lawbook insists that homage must be done in person and in public. While placing his hands between those of his lord, the man swears: 'Hear this, O lord, I become your man for the tenement which I hold of you and I will bear you fidelity in life and limb, in body and goods and earthly honour. So help me God.'[9] The lord then kisses his new man. A serf similarly takes an oath of fidelity to his lord, but he does not swear homage ('I become your man'), nor does he undertake to defend his lord's honour; instead the serf swears to be 'justiciable', meaning that he and his family are subject to the lord's manorial court.

The oath of homage, with its emphasis on fidelity and service, has a model in the relationship between God and mankind enshrined in the Psalter, which was the prayer-book that everyone knew. King David repeatedly calls on his lord, as in these examples taken at random: 'I will extol thee, O Lord, for thou has lifted me up'; 'In thee, O Lord, do I put my trust'; 'Plead my cause, O Lord, with them that strive with me, fight against them that fight against me'; 'O Lord, rebuke me not in thy wrath'.[10] The obligations created by homage were crucial in the strife and civil war of 1258–68. Henry III complained that the rebel barons had deprived him of his honour and dignity, contrary to their oath of homage. On the baronial side it was the oath of homage which justified Richard de Vernon in pleading that he was not a common criminal but a lawful knight who 'in time of war had stood with his lord Robert de Ferrers, earl of Derby, from whom he held his land and to whom he had done homage'.[11] Robert forfeited his earldom, as he had betrayed his homage to the king by joining the rebels, whereas Richard was acquitted of wrongdoing because he had been loyal to his lord.

The concept of 'earthly honour' (as distinct from the service due to God) is included in the aristocratic oath of homage because it encapsulates the lord's feelings about his status. When Henry III complained

that he had been deprived of his honour and dignity, he meant that
he felt humiliated by having his friends and kinsmen removed from
him. To dishonour the king incurred exemplary and public revenge.
In 1242 William de Marisco, who had allegedly attempted to kill the
king, was dragged at a horse's tail to the gallows and cut in pieces.
To drag a knight in his shift along the ground by his feet (a drawing
of this was done by Matthew Paris) was to reverse his status
as an armoured man on horseback. The dismembering of Simon de
Montfort's body at the battle of Evesham served a similar function of
avenging the king's honour. In Henry III's eyes Simon had doubly
betrayed him, as he had married his sister as well as doing homage to
him for the earldom of Leicester.

On the great seal of Henry's last years he is depicted as a magnifi-
cently armoured knight with his sword raised to strike down wrong-
doers. By this time he was over sixty years of age and little use in fact
as a knight, even though he did have two horses killed under him at
the battle of Lewes in 1264. (Henry had had good training in knighthood as a boy, as his tutors were William the Marshal and Peter des
Roches.) The king had also been obliged to fight at the battle of
Evesham a year later, where his identity was mistaken so that he had
to shout out: 'I am Henry of Winchester, your king, do not kill me.'[12]
The old king's participation in the battles of Lewes and Evesham
emphasizes the savagely personal and public nature of lordship. The
lord must be with his men, even though no older man was a physical
match for experienced younger knights. Battles involved feats of horse-
manship along with wearing heavy armour (particularly the helmet)
and wielding massive weapons. Henry III received numerous blows
from swords and maces at Lewes, and survived only because his bodyguard protected him.

At Evesham in 1265 it was Simon de Montfort, now aged fifty-
seven, who was physically overwhelmed. On the morning of the battle
he advised the justiciar Hugh Despenser to remember his age and go
home. Hugh replied, as if he were a hero in one of the *chansons de geste*:
'Sir, let it be. Today we shall drink from one cup, just as we have in
the past.'[13] (This was probably meant literally, as drinking from the
same cup was a way of sealing bonds of friendship.) On Henry III's
side too the senior judges rode into battle with the king. At Lewes the
justiciar Philip Basset refused to surrender and received more than
twenty wounds, and the judge William of Wilton was killed. There

could be no retiring age for lords and little opportunity for hiding themselves behind closed doors, unless they were clerics.

Honour had to be made manifest and lived up to every day. You get honour in the presence of your people, Bishop Grosseteste insisted, by showing yourself daily in your hall with your knights and gentlemen dressed in your livery. The almost liturgical ceremonies of eating in hall described by Grosseteste were reinforced by the furnishings and fabrics using heraldic motifs to display the lord's rank and family connections. In the choir of Henry III's Westminster abbey the coats of arms of his barons are sculpted, as if this too were a baronial hall with shields hanging from the walls. Matthew Paris made one of the earliest inventories of coats of arms and their owners in 1250, and he frequently used the symbolism of heraldry to reinforce the narrative in his chronicle. For example, alongside his drawing of William de Marisco being dragged to the gallows, Matthew showed his heraldic shield split in half and reversed and his shattered banner descending to perdition.

Once coats of arms were designated to particular families, as they had been by 1250 or earlier, they were used on seals and finger-rings, horse trappings and dog collars, ladies' gowns and jewellery, on the liveries of retainers – anywhere where an identifying badge was colourful and useful. Heraldry very successfully designated lordship and distinctions in social class. The heraldic seals of knights show their honourable lineage as well as projecting messages of vigour and authority, as they charge on their warhorses or look as brave as lions, whereas the seals of peasants and merchants are generally smaller in size and use modest floral devices or signs of their trade, a brew-tub for a brewer for example.

An innovation in the thirteenth century are the life-size effigies in churches of knights in armour; sometimes they are shown actually drawing their swords. The effigy of William the Marshal (who died in 1219) in the Temple Church in London is so lifelike that Matthew Paris describes the bishop of Ferns addressing this effigy, as one living person to another, and cursing the Marshal for his robberies in Ireland. At the end of the century the Lincolnshire cleric Robert Manning damned lords 'lying high on their graves' for their pride.[14] A justification for wearing armour in churches is provided by a vision which Ela countess of Salisbury had when she saw her son, who died on St Louis's crusade in 1250, being carried up to heaven fully armed from the battlefield. Ela's husband, William Longespee (who had died in 1226), has

a magnificent effigy in Salisbury cathedral which she may have commissioned. In addition to the life-size heraldic shield on this effigy,
William's helmet and banner would once have hung over the tomb.
The combination of tomb chest, effigy and heraldic accoutrements
made knights' tombs into something approaching shrines.

Women and lordship

The shrine of a lady had existed at Godstow abbey to commemorate
Fair Rosamond, Henry II's lover. When Hugh of Lincoln made an
episcopal visitation in 1191 shortly after the king's death, he noticed the
candlelit tomb with its silk coverings in front of the high altar. The nuns
explained that they honoured Rosamond as a benefactor, but Hugh
insisted that she was a harlot who must be reburied outside the abbey
church. A woman's status depended on that of her lord; once Henry II
was dead, Rosamond was rejected. By contrast, Eleanor of Aquitaine
has a life-size effigy at the abbey of Fontevraud along with the matching
effigies of Henry II and Richard I. She is shown crowned as queen but,
instead of a sceptre or sword as a symbol of lordship, she holds an open
prayer-book to indicate that she is on her way from earthly to heavenly
honour. By 1280 memorials of aristocratic ladies had become more
common; most notable is the bronze effigy in Westminster abbey of
Edward I's queen, Eleanor of Castile. Edward I also honoured his father,
Henry III, with an effigy, but not his mother, Eleanor of Provence. Of
its nature the exercise of lordship was capricious and wilful, and women
of all ranks might be its beneficiaries or casualties.

The same woman at different stages of her life cycle could find
herself playing very different roles. Eleanor of Aquitaine was the sole
heiress of the duke of Aquitaine as a girl, then queen of France, then
(after her divorce from Louis VII) her marriage to his rival Henry II
made her queen of England. As Henry II's viceroy, she occasionally
exercised great power until she was put under house arrest by him in
1173. Following his death in 1189 she recovered her political role
through her influence over her sons, Richard I and King John, and
she died in dignity at Fontevraud in 1204 at the age of eighty or more.
Women at all social levels might exercise lordship and power, provided
it was done by delegation from the men who were their lawful superiors. Eleanor of Aquitaine, during the periods when she had Henry II's

trust, had the power to make war and administer justice. Hence homage could be done *to* a lady who headed a lordship. According to Glanvill, however, homage could not be done *by* a lady (because it involved bodily service), though women did generally take oaths of fidelity to their lords.

The most formidable women were the widows who succeeded in not being compulsorily remarried by their overlords. The church taught that it was wrong for widows to remarry, and this gave them room for negotiation. Magna Carta conceded that widows must be allowed to choose to live without a husband, but equally they could not remarry without the consent of their overlord. At the aristocratic level a remarkable widow is Nichola de la Haye, who outlived two husbands and was appointed castellan and sheriff of Lincolnshire by King John in 1216. The king was in desperate straits after Magna Carta and Lincoln was of strategic importance as it guarded access to the north. She remained castellan after John's death and successfully defended Lincoln castle against the French in 1217. Even more remarkable was Nichola's ability to hold on to her position when it was challenged in the years 1217–26. Yet she was not unique in acting as a sheriff nor in being a castellan, as women were expected to take up the role of their husband in emergencies.

Over a decade of power Nichola proved herself 'neither less attractive nor less capable than a man as a lord' in building a retinue of knights and clerics and rewarding them with property.[15] Other great ladies in Henry III's reign who exercised lordship are Hawise de Quincy, heiress of Ranulf earl of Chester, Margaret de Quincy, countess of Winchester, and Margaret de Lacy, countess of Lincoln. A memorable image of a lordly lady gazes out from the seal of Joanna de Stuteville, the widow of Hugh Bigod who died in 1266. She is shown riding a palfrey side-saddle, so that she faces the viewer, and she holds up a shield displaying the heraldic arms of the Stuteville family. This is as far as representation could go in giving a woman the knightly symbols of a fine horse and arms and armour. In displaying the Stuteville arms, Joanna was emphasizing that her own family lineage was more important to her than her marriages. She may also have wished in 1266 to distance herself from the memory of Hugh Bigod, who had been the rebel barons' justiciar in 1258.

Despite being subordinated to men – indeed because they were totally under their lordship – women at all social levels had well-defined legal rights. This was required by the male members of their families, who had no wish to see the suitors of their daughters, sisters or mothers defrauding the family of property or dishonouring their women. Consequently husbands were obliged on marriage to endow their wives in public 'at the church door' with one-third of their property for the maintenance of the wife and children. Conversely, if the wife were an heiress (which was the most desirable sort of wife), the husband had control of her inheritance as her lord during their joint lives; this included the woman's moveables, her clothes and jewellery for example, as well as her land. On becoming a widow, she was allowed forty days in the family house before removing to a dower house.

Many widows had to litigate in the king's court or in manorial courts for portions of their dowries which might come from different properties. In some parts of England peasant widows were entitled to hold on to all of the property instead of one-third of it. This arrangement might be advantageous to the lord if the dowager paid a new entry fine, but not to the inheritors who had to labour for their mother. In 1252 the widowed countess of Arundel complained to the king: 'Where are the liberties of England which have been written down so often?'[16] Women did indeed have rights which were protected by Magna Carta as well as by customary law. How successfully they defended them against their lords is difficult to assess. In the countess of Arundel's case she ultimately got the property she demanded. For women below the aristocratic class documentation is sparse. Court rolls from manors and villages do not become abundant until after 1300 and they all concern ecclesiastical lords.

All lords – and not just husbands and fathers – supervised women's sexual conduct. Practical considerations about the inheritance of property by unwanted children were involved here as well as patriarchal prejudices. In 1290 at Brightwalton it was declared that 'the custom of the manor is that if a widow is apprehended in adultery, the land which she holds is forfeit to the lord'.[17] Furthermore, the widow in this case was also prosecuted for paying a fine to the ecclesiastical court 'from the lord's goods'. The theory here was that any money she possessed was forfeit to the lord and hence she had wrongfully alienated her lord's goods by paying this fine. This widow, Ellen the wife of Walter the Hayward, was probably of servile status, in which case her property was held at the will of her lord anyway. Whether Ellen, who may still have been young when her husband died, was duly reduced to destitution by her lord, the abbot of Battle, is unknown. This may have been what the aggrieved wife and the village wanted.

Likewise in 1290 the abbot of Crowland's court dealt more generously with a girl, Cecily daughter of Reginald and Maud Saleman, who was accused of having sex outside marriage (*leyrwite* in legal terms). Her suitor, Henry, came forward and agreed that he and Cecily would serve her mother Maud for life; in return she would keep them in food and clothing and give them an acre of land which they were to sow at their own expense. In addition, Henry's father pledged to give them forty shillings. This is in fact a marriage agreement recorded on the court roll for security. In return for this settlement, Cecily's fine for *leyrwite* was converted into a licence to marry, for which the families paid the lord six shillings. Cecily and Henry, with their single acre of land and forty shillings of promised capital, were serfs who stood close to the bottom of respectable peasant society (beneath them was an underclass of the destitute). They were obliged by the abbot of Crowland's court to pay the lord's fines, but for this they won the security of a legally binding agreement with their own parents. At its best, lordship was a reciprocal system which worked to everyone's advantage. At its worst, it constructed wilfulness into a system and justified the exploitation of the vulnerable at all levels of society.

Lords, freemen and serfs

Serfs were despised as the descendants of slaves. For example, a manorial court in 1275 ruled that a free woman who left the village and married a free man elsewhere could return and claim her land at any time, but if she had 'coupled with a serf' she might not return until he died.[18] The implication is that she would not be properly married to a serf, merely 'coupled' (*copulata*) like a cow. In fact such a woman would very probably have been duly married at the church door, as the church insisted on everybody making a Christian marriage and the lord's court reinforced this by fining women for fornication and by selling marriage licences.

A variety of Latin terms was used indiscriminately to describe serfs: *nativus* ('native'), *rusticus* ('rustic'), *servus* ('slave') and *villanus* ('villein'). The additional terms used by historians today, 'peasant' and 'serf', are post–medieval. This plethora of terminology indicates the complexities surrounding lordship over rural workers. Because these words were pejorative, they could be used as personal insults as well as legal terms. *Villanus* literally meant a 'villager', but it was also used to stigmatize a 'villain' in the modern sense of a scoundrel, as well as a 'villein' in the lawyer's sense of a tenant who was treated as unfree in the lord's court. *Nativus* had historical resonances, as the Norman conquerors had despised the rural population as rebellious 'natives'. The *Dialogue of the Exchequer* in the 1170s had equated being English with being of servile status. The king's court provided a writ for a lord to recover his 'native and fugitive'. The word *servus* was extraordinarily ambiguous, as it was used by Bracton in the Roman law sense of a 'slave' and also in the sense of a 'serf' who had some customary rights. In London in 1244 the king's justices declared that:

> Earls, barons and free tenants can lawfully put their rustics in copper but not in iron. It is lawful for them to sell their rustics like oxen or cows, but they cannot and must not kill, maim or wound them because the bodies and members of rustics are solely the lord king's.[19]

It is not known what sort of case occasioned this pronouncement. A lord was indeed entitled to sell a serf, though this was usually done along with his land. There were no slave markets selling people like cattle. The rule that the king had lordship over everyone's body was a crucial legal restriction on the violent enforcement of slavery, though it did not prevent seigniorial bailiffs intimidating rural workers and seizing their animals and goods.

The best protection a serf had was the customary law of the manor court where he held his land. Provided he or she paid the lord his dues, the serf had a title to his or her property which the court would uphold through a local jury. These dues could be large, particularly the fines on taking up the tenement and on marriage, as this was how the lord made his money. A serf could not appeal to the king's court to protect his property, but he was – in theory at least – personally protected from bodily harm. This was the compromise which had been worked out between the king's justices and local landlords through numerous cases in the two decades on either side of Magna Carta. Hence lords continued to have control over the land and its workers, while the king preserved his ancient jurisdiction over all freemen.

A serf might therefore be defined negatively as a person who could not sue for his property in the king's court. Did this matter? Not to the serf perhaps, as litigation was hazardous and expensive. On the other hand, the rule that a serf had no appeal against the wilfulness of his lord's court was an affront to the king's lordship. In 1250 Henry III ordered all sheriffs to examine how the magnates were treating their own men and to report any wrongdoing to him. ('Magnates' was the general term used for the 'great men', meaning the aristocracy.) However, as a consequence of the baronial rebellion of 1258, the crown could not continue with this policy. Furthermore, as national taxation grew more frequent and severe, the officers of the crown who seized livestock and stores – even of seed corn – became the most hated men in the countryside, as the Peasants' Revolt was to show in the fourteenth century.

Everyone was either a serf or a freeman, so freemen can be negatively defined as all those people who were not serfs. Freemen ranged from the two hundred or so aristocratic households (of the earls, barons, bishops and abbots) through knights, gentry and townspeople down to men and women rural workers holding free tenements. All freemen had access to the king's courts, though generally only the rich could pursue property disputes employing lawyers at Westminster. Consequently the division between rich and poor might be more important to a rural worker than the distinction between free and unfree. Money enabled the better-off to prosecute litigation and intimidate their neighbours. Rural workers might be threatened by competing lords as much as by neighbours, as it was common for a village to have more than one manor. In 1267 a radical cleric, Peter of Pecham, wrote a parody of a charter granted by the devil in exchange for homage and service from the rich:

> Be it known to all at present and to come that I, the Prince of Greed, Pride and Envy, have given and granted to the rich, who form my retinue in chief, that they may do everything they can devise by force and deceit, by every sort of wrong and ransom, by seizures and by false pretences, by pledge and by tallage, by privilege and by outrage, or by anything else they can think of, to destroy the common people and to cause them damage and harm.[20]

One way of gauging the extent of class divisions is to see what people ate. At harvest time the lord induced everyone on the manor to work together by offering them free food and drink, which became a customary right recorded in the manorial court roll. At Sedgeford in Norfolk details begin in 1256 of what up to fifty workers were offered for the period of the harvest: wheat for making bread, oats for pottage, malt for ale, together with protein in the form of 1 pig, 20 fowl, 1050 herring (Sedgeford is close to the sea), 120 eggs and quantities of cheese and milk. Likewise in the autumn of each year the king held a feast to celebrate Edward the Confessor, his patron. In 1249 he ordered 18 swans, 18 wild boar, 30 peacocks, 24 roe deer, 14 bucks, 100 rabbits, 600 geese, 8000 chicks and 11,000 eggs. There would have been many more guests at this feast than at the harvest meals in Sedgeford. Nevertheless, the significant point is the difference in the type of diet, notably the exotic birds and game, which the king enjoyed in profusion because he was the lord of the forests and parks which occupied about a quarter of all the land. As head of a hunting band, the king embodied the oldest form of lordship known to man.

What proportion of the total population (an estimated four million or more by 1300) were freemen? Only informed guesses can be made, as there was no census in the thirteenth century. The eminent historian of English law F.W. Maitland concluded from the Hundred Rolls of the 1270s that 'no one can read them without coming to the conclusion that the greater half of the rural population is unfree'.[21] The classic Marxist view of the Russian academician E.A. Kosminsky was similarly that 'a large part of the population of England consisted of serfs bereft of all rights'.[22] On the other hand, Christopher Dyer now argues that 'free tenants accounted for the *majority* of the peasantry'.[23] He suggests that historians have been misled by the coercive language of manorial court rolls: 'Lords exaggerated their arbitrary power over their villeins.'[24] A statement despising 'rustics' like that of the king's justices in London in 1244 may be nostalgic bravado, as lords did not ordinarily have copper shackles and neither were there slave markets. In reality lords depended on their bailiffs in the villages, who had few incentives to make fundamental changes in the custom of the manor, which an incoming lord inherited along with his tenantry.

Rural workers might have greater rights enshrined in law in the custom of the manor than later generations of wage labourers had in the market economy of subsequent centuries. Judging from surviving records, the landlords who were most likely to increase rents and exploit peasants were the great monasteries. Monastic managers were in a better position than lay landlords to pursue consistent economic aims, as they were largely exempt from taxation and they were not subject to the vagaries of family inheritance. However rich they became, monks could make money with a clear conscience, as they were officially God's poor to whom Christian charity was due.

Lordship and management

Faced with inflation and fixed rents, ambitious landlords set up structures to increase the profitability of their estates through direct management. To prevent leases and grants of office becoming the property and hereditary right of their holders, estate officials were made more directly accountable to the lord by organizing them into hierarchies and differentiating their functions: steward, bailiff and reeve (the peasant supervisor of a farm or village) formed a chain of command; essential departmental heads on the estate were the plough-keeper, hayward, woodward, cowherd, swineherd, shepherd and dairy-maid. At frequent intervals all these functionaries had to account for their activities and those of their subordinates in writing. Record-making enabled managers to compare the productivity of one worker with another and to grasp the concepts of efficiency and profitability. Handbooks for lords, like the advice to the countess of Lincoln attributed to Bishop Grosseteste, show how management had become a science: some stewards and accountants may have received their training at an embryo business school in Oxford. A handbook from the 1260s is entitled 'How to manage and improve manors which are in the keeping of stewards and bailiffs'.[25] The lord is advised to ascertain from his account rolls each year which workers have made a profit and to dismiss all those who have made a loss. All these treatises assume that there is a surplus of competent labour to draw on and that improved profitability is the goal of the landlord.

Physical structures in the form of court houses and farm buildings were as important as administrative arrangements for exercising lordship effectively. Famous royal castles, such as the Tower of London and Windsor castle, are less typical as centres of lordship than the thousands of wooden buildings which no longer exist but which can be traced through archaeology. Often these modest manorial buildings stood on an earth mound or motte defended by a ditch. The hall, kitchen, bedchambers, wardrobe and service quarters consisted of separate buildings linked by corridors rather than being planned as a coherent whole. The greatest monuments to managerial lordship still standing are the 'tithe barns', dating mainly from the fourteenth century though there are a few earlier examples. The abbot of Beaulieu's barn at Great Coxwell, as big as a cathedral, still dominates the landscape of his manor of Faringdon. 'Tithe barn' is a misnomer for such a building. With their high arched doorways and partly paved floors, these barns were agricultural factories where the processing of grain and all sorts of other produce was done. They were also of course vast storehouses, which impressed upon the peasants the lord's monopoly of power as a farmer. From the 1220s letters survive to the bishop of Chichester from his steward, Simon of Senlis. He presents himself as the perfect professional:

> You should know, my lord, that I have bought for your use 12 acres of timber from the Chichester woods, selected from the better timber at my choice at 40 shillings an acre . . . The corn in all your manors in your bishopric is ripe and ready for harvesting; it is to be put in your barns provided the heavy rain holds off. Thanks be to God all your business proceeds prosperously in Sussex and I will labour with all my power to keep it that way. I am doing marling [extracting lime-rich fertilizer] at Selsey with two carts, as the very best marl is said to be found there. If you would like me to work with more carts, I advise you to purchase twelve draught horses per cart from Sir Godescal. To expedite matters, these can be bought here in Sussex with cash . . . The windmill at Watersfield is ready, it has been well made and it works.[26]

Simon was pleased with the windmill because windmills were a recent invention; possibly this was the first one on the Sussex Downs. Windmills took the lord's industrial power to the summits of hills to complement the watermills which already dominated the valleys. Simon's letters evoke a landscape of capitalist efficiency with fertile fields, teams of horses, busy mills, full barns and obedient peasants. There were also vexatious problems of course: difficult neighbours, a fugitive serf, a bigamous chaplain and wolves in Aldingbourne park.

The bishop of Chichester to whom Simon of Senlis was writing was Ralph Nevill, the king's chancellor, who in that capacity managed the biggest lordship of all. The title 'lord king' (*dominus rex*) was used from

Henry II's reign onwards, particularly with reference to the sovereignty implicit in the 'crown'. Hence criminal jurisdiction pertained (in the words of Glanvill's lawbook) to 'the crown of the lord king'.[27] The king was also a lord in the ordinary sense of being a landowner, particularly in the home counties west of London comprising the Anglo-Saxon kingdom of Wessex. Direct management of these manors was attempted in 1230s, but they were then returned to leasing. More important than arable lands were the numerous royal forests like the New Forest and Sherwood Forest, which provided the best timber and venison; gifts of oak trees and deer from the king were highly prized. Nevertheless, the bulk of the king's profits as a lord came not from lands but through the patronage he exercised over all the most important appointments in church and state. Appointments to benefices served both as a source of revenue and as a way of rewarding royal servants.

When in 1253 the clergy demanded that the English church should be free from royal interference as promised in Magna Carta, Henry III sardonically reminded the bishops that he had promoted them in the face of better-qualified candidates. He focused in particular on Boniface archbishop of Canterbury, who was the queen's uncle, Aymer bishop of Winchester, who was the king's half-brother, William bishop of Salisbury, who had been a royal justice, and Silvester bishop of Carlisle, 'who as a petty clerk among my clerks survived for a long time as a lick-spittle in the Chancery'.[28] The richest benefices nearly always went to royal appointees. The widow Sybil Giffard, who had responsibility for bringing up Henry III's children, probably never lived to see how four of her own children benefited from royal favour: Walter Giffard became bishop of Bath and Wells and then archbishop of York, Godfrey was bishop of Worcester, Juliana was abbess of Wilton and Mabel was abbess of Shaftesbury; these were the richest convents in England.

Scott Waugh has described the king's control over his lay barons' marriages and inheritances as 'The Lordship of England'. This was the power which allowed Henry III to intrude his wife's Savoyard relatives and his own Poitevin ones into the English nobility. Foreigners like Peter of Savoy and William de Valence were fiercely resented, but they proved useful and enduring. Waugh concludes that (despite Henry III's favourites) the king's lordship 'worked for social stability; it ensured the smooth descent of lands to proper heirs and reduced the opportunities for family quarrels'.[29] The system was effective because of its attention to detail through the interlocking procedures of the Chancery, the Exchequer and the local escheators who kept an eye on the births, marriages and deaths of tenants-in-chief in each county. This was the most elaborate and sustained application of management techniques to lordship anywhere in Europe. Paradoxically, these bureaucratic procedures ensured that the king's relationship with his barons remained a deeply personal one.

The king's lordship was unique because of its monopoly over crime and violence. Enforcing such a wide and general jurisdiction proved harder than controlling baronial marriages and inheritances, though there was money to be made from crime as all fines and confiscated property went to the crown. The statute of Winchester in 1285 declared that 'day by day robberies, homicides and arsons are more often committed than they used to be'.[30] In fact the judicial records, which go back to 1200, show that levels of crime had been remarkably high for a century at least. 'Unknown malefactors killed so-and-so in such-and-such a place, they immediately fled and it is not known who they were'.[31] Entries like this are frequent in the records. When it was unknown who the criminals were, they could not even be outlawed in their absence. Outlaws and vagrants, moving from village to village and county to county, were a constant threat. The real contest between Robin Hood (Robert Hod) and the sheriff of Nottingham (Eustace of Lowdham) probably took place in south Yorkshire between 1226 and 1234.

From sunset to sunrise during the summer months every village and town was meant to have at least four armed men keeping watch, and it was an offence to receive a stranger into one's house except in broad daylight. Prominent individuals might be caught, but banditry persisted. Following a notorious robbery in 'the pass of Alton' on the Southampton–London road in 1249, Henry III appealed in person to the jurors of Hampshire to bring in true verdicts. According to Matthew Paris he said: 'I am only one man, I will not and I cannot bear the burdens of the whole kingdom without the comfort of helpers.'[32] Bracton's lawbook puts this truism into more formal language:

> The lord king commands all his faithful people, in the faith by which they are bound to him and as they wish to save their possessions, to give him effective and diligent counsel and aid for the preservation of

his peace and justice and the suppression and extirpation of
wickedness.[33]

The bond of lordship had to depend on mutual trust and loyalty,
even at the exalted level of the king, because law and order could not
be established by force alone. Paradoxically, such great powers were
invested in the office of the 'lord king' that Henry III may well
have thought himself a failure. All 'wasters and wicked men' (in Piers
Plowman's words) were his responsibility, as the king must do justice
to everybody. The underclass of lordless vagrants, who fed into criminal gangs, probably got bigger during the thirteenth century if the
population increased beyond sustainability. Barbara Hanawalt has
shown how crime increased when the price of wheat went up in years
of dearth (this evidence comes from the first half of the fourteenth
century).[34]

Lordship had many different aspects, brutal and benign, and this
was its strength. The gallows on the hilltop was as characteristic of it
as the bishop of Chichester's windmill. In 1265 in the light of a summer
storm Simon de Montfort watched the earl of Gloucester's banner
moving up, marking the twelve knights who had been chosen to kill
him, alongside the river at Evesham. 'How skilfully they advance',
Simon was reported as saying, 'our bodies are theirs, our souls are
God's.'[35] Romance and reality merge in this contemporary account of
a lord displaying generosity and faith to the last.

EPILOGUE

15

Edward I (1272–1307)

As a king Edward I modelled himself on his father, Henry III, whom he admired and who had loved him very much. When they had briefly been on opposite sides in the civil war, Henry had not permitted himself to see his son, saying: 'If I were to see him, I could not restrain myself from kissing him.'[1] After Edward's victory over Simon de Montfort at Evesham in 1265, Henry had re-established his monarchy on such a secure footing that in 1270 Edward was able to leave England to fulfil his own and his father's crusading vows. The pull of the Jerusalem-centred world was as strong for him as it was for Richard I, though he had even less success there than Richard. Edward reached Acre in May 1271 and remained until September 1272. Acre was the crusaders' fall-back capital, which Richard I had established after Saladin's capture of Jerusalem in 1187. Edward started with high hopes and founded an English order of knights, the confraternity of St Edward at Acre; this turned out to be the most transitory of all the crusading orders. When Acre finally fell to the Moslems in 1291, exactly a century after Richard I had captured it, Edward could do nothing to protect it, a difference between Richard and Edward which commentators in England ruefully noted.

By 1291 Edward I was embroiled in difficulties at home which made returning to the crusade impossible, though that remained his ultimate aim. He died in 1307 not fighting for Jerusalem, as he might have wished, but at Burgh-on-Sands on England's border with Scotland. Since 1291 he had been trying, with intermittent success, to impose his rule on Scotland. In 1298 he had in effect taken over the Scottish monarchy and introduced direct rule, just as he had appropriated the principality of Wales in 1284. Divine providence, the statute of Wales declared, had given Edward complete ownership and the inhabitants had submitted themselves to his will. This was the doctrine that might is right, which had justified the Norman Conquest in 1066. Prince Llywelyn had been harried and killed and his brother Dafydd was captured and hanged, drawn and quartered. Edward had ringed the mountains of Snowdonia with the greatest series of castles in medieval Europe. He could surely do something comparable in Scotland and win a decisive battle there, just as Henry II had done at Alnwick in 1174. Edward was not pursuing an unreasonable or unprecedented objective; victory seemed just round the next corner. Viewed from Scotland, on the other hand, his rule looked ugly and unjust. He had humiliated King John Balliol, taken the Stone of Destiny and the other Scottish regalia to Westminster, and in 1305 William Wallace had been hanged as a traitor like Dafydd of Wales. Edward would not acknowledge that the Welsh and the Scots had legitimate aspirations as nations. They were simply subjects of his kingdom; resistance was treason and was punished accordingly.

Edward I became the victim of his own success. He had failed at Acre, it is true, but on his return to England in 1274 everything seemed to go well for him until the 1290s. He ran the government with fewer crises than Henry III had ever managed. His was an easier task perhaps. His father had had to restore royal authority after his long minority which followed on from Magna Carta, whereas Edward had the most effortless succession to the throne on record in the Middle Ages. He was in Italy when his father died in 1272 and Walter of Merton became Edward's chancellor. Walter symbolized the continuity of government, as he had been Henry III's chancellor and the advocate who had spoken for him at the Mise of Amiens. Walter 'remained at Westminster as in a public place', a chronicler explains, 'until the arrival of the prince'; this interim lasted more than 18 months.[2] Shortly before his death Henry III had exhibited the force of royal justice for the last time, when he made a two-week expedition to Norwich to quell a riot. According to the Bury St Edmunds chronicle, the king had tempered justice with mercy by having only 35 people executed, though thousands had been involved. Edward I claimed to have learned his ruthlessness from Henry III. 'I knew my father's justice very well', he told a Dominican friar, 'and he would have had a scoundrel's eyes torn out.'[3] In this spirit Edward had the bodies of the traitors Dafydd and

Wallace cut in pieces and distributed around the kingdom and he had treated Simon de Montfort's corpse in a similar way at Evesham.

Assessing the king's character

Edward I has proved harder to characterize than King John (bad but formidable) or Henry III (good but weak). We need ready-made characterizations like this in order to fit the rest of the jigsaw into place. Experts can then come forward and point out that John was not so bad, or Henry III was not so weak, and gradually a completer picture of the king builds up. For Edward I there is no such readily agreed characterization. Certainly he was physically formidable. He is described towering above his contemporaries and this was confirmed at the opening of his tomb in Westminster abbey in 1774, when he was found to measure 6 foot 2 inches. But was he good or bad? On his tomb is inscribed (though this may not have been done until the Tudor period): *Scottorum Malleus Hic Est* ('Here is the Hammer of the Scots') and *Pactum Serva* ('Keep Troth'). To a Scot these claims may well look contradictory: Edward did not live up to his motto of 'Keep Troth' with the Scots; following the treaty of Birgham in 1290, which had recognized the integrity of Scotland, he repeatedly deceived them. To an English supporter, on the other hand, being the 'Hammer of the Scots' demonstrates what 'Keep Troth' means; Edward demonstrated his loyalty to England by his ruthlessness towards criminals like Wallace. As Peter Langtoft (an Augustinian canon at Bridlington in Yorkshire) wrote in his chronicle: 'Wales has always been full of treason'; as for Wallace, his execution showed 'what reward belongs to traitor and thief'.[4]

Describing Edward I in terms of modern football rivalries (English fans v. Scottish fans), or in the harsher terms of the unfinished war in Ireland between loyalists and republicans, illustrates how he still rouses partisan emotions, like William the Conqueror or William of Orange. In 1952 Scottish nationalists broke into Westminster abbey and took the Stone of Destiny out of the coronation chair, which Edward I had had specially made for it in 1299, though it was recovered in time for the coronation of Elizabeth II. In 1996 the government of the United Kingdom ceremonially returned the Stone of Destiny to Scotland as a gesture to nationalists. But the provocative inscription 'Here is the

Hammer of the Scots' on Edward's tomb still stands in Westminster abbey. Like other rulers famed primarily for their military success, Edward I fuels modern debates about justice and humanity. Was he a hero or a war criminal? He has affinities with Hitler, as he expelled the Jews from England in 1290. In 1296 he had all the men of Berwick-upon-Tweed, numbering 11,160 according to the Hagnaby chronicle, killed. But should a medieval ruler be judged by modern standards of international law? Edward was a Christian crusader; it was his duty to kill Jews and Moslems and Christian enemies too, if – collectively or individually – they resisted the righteousness of God which he embodied.

'Historians, so we have been assured, are quiet men. Nevertheless they have a soft spot for conquest, the more sudden, clear-cut and overwhelming the better.'[5] These are the opening words of Sir Rees Davies's *Domination and Conquest: the Experience of Ireland, Scotland and Wales 1100–1300* (1990). In this view from the subjected peripheries of the United Kingdom (the book is based on lectures given at Belfast in 1988), Edward I is characterized as ruthless, sinister and chilling.[6] Such epithets would have disappointed Davies's predecessor as professor of medieval history in Oxford, Sir Maurice Powicke. In the aftermath of the Second World War, he had constructed a portrait of Edward I, which he hoped would have the authority to bridge old divisions. His two big books, *King Henry III and the Lord Edward* (1947) and *The Thirteenth Century* (1953), culminated Powicke's career (he had been professor in Oxford since 1928) and they were applauded by reviewers as the final word of a great historian on a great king. 'Edward was a great man', Powicke argued, 'not in virtue of any subtlety or exaltation in his nature but because, an ordinary Christian gentleman, he could fill a great position.'[7]

Powicke urged his readers 'to try to forget everything that has happened since 1307 and to look at the world as he (Edward I) saw it'. Then the king would stand out as the fine character whom his contemporaries had described: 'clear and emphatic in speech, uncertain in temper, reasonable in counsel'.[8] This description of Edward's manner of speaking is over-simplified, however, as Thomas Trivet made the subtler observation that the king had a stammer, which seemed to give emphasis to what he said.[9] By and large, though, Powicke's portrait does accord with the eulogies written at Edward's death in 1307 by his English admirers. Peter Langtoft wrote: 'He reigned over England by established law; by reason and right he maintained the monarchy.'[10] A ballad-writer agreed: 'He was a king who knew much of war, in no book can one read of a king who better sustained his land; all that he wished to do he brought wisely to a conclusion.'[11] Another, writing in English (instead of French) for a wider audience, wanted 'all England to know of whom I sing: he was the truest man in all things'.[12] Feelings were running high in 1307 because Edward had died in the middle of the war with Scotland. Writers in England were likely to take a partisan view and Langtoft is explicit in his animosity to Edward's Welsh and Scottish opponents.

Powicke's way of looking at the world as Edward I saw it is valid for a biographer, but it is too partial – in every sense – to be durable history. He took little account of contemporary comments unfavourable to the king and he did not analyse the documentary evidence systematically. He was not familiar with the mass of material concerning Edward's government, particularly in its legal and financial aspects, which exists in manuscript only in the royal archives. Furthermore, forgetting 'everything that has happened since 1307' precluded Powicke from assessing Edward's government in the light of the later development of the United Kingdom. The best he could do was to insist on Edward's personal integrity: 'we are not justified in casting doubts on his sincerity; we must hold the balance even'.[13] But Powicke has not convinced subsequent historians of Wales and Scotland that he did hold the balance even. Rees Davies has a contrary interpretation of Edward in *Domination and Conquest*, and Geoffrey Barrow has argued in *Robert Bruce* that Powicke was partial to Edward in the crucial case of Wallace.[14] Powicke's unfamiliarity with the royal archives can be defended, however, as no official document is likely to be definitive about the king's character. His own teacher, T.F. Tout, had worked there for years and had published six volumes of *Chapters in the Administrative History of Medieval England* (1920–33). These have been an inspiration to research students, but they did not resolve the questions about the king's personality which interested Powicke.

Powicke's ideal of Edward I as a Christian gentleman is remarkably endorsed by the discovery of a memorial sermon in a Vatican manuscript, which David d'Avray published for the first time in 1994. The preacher, who was probably the king's former confessor, likens Edward to Alexander the Great: 'in the equity of his justice, in the power of warring down his enemies, and in energy and wisdom of mind'.[15] Each of these themes is carefully developed. The preacher makes no apology for Edward's wars and he praises him in the words of the Book of Maccabees: 'Like a lion's cub roaring in his hunting, he went after evil men, and he burnt with flames those who were disturbing his people.'[16] The righteousness of the just war was a commonplace that went back in Christian thinking to St Augustine and the conversion of the Emperor Constantine. In the Painted Chamber at the Palace of Westminster (which was destroyed by fire in 1834) the main theme of the frescoes was the life and military campaigns of Judas Maccabeus. These had been commissioned by Edward I and the preacher may have had them in mind, when he made his memorial sermon before Pope Clement V in 1307.[17] (The pope was a Gascon who had owed allegiance to Edward.) This sermon is the most authoritative portrait of Edward that we have; it certainly helps us 'to look at the world as he saw it' (in Powicke's words). Like the English chroniclers' obituaries, however, its applicability is limited by its purpose as a eulogy made on the king's death.

'There are no simple judgements to be made on Edward I. An assessment of his personality presents great problems. It is hard to know how far documents issued in the king's name reflect his own view: they may have been the work of his ministers or clerks, and issued without specific consultation with Edward himself.'[18] These conclusions from Michael Prestwich's *Edward I* (1988) point out the difficulties of both Powicke's and Tout's approaches even at their best. Over a series of books on Edward I (publishing documents from the royal archives and discussing all sort of problems about the evidence), Prestwich has produced the best explanations we have: 'Edward met most of the contemporary requirements for a king'; his career can provide 'a multitude of arguments, some in his favour, some against him'; 'Edward I was a man of action, and it would be wrong to expect him to have had a consistent and clear philosophy of government.'[19] Prestwich points out that in the *Song of Lewes* the young Edward had been compared to a leopard.[20] The medieval *leopardus* had a dual character: it combined the courage and strength of a lion (*leo*) with the dark inconstancy of a panther (*pardus*). No one denied Edward's personal courage and physical strength. A variety of anecdotes about falconry and hunting attest this. The darker side of his rule: his inconsistency – or ability to adapt in political terms – seems equally evident. Such a combination of characteristics made sense in a king 'who knew much of war'.[21]

This chapter stresses one additional idea about Edward I: that he had been shaped by the strife and civil war of 1258–65. He himself had been a prisoner of the barons and he had seen his father and the monarchy humiliated. He was more like his father than has generally been recognized; he certainly pursued similar objectives. This is not surprising, as the government machine with its writs and accounts – the panoply of justice and finance – was at least two centuries old and it had a greater momentum than any individual, including the king. Possibly Edward wanted to avenge his father's humiliations, as well as his own. In one way though, he was very unlike Henry III, as he never seems to have lost his appetite for a fight. If he had quietened down, he might have been more successful, particularly in his negotiations with Scotland and France in the 1290s, and arguably at home as well. But, in the words of another memorial sermon in the Vatican manu-script: 'he never knew how to be at rest; he fits that which is written in *Ecclesiastes* – "Whatsoever your hand is able to do, do it instantly".'[22]

The enforcement of royal rights

Less than two months after his coronation in 1274 Edward I undertook an inquiry into his rights. Jurors from every group of villages (known as a 'Hundred') answered questions of all sorts concerning encroach-ments 'on the king or the royal dignity'.[23] Here was a time-honoured formula. Offences against 'the royal dignity', so recently solemnified by Edward's coronation in the new Westminster abbey, might com-prise anything from attempting to rescue confiscated goods from a local bailiff to treason and felony. (Llywelyn prince of Wales had offended the royal dignity by failing to attend the coronation.) Every detail was demanded from the 'Hundred' jurors: 'how?', 'how much?', 'since when?', 'by whom?', 'from whom?', 'by what warrant?', 'in what way?'. These questions come up repeatedly in the articles of the inquiry. They produced thousands of replies, particularly on the mis-conduct of officials, which were recorded in the 'Hundred Rolls'. These are preserved in the royal archives and they comprise the largest coherent body of evidence about any medieval kingdom, particularly when they are combined with a further inquiry in 1279. The latter would have served as a comprehensive register of landholders, but –

like many of Edward I's attempts at law reform – it was left incomplete, when it turned out to be much more complex than his advisers had allowed for.

To undertake reforms and then fail to carry them through risked bringing 'the royal dignity', as much as the rule of law, into disrepute. The masses of records made in Edward I's reign are a superb resource for historians today and they demonstrate the industriousness of his bureaucracy. Whether they were a wise use of scarce government resources is a different matter, however. No individual, either then or now, least of all the king with his multifarious commitments, could master all this information. Inquiries like the 'Hundred Rolls' were not novel in England, where William the Conqueror's Domesday Book and Henry II's Inquest of Sheriffs are obvious precedents. Through the justices in eyre going on regular circuits, the king's government had been asking such questions of local jurors for a century or more. Like any incoming lord, Edward I certainly needed to survey his inheritance, particularly as he had been absent from England for four years. On the day his father had died (16 November 1272) the justices in eyre were stopped in their tracks (they were at Chelmsford, Shrewsbury and Bedford) because their commissions became invalid. As interim chancellor, Walter of Merton had kept the government in a state of suspended animation at Westminster, but that was all he was entitled to do. The judicial machine would not restart until the new king was crowned and duly authorized to prosecute 'the pleas of the crown' through his justices.

The test for Edward I's own government would come when his new chancellor, Robert Burnell, attempted to follow up the allegations in the 'Hundred Rolls'. By this criterion 'no good came of it', in the opinion of the Dunstable chronicler.[24] He probably meant that royal officials, who made demands on the priory, had not been disciplined. His self-interest is evident in his rejoicing in 1276 when Roger of Seaton, the judge heading the follow-up inquiries, was struck with paralysis and lost the use of his tongue.[25] Of all the magnates, it was religious houses who were most self-righteous and vociferous in defence of their privileges because they believed they were God-given. Good certainly came of the 'Hundred Rolls' in the form of legislation. The first and longest article of the statute of Westminster in 1275 defended religious houses (like Dunstable) from giving compulsory 'hospitality' to laymen, and fifty other articles acted on the 'Hundred Rolls' by

making numerous regulations about crime, corrupt officials and property law. This statute is longer than Magna Carta and it was duly
copied into the books of statutes, which lawyers and landowners were
beginning to compile.

Edward I has achieved a posthumous reputation as a lawgiver, even
being called the English Justinian (the emperor who codified Roman
Law), because of the number and importance of the statutes recorded
in his name. Looking back over their books, later generations of
lawyers (particularly in the seventeenth century in disputes with
Charles I) saw Edward I's reign as a formative time. His predecessors
– Henry II, John and Henry III – had probably done just as much
law-making, but their work had taken the form of instructions given
directly to judges and officials, which were not systematically recorded.
Details of Henry III's legislation, for example, are spread haphazardly
among the Chancery rolls, the Memoranda rolls of the Exchequer and
material in chronicles. By Edward's reign what was beginning to
change was the way in which legislation was issued: no longer simply
in the form of instructions, but as solemn and public parliamentary
statutes. A 'statute' was so called because it 'stood' as law in perpetuity.
Henry III's statute of Marlborough in 1267, 'ordained in an assembly
of discrete men, both high and low', and 'put in writing to be observed
by all the inhabitants of the realm for ever', was a model for
Edward I.[26]

From the rebellion and civil war of 1258–65, Henry III's government had concluded that laws were best made in formal public assemblies or parliaments. Edward I seems to have accepted this principle,
though not every one of his statutes was made in parliament and
recorded in the form of a public enactment. The statute of Mortmain
in 1279, for example, which regulated gifts to religious houses, is cast
in the traditional form of a royal letter to the judges, instructing them
to act on what we 'on the advice of our council' have ordained.[27] There
is no reference to consulting 'high and low' in a public assembly.
Edward I took advice before legislating, but this advice did not have
to take the form of an act of parliament, approved and recorded by
Lords and Commons in their separate houses (that development starts
in the fourteenth century, not in the thirteenth). At the end of Edward's
reign in 1305 his chief justice, Hengham, testily warned a lawyer in
court: 'Don't comment on the statute. We know it better than you
because we made it.'[28] In this view from the top, law-making had to

be the business of experts and especially of the senior judges, because they were most familiar with its shortcomings. Ordinary people, the 'inhabitants' of England (as statutes refer to them), should be grateful to benefit from this superior wisdom.

This authoritarian and royalist view was made most explicit in Edward I's challenge to the magnates to show 'by what warrant?' (*quo waranto*) they exercised royal justice in their localities. These 'liberties' meant that law enforcement was the responsibility of lords and not of the sheriff. The liberty-holder executed royal writs and he had powers of arrest and of confiscating animals and goods to ensure that he was obeyed. This arrangement signified the compromise made a century earlier between Henry II and the magnates. The 'royal dignity' had been preserved, as legal actions were initiated by royal writs, but real power remained with the liberty-holders. Like the law's use of jury verdicts to settle all sorts of questions, 'liberties' ensured that legal decisions made in the king's name were rooted in local opinion and local interests. Edward I's intentions in challenging this compromise can only be guessed at. At first he may have been advised simply to follow up individual complaints which the 'Hundred Rolls' inquiry had revealed. But in 1278 the statute of Gloucester went further than this, as it declared that the law concerning liberties was 'defective' and had caused 'the most grievous damages and innumerable disinheritances'.[29] 'For the betterment of the realm' and for that 'fuller manifestation of justice which the worth of the kingly office requires', all holders of 'liberties' were required to come before the justices in eyre and show their warrants for them.

The statute of Gloucester was a challenge to the greatest men in the realm, the 'prelates, earls and barons'. The most powerful and experienced of them, Gilbert de Clare, earl of Gloucester, argued in a petition to Edward I that, 'if it please the king', nothing should be done to him wilfully and 'contrary to the law of the realm'; he should be allowed to enjoy his existing 'liberties' in peace.[30] This argument implied that a newly-made statute did not have the authority to disturb the peace by overriding established custom. The Earl Warenne is reported to have answered the king's justices in a more threatening way by producing a rusty sword, which his ancestor had used at Hastings, saying: 'This is my warrant! My ancestors came with William the Bastard and conquered their lands with the sword, and by the sword I will defend them from anyone intending to seize them.'[31] Historically and politically, Warenne was right. The king could not monopolize justice and power. In 1276 the sheriff of Lincolnshire reported that he had been unable to execute a writ within Warenne's liberty of the town of Stamford; he claimed he would have required a force of 5000 men to do it.[32] Nevertheless, despite resistance both in and out of court, Edward I had his lawyers persist with the *quo waranto* prosecutions throughout the 1270s and 1280s.

In 1281 the king's attorney, Gilbert of Thornton, argued against the Earl Warenne that even a charter granted by Edward himself was insufficient as a warrant because it had been made in Henry III's reign, when Edward had been as it were 'another person'.[33] In legal theory Thornton was right, as a king was made by his coronation and he started anew from that day. In personal and political terms, on the other hand, it was an insult to Edward's leading men, who had been his companions in the civil war, to allow newly promoted lawyers to argue that he was no longer bound by his former obligations. The Earl Warenne had supported Simon de Montfort for a while, it is true; but he had been a friend of Edward as a young man and he had fought with him at the battle of Evesham. The king's attorneys risked undermining the delicate balance of interests which Henry III had constructed after the strife and civil war of 1258–65. They were not succeeding in winning judgements, let alone executions of judgements, against men like the Earl Warenne. By 1290 there were at least 250 *quo waranto* cases awaiting resolution. To push them forward, Edward I appointed Gilbert of Thornton as chief justice in that year. But in the same year, in the Easter parliament of 1290, the king had to make concessions and the *quo waranto* cases were adjourned once more. In 1294 he had finally to concede in parliament that all *quo waranto* writs should be adjourned 'until he or his heirs wish to speak about them'.[34] The saving phrase 'wish to speak' preserved the royal dignity.

'The *quo waranto* business', in the opinion of its historian, D.W. Sutherland, 'was always slow, usually incomplete, and often futile'; it exemplified the 'mediocrity' of Edward I's government.[35] But the consequences may have been worse than that. Over a period of nearly twenty years the greatest men in the kingdom, clerics as well as lay lords, had been challenged over the crucial matter of their legal powers. As these public prosecutions had rarely proceeded as far as judgements, the bailiffs in the localities, whether they answered to a sheriff or to a liberty-holder, had had their authority brought into doubt. The statute of Winchester in 1285 had declared that 'day by day robberies, homicides and arsons are more often committed than they used to be'.[36] Edward I himself acknowledged, in the 'trailbaston' commissions in his last years in the early 1300s, that law and order had deteriorated over the thirty years of his reign. If this really was what had occurred, the *quo waranto* proceedings may have been the primary cause, as they had initiated a destabilization of the traditional judicial system, which Edward's wars in Wales and Scotland then compounded.

Why did the king persist with prosecutions against the magnates, which he could not win, and which risked undermining the structure of government? To ask such questions is to be wise after the event. Edward presumably thought he could win, just as he had won against Simon de Montfort in 1265 and Llywelyn in Wales in 1277, the year before the statute of Gloucester. Moreover, he did win against the earl of Gloucester in one way, as he was compelled in 1292 to make a fine of 10,000 marks for his liberty of Glamorgan. But even this was not a decisive victory, as fines like this were not paid in cash and frequently they were not paid in full. As a young man, Edward had triumphed over the rebel barons and taken terrible revenge on them at the battle of Evesham. Once he became king, he never had such successes again in England. He was obliged to proceed by legal means and this condemned him to the 'mediocrity' (Sutherland's phrase) of the *quo waranto* proceedings. In 1297 he suffered humiliations as gross as anything his father had faced, when a group of barons led by the earls of Norfolk and Hereford, Roger Bigod and Humphrey de Bohun, refused to do military service overseas. Bigod and Bohun would not even act in their capacities as marshal and constable to muster the troops. (It was defiance of this sort which had started the revolution of 1258.) In 1297 Edward had to overlook the earls' defiance and cross the Channel without them. On his return, he had to reissue Magna Carta and promise to abide by it, just as his father had been obliged to do on various occasions before 1258.

The conquest of Wales

Edward I compensated for his humiliations in England by his wars in Wales and Scotland. As the preacher said at his exequies, he 'warred down' his enemies by his power like Alexander the Great.[37] His military campaigns were *quo waranto* cases prosecuted at full force, in accordance with the laws of war, instead of the restrictive common law of England, and encouraged – rather than being negated – by magnates like the earl of Gloucester and the Earl Warenne (who commanded Edward's forces in Scotland in (1296–7). When Llywelyn of Wales failed to appear at the coronation in 1274 and repeatedly failed to do homage thereafter, because he was in dispute with Edward over various grievances, the king declared war in 1276. Llywelyn surrendered in 1277. Edward allowed him to continue as prince of Wales, but he fined him £50,000, which was tantamount to saying that Llywelyn was at his mercy, as he could never find such a sum. Henceforward Llywelyn was dependent on the lawcourts at Westminster. He was treated there like any other litigant and subjected to delays; but, unlike ordinary English litigants, he was too prominent a person to bribe the judges and too proud to do nothing. In 1281 the king's court claimed in one case concerning Llywelyn that it did not have his original writ and he would therefore have to start all over again. Edward I told him not to take offence at this, as his courts had to do their duty.[38] When Llywelyn and his brother Dafydd lost patience with this sort of prevarication and rebelled in 1282, Edward treated them as traitors and destroyed them entirely.

Edward I became the owner of Llywelyn's lands and the absolute lord of all his people by right of conquest (as the statute of Wales of 1284 declared), though the title of 'Prince of Wales' was not revived until 1301, when it was conferred on the future Edward II and thenceforward on the heir to the English throne. The great castles which Edward built to control Snowdonia and Anglesey demonstrated the scale of his triumph. They were built very fast but exceptionally well, primarily between 1282 and 1286. Like the fortresses Edward had seen in Palestine, they served as planted havens of 'civilization' and Englishness in an alien land. The archbishop of Canterbury did his bit to justify the war by maintaining that Welsh laws were primitive and contrary to the Bible (this was the ecclesiastical argument that had justified the English invasion of Ireland in the preceding century). Under Edward's regime the natives became 'mere Welshmen', disadvantaged at law when in competition or conflict with the English incomers. The castles were the outward form of Edward's victory. It was the modest English burgesses, sheltering in their neat little new towns under the castles, who were the long-term means of control. Like the Anglo-Norman settlers, who had come into Wales with the Marcher lords in the twelfth century, Edward's colonists showed the natives the advantages of obedience. They intermarried and spread English habits. But their victory was never total, as the resilience of the Welsh language in Llywelyn's former lands in North Wales shows to this day.

Edward I had succeeded in Wales by bringing overwhelming force against Llywelyn. The English government machine could not be turned in on itself to enforce the 'Hundred Rolls' inquiry or harry the magnates by *quo waranto*, but Edward showed how it could be directed outwards to bear down on Llywelyn. Finance, supplies, ships, wagons, troops, craftsmen and thousands of labourers were assembled for the campaign of 1277. They came from many parts of England, from the Marcher lordships of Wales (and from rival Welsh rulers), from Ireland, and from Gascony (which sent crossbowmen in particular). These varied forces were coordinated on the instructions of the royal Exchequer, Chancery and Wardrobe (Edward's huge informal or 'bedroom' funds, laundered by his Italian bankers). Although sums like the £1551 spent on Flint and Rhuddlan castles in 1277 do not look large today, the war was a financial operation on an unprecedented scale in England.[39] Numbers of men and supplies best indicate the size of Edward's enterprise: 200,000 crossbow bolts to be made at St Briave's castle in Gloucestershire; 968 diggers (or 'ditchers' – *fossatores*) at Rhuddlan employed in diverting the river Clwyd and making the earthworks for the castle and new town; 15,640 men receiving pay as infantry (including 9000 Welshmen) on 20 August 1277; 360 men with scythes, landed on the island of Anglesey to harvest Llywelyn's crops and feed Edward's men.[40] The organization of the war has been reconstructed in detail in J.E. Morris's classic *The Welsh Wars of Edward I* (1901).

Edward's strategy was elementary in principle: to proceed westwards from his headquarters at Chester along the coast of north Wales until Anglesey was reached; then cut off Anglesey from the mainland and pen Llywelyn into the mountains of Snowdonia; finally await the onset of winter to force him out. Today trains, full of holiday-makers bound for the beaches of North Wales, follow this route from Chester or Anglesey. Until 1277, however, there was no coastal road because tidal estuaries, marshes and woodland extended down to the sea.

Edward knew this very well because he had been earl of Chester in his father's reign. He was a chess player (there are records of his losses at the game in 1278); he presumably understood the various strengths of each piece on the board and how to bide his time. Although he had a reputation for restlessness and wanting to do things instantly, in war he also knew how to wait. In 1277 his forces proceeded cautiously but inexorably; supply lines were kept intact, for example, by building Flint and Rhuddlan castles at the Chester end of the line before advancing further west. Success depended on the 'civil engineers' as they would be called today: the diggers, foresters, carpenters, masons and water-men (some from the Fenlands of East Anglia), who cleared trees, built bridges and forts, and made huge embankments and ditches. As these men gradually made their way westwards by land, they were supported and supplied from the sea.

The skilled men – whether they were sailors or craftsmen or cross-bowmen – were compelled to muster in Wales and do the work, but they were not slave labourers. The greatest achievement of Edward's governmental machine was to pay them wages in silver pennies. Although there was certainly peculation and delay in this, Edward's restlessness and energy was here a great advantage. He saw to it that unprecedented numbers of men and supplies were placed where he wanted them. There were no pitched battles and few heroics, and Llywelyn duly surrendered on 9 November 1277. Edward did not destroy him on this occasion, but systematically humiliated him. As he triumphantly reported to his confidants on 21 March 1278, 'Look at this! Llywelyn prince of Wales has appeared before our judges and most agreeably (*benigne*) seeks and submits to justice and judgement.'[41] For the time being Edward allowed him to go on calling himself 'Prince of Wales', provided he submitted to royal justice like everybody else. Furthermore, Llywelyn had sworn homage and loyalty to Edward as his overlord. If he disobeyed him, Edward could call him a traitor. Fortunately for himself, Llywelyn was killed in a skirmish in 1282; but Dafydd, his brother, was taken prisoner and executed by the worst death that English law could devise: hanging, drawing and quartering.

Judging by contemporary English accounts, the executions of aris-tocratic prisoners of war were Edward's most celebrated and novel achievements. In the baronial war of 1264–5 this had not occurred and neither had it in the wars between King John and his barons. Edward judged his Scottish and Welsh opponents not to be fellow Christian knights fighting for their lords, but criminals subject to the penalties of English law. His rigour was applauded by English commentators. 'Listen, lords, a new song I shall begin,' writes one, describing in detail the execution of Sir Simon Fraser in 1306: how he was brought out of the Tower of London, dragged half-naked down Cheapside, hanged but kept alive, disembowelled, and so on.[42] Now that severed heads and limbs are no longer displayed on Edward I's castles, their majestic architecture stands out as his most remarkable achievement. The most magnificent of them is Caernarfon, which Edward built as the capital of conquered Wales. Arnold Taylor has suggested that the design was intended to make a reality of 'the fairest fortress man ever saw' dreamed of in the Mabinogion, the great collection of old Welsh tales.[43] Edward was proud of Wales, now that it belonged to him, and in his castles he showed its poor and primitive inhabitants what a real prince could do.

Caernarfon was in origin a Roman town, which was believed to have been the birthplace of the Emperor Constantine. This was celebrated in the design of Edward's castle by the unusual polygonal towers and walls of banded coloured stone, which recall the walls of Constantinople. The similarity is so close that the effect was probably deliberate. On his crusade Edward had seen many imperial buildings in the Mediterranean and, though he had not been to Constantinople, he employed officials who knew it well. The design of Caernarfon (and Edward's other castles in Wales) has a variety of Mediterranean and imperial features. Golden statues of eagles topped the principal towers at Caernarfon and over the main gate was a figure of the king in majesty, perhaps recalling the statue of the Emperor Frederick II on the portal of justice at Capua. When returning from the crusade in 1272, Edward had travelled up through Italy and he had been received in Sicily by Charles of Anjou, the brother of St Louis and successor by conquest to Frederick II's Italian kingdom. There Edward was told of the death of his father, Henry III. Charles of Anjou was surprised at how hard he seemed to take the news.[44] The international references of Edward's castles in Wales seem to recall his wide travels and concerns: in southern France, Savoy, Italy and the Mediterranean. Their grandeur and theatricality may also be a tribute to his father: Caernarfon was Edward's answer to Henry III's palace and abbey at Westminster.

To a modern visitor from London the remotest part of Wales may seem a strange place to put up buildings rivalling Constantinople and imperial Rome. To a medieval person equally, Wales stood on the edge of the world, as the Jerusalem-centred map in Hereford cathedral (which is contemporary with Edward's conquests) shows. Why was Wales so important to Edward I? The answer may be that the edge of the medieval world was a place for new beginnings. Edward was ambitious and to that extent he may have been a romantic, matching himself against the Roman emperors and the medieval image of Alexander the Great, who was credited with conquering the world. At Caernarfon Edward had been presented with the crown of King Arthur and he held Arthurian feasts there. Tales from the Mabinogion, or of Arthur and his knights, or of unexplored lands shown on Jerusalem-centred maps beyond the edge of the world in the Ocean Sea, told Edward of places and peoples yet to be conquered. He and his advisers took such information seriously, as his letter to the pope in 1301 shows: to justify his own conquests, Edward describes how Brutus and his Trojans first came to Britain and later on King Arthur 'held a most famous feast at the City of the Legions, at which were present all the kings subject to him', including the king of Scotland who demonstrated his subjection by bearing the sword of King Arthur before him.[45] This was history with a vengeance as far as Edward was concerned, as Alexander III had refused to bear such a sword at Edward's coronation.

The subjection of Scotland

Edward's subjection of Scotland had its origin in the conquest of Wales. In his letter of 21 March 1278, rejoicing over the submission of Llywelyn, Edward went on to report that Alexander III had offered to do homage 'unconditionally' and 'we have given him a day to do it in London.'[46] By giving the Scottish king 'a day in London', Edward was emphasizing his superiority over him: Alexander was to present himself at Westminster after Michaelmas. When Alexander met Edward at Tewkesbury on the way to London and offered to do homage there and then, Edward refused. Alexander must go through the whole humiliating experience within Edward's palace at Westminster. Unlike Llywelyn, Alexander had attended Edward's coronation in his capacity as a fellow king and his brother-in-law. But he had not done homage and neither had he borne a sword before Edward at the ceremony. In 1274 Edward had accepted these snubs, however unwillingly. Llywelyn's surrender in November 1277 changed the balance of power; it served as a warning to Alexander and it also released Edward's forces for an invasion of Scotland. No contemporary explains why Alexander changed his policy and offered, early in 1278, to come to London specially to do homage. As a compromise, he might have offered to do homage on the border between England and Scotland. To come as far south as London at Edward's behest was in itself a public acknowledgement of Alexander's inferior status.

The coupling of Llywelyn's case with Alexander's in Edward's letter suggests that Alexander was frightened into doing homage in 1278. At the same time he could draw some comfort from the way Edward had reinstated Llywelyn as prince of Wales after his surrender. If Alexander came promptly to Edward, he too might be reinstated and continue his outwardly friendly relations with his brother-in-law. This was a bit of a gamble, as Edward might keep him in London and compel him to do homage for the kingdom of Scotland, as well as for his lands in England. In October 1278 'in parliament' and 'in the king's chamber at Westminster' Alexander certainly did homage in some form.[47] Years later Edward claimed (in his letter to the pope in 1301) that 'Alexander king of Scots did homage to our father Henry for the kingdom of Scotland and later on to us', though the Scots maintained that Alexander had 'protested' that this was only for his lands in England.[48] Edward may have discounted this protest, so that – in his own mind, if not in reality – his achievement in getting Alexander's homage was no less than his father's.

When the Scottish throne became 'vacant' (Edward's expression) on the death of the 'Maid of Norway' (Alexander III's heiress) in 1290, Edward took the opportunity to get a total submission from the Scots. He made no secret of this. In 1291 he had required all the leaders of Scotland to come to him 'as they were bound to do by law', since he was 'the chief lord of the vacant kingdom', and they had sworn loyalty to him 'as the superior and direct lord of Scotland'.[49] Then, after duly investigating who should be king, Edward gave judgement in 1292 in favour of John Balliol, who did 'the due and accustomed homage'. 'He came to our parliaments at our command', Edward continued (in his letter to the pope in 1301) 'and he was present in them as our subject like the other people of our kingdom'.[50] (John's coming to Edward's parliaments 'at our command' is comparable with Alexander III duly presenting himself at the Westminster parliament in 1278.) Because John was in a weaker position than Alexander III had ever been, Edward subjected him – like the defeated Llywelyn – to repeated indignities in his lawcourts. In 1293 John was summoned to appear before the King's Bench at Westminster and, like Llywelyn, he was told to make sure he came along with the correct initiating writs.[51] John replied that he could not answer without consulting the leading men of his kingdom. In 1294 he again duly appeared in person at Westminster, only to be told that the king was too busy to deal with his case.[52]

The English legal system, with its delays and adjournments, which had worked against Edward in the *quo waranto* proceedings, worked in his favour when it came to demonstrating to the prince of Wales or the king of Scots that they were merely ordinary subjects of Edward I. John Balliol was finally provoked into rebellion in 1296. This made him a traitor, but Edward did not have him hanged, drawn and quartered like Dafydd. Instead he made John stand up and have the royal arms of Scotland stripped from his surcoat and torn to shreds. He was humiliated and dishonoured as a non-person, a knight without a coat of arms, and the advantage of this for Edward was that by the same token Scotland became a non-kingdom. Henceforward he referred to it only as a 'land' (*terra* as distinct from *regnum*). This is when he seized the Scottish regalia and had the coronation Stone of Destiny sent to Westminster. 'And so', Edward concluded his story to the pope, 'the kingdom of Scotland was subjected by right of ownership to our direction.'[53] Like Wales, Scotland became Edward's property and – in accordance with the theory of government by right of conquest – he could do whatever he pleased with it and its people.

In reality, however, Edward found himself with a war on his hands that proved more protracted than his campaigns in Wales, though he acted throughout with characteristic vigour. His response to William Wallace's victory at Stirling Bridge in 1297 was to transfer the government machine from Westminster to York in 1298, so that the whole weight of its organization could be brought to bear on Scotland as formerly it had been brought against Wales. After bitter years of campaigning it looked as if Edward had won by 1305, when he executed Wallace and other traitors and issued his 'ordinance for the stability of the land of Scotland'.[54] His immediate solution was to put English loyalists into all the posts and, as in Wales, he emphasized his superiority by declaring some Scottish laws to be 'patently contrary to God and to reason'.[55] But Edward's triumph was only temporary, as Robert Bruce revived the Scottish monarchy in 1306 and Edward died on the Scottish border without a decisive victory in 1307.

In Edward's defence it has often been argued that he did not understand what he was up against in Wales and Scotland. He was a typical medieval king and national feeling was something novel and alien to him. It is true that the Plantagenet family, and Henry III in particular, regarded themselves as being above local rivalries. They belonged (along with the pope, the emperor, the kings of Spain and St Louis) to a super-league of rulers with titles and interests extending across Latin Christendom. Edward had been educated in this tradition and he had lived up to it by going on crusade from 1270 to 1274 and then absenting himself from England again in 1286–9, when he was involved in all sorts of business in his duchy of Gascony. This is also when he fortified the Dordogne area with planned towns (*bastides*) to control local markets. In the 1290s he had been primarily concerned with the threat from France where, as duke of Gascony, he was obliged to do homage to the king of France, much as the king of Scots did homage to him. Indeed it was even clearer in legal terms that Edward, as duke of Gascony, owed homage to France, as this had been agreed by the treaty of Paris in 1259. It was only in 1298, after the success of Wallace's rebellion, that Edward moved the centre of government to York and concentrated on Scotland.

Edward certainly underestimated the resistance he aroused and perhaps he failed to understand it. He thought he would make a united kingdom of the British Isles by subjecting everyone to his 'dictates' (*dictio* – 'dictatorship' – is the Latin word he uses) by right of history and by right of conquest; divine providence was on his side, he had declared in the statute of Wales.[56] Where he misled the pope in his letter of 1301 was in stating that the Scottish representatives in 1291 had come 'freely and spontaneously' to swear oaths of loyalty to him.[57] His officials may have concealed from him how fierce a debate there had been and how coherent and lawful were the objections which the Scots had made. Later on, Edward had his own version of these events, supported by carefully selected and corrected documents, copied up in triplicate into great rolls of parchment by the international notaries John of Caen and Andrew de Tange, as if writing down his wishes would somehow make them come true. Edward had had neither the time nor the money to ring Scotland with castles like Llywelyn's Wales, even if such a project were strategically or geographically feasible. Instead, he put his trust in his great rolls; they proved his righteousness and justified his making and destroying King John Balliol.

English law and nationalism

The panoply of written law may have beguiled Edward I more than he knew. He may not have been a great legislator, but he was certainly the most record-conscious English king since Alfred. In the royal palace at Westminster Edward was in daily contact with his clerks, with their writs and rolls of parchment, and he had added to their number by appointing internationally authorized notaries. His letter to the pope in 1301 shows how impressed he had been by the testimonies his clerks had gathered, from religious houses and elsewhere, about the Trojan Brutus and King Arthur and much other dubious history. In the anti-clerical propaganda produced against the pope (Boniface VIII) in the 1290s a knight says:

> I had a good laugh when I heard that Lord Boniface had just decreed that he is and ought to be over and above all other governments and kingdoms. That way he can easily acquire a right for himself over anything whatever: all he has to do is to write it down, and everything will be his as soon as he has written.[58]

For Edward's opponents, though, this was no laughing matter because he – unlike the pope – had armies and executioners to make his ideas a reality. To this treatment the Scots famously replied in the Declaration of Arbroath:

> As long as a hundred of us remain alive, we will never on any conditions be subjected to the lordship of the English. For we fight not for glory, nor riches, nor honours, but for freedom alone, which no good man gives except with his life.[59]

This was published after Edward's death in 1320, but he was familiar with its arguments and he would simply have replied, as he had done to the pope, that Scotland belonged to him. Edward also knew that it was untrue to say that a good man values freedom more than his life. Over a lifetime of war he had seen many frightened prisoners (from King John Balliol downwards) preferring to save themselves and their families once the hanging, drawing and quartering began. Llywelyn, the great prince of Wales, had preferred humiliation to death after his surrender in 1277. Edward had not responded when Llywelyn's attorneys eloquently stated the national case for Wales in 1279. He had no need to respond, as he knew he had made Llywelyn 'most agreeably seek and submit to justice and judgement' in the English courts.[60] Llywelyn's attorneys put his case in terms of international law:

> Every province constituted under the lord king's empire [or 'rule' – *imperium*] has its own laws and customs in accordance with the manner and usage of the parts where it is situated, as the Gascons have in Gascony, the Scots in Scotland, the Irish in Ireland and the English in England. This is to the advantage of the lord king's crown rather than its detriment. The prince [Llywelyn] therefore claims that he likewise should be able to have his own Welsh law . . . by common right, just as the other nations constituted under the lord king's empire each have their own laws and customs in accordance with their language [*lingua*].[61]

To this the lawyers opposing Llywelyn replied:

> All the aforesaid nations are governed in the lord king's court in accordance with a single common law and they proceed in that same court in accordance with the same law and not by diverse and mutually contradictory laws in one and the same court.[62]

This statement was inaccurate, as Gascons were not ordinarily subjected to the courts at Westminster and neither were the Scots as yet, though these lawyers may have had Alexander III's submission in the Westminster parliament in 1278 in mind, as that had been only three months earlier and it had been done in the presence of the English judges. The lawyers' statement was correct, however, as far as the Welsh and Irish were concerned, as their lands had been conquered and any jurisdictions they had were at the say-so of the English government. Essentially a 'single common law', administered uniformly from Westminster through the royal courts, has indeed been the most distinctive characteristic of the English state from the Anglo-Norman period up to the present day.

In theory English common law favours no one individual, or class, or race or creed. The medieval ideal was that everyone, be he churl or earl, Cornishman or Yorkshireman, Christian or Jew, was equally subject to the king's majesty and bound to accept the judgements of his courts. This uniformity can be seen either as liberating and democratic or as tyrannical and arbitrary. English nationalists have admired it, whereas those with experience of colonial rule have been more dubious. Edward I's persistence with the *quo waranto* prosecutions and his use of the lawcourts to humiliate Llywelyn and John Balliol suggest that he thought the common law was liberating (as it was in many ways for him) and democratic (as it was in the sense that everyone was equally his subject). The common law was the basis of the king's peace in a united kingdom; this seems to have been Edward's ideal of government. Some aspects of the system might prove defective, but he would reform it and enforce it more rigorously: hence the 'Hundred Rolls' inquiry, the new statues, the dismissal of corrupt judges in 1289, the expulsion of the Jews in 1290, the threats made to the earls who refused military service in 1297, the reissue of Magna Carta in the same year, the 'trailbaston' commissions against the subversion of justice in 1305, the execution of Wallace and other Scottish criminals in London, and so on.

All this would have worked very well in Edward I's opinion, if people had done their duty and not resisted him; there was no justification for that. 'The western state', in the words of R.W. Kaeuper, 'was launched on its remarkable course as the agency defining and practising legitimate violence, while working to suppress the violence of private persons of every social rank within its boundaries.'[63] Edward I underestimated his opponents because he could not or would not recognize that the common law, in which he put his trust, had racist and elitist elements since it had been shaped by the Norman Conquest. In the conquered territories the natives were overtly discriminated against by being designated 'mere' Welshmen or 'mere' Irishmen. Within England the king's courts would not protect the property of the unfree, those whom the Norman conquerors had called the 'natives' or peasants. They were subject to local manorial courts. Possibly this was one of the injustices which Edward hoped to reform through the *quo waranto* proceedings. He did his best to humble the English magnates, even though he failed, and he did at least ensure that everyone in England continued to be subject to the criminal law, though he had to admit (in the 'trailbaston' commissions) that there had been many local conspiracies to pervert justice.

'Do as you would be done by' was not the rule by which Edward I's government operated. When in 1295 England was threatened with a French invasion, a letter was sent out in king's name to all senior clergy (because they were the chief articulators of public opinion), which acknowledged the strength and justice of English national feeling. The letter spoke not of blind subjection to Edward's will, but of solidarity and democracy: 'a most just law has established that what concerns everybody should be approved by everybody'.[64] (This quotation from the lawcode of the Emperor Justinian shows how there was one rule for the English and another for their subject peoples, as Edward I repeatedly failed to win Welsh and Scottish approval for his measures.) Common dangers, the letter of 1295 continues, require common remedies. (In other words, the government needed unprecedented sums of money, from the clergy as well as the laity, to conduct this war.)

> You already know well enough how the king of France has fraudulently and wickedly detained our land of Gascony. Not content with this fraud and viciousness, he has now assembled a huge fleet and army for the conquest of our kingdom and the enemy has already invaded our kingdom and its inhabitants. If he has the power to do all the evil he intends, from which God protect us, he is planning to wipe out the English language [*lingua*] entirely from the earth.

When faced with an aggressor as big as itself (as distinct from Scotland, Wales or Ireland), Edward's government recognized that his kingdom too was a national entity. This was the reality, rather than all the Plantagenet boasting about the king heading some revived sort of supranational Roman or Arthurian empire. Like the claim Llywelyn's attorneys had made for Wales in 1279, Edward's kingdom too was distinguished by its language. There were ironies here, as the letter stating this is written in Latin, because it was addressed to the clergy, and Edward I and his clerks were much more accustomed to French as a written language than English. Nevertheless, by the beginning of the fourteenth century a few writers, most notably the author of *Cursor*

Mundi (a popularization of the Bible story in northern English), explicitly associated their use of English with nationalism:

> Of England the nation
> Is Englishman there in common.
> The speech that man with most may speed
> Most therewith to speak was need.
> Seldom was for any chance
> Praised English tongue in France.[65]

But Peter Langtoft, the most virulently nationalist of English chroniclers in Edward I's reign, wrote in French. He compared Edward's conquests with those of King Arthur and described him as the flower of Christendom:

> Of him may one speak as long as the world lasts.
> For he had no equal as a knight in armour
> For vigour and valour, neither present nor future.[66]

As a eulogistic obituary, this does very well. In England's history Edward I can indeed stand as the once and future king, like Arthur: looking back to the Roman Empire and forward to the worldwide British colonial empire.

Notes

ABBREVIATIONS

EHD 2 *English Historical Documents 1042–1189* ed. D.C. Douglas and
G.W. Greenaway (2nd edition, 1981)

EHD 3 *English Historical Documents 1189–1327* ed. H. Rothwell
(1975)

RS Rolls Series (*Chronicles and Memorials of Great Britain*)

1. ENGLAND'S PLACE IN MEDIEVAL EUROPE

[1] *Annales Monastici* (RS 36), vol. 1, p. 339. Cf. ch. 11, n. 22 below.

[2] *Historia Ecclesiastica* ed. M. Chibnall (1969–81), vol. 2, p. 269.

[3] Letter to the bishop of Metz, trans. B. Pullan, *Sources for the History of Medieval Europe* (1966), p. 150.

[4] T.A. Heslop, 'Eadwine and his Portrait', *The Eadwine Psalter* ed. M. Gibson, T.A. Heslop, R.W. Pfaff (1992), p. 180.

[5] *De Gestis Pontificum* (RS 52), p. 4.

[6] *De Gestis Regum* (RS 90), p. 395.

[7] *Lives of the Saints* vol. 2, pp. 290–1, cited by F. Barlow, *The English Church 1000–1066* (2nd edition, 1979), p. 22.

[8] EHD 3, p. 998.

[9] *Historia Regum Britanniae* ed. A. Griscom (1929), p. 221.

[10] *De Gestis Pontificum*, p. 292.

[11] *Vita Lodovici VI* ed. H. Waquet (1929), p. 8.

[12] *Henrici Huntendunensis Historia* (RS 74), p. 231. R.H.C. Davis, *The Normans and their Myth* (1976), p. 121.

[13] *De Gestis Regum*, p. 379.

[14] *Estoire des Engleis* ed. A. Bell (Anglo-Norman Text Soc. 1960), lines 5963–8.

[15] *Historia Regum Britanniae*, p. 239.

[16] *Chronicles* (RS 82), vol. 1, p. 12.

[17] *Becket Materials* (RS 67), vol. 3, p. 8. C. Brooke and G. Keir, *London 800–1216* (1975), pp. 258–9.

[18] *Henrici Huntendunensis*, p. 262. J. Le Patourel, *The Norman Empire* (1976), p. 353. Davis, *The Normans*, pp. 66–7.

[19] *History of Friedrich II of Prussia* (1858), vol. 1, p. 415.

[20] *Historical Essays: First Series* (1871), p. 50.

[21] *Select Charters* (8th edition, 1895), p. v (preface of 1870).

[22] ibid, p. vii.

[23] ibid., p. viii.

[24] ibid., p. vii.

[25] F. Barlow, *Edward the Confessor* (1970), p. 136.

[26] *Letters of Lanfranc* ed. H. Clover and M. Gibson (1979), p. 51.

[27] ibid., p. 67.

[28] R.R. Davies, *The First English Empire* (2000), pp. 49, 52, 202.

PART I. THE NORMANS

[1] D.C. Douglas, *The Norman Achievement* (1969), p. 56. J. Hermans, 'The Byzantine View of the Normans', *Proceedings of the Battle Conference 2* (1979), ed. R. Allen Brown, p. 87. *The Alexiad of Anna Comnena* trans. E.R.A. Sewter (1969), p. 422.

[2] *Carmen de Hastingae Proelio* ed. C. Morton and H. Muntz (1972), p. 19.

[3] *De Gestis Regum* (RS 90), p. 306.

[4] *Carmen*, p. 17.

[5] *De Gestis Regum*, p. 306.

2. THE NORMAN CONQUEST

[1] D.C. Douglas, *William the Conqueror* (1964), p. 251, n. 4.

[2] *De Gestis Regum* (RS 90), p. 304.

[3] *Dialogus de Scaccario* ed. C. Johnson (1950), p. 52.

[4] *EHD* 2, p. 150 (translation adapted).

[5] *Historia Ecclesiastica* ed. M. Chibnall (1969–81), vol. 2, p. 322.

[6] *Transactions Royal Historical Soc.* 23 (1973), p. 246.

[7] *Governance* (1963), p. 27.

[8] *The Norman Conquest and British Historians* (Glasgow University Publications, 67, 1946), p. 33.

[9] *Historia Ecclesiastica*, vol. 2, p. 190.

[10] ibid., p. 272.

[11] *De Gestis Regum*, pp. 277–8.

[12] *Patrologia Latina*, vol. 195, pp. 773–4. *Vita Edwardi Regis* ed. F. Barlow (1962), pp. 89–90.

[13] *Dialogus de Scaccario*, p. 53.

[14] *History of English Law* (1898), vol. 1, p. 81.

[15] *Dialogus de Scaccario*, p. 63.

[16] 'The Norman Conquest', *History* 51 (1966), p. 283.

[17] *Chronicle of Battle Abbey* ed. E. Searle (1980), p. 310.

3. NORMAN GOVERNMENT

[1] *De Gestis Regum* (RS 90), p. 468.

[2] ibid., p. 488.

[3] ibid., p. 364.

[4] *Chronicle of Battle Abbey* ed. E. Searle (1980), p. 94.

[5] *Anthology of Troubadour Lyric Poetry* ed. A.R. Press (1971), p. 24.

[6] *EHD* 2, p. 195 (translation adapted).

[7] R.W. Southern, *Medieval Humanism and Other Studies* (1970), p. 219.

[8] *Leges Henrici Primi* ed. L.J. Downer (1972), p. 97.

[9] *Select Charters* ed. W. Stubbs (9th edition, 1913), p. 122.

[10] Southern, *Medieval Humanism*, pp. 184–5.

[11] *Dialogus de Scaccario* ed. C. Johnson (1950), p. 6.

[12] *Opera* ed. J.S. Brewer (RS 21), vol. 3, p. 28.

[13] *Dialogus de Scaccario*, p. 15.

[14] ibid., p. 2.

[15] ibid., p. 14.

[16] *Registrum Antiquissimum* ed. C.W. Foster (Lincoln Record Soc., 27, 1930), p. 26. *EHD* 2, pp. 520–1, nos. 63 and 64.

[17] *The Exchequer in the Twelfth Century* (1912), p. 57.

[18] *Medieval Humanism*, p. 211.

[19] Trans. L.A. Manyon (1961), p. 446 (abbreviated).

[20] Stenton (2nd edition, 1961), p. 124, n. 2. Maitland, *Domesday Book* (1897), pp. 305–7. For debates about feudalism, Susan Reynolds, *Fiefs and Vassals* (1994) is essential reading.

[21] Stenton, p. 130.

[22] *EHD* 2, p. 171.

4. CHURCH REFORM

[1] *Letters of Lanfranc* ed. H. Clover and M. Gibson (1979), p. 35.

[2] ibid., p. 153.

3 *De Gestis Pontificum* (RS 52), p. 69. T.S.R. Boase, *English Art 1100–1216* (1953), p. 1.

4 M. Gibson, *Lanfranc of Bec* (1978), p. 161.

5 *Life of Anselm* ed. R.W. Southern (1962), pp. 50, 52. 'Novus Anglus', *Letters* ed. Clover and Gibson, p. 38.

6 *Life of Anselm*, p. 51.

7 'Acta Lanfranci' in *Two Saxon Chronicles* ed. J. Earle and C. Plummer (1892), vol. 1, p. 291.

8 *Historia Novorum* (RS 81), p. 23.

9 ibid., p. 83.

10 *S. Bernardi Opera* ed. J. Leclercq and H. Rochais, vol. 7 (1974), no. 92, p. 241 (abbreviated).

11 *EHD* 2, pp. 207, 208 (translation adapted).

12 *Walter Daniel's Life of Ailred* ed. F.M. Powicke (1950), p. 11.

13 ibid.

14 *Cartulary of the Priory of St Gregory* ed. A.M. Woodcock (Camden Soc. Third Series, 88, 1956), p. 1.

15 M.L. Coker, 'A Hagiographic Polemic', *Mediaeval Studies* (Toronto) 39 (1977), p. 65.

5. THE CREATION OF WEALTH

1 *Domesday Book: A Complete Translation* ed. A. Williams and G.H. Martin (Alecto/Penguin edition, 2002), p. 1249.

2 ibid., p. 1248.

3 William of Malmesbury, *Gesta Regum Anglorum* ed. R.A.B. Mynors and R.M. Thomson, vol. 1 (1998), p. 587.

4 ibid., p. 588.

5 C. Harper-Bill, 'The Religious Houses', in C. Rawcliffe and R. Wilson (eds), *Medieval Norwich* (2004), p. 74.

6 *Domesday Book*, p. 679.

7 C. Daniell, *From Norman Conquest to Magna Carta* (2003), p. 173.

8 *EHD* 2, pp. 201–2.

9 *Life of Anselm* ed. R.W. Southern (1962), p. 71.

10 *Domesday Book*, p. 158.

11 *Dialogus de Scaccario*, p. 122.

12 *Domesday Book*, p. 158 (my translation).

13 *God's Peace and King's Peace* ed. R.R. O'Brien (1999), p. 164, nos. 7 and 8.

14 C. Dyer, *Making a Living in the Middle Ages* (2002), p. 70.

15 *Leges Henrici Primi* ed. L.J. Downer (1972), p. 244, no. 78.2b.

[16] F.W. Maitland, *Domesday Book and Beyond* (1897), p. 61.

[17] *Domesday Book*, p. 598.

[18] R. Lennard, *Rural England 1086–1135* (1959), pp. 69–70, 210–12.

[19] E. Fernie, *The Architecture of Norman England* (2000), p. 24.

PART II. THE ANGEVINS

[1] *Proceedings of the British Academy* 61 (1975), pp. 239–40.

[2] *Chroniques des Comtes d'Anjou* ed. L. Halphen and R. Poupardin (1913), p. 71.

[3] *Gesta Stephani* ed. K.R. Potter and R.H.C. Davis (1976), p. 224.

[4] *EHD* 2, p. 419.

[5] *Anthology of Troubadour Lyric Poetry* ed. A.R. Press (1971), p. 163.

[6] 'L'empire angevin était donc conçu comme un état très fort, mais dans le cadre du système féodal', *Le Gouvernement d'Henri II Plantagenêt* (1956), p. 569.

[7] *Dialogus de Scaccario*, p. 27. *Glanvill* ed. G.D.G. Hall (1965), p. 1.

6. STRUGGLES FOR THE KINGDOM

[1] *Gesta Stephani* ed. K.R. Potter and R.H.C. Davis (1976). p. 2.

[2] ibid., p. 222.

[3] *Regesta Regum Anglo-Normannorum* vol. 3, ed. H.A. Cronne and R.H.C. Davis (1967), no. 276, p. 103.

[4] *Select Charters* ed. W. Stubbs (9th edition, 1913), p. 176.

[5] *Angevin Kingship* (2nd edition, 1963), p. 87.

[6] *Charters* ed. Stubbs, pp. 137–8.

[7] *Gesta Stephani* p. 198.

[8] ibid., p. 206.

[9] *Chronicle of Richard of Devizes* ed. J.T. Appleby (1963), p. 49.

[10] *Historia Novella* ed. K.R. Potter (1955), p. 16.

[11] *History* 59 (1974), p. 182.

[12] ibid., p. 181.

[13] *The Becket Conflict and the Schools* (1973), p. 238.

[14] *Becket Materials* (RS 67), vol. 4, p. 28. *EHD* 2, p. 765.

[15] *Recueil des Historiens des Gaules*, vol. 12, pp. 419–20.

[16] *Anthology of Troubadour Lyric Poetry* ed. A.R. Press (1971), p. 162.

[17] *Historia* (RS 82), vol. 1, p. 283.

[18] *Giraldi Cambrensis Opera* (RS 21), vol. 8, p. 208.

[19] J. Gillingham, *Richard I* (1999), p. 348.

7. LAW AND ORDER

[1] *Glanvill* ed. G.D.G. Hall (1965), p. 148 (my translation).

[2] *Select Charters* ed. W. Stubbs (9th edition, 1913), p. 171.

[3] *Leges Henrici Primi* ed. L.J. Downer (1972), p. 108.

[4] *Royal Writs* ed. R.C. van Caenegem (Selden Soc. 77, 1959), p. 217.

[5] *Henry II* (1973), p. 375.

[6] *Charters*, ed. Stubbs, p. 166.

[7] *Glanvill*, p. 3.

[8] ibid., pp. 5, 10.

[9] ibid., pp. 28, 149.

[10] *Charters* ed. Stubbs, p. 172.

[11] Van Caenegem (1973), p. 100. D.M. Stenton, *English Justice* (1965), p. 26.

[12] *De Nugis Curialium* ed. M.R. James (Anecdota Oxoniensa, Medieval and Modern series, 14, 1914), p. 237.

[13] *Policraticus* ed. C.C.J. Webb (1919), vol. I, pp. 345–6.

[14] *Charters* ed. Stubbs, p. 163.

[15] *Glanvill*, p. 137. Cf. ibid., p. 148.

[16] *The Birth of the English Common Law*, p. 85.

[17] ibid., p. 97, note *e*.

[18] *Glanvill*, p. xxxi.

[19] ibid., p. 3.

8. THE TWELFTH-CENTURY RENAISSANCE

[1] *Metalogicon* ed. C.C.J. Webb (1929), p. 136.

[2] *Cligés*, lines 27–42. E.R. Curtius, *European Literature and the Latin Middle Ages* trans. W.R. Trask (1953), pp. 384–5.

[3] *Medieval Humanism* (1970), p. 158.

[4] Rickman (6th edition, 1862), p. 45.

[5] *A Mirror for Fools* trans. J.H. Mozley (1963), p. 39.

[6] Ed. M.R. James (1914), p. 1.

[7] *Medieval Humanism*, p. 176.

[8] *Poetria Nova* trans. M.F. Nims (1967), p. 16.

[9] ibid., p. 15.

[10] *De Nugis Curialium* ed. James (1914), p. 5.

[11] ibid., p. 203.

[12] ibid.

[13] M.D. Legge, *Anglo-Norman Literature* (1963), p. 94.

[14] Ed. N. Cartlidge (2001), p. 43. Cartlidge (p. xv) argues that the poem was most likely composed after 1272, rather than after 1189, which is the generally accepted date.

[15] *Chronicle of Jocelin of Brakelond* ed. H.E. Butler (1949), p. 40.
[16] *Historical Works of Gervase of Canterbury* (RS 73), vol. 1, p. 21.

9. THE MATTER OF BRITAIN

[1] R.R. Davies, *The First English Empire* (2000), p. 17, n. 38.
[2] S. Duffy, *Ireland in the Middle Ages* (1997), p. 75.
[3] R. Bartlett, *Gerald of Wales* (1982), p. 59.
[4] *Wace's Roman de Brut: A History of the British* ed. J. Weiss (1999), p. 246, lines 9794–6 (my translation).
[5] ibid., p. 246, lines 9762–5 (my translation).
[6] Geoffrey of Monmouth, *History of the Kings of Britain* trans. L. Thorpe (1966), p. 227.
[7] *Wace's Roman de Brut*, pp. 332–4, lines 13275–86 (my translation).
[8] *Lawman's Brut* trans. R. Allen (1992), p. 365, lines 14293–7.
[9] Gerald of Wales, *The Description of Wales* trans. L. Thorpe (1978), p. 220, bk. 1, ch. 1 (my translation).
[10] *The Life of Gruffudd ap Cynan* ed. D.S. Evans (1990), pp. 35, 66.
[11] M. Richter, 'The Political and Institutional Background to National Consciousness in Medieval Wales', in T.W. Moody (ed.), *Nationality and the Pursuit of National Independence* (1978), p. 43.
[12] M. Lapidge, 'Welsh-Latin Poetry', *Studia Celtica* 9 (1974), p. 92.
[13] *Description of Wales*, p. 273, bk. 2, ch. 9 (my translation).
[14] R.R. Davies, *The Age of Conquest: Wales 1063–1415* (1991), p. 15.
[15] *The Law of Hywel Dda* trans. D. Jenkins (1986), pp. 141, 1.
[16] *Description of Wales*, p. 231, bk. 1, ch. 6 (my translation).
[17] Davies, *The Age of Conquest*, pp. 17–18.
[18] *The Law of Hywel Dda*, p. 120.
[19] William of Newburgh, *History* (RS 82), bk. 2, ch. 5, vol. 1, p. 107.
[20] *Description of Wales*, p. 220, bk. 1, ch. 1 (my translation).
[21] Walter Map, *De Nugis Curialium* ed. M.R. James (1983), distinction 2, ch. 23, p. 192.
[22] Davies, *The First English Empire*, p. 4.
[23] *The Chronicle of John of Worcester* ed. P. McGurk, vol. 3 (1995), pp. 64–5.
[24] *De Invectionibus* (RS 21), vol. 3, p. 24, and see Gerald's *Expugnatio Hibernica* ed. A.B. Scott and F.X. Martin (1978), p. 246, line 9 (*Anglorum gens*).
[25] *Domesday Book* ed. A. Williams and G.H. Martin (Alecto/Penguin edition, 2002), pp. 515, 506.
[26] J. Gillingham, 'Slaves of the Normans?', in P. Stafford, J.L. Nelson and J. Martindale (eds), *Essays in Honour of Susan Reynolds* (2001), pp. 162–4.

[27] *Description of Wales*, p. 274, bk. 2, ch. 10 (my translation).

[28] William of Newburgh, *History* (RS 82), bk. 2, ch. 4 vol. 1, p. 105.

[29] E.L.G. Stones, *Anglo-Scottish Relations 1174–1328* (1965), pp. 2–3.

[30] William of Newburgh, *History, Book 1* ed. P.G. Walsh and M.J. Kennedy (1988), ch. 24, p. 107.

[31] A.O. Anderson, *Early Sources of Scottish History* (1922), vol. 2, p. 258.

[32] A.A.M. Duncan, *Scotland: The Making of the Kingdom* (1975), p. 263, n. 10.

[33] *Memorials* (RS 58), vol. 2, p. 206.

[34] D. Crouch, *The Reign of King Stephen* (2000), p. 321, n. 2.

[35] R. Bartlett, *England under the Norman and Angevin Kings* (2000), p. 78.

[36] *Jordan Fantosme's Chronicle* ed. R.C. Johnston (1981), p. 52, lines 686–7.

[37] William of Malmesbury, *Gesta Regum Anglorum*, para. 400, ed. R.A.B. Mynors and R.M. Thomson, vol. 1 (1998), pp. 726–7.

[38] J. Gillingham, *The English in the Twelfth Century* (2000), pp. 17–18, and see p. 48.

[39] *Gesta Stephani* ed. K.R. Potter and R.H.C. Davis (1976), p. 54. *Jordan Fantosme's Chronicle*, p. 54, line 706.

[40] *EHD* 2, p. 832, no. 162.

[41] D. Ó Cróinín, *Early Medieval Ireland* (1995), p. 288.

[42] *Annals of Loch Cé* (RS 54), p. 145.

[43] *Expugnatio Hibernica*, p. 104, line 22.

[44] *Gesta Stephani*, p. 16.

[45] Matthew Paris, *Chronica Majora* (RS 57), vol. 5, pp. 492–5.

[46] S. Painter, *William Marshal* (1933), p. 149, and see p. 167.

PART III. THE POITEVINS

[1] *Constitutional History*, vol. 1 (1874), p. 519.

[2] T. Wright, *Political Songs of England* (Camden Soc. 1839), p. 10. The origins of Peter des Roches and the meaning of 'Poitevin' are discussed by N. Vincent, *Peter des Roches* (1996), ch. 1.

[3] *Chronica Majora* (RS 57), vol. 3, p. 272. Vincent, *Peter des Roches*, pp. 17, 28, discusses *capicerius*.

10. KING JOHN AND THE MINORITY OF HENRY III

[1] *Radulphi de Coggeshall Chronicon* (RS 66), p. 138. W.L. Warren, *King John* (Penguin edition, 1966), p. 95.

[2] *Chronica Rogeri de Wendover* (RS 84), vol. 2, p. 100. Warren, *John*, p. 240.

[3] *Memoriale Walteri de Coventria* (RS 58), vol. 2, p. 232. Cf. the translations of J.C. Holt, *King John* (Historical Assoc., 1963), pp. 24–5, and of A. Gransden, *Historical Writing in England* (1974), p. 343.

[4] *Chronica Majora* (RS 57), vol. 2, p. 699. Cf. V.H. Galbraith, *Roger Wendover and Matthew Paris* (1944), p. 36, and Warren, *John*, p. 30.

[5] *Constitutional History*, vol. 2, p. 17.

[6] *Pipe Roll 11 John*, p. 172. Warren, *John*, p. 162.

[7] *Memorials of St Edmunds Abbey* (RS 96), vol. 2, p. 25. Warren, *John*, p. 27. Cf. S. Painter, *Reign of King John* (1949), pp. 270–3.

[8] *Wendover*, vol. 2, p. 84. *Chronica Majora*, vol. 2, p. 552. J.C. Holt, *Magna Carta* (1965), pp. 137–8.

[9] *Annales Monastici* (RS 36), vol. 2, p. 277. F.M. Powicke, *Stephen Langton* (1928), pp. 42–3. 115–16.

[10] *Magna Carta* (1965), p. 20.

[11] *Wendover*, vol. 2, p. 199.

[12] *Life of St Hugh of Lincoln* ed. D.L. Douie and H. Farmer (1961), vol. 2, p. 185.

[13] *Histoire de Guillaume le Maréchal* ed. M.P. Meyer (1891–1901), vol. 2, lines 15183–8.

[14] Wright, *Political Songs*, p. 22.

[15] *Chronica Majora*, vol. 3, p. 28.

[16] *Guillaume le Maréchal*, vol. 2, lines 18041–3.

[17] ibid., vol. 2, lines 19149–52.

[18] *Dialogus de Scaccario* ed. C. Johnson (1950), p. 109.

[19] *Pipe Roll 3 Henry III*, pp. xxiii, 205.

11. THE PERSONAL RULE OF HENRY III

[1] *Select Charters* (9th edition, 1913), p. 37.

[2] *The Thirteenth Century* (1953), p. 130.

[3] *Laws and Customs of England* ed. S.E. Thorne (1968), vol. 2, p. 22.

[4] *Chronica Majora* (RS 57), vol. 3, p. 620.

[5] *Wendover* (RS 84), vol. 3, p. 51.

[6] *Annales Monastici* (RS 36), vol. 1, pp. 463–4.

[7] R.F. Treharne and I.J. Sanders, *Documents of the Baronial Movement* (1973), pp. 236–9.

[8] Matthew Paris, *Chronica Majora*, vol. 5, p. 52.

[9] II *Chronicles*, ch. 26, verse 19. *Letters of Grosseteste* (RS 25), p. 351.

[10] *Letters of Grosseteste*, p. 352.

[11] *Close Rolls 1251–3*, p. 225.

[12] *Chronica Majora*, vol. 5, p. 339.
[13] *Walter of Henley and other Treatises* ed. D. Oschinsky (1971), p. 402.
[14] *Chronica Majora*, vol. 5, p. 20.
[15] *Close Rolls 1254–6*, p. 326.
[16] *Chronica Majora*, vol. 5, pp. 339, 617.
[17] Above, ch. 10, note 16.
[18] *Close Rolls 1234–7*, p. 271.
[19] *Chronica Majora*, vol. 3, p. 388.
[20] ibid., vol. 5, p. 457.
[21] Above, note 18.
[22] *Annales Monastici*, vol. 1, p. 339.
[23] *Purgatorio*, canto 7, lines 130–1.

12. NATIONAL IDENTITY

[1] *Gesta Regum* (RS 90), vol. 1, pp. 277–8.
[2] *Wendover* (RS 84), vol. 3, p. 49.
[3] R.F. Treharne and I.J. Sanders, *Documents of the Baronial Movement* (1973), p. 80.
[4] ibid., p. 80.
[5] T. Wright, *Political Songs*, p. 72, lines 9, 11–12; p. 92, lines 414, 416.
[6] ibid., pp. 23, 22.
[7] *Wendover*, vol. 2, p. 212.
[8] *Flores Historiarum* (RS 95), vol. 3, pp. 266–7.
[9] *Chronicon Willelmi de Rishanger* ed. J.O. Halliwell (Camden Soc. 1840), p. 18.
[10] *Wendover*, vol. 3, p. 16.
[11] *Chronicon Abbatiae de Evesham* (RS 29), p. 189.
[12] Walter Map, *De Nugis Curialium* ed. M.R. James (1914), p. 25.
[13] *Rishanger* ed. Halliwell, pp. 17–18.
[14] Above, ch. 1, note 27.
[15] *EHD* 3, p. 307.
[16] *Chronicle of Richard of Devizes* ed. J.T. Appleby (1963), p. 66.
[17] *EHD* 3, pp. 881–4.
[18] *Radulphi de Coggeshall Chronicon* (RS 66), p. 185.
[19] *Rotuli Litterarum Clausarum* (1833), vol. 1, p. 329 (to sheriff of Somerset).
[20] *Curia Regis Rolls*, vol. 16, p. 290.
[21] Matthew Paris, *Chronica Majora*, vol. 4, p. 118.
[22] *Select Charters* ed. W. Stubbs (9th edition, 1913), p. 356.
[23] *Chronica Johannis de Oxenedes* (RS 13), pp. 224–5.

[24] *Annales Monastici* (RS 36), vol. 2, pp. 349–50.

[25] A.H. Hershey (ed.), *The 1258–9 Special Eyre of Surrey and Kent* (Surrey Record Soc. 38, 2004), p. 76, no. 146, comment at pp. lviii–lx.

[26] *Annales Monastici*, vol. 1, p. 463.

13. THE COMMUNE OF ENGLAND

[1] *Chronica Majora*, vol. 5, p. 706.

[2] ibid., vol. 5, p. 313.

[3] T. Wright, *Political Songs*, p. 85, lines 265–9. In general see J.R. Maddicott, *Simon de Montfort* (1994), ch. 3 'Religion and Virtue'.

[4] *Annales Monastici* (RS 36), vol. 1, p. 164.

[5] *Chronicle* ed. J.T. Appleby (1963), p. 49, cf. p. 141 above.

[6] F. Pollock and F.W. Maitland, *History of English Law* (1898), p. 688.

[7] *EHD* 3, p. 367.

[8] *Crusader Institutions* (1980), p. 59.

[9] *Close Rolls 1256–9*, p. 328.

[10] R.F. Treharne and I.J. Sanders, *Documents of the Baronial Movement* (1973), pp. 238–41.

[11] ibid., p. 98.

[12] *Close Rolls 1256–9*, p. 328.

[13] Treharne and Sanders, p. 258.

[14] ibid., p. 216, clause 19 (my translation).

[15] ibid., p. 168.

[16] ibid., pp. 206–7.

[17] ibid., pp. 242–3.

[18] ibid., p. 265.

[19] ibid., pp. 288–9.

[20] ibid., pp. 296–7.

[21] Wright, *Political Songs*, pp. 110–11, lines 763–70.

[22] P. Binski, *Westminster Abbey and the Plantagenets* (1995), p. 97.

[23] *Willelmi Rishanger* (RS 28), vol. 2, p. 75.

14. LORDSHIP AND THE STRUCTURE OF SOCIETY

[1] D. Oschinsky, *Walter of Henley* (1971), p. 403, no. xxii.

[2] *Glanvill* ed. G.D.G. Hall (1965), p. 107 (my translation).

[3] *Piers Plowman*, C-Text, passus ix, lines 24–31, cited in G.C. Homans, *English Villagers of the Thirteenth Century* (1970 edition), p. 256.

[4] *Bracton* ed. S.E. Thorne (1968), vol. 2, p. 32.

[5] ibid., p. 259 (my translation).

6 *Rotuli Litterarum Patentium* ed. T.D. Hardy (1935), p. 33.

7 *Bracton*, vol. 2, p. 354.

8 Oschinsky, *Walter of Henley*, p. 399, no. xii.

9 *Bracton*, vol. 2, p. 232 (my translation).

10 Psalms (Authorized Version), the first verse of Psalms 30, 31, 35, 38.

11 D.A. Carpenter, 'The Second Century of English Feudalism', *Past and Present* 168 (2000), pp. 66–7.

12 D.A. Carpenter, *The Battles of Lewes and Evesham* (1987), p. 64.

13 O. de Laborderie, 'The Last Hours of Simon de Montfort', *English Historical Review* 115 (2000), pp. 408, 410.

14 *Handling Sin*, lines 8777–82, cited in J. Alexander and P. Binski (eds.), *Age of Chivalry* (1987), p. 289.

15 L.J. Wilkinson, 'Thirteenth-Century Women in Lincolnshire' (University of London Ph.D. thesis, 2000), p. 47.

16 Matthew Paris, *Chronica Majora* (RS 57), vol. 5, p. 337.

17 L.R. Poos and L. Binfield, *Select Cases in Manorial Courts* (Selden Soc. 114, 1997), p. 97.

18 F.W. Maitland, *Select Pleas in Manorial and Other Seignorial Courts* (Selden Soc. 2, 1888), pp. 24–5.

19 H.M. Chew and M. Weinbaum, *The London Eyre of 1244* (London Record Soc. 6, 1970), pp. 135–6, no. 346.

20 D.L. Jeffrey and B.L. Levy, *The Anglo-Norman Lyric* (1990), pp. 137–8 (excerpts).

21 F. Pollock and F.W. Maitland, *The History of English Law* (second edition, 1898), vol. 1, p. 432.

22 E.A. Kosminsky, *Studies in the Agrarian History of England* (1956), p. 200, n. 2.

23 C. Dyer, *Making a Living in the Middle Ages* (2002), p. 178 (my emphasis).

24 ibid., p. 179.

25 Oschinsky, *Walter of Henley*, p. 264 (my translation).

26 W.W. Shirley, *Royal and Other Historical Letters of the Reign of Henry III* (RS 27), vol. 1, pp. 288–9, no. 239 (excerpts).

27 *Glanvill*, p. 3.

28 *Chronica Majora*, vol. 5, p. 374.

29 S.L. Waugh, *The Lordship of England* (1988), p. 278.

30 W. Stubbs, *Select Charters* (ninth edition, 1913), p. 464. *EHD* 3, p. 460.

31 A. Harding, *The Roll of the Shropshire Eyre of 1256* (Selden Soc. 96, 1980), p. 271, no. 784.

32 *Chronica Majora*, vol. 5, p. 57.

[33] *Bracton*, vol. 2, p. 327 (my translation).

[34] B.A. Hanawalt, *Crime and Conflict in English Communities* (1979), pp. 243–50.

[35] Laborderie, 'The Last Hours of Simon de Montfort', pp. 408, 411.

EPILOGUE
15. EDWARD I

[1] M. Prestwich, *Edward I* (1988), p. 33, n. 34.

[2] *Select Charters* ed. W. Stubbs (9th edition, 1913), p. 421.

[3] *Willelmi Rishanger* (RS 28), vol. 2, p. 98. A. Gransden, *Historical Writing in England* (1974), p. 507.

[4] Gransden, *Historical Writing*, p. 478. *EHD* 3, p. 259.

[5] Davies, *Domination and Conquest*, p. 1.

[6] ibid., pp. 106, 114, 125.

[7] Powicke, *King Henry III and the Lord Edward*, pp. 690–1.

[8] Powicke, *The Thirteenth Century*, p. 228.

[9] This passage from Trivet (*alias* Trevet) is translated in differing ways by: Powicke, *King Henry III and the Lord Edward*, pp. 686–7; G.W.S. Barrow, *Feudal Britain* (1956), p. 308; E.L.G. Stones, *Edward I* (1968), p. 2; Gransden, *Historical Writing*, p. 506.

[10] *EHD* 3, p. 265.

[11] T. Wright, *Political Songs* ed. P.R. Coss (1996), p. 242.

[12] ibid., p. 246.

[13] Powicke, *King Henry III and the Lord Edward*, p. 677.

[14] Barrow, *Robert Bruce* (1965), pp. 195, 183, n. 4.

[15] D.L. d'Avray, *Death and the Prince: Memorial Preaching before 1350* (1994), pp. 71, 263.

[16] ibid., pp. 72, 264.

[17] Prestwich, *Edward I*, p. 558. P. Binski, *The Painted Chamber in Westminster* (1986), pp. 96ff.

[18] Prestwich, *Edward I*, p. 558.

[19] ibid., pp. 559, 560, 563.

[20] Prestwich, *The Three Edwards* (1980), p. 6, n. 1.

[21] See n. 11 above.

[22] D'Avray, *Death and the Prince*, pp. 76, 268.

[23] H.M. Cam, *The Hundred and the Hundred Rolls* (1930), pp. 250–1, article 13.

[24] *Annales Monastici* (RS 36), vol. 3, p. 263. Cam, *The Hundred*, p. 240.

[25] *Annales Monastici*, vol. 3, p. 272.

[26] *EHD* 3, pp. 384–5.

[27] *EHD* 3, pp. 419–20, and see P.A. Brand, *The Making of the Common Law* (1992), pp. 233–44.

[28] *Year Books 34–35 Edward I* (RS 31), p. 82.

[29] *Statutes of the Realm*, p. 45 (my translation).

[30] Prestwich, *Edward I*, p. 261.

[31] Clanchy, *From Memory to Written Record* (2nd edition, 1993), p. 36.

[32] R.C. Palmer, *The County Courts of Medieval England* (1982), pp. 265–6.

[33] Prestwich, *Edward I*, p. 261.

[34] D.W. Sutherland, *Quo Warranto Proceedings in the Reign of Edward I* (1963), pp. 30, 213.

[35] ibid., pp. 188–9.

[36] *EHD* 3, p. 460.

[37] See n. 15 above.

[38] Powicke, *King Henry III and the Lord Edward*, p. 675.

[39] A. Taylor, *The Welsh Castles of Edward I* (1986), p. 117.

[40] Prestwich, *Edward I*, p. 179. Taylor, *The Welsh Castles*, p. 27. Prestwich, *Edward I*, p. 180.

[41] Powicke, *King Henry III and the Lord Edward*, p. 672.

[42] Wright, *Political Songs*, pp. 213, 221.

[43] Taylor, *The Welsh Castles*, pp. 78–9.

[44] Prestwich, *Edward I*, p. 82.

[45] E.L.G. Stones, *Anglo-Scottish Relations 1174–1328* (2nd edition, 1970), p. 196.

[46] Rymer, *Foedera*, vol. 1, part 2, p. 554, and see n. 41 above.

[47] Stones, *Anglo-Scottish Relations*, pp. 76–83.

[48] ibid., pp. 208, 230.

[49] ibid., p. 208.

[50] ibid., p. 210.

[51] ibid., p. 132, and see n. 38 above.

[52] ibid., p. 134.

[53] ibid., p. 214.

[54] ibid., p. 240.

[55] ibid., p. 250.

[56] ibid., p. 214.

[57] ibid., p. 208.

[58] Clanchy, *From Memory to Written Record* (2nd edition, 1993), p. 183.

[59] A.A.M. Duncan, *John Barbour, The Bruce* (1997), pp. 780–1.

[60] See n. 41 above.

[61] *Welsh Assize Roll 1277–84* ed. J. Conway Davies (1940), p. 266.

[62] ibid.

[63] R.W. Kaeuper, *War, Justice and Public Order: England and France in the Later Middle Ages* (1988), p. 381.

[64] Stubbs, *Charters*, p. 480.

[65] *Cursor Mundi*, lines 241–6, and see T. Turville-Petre, *England the Nation* (1996), pp. 16, 39–40.

[66] *EHD* 3, p. 264.

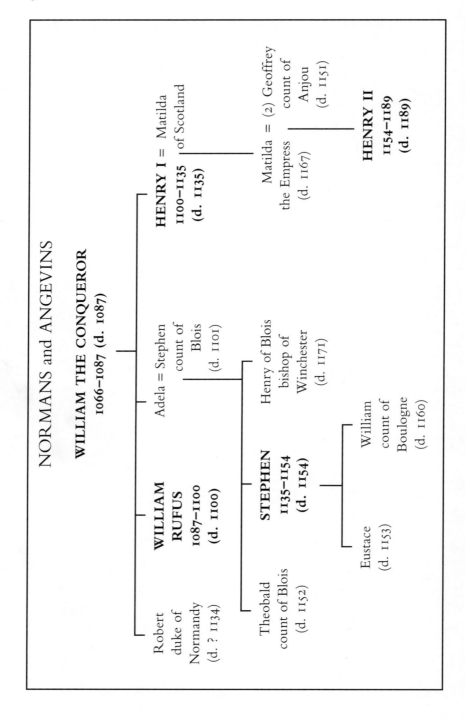

NORMANS and ANGEVINS

WILLIAM THE CONQUEROR
1066–1087 (d. 1087)

Robert
duke of
Normandy
(d. ? 1134)

**WILLIAM
RUFUS
1087–1100
(d. 1100)**

Adela = Stephen
count of
Blois
(d. 1101)

HENRY I = Matilda
1100–1135   of Scotland
(d. 1135)

Theobald
count of Blois
(d. 1152)

**STEPHEN
1135–1154
(d. 1154)**

Henry of Blois
bishop of
Winchester
(d. 1171)

Matilda = (2) Geoffrey
the Empress   count of
(d. 1167)   Anjou
                   (d. 1151)

**HENRY II
1154–1189
(d. 1189)**

Eustace
(d. 1153)

William
count of
Boulogne
(d. 1160)

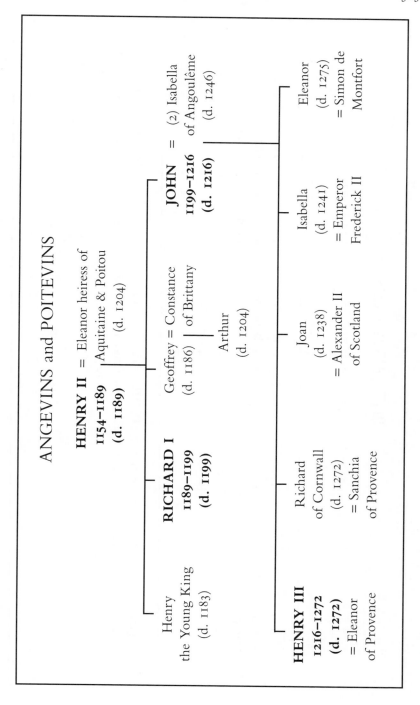

ANGEVINS and POITEVINS

HENRY II = Eleanor heiress of
1154–1189   Aquitaine & Poitou
(d. 1189)   (d. 1204)

JOHN = (2) Isabella
1199–1216   of Angoulême
(d. 1216)   (d. 1246)

Henry
the Young King
(d. 1183)

RICHARD I
1189–1199
(d. 1199)

Geoffrey = Constance
(d. 1186)   of Brittany

Arthur
(d. 1204)

HENRY III
1216–1272
(d. 1272)
= Eleanor
of Provence

Richard
of Cornwall
(d. 1272)
= Sanchia
of Provence

Joan
(d. 1238)
= Alexander II
of Scotland

Isabella
(d. 1241)
= Emperor
Frederick II

Eleanor
(d. 1275)
= Simon de
Montfort

THE SAVOYARDS

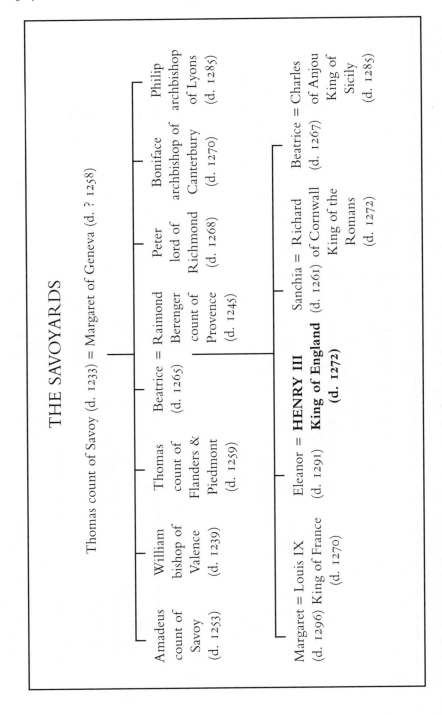

Thomas count of Savoy (d. 1233) = Margaret of Geneva (d. ? 1258)

Amadeus
count of
Savoy
(d. 1253)

William
bishop of
Valence
(d. 1239)

Thomas
count of
Flanders &
Piedmont
(d. 1259)

Beatrice = Raimond
(d. 1265)   Berenger
            count of
            Provence
            (d. 1245)

Peter
lord of
Richmond
(d. 1268)

Boniface
archbishop of
Canterbury
(d. 1270)

Philip
archbishop
of Lyons
(d. 1285)

Margaret = Louis IX
(d. 1296) King of France
          (d. 1270)

Eleanor = HENRY III
(d. 1291) King of England
          (d. 1272)

Sanchia = Richard
(d. 1261) of Cornwall
          King of the
          Romans
          (d. 1272)

Beatrice = Charles
(d. 1267) of Anjou
           King of
           Sicily
           (d. 1285)

Suggestions for Further Reading

INTRODUCTORY

F. Barlow, *The Feudal Kingdom of England 1042–1216* (5th edition, 1999).

R. Bartlett, *England under the Norman and Angevin Kings 1075–1225* (2000).

D. Carpenter, *The Struggle for Mastery: Britain 1066–1284* (2003).

M. Chibnall, *Anglo-Norman England 1066–1166* (1986).

C. Daniell, *From Norman Conquest to Magna Carta: England 1066–1215* (2003).

D.C. Douglas and G.W. Greenaway (eds), *English Historical Documents 1042–1189* (2nd edition, 1981).

C. Dyer, *Making a Living in the Middle Ages: The People of Britain 850–1520* (2002).

R. Horrox and M. Ormrod (eds), *A Social History of England 1200–1500* (2006).

R. Huscroft, *Ruling England 1042–1217* (2005).

E. King, *Medieval England: From Hastings to Bosworth* (2005).

D. Matthew, *Britain and the Continent 1000–1300* (2005).

R. Mortimer, *Angevin England 1154–1258* (1994).

M. Prestwich, *Plantagenet England 1225–1360* (2005).

H. Rothwell (ed.), *English Historical Documents 1189–1327* (1975).

N. Saul (ed.), *The Oxford Illustrated History of Medieval England* (1997).

C. Tyerman, *Who's Who in Early Medieval England 1066–1272* (1996).

M. Wood, *The Domesday Quest: In Search of the Roots of England* (2005).

WILLIAM THE CONQUEROR, WILLIAM RUFUS AND HENRY I

F. Barlow, *William Rufus* (1983).

M. Chibnall, *The Debate on the Norman Conquest* (1999).

D. Crouch, *The Normans: The History of a Dynasty* (2002).

H.C. Darby, *Domesday England* (1977).

R.H.C. Davis and M. Chibnall (eds), *The Gesta Guillelmi* [*Deeds of William I*] *of William of Poitiers* (1998).

D.C. Douglas, *William the Conqueror* (1964).

R. Gameson (ed.), *The Study of the Bayeux Tapestry* (1997).

B. Golding, *Conquest and Colonization: The Normans in Britain 1066–1100* (2001).

J.A. Green, *The Aristocracy of Norman England* (1997).

J.A. Green, *Henry I* (2005).

E.M. Hallam and D. Bates (eds), *Domesday Book* (2001).

C. Harper-Bill and E. van Houts (eds), *A Companion to the Anglo-Norman World* (2003).

D. Henson, *The English Elite in 1066* (2001).

N.J. Higham, *The Death of Anglo-Saxon England* (1997).

C.W. Hollister and A.C. Frost, *Henry I* (2001).

E. Mason, *William II Rufus – the Red King* (2005).

P. McGurk (ed.), *The Chronicle of John of Worcester*, vol. 3: *1067–1140* (1995).

G.R. Owen-Crocker (ed.), *King Harold II and the Bayeux Tapestry* (2005).

P. Rex, *The English Resistance: The Underground War against the Normans* (2004).

H. Thomas, *The English and the Normans 1066–1220* (2003).

E. van Houts (ed.), *The Normans in Europe* (2000).

A. Williams, *The English and the Norman Conquest* (1995).

A. Williams and G.H. Martin (eds), *Domesday Book: A Complete Translation* (2002).

STEPHEN, MATILDA AND HENRY II

E. Amt, *The Accession of Henry II: Royal Government Restored 1149–1159* (1993).

F. Barlow, *Thomas Becket* (1986).

J. Bradbury, *Stephen and Matilda: The Civil War of 1139–53* (1995).

M. Chibnall, *The Empress Matilda* (1991).

D. Crouch, *The Reign of King Stephen* (2000).

P. Dalton, *Conquest, Anarchy and Lordship: Yorkshire 1066–1154* (1994).

A.J. Duggan (ed.), *The Correspondence of Thomas Becket 1162–70*, 2 vols. (2000).

A.J. Duggan, *Thomas Becket* (2004).

Henry of Huntingdon, *The History of the English People 1000–1154* trans. D. Greenway (2002).

E. King (ed.), *The Anarchy of King Stephen's Reign* (1994).

E. King and K.R. Potter (eds), *The Historia Novella by William of Malmesbury* (1998).

D. Matthew, *King Stephen* (2002).

K.R. Potter and R.H.C. Davis (eds), *Gesta Stephani: The Deeds of Stephen* (1976).

M. Staunton (ed.), *The Lives of Thomas Becket* (2001).

W.L. Warren, *Henry II* (1973).

G.J. White, *Restoration and Reform 1153–65: Recovery from Civil War in England* (2000).

RICHARD I AND JOHN

J.T. Appleby (ed.), *The Chronicle of Richard of Devizes of the Time of Richard I* (1963).

N. Barratt, 'The Revenue of King John', *English Historical Review* 111 (1996), pp. 835–55.

C.R. Cheney and W.H. Semple (eds), *Selected Letters of Pope Innocent III Concerning England 1198–1216* (1953).

S.D. Church, *The Household Knights of King John* (1999).

S.D. Church (ed.), *King John: New Interpretations* (1999).

D. Crouch, *William Marshal 1147–1219* (2nd edition, 2004).

J. Gillingham, *Richard I* (1999).

J. Gillingham, *The Angevin Empire* (2nd edition, 2001).

A.J. Holden, S. Gregory and D. Crouch (eds), *History of William Marshal* (2002).

J.C. Holt, *Magna Carta* (2nd edition, 1992).

D. Power, *The Norman Frontier in the Twelfth and Early Thirteenth Centuries* (2004).

R.V. Turner, *King John* (1994).

R.V. Turner, *Magna Carta through the Ages* (2003).

R.V. Turner and R.R. Heiser, *The Reign of Richard Lionheart* (2000).

W.L. Warren, *King John* (1961).

HENRY III AND EDWARD I

D.A. Carpenter, *The Minority of Henry III* (1990).

D.A. Carpenter, *The Reign of Henry III* (1996).

P.R. Coss (ed.), *Thomas Wright's Political Songs of England* (1996).

A. Harding, *England in the Thirteenth Century* (1993).

M. Howell, *Eleanor of Provence* [queen 1236–72] (1998).

A. Jobson (ed.), *English Government in the Thirteenth Century* (2005).

S.D. Lloyd, *English Society and the Crusade 1216–1307* (1988).

J.R. Maddicott, *Simon de Montfort* (1994).

M. Morris, *The Bigod Earls of Norfolk in the Thirteenth Century* (2005).

W.M. Ormrod, 'State-Building and State Finance under Edward I', in *England in the Thirteenth Century: Proceedings of the 1989 Harlaxton Symposium* (1991).

J.C. Parsons, *Eleanor of Castile* [queen 1272–90] (1995).

M. Prestwich, *Edward I* (1988).

M. Prestwich, *English Politics in the Thirteenth Century* (1990).

R. Stacey, *Politics, Policy and Finance under Henry III 1216–1245* (1987).

R.F. Treharne and I.J. Sanders (eds), *Documents of the Baronial Movement* (1973).

R. Vaughan (ed.), *The Illustrated Chronicles of Matthew Paris 1247–1250* (1993).

N. Vincent, *Peter des Roches: An Alien in English Politics* (1996).

B.K.U. Weiler (ed.), *England and Europe in the Reign of Henry III* (2002).

ARCHAEOLOGY AND ARCHITECTURE

J. Alexander and P. Binski (eds), *Age of Chivalry: Art in Plantagenet England* (1987).

G. Astill and A. Grant (eds), *The Countryside of Medieval England* (1988).

M.W. Beresford and M.K. St Joseph, *Medieval England: An Aerial Survey* (2nd edition, 1979).

P. Binski, *Becket's Crown: Art and Imagination in Gothic England 1170–1300* (2004).

P. Binski, *Westminster Abbey and the Plantagenets 1200–1400* (1995).

J. Blair and N. Ramsey (eds), *English Medieval Industries* (1991).

H. Clarke, *The Archaeology of Medieval England* (1984).

N. Coldstream, *The Decorated Style* (1994).

P. Fergusson and S.A. Harrison, *Rievaulx Abbey* (2000).

E. Fernie, *The Architecture of Norman England* (2000).

R. Gilchrist, *Gender and Material Culture: The Archaeology of Religious Women* (1984).

L. Grant and R. Mortimer (eds), *Westminster Abbey: The Cosmati Pavements* (2002).

J. Hunt, *Lordship and Landscape: A Documentary and Archaeological Study of the Honour of Dudley 1066–1322* (1997).

R. Liddiard (ed.), *Anglo-Norman Castles* (2003).

C. Platt, *Medieval England: A Social History and Archaeology* (1978).

D. Rollason, M. Harvey and M. Prestwich (eds), *Anglo-Norman Durham* (1994).

M. Thurlby, *The Herefordshire School of Romanesque Sculpture* (1999).

T. Williamson, *Shaping Medieval Landscapes* (2003).

BOOKS, DOCUMENTS AND LEARNING

C. Burnett (ed.), *Adelard of Bath, Conversations with his Nephew* (1998).

J.I. Catto (ed.), *The Early Oxford Schools*, vol. 1 of *The History of the University of Oxford*, ed. T.H. Aston (1984).

P. Chaplais, *English Royal Documents 1199–1461* (1971).

M.T. Clanchy, *From Memory to Written Record: England 1066–1307* (2nd edition, 1993).

A. Coates, *English Medieval Books: The Reading Abbey Collections* (1999).

C. de Hamel, *A History of Illuminated Manuscripts* (2nd edition, 1994).

C. Donovan, *The De Brailes Hours: Shaping the Book of Hours in Thirteenth-Century Oxford* (1991).

R. Gameson, *The Manuscripts of Early Norman England* (1999).

A. Gransden, *Historical Writing in England 550–1307* (1974).

P.D.A. Harvey and A. McGuinness, *A Guide to British Medieval Seals* (1996).

C. Johnson (ed.), *The Course of the Exchequer by Richard Son of Nigel* (1950).

S. Lewis, *The Art of Matthew Paris in the Chronica Majora* (1987).

M.B. Parkes, *Scribes, Scripts and Readers* (1991).

R.B. Patterson, *The Scriptorium of Margam Abbey 1150–1225* (2002).

R.M. Thomson, *William of Malmesbury* (1987).

T. Webber, *Scribes and Scholars at Salisbury Cathedral 1075–1125* (1992).

CHURCH, RELIGION AND BELIEF

F. Barlow, *The English Church 1066–1154* (1979).

J. Burton, *Monastic and Religious Orders in Britain 1000–1300* (1994).

J. Burton, *The Monastic Order in Yorkshire 1069–1215* (1999).

H. Clover and M. Gibson (eds), *The Letters of Lanfranc* (1979).

H.E.J. Cowdrey, *Lanfranc: Scholar, Monk, Archbishop* (2003).

P. Dalton, 'Churchmen and the Promotion of Peace in King Stephen's Reign', *Viator* 31 (2000), pp. 79–119.

B. Golding, *Gilbert of Sempringham and the Gilbertine Order* (1994).

E. Jamroziak, *Rievaulx Abbey and its Social Context 1132–1300* (2004).

Jocelin of Brakelond, *Chronicle of the Abbey of Bury of St Edmunds* trans. D. Greenway and J. Sayers (1989).

C.H. Lawrence, *The Life of St Edmund by Matthew Paris* (1996).

E. Mason, *St Wulfstan of Worcester* (1990).

D. Rollason (ed.), *Symeon of Durham* (2000).

J. Sayers and L. Watkiss (eds), *Thomas of Marlborough's History of the Abbey of Evesham* (2003).

R.W. Southern, *Robert Grosseteste* (1986).

R.W. Southern, *St. Anselm* (1990).

N. Vincent, *The Holy Blood: King Henry III and the Westminster Blood Relic* (2001).

B. Ward, *Miracles and the Medieval Mind 1000–1215* (1982).

C. Watkins, *History and the Supernatural in Medieval England* (2005).

S. Yarrow, *Saints and their Communities: Miracle Stories in Twelfth-Century England* (2005).

ECONOMY AND SOCIETY

M. Bailey (ed.), *The English Manor 1200–1500* (2002).

C.M. Barron, *London in the Later Middle Ages 1200–1500* (2004).

J.L. Bolton, *The Medieval English Economy 1150–1500* (1980).

R.H. Britnell, *The Commercialisation of English Society 1000–1500* (2nd edition, 1996).

R.H. Britnell and B.M.S. Campbell (eds), *A Commercialising Economy: England 1086–1300* (1995).

B.M.S. Campbell, *English Seigniorial Agriculture 1250–1450* (2000).

P. Coss, *The Origins of the English Gentry* (2003).

D. Crouch, *The Image of Aristocracy in Britain 1000–1300* (1992).

C. Dyer, *Everyday Life in Medieval England* (1994).

R. Faith, *The English Peasantry and the Growth of Lordship* (1997).

R. Goddard, *Lordship and Medieval Urbanization: Coventry 1043–1355* (2004).

J. Hatcher and M. Bailey, *Modelling the Middle Ages: The History and Theory of England's Economic Development* (2001).

A. Haverkamp and H. Vollrath (eds), *England and Germany in the High Middle Ages* (1996); N. Orme on literacy, D.A. Carpenter on crime,

P.R. Hyams on Jews, S. Reynolds on towns, C. Dyer on manorialism and J. Gillingham on social mobility.

R. Lennard, *Rural England 1086–1135* (1959).

J. Masschaele, *Peasants, Merchants and Markets: Inland Trade in England* (1997).

E. Miller and J. Hatcher, *Medieval England: Towns, Commerce and Crafts* (1995).

R.R. Mundill, *England's Jewish Solution 1262–1290* (1998).

D.M. Palliser (ed.), *The Cambridge Urban History of Britain*, vol. 1: *600–1500* (2000).

D.A.E. Pelteret, *Slavery in Early Medieval England* (1995).

C. Rawcliffe and R. Wilson (eds), *Medieval Norwich* (2004).

S. Reynolds, *An Introduction to the History of English Medieval Towns* (1977).

P. Skinner (ed.), *The Jews in Medieval Britain* (2003).

ENGLAND, BRITAIN AND IRELAND

W.R.J. Barron and S.C. Weinberg (eds), *Layamon's Arthur* (2001).

G.W.S. Barrow, *Kingship and Unity: Scotland 1000–1306* (2nd edition, 2003).

R. Bartlett, *Gerald of Wales 1146–1223* (1982).

R.M. Blakely, *The Brus Family in England and Scotland 1100–1295* (2005).

R. Britnell, *Britain and Ireland 1050–1530* (2004).

R.R. Davies, *The Age of Conquest: Wales 1063–1415* (1991).

R.R. Davies, *The First English Empire: Power and Identities in the British Isles 1093–1343* (2000).

S. Duffy, *Ireland in the Middle Ages* (1997).

A.A.M. Duncan, *The Kingship of the Scots 842–1292* (2002).

M.T. Flanagan, *Irish Society, Anglo-Norman Settlers, Angevin Kingship* (1989).

R. Frame, *The Political Development of the British Isles 1100–1400* (1990).

Geoffrey of Monmouth, *The History of the Kings of Britain* trans. L. Thorpe (1966).

Gerald of Wales, *The Journey through Wales* and *The Description of Wales* trans. L. Thorpe (1978).

Gerald of Wales, *The History and Topography of Ireland* trans. J.J. O'Meara (1982).

J. Gillingham, *The English in the Twelfth Century* (2000).

R.C. Johnston (ed.) *Jordan Fantosme's Chronicle* [of the Scottish War] (1981).

E. Mullally (ed.), *The Deeds of the Normans in Ireland* (2002).

S.H. Rigby (ed.), *A Companion to Britain in the Later Middle Ages* [1100–1500, includes Ireland] (2003).

A.B. Scott and F.X. Martin (eds), *Expugnatio Hibernica: The Conquest of Ireland, by Giraldus Cambrensis* (1978).

B. Smith, *Colonization and Conquest in Medieval Ireland: The English in Louth* (1999).

J.B. Smith, *Llywelyn ap Gruffudd Prince of Wales* (1998).

E.L.G. Stones (ed.), *Anglo-Scottish Relations 1174–1328* (1965).

K.J. Tiller, *Layamon's Brut and Anglo-Norman Historiography* (2006).

R. Turvey, *The Welsh Princes 1063–1283* (2002).

B. Webster, *Medieval Scotland: The Making of an Identity* (1997).

J. Weiss (ed.), *Wace's Roman de Brut: A History of the British* (2002).

GENDER, FAMILY AND INHERITANCE

J.M. Bennett, *Women in the Medieval English Countryside* (1987).

P. Brand, 'Family and Inheritance, Women and Children', in C. Given-Wilson (ed.), *An Illustrated History of Late Medieval England* (1996).

P. Coss, *The Lady in Medieval England 1000–1500* (1998).

S. Fanous and H. Leyser (eds.), *Christina of Markyate* (2005).

S.M. Johns, *Noblewomen, Aristocracy and Power in the Anglo-Norman Realm* (2003).

H. Leyser, *A Social History of Women in England 450–1500* (1995).

C. McCarthy, *Marriage in Medieval England* (2004).

B. Millett and J. Wogan-Browne (eds), *Medieval English Prose for Women* (1990).

L.E. Mitchell, *Portraits of Medieval Women: Family, Marriage and Politics in England 1225–1350* (2003).

V. Morton and J. Wogan-Browne (eds), *Guidance for Women in Twelfth-Century Convents* (2003).

S. Thompson, *Women Religious: The Founding of English Nunneries after the Norman Conquest* (1991).

J.C. Ward, *Women of the English Nobility and Gentry 1066–1500* (1995).

S.L. Waugh, *The Lordship of England: Royal Wardships and Marriages* (1988).

B. Wheeler and J.C. Parsons (eds), *Eleanor of Aquitaine: Lord and Lady* (2002).

LANGUAGE, LITERATURE AND EDUCATION

G.S. Burgess (ed.), *Two Medieval Outlaws: The Romances of Eustace the Monk and Fouke Fitz Waryn* (1997).

H.E. Butler and J. Gillingham (eds), *The Autobiography of Gerald of Wales* (2005).

N. Cartlidge (ed.), *The Owl and the Nightingale: Text and Translation* (2001).

P. Damian-Grint, *The New Historians of the Twelfth-Century Renaissance* (1999).

R.J. Dean, *Anglo-Norman Literature: A Guide to Texts and Manuscripts* (1999).

A. Lupack, *The Oxford Guide to Arthurian Literature and Legend* (2005).

T.W. Machan, *English in the Middle Ages* (2003).

C.M. Meale (ed.), *Women and Literature in Britain 1150–1500* (1993).

N. Orme, *From Childhood to Chivalry: The Education of the English Kings and Aristocracy 1066–1530* (1984).

N. Orme, *Medieval Children* [England 1100–1550] (2001).

A.G. Rigg, *A History of Anglo-Latin Literature 1066–1422* (1992).

T. Turville-Petre, *England the Nation: Language, Literature and National Identity* (1996).

D. Wallace (ed.), *The Cambridge History of Medieval English Literature* (1999).

Walter Map, *Courtiers' Trifles – De Nugis Curialium* ed. M.R. James, C.N.L. Brooke and R.A.B. Mynors (1983).

LAW AND ORDER

P.A. Brand, *The Making of the Common Law* (1992).

P.A. Brand, *Kings, Barons and Justices* (2003).

M.T. Clanchy, 'Highway Robbery and Trial by Battle', in R.F. Hunnisett and J.B. Post (eds), *Medieval Legal Records Edited in Honour of C.A.F. Meekings* (1978).

R. Fleming, *Domesday Book and the Law* (1998).

G.D.G. Hall (ed.), *The Treatise on the Laws Commonly Called Glanvill* (1965).

A. Harding, *Medieval Law and the Foundations of the State* (2002).

R.H. Helmholz, *The Oxford History of the Laws of England: The Canon Law* (2004).

A.H. Hershey (ed.), *The 1258–9 Special Eyre of Surrey and Kent* (Surrey Record Soc. 38, 2004).

J. Hudson, *Land, Law and Lordship in Anglo-Norman England* (1994).

J. Hudson, *The Formation of the English Common Law* (1996).

P.R. Hyams, *Rancor and Reconciliation in Medieval England* (2003).

J.M. Stenton, *English Justice between the Norman Conquest and the Great Charter* (1965).

H. Summerson (ed.), *Crown Pleas of the Devon Eyre 1238* (Devon and Cornwall Record Soc. 28, 1985).

R.V. Turner, *Judges, Administrators and the Common Law in Angevin England* (1994).

R.C. van Caenegem (ed.), *English Lawsuits from William I to Richard I*, 2 vols (Selden Soc., 1990, 1991).

WAR AND CHIVALRY

R. Barber, *The Knight and Chivalry* (2nd edition, 1996).

J.R.V. Barker, *The Tournament in England 1100–1400* (1986).

J. Bradbury, *The Battle of Hastings* (1998).

D. Carpenter, *The Battles of Lewes and Evesham 1264–65* (1987).

P. Coss, *The Knight in Medieval England 1000–1400* (1993).

C. Coulson, *Castles in Medieval Society* (2003).

D. Crouch, *Tournament* (2005).

R.H.C. Davis, *The Medieval Warhorse* (1989).

M. Keen, *Chivalry* (1984).

M.K. Lawson, *The Battle of Hastings* (2002).

S. Morillo, *Warfare under the Norman and Angevin Kings* (1994).

J.E. Morris, *The Welsh Wars of Edward I* (1901, reissued 1995).

J.O. Prestwich, *The Place of War in English History 1066–1214* (2004).

M. Prestwich, *Armies and Warfare in the Middle Ages: The English Experience* (1996).

M. Strickland (ed.), *Anglo-Norman Warfare* (1990).

M. Strickland, *War and Chivalry: The Conduct and Perception of War in England and Normandy 1066–1216* (1996).

M. Strickland and R. Hardy, *From Hastings to the Mary Rose: The Great Warbow* (2005).

KEEPING UP TO DATE

Consult the annual volumes of *Anglo-Norman Studies* (Proceedings of the Battle Conference 1978–), ed. R. Allen Brown, M. Chibnall, C. Harper-Bill, J. Gillingham, and the biannual volumes of *Thirteenth-Century England* ed. P.R. Cross, S.D. Lloyd, M. Prestwich, R.H.

Britnell, R. Frame, B. Weiler (1986–). See also *The Haskins Society Journal*, beginning with vol. 1 (1989). The Royal Historical Society has a free online *Bibliography on British History* at <www.rhs.ac.uk/bibwel. html>.

Index